Westminster Abbey Chapter House

the history, art and architecture of
'a chapter house beyond compare'

Westminster Abbey Chapter House

the history, art and architecture of
'a chapter house beyond compare'

Edited by Warwick Rodwell and Richard Mortimer

with contributions from Jeremy Ashbee, Paul Binski, Martin Bridge, Steven Brindle, David Carpenter, Richard Foster, Elizabeth Hallam Smith, Barbara Harvey, Helen Howard, Laurence Keen, Daniel Miles, Warwick Rodwell, Tim Tatton-Brown, Pamela Tudor-Craig and Christopher Wilson

The Society of Antiquaries of London

First published 2010 by
The Society of Antiquaries of London
Burlington House
Picccadilly
London W1J 0BE

<www.sal.org.uk>

The Society of Antiquaries gratefully acknowledges the
financial support of English Heritage and Westminster Abbey
Enterprises Ltd in the publication of this book.

ISBN 978-0-85431-295-5

British Library Cataloguing in Publication Data
A CIP catalogue record for this book is available from the
British Library.

Original series design by Tracy Wellman and Sue Cawood
Designed and laid out by Sue Cawood
Printed and bound in Belgium by Deckers Snoeck

Westminster Abbey Chapter House is normally open from
10am to 4pm daily.
Visiting details can be found on the English Heritage website:
<www.english-heritage.org.uk>.

Cover illustrations: (front) an aerial view of Westminster Abbey
from the south west, showing the setting of the chapter house
(located centre right). *Photograph*: © English Heritage Photo
Library; (back) a detail from the wall painting of the
Apocalypse of St John in the chapter house (north-west wall,
bay 3), showing Christ in Majesty, surrounded by elders
playing musical instruments, *c* 1400. *Photograph*: © English
Heritage Photo Library 2002

Frontispiece: the interior of Westminster Abbey Chapter House
from the entrance looking east. *Photograph*: © Malcolm
Crowthers

Contents

Figures

Foreword

London is blessed with many fine buildings from the last twenty centuries, but the further we go back in time, the more their remains become fragmentary and to understand them fully, we have to discover their history, their adaptations over the centuries and the significance of any restorations that may have been undertaken.

Westminster Abbey chapter house is an excellent example of a medieval monument created to impress its importance, by the use of a striking architectural style, adapting the cutting edge of the engineering possibilities for the combination of minimal stone structure and the maximum amount of glass to create a space of super-human proportions.

Westminster Abbey was the place where the power of the state, manifest in the person of the King, was most strongly allied to the power of the Church. The chapter house was a debating chamber where the right to speak and the need to listen were most eloquently expressed by the architecture and the form of the chamber with its unnecessarily high roof.

Its place in the history of the nation lies in its use as a venue for the King to discuss policy, before Parliament had created a permanent chamber in which to meet. As this role was gradually superseded by other buildings, the chapter house became more exclusively used by the abbey and at the Dissolution it was adapted for more humble purposes, which continued until it was restored to its former glory, as well as he could, by Sir George Gilbert Scott in the 1860s.

Since then, of course, Gothic architecture has been much more competently and comprehensively studied and the techniques of historic construction more fully understood. The purpose of this publication is to illuminate the scholar and to introduce the visitor to the date and function of everything he or she sees, and also to reveal, through its history, the significance of the building's role in the history of this city and this nation.

HRH The Duke of Gloucester KG GCVO
Royal Patron, Society of Antiquaries of London

Preface

Chapter houses occur in a variety of forms and comprise one of the most distinctive components of major medieval ecclesiastical complexes, both monastic and secular. Remarkably these structures have never been the subject of a comprehensive assessment, and the first seminar on 'The Gothic Chapter House in England' was held as recently as 1999, organized by Sarah Brown for English Heritage in York. The principal outcome of that event was the recognition of the enormous potential for further chapter house studies, based on individual structures and stylistic groups. Nowhere was that potential more apparent than in the case of Westminster Abbey, and it was subsequently determined that an in-depth study of the abbey's remarkable chapter house complex should be undertaken. The results were presented on 4 and 5 July 2008 in a series of papers given to the Tercentenary Research Symposium of the Society of Antiquaries, held in collaboration with the Dean and Chapter of Westminster and English Heritage.

The symposium brought together scholars who had been working on various aspects of Westminster Abbey and its chapter house for a decade or more, and the papers given on that occasion have been recast to form the contents of the present volume, with the addition of an introductory chapter attempting to provide a general overview of the structure and history of its fabric.

Acknowledgements

Our first debt is to the contributors, all of whom gave papers at the symposium and subsequently honed them for publication with attention to our exceptionally tight publication schedule, often under difficult circumstances; we are very grateful for their forbearance and efficiency.

The symposium and the resulting publication have been very much a collaborative enterprise between Westminster Abbey, English Heritage and the Society of Antiquaries. Generous funding has been provided by English Heritage and Westminster Abbey Enterprises Ltd. At English Heritage, we are indebted to Jeremy Ashbee, Steven Brindle, Robert Gowing, Edward Impey, Barney Sloane and Simon Thurley for supporting the study and recording of the chapter house complex.

We owe a great debt to our colleagues at Westminster Abbey: the Dean and Chapter, Major-General David Burden (formerly Receiver General), Diane Gibbs-Rodwell (Museum Co-ordinator), Christine Reynolds (Assistant Keeper of the Muniments), Tony Trowles (Head of the Collections and Librarian), Jim Vincent (Clerk of the Works) and Christopher Vyse (Legal Secretary). For assistance with the illustrations we are grateful to Rosie Daswani and Claudio Costantino.

Officers and staff of the Society of Antiquaries have lent much practical support, namely Eric Fernie (President during the planning of the symposium and chair of the proceedings), Geoffrey Wainwright (President when the symposium was held), David Gaimster (General Secretary) and Georgia Toutziari (Office Manager). Kate Owen and Christopher Catling managed the text editing, design and production. We are immensely grateful to them all.

Warwick Rodwell
Consultant Archaeologist, Westminster Abbey
Richard Mortimer
Keeper of the Muniments, Westminster Abbey

Summary

Westminster Abbey chapter house ranks as one of the spectacular achievements of European Gothic architecture; and that is precisely what its builder, King Henry III, wished. Begun in the mid-1240s, and completed within a decade, its pre-eminence was recognized in its own day, when the chronicler Matthew Paris described Westminster as having 'a chapter house beyond compare'. It exhibits many features of distinction, from the elevation of its main chamber above a vaulted undercroft to the prominent display of Henry's arms – sixty-two times – in the tile pavement.

Lying adjacent to the principal royal palace in England of its day, Westminster Abbey has always had a uniquely complex relationship with the Crown and monarchy, enjoying the status of Royal Peculiar from the sixteenth century. In the Middle Ages, the king's great court, the predecessor of the English Parliament, sometimes met in the chapter house or in the refectory, and the royal Wardrobe established one of its repositories within the walls of the abbey. The undercroft ('crypt') and a nearby room known as the Pyx chamber were commandeered as royal treasuries from the reign of Edward I, if not earlier, and in 1303 the abbey became the focus of a scandal when one of the chambers was broken into and robbed.

After the Dissolution, the chapter house and Pyx chamber became repositories for government archives, while the undercroft fell out of use. The Public Record Office was thus born in the chapter house, and stayed there until the late 1850s. During the following decade, the building, which had been terribly mutilated over the centuries, underwent a comprehensive restoration at the hands of Sir George Gilbert Scott, to become what it is today. Still a 'Crown enclave' within Westminster Abbey, the chapter house and Pyx chamber are under the care of English Heritage, although, by a management agreement signed in 2003, day-to-day running of the buildings is now the responsibility of the Dean and Chapter.

Résumé

La salle du chapitre de l'abbaye de Westminster compte parmi les réalisations les plus spectaculaires de l'architecture gothique européenne; et c'est précisément ce que désirait son constructeur, le roi Henri III. Commencée au milieu des années 1240 et terminée en moins d'une décennie, sa prééminence était reconnue à l'époque même, lorsque le chroniqueur Matthew Paris décrivit Westminster et en dit qu'elle avait 'une salle du chapitre incomparable'. Elle présente nombre de remarquables caractéristiques, de l'élévation de sa salle principale au-dessus d'une crypte voûtée à l'affichage bien en évidence des armes du roi Henri – à soixante-deux reprises – dans le carrelage du sol.

Située à côté du principal palais royal d'Angleterre de l'époque, l'abbaye de Westminster a toujours eu des rapports vraiment complexes et uniques avec la couronne et la monarchie, car elle jouissait du titre de 'Royal Peculiar' [lieu de culte relevant de la juridiction personnelle du monarque et non pas d'un diocèse]. Au moyen-âge, la grande cour du roi, le prédécesseur du Parlement anglais, se réunissait parfois dans la salle du chapitre ou bien dans le réfectoire, et la garde-robe royale avait établi l'un de ses dépôts à l'intérieur des murs de l'abbaye. La crypte et une salle à proximité, connue sous le nom de salle Pyx, furent réquisitionnées pour servir de trésoreries royales à partir du règne d'Edouard I, sinon plus tôt, et, en 1303, l'abbaye devint le centre d'un scandale lorsque l'une des salles fit l'objet d'une effraction et d'un cambriolage.

Après la dissolution des monastères, la salle du chapitre et la salle Pyx furent transformées en dépôts pour les archives gouvernementales et la crypte ne fut plus utilisée. Ce fut ainsi que le Public Record Office [Archives nationales] vit le jour dans la salle du chapitre, et y resta jusqu'à la fin des années 1850. Au cours de la décennie suivante, le bâtiment, qui avait été terriblement mutilé au cours des siècles, fit l'objet d'une complète restauration, laquelle fut confiée à Sir Gilbert Scott, pour devenir ce qu'il est à l'heure actuelle. A ce jour, la salle du chapitre et la salle Pyx restent encore une 'enclave de la couronne' à l'intérieur de l'abbaye de Westminster, et elles sont entretenues par English Heritage bien que, de par un accord de gestion signé en 2003, le doyen et le chapitre soient dorénavant responsables de la gestion au quotidien des bâtiments.

Zusammenfassung

Das Kapitelhaus der Westminster Abtei gilt als eines der eindrucksvollsten Errungenschaften europäischer gotischer Architektur; ganz nach dem Wunsch seines Erbauers, König Henry III. Angefangen in der Mitte der 40er Jahre des 13. Jahrhunderts, und innerhalb eines Jahrzehnts vervollständigt, war ihre Besonderheit schon während ihrer Zeit anerkannt, als der Chronist Matthew Paris die Westminster Abtei als 'ein Kapitalhaus ohne Vergleich' beschrieb. Sie besitzt viele ausgezeichnete Merkmale, von der Erhebung ihres Hauptkapitels über einer gewölbten Kellergruft bis zur markanten Darstellung von Henry's Wappen – zweiundsechzig Mal – im Fliesenboden.

Durch die direkte Nähe zum damaligen königlichen Palast der englischen Krone, hatte die Westminster Abtei schon immer eine einzigartig komplexe Beziehung mit der Krone und der Monarchie, und nahm den Status einer Eigenkirche der Monarchie ein. Im Mittelalter traf der Königshof, der Vorläufer des englischen Parlaments, manchmal in Kapitelsaal oder im Refektorium zusammen, und die königliche Garderobe errichtete eine ihrer Aufbewahrungskammern innerhalb der Abtei. Die Kellergruft ('crypt') in einem benachbarten Raum, der sogenannten 'Pyx'-Kammer wurde seit der Regierungszeit von Edward I, eventuell schon früher, für den königlichen Schatz requiriert und im Jahr 1303 wurde die Abtei Brennpunkt eines Skandals, als einer der Kammern aufgebrochen und ausgeraubt wurde.

Nach der Auflösung der englischen Klöster wurden das Kapitelhaus und die 'Pyx'-Kammer zur Verwahrung von Regierungsarchieven genutzt, und das Kellergewölbe war nicht weiter in Gebrauch. Damit war das Britische Staatsarchiv im Kapitelhaus geboren, und war dort bis 1850 untergebracht. Im nachfolgendem Jahrzehnt erlebte das Gebäude, das in den vorhergehenden Jahrhunderten schrecklich verschandelt wurde, von Sir George Gilbert Scott eine umfassende Restauration, und wurde das, was es heute ist. Bis heute bleiben das Kapitelhaus und die 'Pyx'-Kammer eine Enklave der königlichen Krone innerhalb der Westminster Abtei und werden von English Heritage verwaltet. Die tägliche Verwaltung der Gebäude ist jedoch durch ein Management Abkommen, das 2003 unterschrieben wurde, jetzt die Verantwortung des Dekan und Stifts.

Contributors

Jeremy Ashbee MA PhD FSA
Head Properties Curator, English Heritage

Paul Binski MA PhD FBA FSA
Professor of the History of Medieval Art, University of Cambridge, and Fellow of Gonville and Caius College, Cambridge

Martin Bridge BSc PhD FSA
Oxford Dendrochronology Laboratory; Lecturer, Institute of Archaeology, University College London

Steven Brindle MA DPhil FSA
Senior Properties Historian, English Heritage

David Carpenter MA DPhil FRHistS
Professor of Medieval History, King's College, London

Richard Foster BA PhD FSA
Medieval Cultural Historian

Elizabeth Hallam Smith BA PhD FSA FRHistS
Director of Information Services and Librarian, House of Lords

Barbara Harvey CBE BLitt MA FBA FSA FRHistS
Emeritus Fellow, Somerville College, Oxford

Helen Howard BFA MA PhD
Scientific Department, National Gallery, London

Laurence Keen OBE MPhil FSA FRHistS
Medieval Archaeologist and Historian

Daniel Miles DPhil FSA
Oxford Dendrochronology Laboratory

Richard Mortimer MA PhD FSA FRHistS
Keeper of the Muniments, Westminster Abbey

Warwick Rodwell OBE BSc MA DPhil DLitt DLit FSA FRHistS
Visiting Professor in Archaeology, University of Reading; Consultant Archaeologist, Westminster Abbey and Wells Cathedral

Tim Tatton-Brown BA
Consultant Archaeologist, Salisbury Cathedral and formerly Westminster Abbey

Pamela Tudor-Craig (Lady Wedgwood) BA PhD FSA
Medieval Art Historian

Christopher Wilson BA PhD FSA
Emeritus Professor of Architectural History, University College, London

The chapter house complex:
morphology and construction

Warwick Rodwell

The chapter house of St Peter's Abbey, Westminster, is approached from the mid-point of the east cloister walk, through a long vestibule which passes under the dormitory range (figs 1 and 2). The structure is octagonal in plan and projects into what was formerly the monastic cemetery. Several aspects of the form and layout of the chapter house complex are unusual. First, the vestibule is divided into two distinct parts: outer and inner. Second, not only is the octagonal chamber attached on its west side to the vestibule, but its north-west face is also integrated with the corner of the transept; consequently, only six faces are presented externally. Third, the principal chamber is not at ground level, but is elevated by half a storey and is reached by a flight of ten steps situated in the inner vestibule. Fourth, the base of the octagon comprises a massively constructed podium; inside this is a vaulted undercroft (known as 'the crypt'), also of octagonal plan but only half the size of the chapter house above. Access to the subterranean chamber is via a tortuous passage and flight of steps leading off the south transept.

From the time that it was built in the 1250s to its restoration as an ancient monument in the 1860s, the chapter house and its adjuncts have fulfilled a variety of functions and have undergone numerous alterations to accommodate these. Some of the changes were drastic: particularly those associated with the use of the main chamber as a record office after the Dissolution when a huge amount of medieval fabric and decoration was lost. Consequently, the Victorian restoration had also to be drastic, but it, too, has suffered from dilapidation so that major external repair programmes were necessitated on the masonry in 1948–51 (following war damage), the early

1970s, the mid-1980s and again in 2009–10. Internally, some of the techniques employed in the nineteenth and twentieth centuries to protect and conserve the medieval sculpture, wall paintings and tile pavement have proved to be ineffective, or even seriously damaging, and these are a subject of continuing concern.

Although mentioned by numerous antiquaries, the chapter house was first effectively brought to the attention of scholars by Sir George Gilbert Scott in the 1860s, when he was engaged on a major restoration of the structure (see chapter 9). He published a number of papers describing the debilitated condition in which he found the building and the works that he undertook to bring it to its present state (figs 3 and 4).[1] Many scholars have subsequently discussed aspects of the history, architecture, art and restoration of the chapter house,[2] but it was not until 1924 that a systematic description was published by the Royal Commission on Historical Monuments.[3] This was followed in 1935 by the first of many editions of the official guide book.[4]

This chapter presents a brief description of the principal component parts of the vestibules, chapter house and undercroft (Plan 1), dwelling only on those aspects that are not more fully covered elsewhere in this volume.

Outer vestibule

The outer vestibule has twin entrances from the cloister, which are integrated with the bay structure of the outer wall (fig 5). The arches of the outer portal are low and pointed and have a continuous hollow chamfer, decorated with sprigs of foliage; there are no imposts. Outlining each

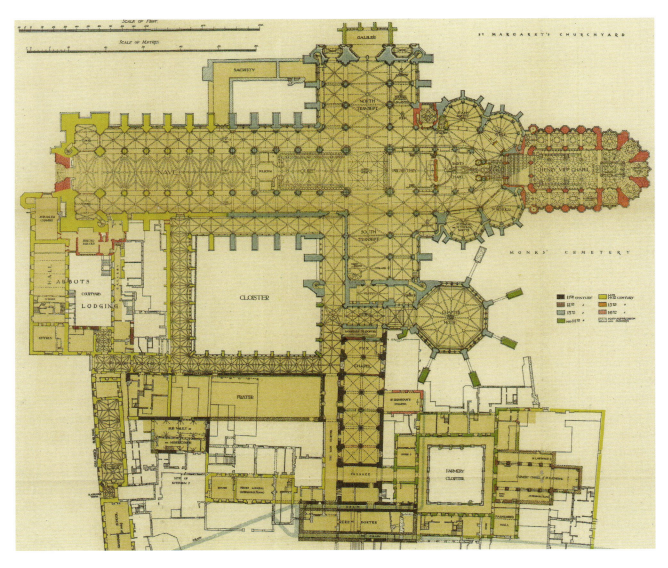

Fig 1 General plan of Westminster Abbey, 1921. *Drawing*: after RCHME 1924

opening is a hood-moulding with head-stops. The large tympanum above carries three ornate brackets for statuary, and the surrounding field is decorated with scrollwork, now eroded almost to extinction (for the sculpture, see chapter 10). Notwithstanding, vestigial traces of red and blue pigment can still be seen on the ashlar, and gilding was also formerly present.[5] In 1790, it was described as 'a most rich and magnificent Gothic portal',[6] and an account of the colour and gilding was given by Ackermann in 1812.[7] Encompassing the whole tableau is the wall-arch of the cloister vault, which in this bay is elaborated with two sculptured orders. These rise from the capitals of the clustered vaulting-shafts that punctuate the cloister bay divisions. The shafts, their capitals and bases, and the *trumeau* between the entrance arches are all made from Purbeck marble, whereas the remainder of the portal is of Reigate stone.

Inside, the vestibule is three bays in length and two in width, and on the central axis is a line of Purbeck marble columns with moulded capitals and bases (figs 6 and 68). Stone wall-benches along the northern and southern sides carry a complementary series of marble vaulting-shafts, which support the springers and moulded wall-arches of pointed form. There are two wall-arches per bay, except in the easternmost bays, where one is replaced by a doorway to both north and south.[8]

The ceiling of the vestibule is low and comprises six bays of quadripartite vaulting. The ribs are moulded and have carved foliage bosses that are now fragmentary. The vault in the north-west bay, and three-quarters of that in the adjoining bay to the east, were reconstructed by Scott, the original having been broken out in the late sixteenth century so as to install a timber staircase giving access to the library above. The bosses in the three northern bays are replacements. Scott based his designs for the new bosses on those surviving in the southern bays. The first

Fig 2 Cutaway view from the south west of the chapter house and adjacent structures in the east cloister. *Drawing*: Terry Ball; *photograph*: © English Heritage Photo Library

(western) bay has an asymmetrical foliate design incorporating a lizard-like creature, the second contains a symmetrical foliate boss with bunches of grapes and the third has swirling foliage.[9] The vault is constructed in Reigate stone, most of which has lost its original surface and hence any painted decoration; the plaster has also gone from the webs, which mainly comprise chalk blocks. Similarly, the comprehensive erosion of the wall arcades has left no evidence of painting. An indication of what has probably been lost is provided by Salisbury Cathedral (p 101).

The two opposing doorways in the easternmost bays are primary, and interconnect with chambers adjoining the vestibule to north and south. The doorway on the north gave access to the principal sacristy (which also housed an altar to St Faith), and through that to the transept. Known today simply as St Faith's chapel, the former sacristy is structurally an integral part of the chapter house complex.

The orientation of this doorway is interesting. As seen from the vestibule, the opening is recessed and has a lintelled head of Purbeck marble and chamfered jambs. This is, however, only the rear-arch: the 'outer' face, which is chamfered all round, is inside the sacristy. Thus the door opened into the vestibule.[10] The present oak door comprises a pair of leaves hanging in a frame and was installed before 1871. Nothing is known of its medieval predecessor, the door having been removed in the sixteenth century and the aperture blocked.[11]

The doorway in the south wall has a shouldered lintel of Purbeck marble and chamfered jambs. The door opens outwards from the vestibule into a small store-room under the Victorian stair that leads to the library above; since 1591, the chapter library has been housed in the northern end of the former dormitory. The entry to that stair is from the east cloister, in the bay adjoining the vestibule to the south, where there is an ornate

3

Fig 3 The chapter house from the east in the early twentieth century. *Photograph*: English Heritage. NMR

thirteenth-century doorway (Plan 1). Here originally lay the monks' day-stair, which was also contemporary with the construction of the chapter house. The door in the south wall of the vestibule thus accessed an awkwardly disposed chamber under, and to the rear of, the day-stair. It is debatable whether there was also at that time an opening from the understair chamber into the adjacent bays of the dormitory undercroft, a space that later became known as the Pyx chamber (Plan 1). The provision of a door in the south wall of the vestibule does, in any event, indicate an anticipated need to access the dorter undercroft from the vestibule. Whether Henry III intended to remodel the remainder of the east cloister range is unknown, but he would almost certainly have anticipated rebuilding the four cloister walks in the Gothic style. Having reconstructed most of the east walk, he would hardly have wished to leave the others in their eleventh-century form.

The day-stair was demolished in or soon after 1591, and was superseded by a timber staircase in the outer vestibule; the original arrangement was restored by Scott in 1860. In 1823 the former day-stair space was described as 'a vaulted part of the old buildings, now used as a wine cellar';[12] the plan of 1820 (fig 32) indicates that entry was from the cloister, and the door from the vestibule appears to have been closed up, but other evidence conflicts with this.[13] Not long after, the space was somehow appropriated for the storage of public records.[14] The door hanging in the opening is of exceptional interest: it dates from Edward the Confessor's reign, and was reduced in size in the thirteenth century for reuse here (door 1 in fig 242).

The floor is stone flagged and is now one step up from the cloister level.[15] The paving in the northern half of the vestibule is irregular in layout and is now mostly of Yorkstone. Dating from 1987, it replaced a similarly irregular arrangement of worn limestone slabs, which have often been claimed as medieval (fig 7).[16] If this had been medieval paving, it is unlikely to have been primary, since squares of Purbeck stone were employed in the thirteenth century for flooring both the church and the east cloister. The larger and more regimented slabs of Yorkstone in the southern bays were possibly first introduced by Scott, but have been relaid subsequently. Photographs show that the paving in the two halves of the vestibule was at different levels with a low stone step (now gone) running east–west along the axis between the columns.[17] The entrance was not designed to accommodate doors, and the present iron gates date from the 1860s.[18]

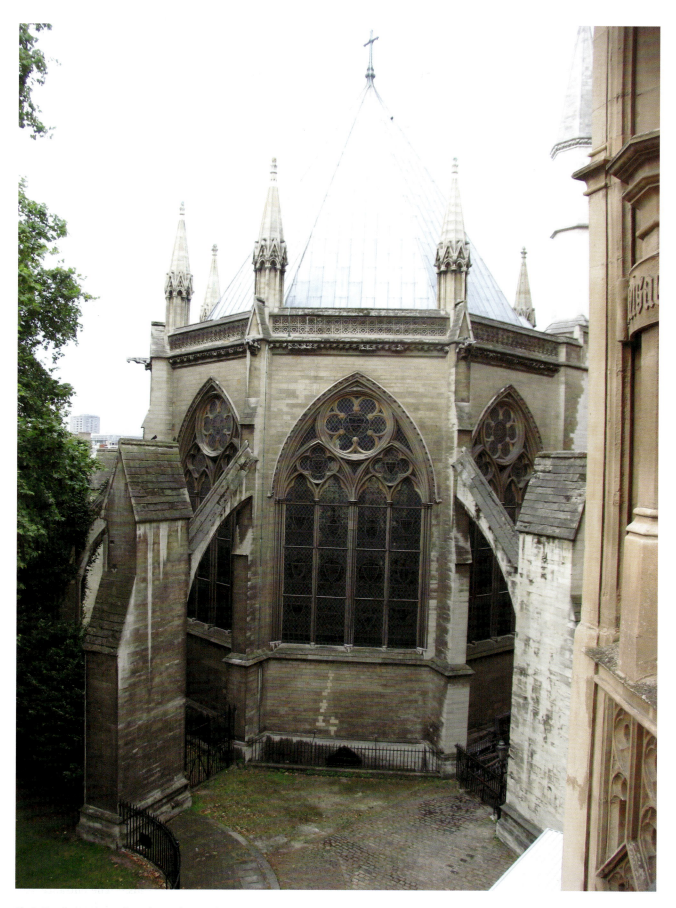

Fig 4 The chapter house from the north east. The tops of the undercroft windows show just above ground level. *Photograph*: Warwick Rodwell
© Dean and Chapter of Westminster

Fig 5 The entrance to the chapter house vestibule (outer portal) from the east cloister. *Photograph*: © Dean and Chapter of Westminster

Fig 6 The outer vestibule: view east through the southern portal, with the steps of the inner vestibule beyond. *Photograph*: Warwick Rodwell © Dean and Chapter of Westminster

Fig 7 The outer vestibule: view east, showing the possible medieval paving in the northern half prior to its renewal in 1987. *Photograph*: © English Heritage. NMR

At the eastern end of the vestibule is a second pair of pointed arches with moulded jambs carved with sprigs of foliage (middle portal); the inner vestibule lies beyond. Again, there are no rebates for medieval doors, and the openings are filled with pairs of wrought iron gates, introduced by Scott.[19]

Inner vestibule

This is of two unequal bays, both vaulted with a single span; there is no axial division of the space, nor a central column.[20] The inner vestibule projects eastwards beyond the dormitory range, and is much loftier than the outer vestibule on account of there being no structure over it. Above the vault is a flat lead roof, which was renewed in 1994. The joists and boarding were found to be of deal and dated from *c* 1870; no evidence for the form of the medieval roof was recoverable. The external masonry and parapet of the vestibule had also been renewed by Scott in Chilmark stone.[21]

The interior is almost entirely filled with a broad flight of nine steps (2 + 7) and two landings (fig 8).[22] Flanking the steps to north and south are wide stone-capped ledges, on top of which are narrower wall-benches carrying the shafts supporting the quadripartite vaulting. That has moulded ribs of Reigate stone and the webs are filled with a mixture of Reigate and chalk blocks; there is a central foliate boss in the eastern bay only.

The middle portal has twin openings at the point of entry from the outer vestibule. On the west side these have continuously moulded jambs and arches, and one order is carved with foliage (fig 66). The label-mouldings have head-stops. Facing east, above the entrance, is a Purbeck marble string-course, upon which rest three blind wall-arches of pointed form, springing from shafts with moulded capitals. Over those arches are three blind quatrefoils. At the base of each wall-arch is a corbel to support a figure-sculpture. The whole of this work is enclosed by a pointed wall-arch of two moulded and one carved order, springing from Purbeck marble shafts with moulded capitals and bases.

In the north wall, above the string-course, are two pairs of lancet windows that provide borrowed light for St Faith's chapel (fig 64). The two windows in the south wall admitted light from the exterior (figs 65 and 66). The eastern is a lancet with a moulded rear-arch and shafted reveals, while the western has three graduated, trefoil-headed lights, a moulded rear-arch and flanking shafts with foliate capitals. This window is a reconstruction by Scott.[23] In the lower register, beneath the eastern window is a tall, narrow locker formed within the wall. It has a square head and rebated jambs for a door. The interior is divided into two unequal compartments by a stone shelf.[24]

The stone steps and the decorated tile paving of the landings all date from the mid-nineteenth century. However, there was a medieval inlaid tile floor here, described in 1842 as 'paved with variegated tiles, the patterns of which are now nearly obliterated'.[25] Five

Fig 8 The inner vestibule: steps leading up to the west face of the inner portal to the chapter house. *Photograph*: Warwick Rodwell © Dean and Chapter of Westminster

original tiles have been reset on the upper landing. These are products of the 'Westminster' tiler and probably date from the late thirteenth or early fourteenth century.[26] Scott's reproduction tiles are of similar type, having been copied from the worn medieval examples that he replaced

(figs 9 and 10; Plan 2). His brass heating grilles are decoratively pierced in emulation of the tile designs. The upper landing is one step below floor level in the chapter house, which is entered through yet another pair of arches without doors: the inner portal.

Fig 9 The inner vestibule: Victorian tile pavement on the landing in front of the inner portal. The designs are based on the medieval 'Westminster' tiles that Scott replaced. The pierced brass heating grilles embody the same designs. *Photograph*: Warwick Rodwell © Dean and Chapter of Westminster

Fig 10 Inner vestibule: detail of the Victorian tile pavement adjacent to the *trumeau* of the inner portal, with five reset medieval 'Westminster' tiles. *Photograph*: Warwick Rodwell © Dean and Chapter of Westminster

Chapter house

The chapter house is a regular octagon in plan, and externally measures 19.8 m (65 ft) across the faces at plinth level; internally it is 18 m (59 ft 6 in). The thirteenth-century structure was faced externally with Reigate stone, nearly all of which was replaced by Scott using Chilmark stone.[27] The window mullions and responds, together with their shafts, capitals and bases, were of Purbeck marble,

and mirrored exactly the internal arrangement (for which see below, p 11). However, the external features have all been renewed in Devonshire and Kilkenny marbles (figs 11 and 12).[28] The latter was also used in the 1870s as a substitute for shafts of blue lias on the west front of Wells Cathedral. Since these materials bore little visual resemblance to Purbeck marble, they were toned with an oil-based concoction.[29] The window tracery is of oolitic limestone, probably from the Bath area; the original may have been of Caen stone. Although Scott's restoration was thoroughgoing, he adopted an archaeological approach and carried out extensive investigations in order to recover evidence for the authentic detailing. It is therefore likely that, up to parapet level, the external envelope is a more-or-less faithful replica of what was originally built, except in respect of the stone types employed. The parapets and pinnacles are entirely Scott's own design, there being no surviving evidence for the form of the originals. He was however unaware of an early seventeenth-century drawing showing that the parapet had a quatrefoil frieze (fig 30).

A few original mouldings and areas of medieval ashlar-work were preserved, but these too have now been lost through twentieth-century restoration.[30] The tall lead-covered pyramidal roof is also Scott's and is a remarkable piece of engineering: the structural framing consists not of timber but of cast iron sections bolted together (fig 137).

The exterior elevations comprise three stages plus parapet, and a buttress of three weathered stages clasps each of the six visible angles (fig 4). The first stage comprises the deep plinth, which has a single window in each face and corresponds to the visible part of the semi-subterranean undercroft (see below). Above a chamfered offset is the second featureless stage, which is topped by a string-course at window sill level. The third stage is dominated by huge four-light windows; the lights are

paired and each has a trefoil head with a quatrefoil in the tracery above, all surmounted by a roundel containing a sexfoil and a two-centred outer arch with hood-moulding. In three instances, there are carvings in the cavetto of the hood.[31] The wall-tops were finished by Scott with a corbel-table, a solid parapet with shallowly carved decoration and tall aedicular pinnacles.

In the fourteenth century the walls evidently began to lean outwards, threatening the stability of the vault, and additional support was provided by the construction of massive flying buttresses in 1377.[32] These seem to have comprised a mixture of Reigate stone, Caen stone (for the copings) and other limestones. The addition of pinnacles, for which Scott detected slight evidence (p 144), will have occurred at the same time. It was also probably in the

Fig 12 The chapter house south-east window: Scott's king-mullion, after partial cleaning in 2009. The triple roll is made of coursed Devonshire marble of strikingly variegated colour, and the base is grey Carboniferous limestone. The lowest mullion block has been cleaned, whereas that above retains some of Scott's oil-based treatment to simulate Purbeck marble. *Photograph*: Warwick Rodwell © Dean and Chapter of Westminster

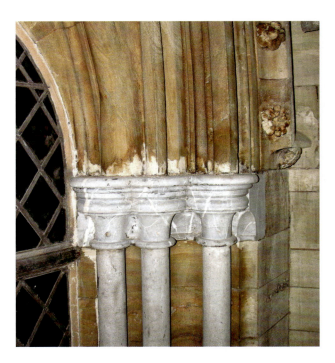

Fig 11 The chapter house, east window: Scott's north respond, after cleaning in 2009. The capital is Devonshire marble, the shafts probably Kilkenny marble, the mouldings above are Bath stone and the ashlar is Chilmark stone. *Photograph*: Warwick Rodwell © Dean and Chapter of Westminster

fourteenth century that the tracery in the west window of the chapter house (above the inner vestibule roof) was changed, possibly after fire damage: it was now given five lights instead of four, and the sexfoiled roundel was replaced by an octofoil, which was aesthetically more pleasing for the proportions of such a short window.[33] The original four-light arrangement was reinstated by Scott, who jettisoned his first scheme to retain the modified west window (figs 132 and 140).

When Wren was carrying out repairs to the south ambulatory in 1705–7 he entirely removed the northernmost flying buttress from the chapter house, deeming it to be an unnecessary obstacle: it was replaced by Scott.[34] The age of the small flying buttress in the angle between the vestibule and the south-west side of the chapter house may also be questionable since it does not appear on a plan of 1820 (fig 32).[35]

The interior of the chapter house need not be described in detail since all its major aspects are covered in subsequent chapters (Plan 2). The entry from the inner vestibule consists of a moulded and profusely carved two-centred arch of four orders, within which is a pair of trefoil-headed openings surmounted by a large quatrefoil in the tracery (the inner portal; figs 8 and 142). The responds and central column are all of Purbeck marble and the capitals are profusely carved with stiff leaves and other details. On the east face the arch has two orders: one moulded and the other exquisitely carved. The spandrels to either side of the entrance are filled with trefoils containing sculptures of censing angels, and the whole composition is flanked by the figures of the Annunciation standing on surprisingly crude pedestals in trefoil-headed niches (fig 142).

Two aspects of Scott's treatment of this portal require comment. First, the large circle containing an open quatrefoil (or possibly a sexfoil) had been badly damaged, and he restored it, but inexplicably he filled the opening with two sculptured roundels depicting Christ in Majesty, placed back to back. Although the subject of frequent adverse comment (see pp 152 and 168), the motivation for this extraordinary intervention has yet to be discovered. Almost certainly he was influenced by the inner portal of the chapter house at Salisbury Cathedral, where there is a blind quatrefoil in a similar position (fig 69). It faces into the chapter house and incorporates a Victorian figure of Christ; on the vestibule side there is a wide niche with a foiled head and a statue bracket.[36]

Second, Scott applied his usual shellac-based treatment – which he termed 'induration' – to the Reigate stone carving, in the belief that this would preserve the friable surface from further decay.[37] However, examination from scaffolding in 2008 revealed how tragically damaging this

intervention has been (see chapter 10, appendix B). On the figure of St Mary, for example, Scott's mixture was carelessly applied and only part of her sinister arm and side were indurated: the brush-marks at the extremity of the treated area were clearly visible, as was the effect of the application. The stone that had not been indurated still retains a smooth surface with much evidence of polychromy, whereas the adjacent treated area has almost completely lost its original surface and is now powdery. Scott also indurated the portal in the cloister, the subsequent decay of which has been similarly accelerated.[38]

The lofty interior of the chamber is stone vaulted, supported at the centre by a slender, compound pillar of Purbeck marble, 10.7 m high (frontispiece and fig 47). The octagonal base supports a circular central core, ringed with eight subsidiary shafts. The core is fabricated from multiple blocks with thin bedding joints, and the pillar is divided into three sections by shaft-rings. The marble capital is carved with luxuriant stiff-leaf foliage (fig 143), and the base has waterholding mouldings. It is uncertain to what extent Scott dismantled and rebuilt the central column. Although he repaired it, together with the capital and base, he did not renew them entirely.[39] Instead, he skilfully pieced-in stone to restore damaged mouldings and carving; some sections of the *en délit* shafts have, however, been renewed. The springers and first few sections of vaulting rib, on both the column and the wall-shafts, are thirteenth century, but the remainder of the vault is Scott's. He also introduced four fine historiated bosses (fig 13), and four with foliate carving.

Radiating from the abacus are eight wrought iron hooks. Iron tying-bars with looped ends were originally attached to these and to the corresponding hooks placed at the angles in the outer wall. Similar bars, linking together the arcade piers and vaulting-shafts in the ambulatory and transepts of the abbey, are still *in situ* (fig 51). The bars in the chapter house do not appear on the 1807 sectional view (fig 123), and had thus presumably been discarded during the eighteenth-century refit.[40] The antiquity of the hooks in the pillar and walls has been questioned, but most, if not all, are medieval.[41] The method of embedding the hooks in the abacus of the pillar is well illustrated at Salisbury (fig 105).

Each wall contains a four-light window with Geometrical tracery, although in the north-west face it is blind on account of the juxtaposition of the transept staircase (fig 50). The integration of these features establishes beyond doubt that the chapter house complex was designed and built with the transept. The window reveals carry three freestanding Purbeck marble shafts; the king-mullion has an attached triple roll and the

Fig 13 Chapter house: boss on the east side of the vault depicting the Annunciation. It is one of four new historiated bosses introduced by Scott in his reconstructed vault. *Photograph*: © English Heritage. NMR 1951

intermediate mullions have single rolls. All the shafts and rolls, including their capitals and bases, are wrought in Purbeck marble (fig 56). Below window sill level is a marble string-course and continuous circuit of blind arcading, founded on a wall-bench, except where it is interrupted by the entrance (fig 58). There are two further tiers of continuous stone benching in front, which would have allowed the seating capacity to be tripled. The trefoil arches of the wall-arcade are moulded and are carried on Purbeck marble shafts with carved capitals. The spandrels are enriched with a variety of diapering and other repetitive detail, all in Reigate stone.

The arcading defines five seats per side, except on the west, where there are only two, making a total of thirty-seven (Plan 2). The five bays on the east are deeper than the rest and have an extra tier of benching, giving added dignity to the abbot and senior monks; the same occurs at Salisbury (p 94). Little is known about the thirteenth-century decoration of the arcaded zone; traces of colour and gilding remain on the arcade mouldings of the east wall and though it has not been confirmed whether this polychromy is primary, it seems highly likely. Cole published a drawing of one bay, recorded while the colours were still vibrant: the roll-mouldings of the trefoil-heads were crimson, maroon and gold, and the hollows in between were pale blue; the

stiff-leaf capitals were red and blue and the spandrels were red with gilded diapering (fig 34).[42]

The two niches on the west (nos 1 and 37) are much taller than the rest, and give the impression that they were designed to accommodate standing figures somewhat larger than life-size (figs 132 and 142). Whether these were intended to be sculptures, or painted images, cannot now be determined.

The surviving wall paintings in the arcades are all secondary, and are divisible into four distinct groups (see chapter 11):

(i) The five eastern bays and three of those flanking them on the north-east and south-east (eleven in all: nos 14–24) depicted Christ in Judgement (frontispiece and fig 173). The scenes have been entirely lost from the north-east bays. Date: *c* 1400.

(ii) The remaining arcade bays, all round the chapter house except on the west (nos 2–13, 25–36), each contained four scenes from the Apocalypse (figs 174 and 180). The total number of scenes was ninety-six.[43] Date: *c* 1400.

(iii) A series of angels playing musical instruments, in the upper lobe of each wall-arch, except on the east (figs 178 and 179). Date: *c* 1400.

(iv) Beneath the Apocalypse scenes were two panels in each bay, depicting beasts and birds confronting one another (figs 181 and 183). The total number of creatures was probably forty-eight. Date: late fifteenth century, or possibly early sixteenth.

The complete absence of decoration today on the northern and north-eastern sides of the chamber is the result of the masonry having been substantially reconstructed by Scott. In the early nineteenth century, a single doorway was broken through the north wall for external access (fig 33), and two more through the north-east, to connect with a new office that was built outside the chapter house. Reconstruction of the ashlar masonry in these bays has been so thorough that the outlines of the openings are undetectable. Two further doorways were created in the east wall for access to another office, causing partial destruction of the paintings in the first and fifth bays of the arcade. The Victorian masonry filling these openings is readily discernible, and the wall-benches below are largely reconstructions too.

Full exposure of the wall paintings in the 1860s led to a succession of ill-fated attempts to carry out 'preservative' treatments. In 1891, W J Loftie urged that the paintings 'should be carefully examined while they are yet visible. Unfortunately, by way of securing their preservation, they were coated by some sort of varnish by Scott, and the past few years have wrought more harm to them than the centuries they passed in neglect behind the wainscoting'.[44]

The decorated tile floor in the chapter house stands 1.75 m above the level of the cloister paving. In part, it became heavily worn before being concealed beneath a timber floor that was installed at an uncertain date, but probably not before the late seventeenth century (it was most likely Wren's work). The pavement had suffered considerable wear before it was boarded over, and visitors were permitted to walk freely on it after Scott's restoration. By the late nineteenth century access was restricted and linoleum was laid down to protect the tiles. When the floor was re-exposed in 1923, visitors were again allowed onto the tiles so long as they wore the felt-soled overshoes that were provided.[45] As a result of bomb damage the chapter house was closed to the public from 1940 to 1951; the floor was fully exposed and overshoes were again provided, an arrangement that persisted for some decades.[46] Then, in the late twentieth century, mats were reinstated and visitors were constrained to walk on those alone. Although the chapter house boasts the finest thirteenth-century tile pavement in Britain, it has not hitherto been systematically studied; such accounts of it as have been published are very incomplete, and the plans notable for their inaccuracy. The pavement was comprehensively cleaned and an orthophotographic record made in 1997 (fig 215); a detailed plan was drawn in 2009 (Plan 2).

During the nineteenth and early twentieth centuries the chapter house gradually became cluttered with exhibition material and museum cases containing documents, seals and other artefacts. The vestibules were used to display the Roman sarcophagus discovered on North Green in 1869 and a lapidary collection.[47] Since the 1980s these exhibits have progressively been removed.

Major works were carried out by Wren. In 1663–64, one of the Gothic windows was bricked up;[48] in 1672–73 two of the buttresses were mutilated and c 1707 the flying buttress on the north side was demolished. Sometime before 1686 one of the canons caused aggravation by building a brewhouse against the south side of the chapter house.[49] The chapter house was in poor condition in 1703, when the increasing volume of archives caused an accommodation crisis. Wren built the gallery soon after, and that must have been the time when the large medieval openings were infilled and pairs of much smaller classical round-headed windows substituted.[50] By 1728 the chapter house was a 'commodious repository for records'.

By 1737 the structure was again in a parlous state and more repairs followed, culminating in the removal of the stone vault and roof in 1751–52.[51] An attic storey was now formed, lit by lunette windows with Y-tracery, which were inserted into the heads of the already blocked medieval openings. The new roof had a flat top, was square in plan, and hipped all round; it was finished with a crenellated brick parapet coped with Portland stone. Several illustrations of this structure have survived (figs 123, 124 and 133).[52] At ground level, a door was broken through the north wall, so that access to the record office could be obtained without entering the abbey.

The restoration by Scott is discussed in chapter 9. The form of the original roof has caused much speculation, but was almost certainly near-flat, as seen in early views of the abbey and maps (figs 31 and 62). Salisbury and Wells cathedrals provide close analogues (pp 98 and 81). Scott's soaring pyramidal structure was inspired by the tall 'candle snuffer' roofs at Lincoln, Southwell and York,[53] but he was also heavily influenced by the falsely authoritative assertion of his mentor, Henry Clutton: 'The high-pitched roof at Westminster was removed in 1714; this is a recorded fact, and confirms the opinion set forth in my report, that no chapter-house of a polygonal shape was ever entirely finished without the addition of this very characteristic feature.'[54] Although Clutton had restored Salisbury's chapter house in 1855, he was evidently unaware that its surviving low pitched roof was primary (fig 107).

After Scott, little seems to have been done to the fabric until the late 1940s, when war damage was repaired. That was largely confined to the window tracery and glazing (chapter 13).[55] By 1970, the masonry of the flying buttresses and pinnacles was in dire condition and repairs were put in hand, while the roof was re-leaded in 1976.[56]

Undercroft (crypt)

'Beneath the Chapter House at Westminster is a Crypt of so remarkable a character that it is surprising no efforts should have been made to ascertain the purpose of its construction, or, if such efforts have been made, that they should have produced no result.' So wrote Henry Harrod in 1873 at the opening of his paper on the undercroft.[57] He then proceeded to argue that the undercroft had been constructed expressly as a royal treasury, and that it was the scene of the great robbery in 1303 (chapter 7).

The undercroft is one of the least studied spaces in the abbey and notwithstanding its frequent mention in discussions of the events of 1303, it has never been systematically described; most architectural publications concerning the chapter house have either omitted it altogether or provided only a cursory account.[58] There are two components: the octagonal chamber and the dog-legged passage by which it is approached from the south transept. We shall begin with the passage, which contains nineteen steps and is in three distinct sections (A, B and C on figs 14 and 15).

Entrance Passage

In the south-east corner of the south transept (Poets' Corner) is an undistinguished doorway with a low, two-centred head (door 3 on Plan 1; fig 250). It opens into a passage (A) with a part-vaulted and part-corbelled roof (fig 16). The passage is skewed towards the south-east, and

is responsible for the asymmetrical plan and canted corner in St Faith's chapel (Plan 1). Although the passage is integral with the 1240s construction, the door itself was renewed in the mid-fourteenth century (p 258).

Within the passage, off to the left, is the substantial newel stair that provides the principal means of access to the triforium and the roofs in the eastern arm of the abbey. The passage continues south-eastwards, past the stair, the floor descending by four steps to a quadrangular landing (steps 1–4) outside the door opening into the second leg of the passage (B).[59] This lies at right-angles to the first

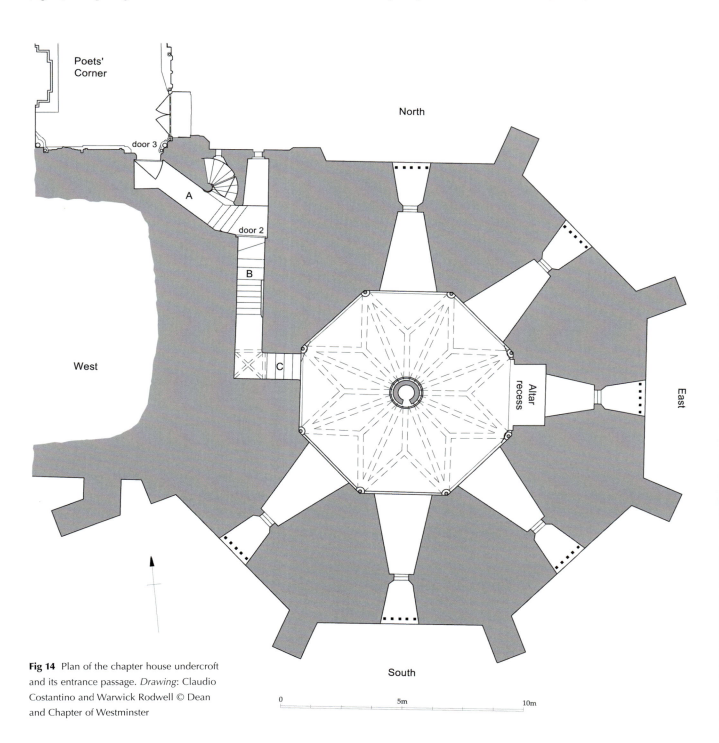

Fig 14 Plan of the chapter house undercroft and its entrance passage. *Drawing*: Claudio Costantino and Warwick Rodwell © Dean and Chapter of Westminster

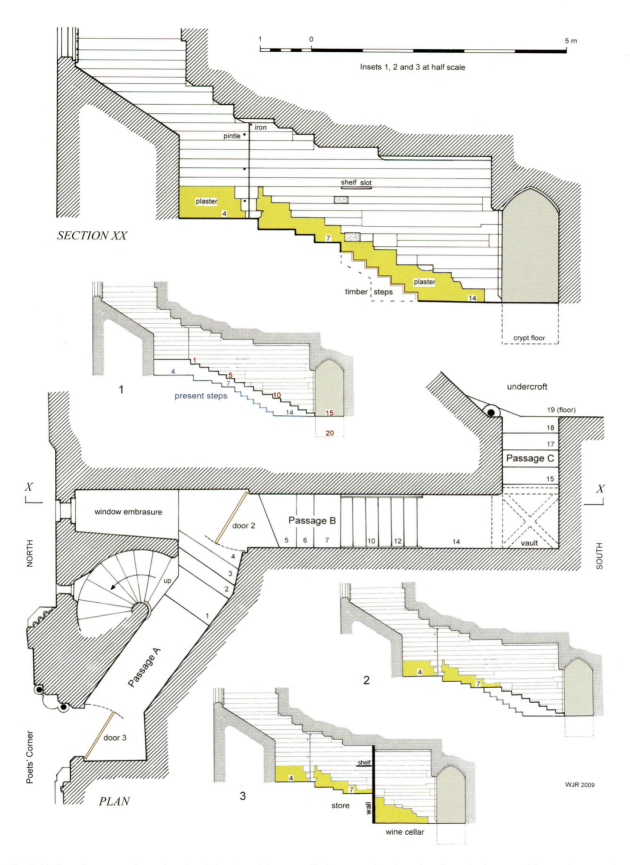

SECTION XX

Fig 15 Undercroft passage: plan and sectional elevation of the east wall, showing archaeological evidence for the original floor and steps in the central portion (B) of the passage. *Insets*: (1) reconstruction of the original mid thirteenth-century steps (numbered in red) in passage B, in relation to the present arrangement (blue); (2) late thirteenth-century rearrangement to create a landing for a secure door at the junction between passages A and B, and to improve headroom in B; (3) post-medieval removal of some steps from passage B, inserting a blocking wall to close it off at the mid-point, and converting the upper part into a store and the lower part into a wine cellar. *Drawing*: Warwick Rodwell © Dean and Chapter of Westminster

Fig 16 Undercroft passage, section A. View south east along the passage, from the doorway in the south transept to the inner door at the beginning of section B. *Photograph*: Warwick Rodwell © Dean and Chapter of Westminster

Fig 17 Undercroft passage, section B. View north, showing the six Victorian timber steps and scarring on the side walls where the original stone steps have been removed. *Photograph*: Warwick Rodwell © Dean and Chapter of Westminster

passage and at its northern end is a small rectangular window set high up, in a deep embrasure. To the south, is a square-headed oak door hanging in an opening which has rebated jambs but no proper head (door 2 on fig 15; fig 246). Above the door is a corbelled arrangement of lintels of Purbeck marble forming the complex roof of the passage. The lintels do not cross the passage at right-angles but are markedly skewed, the reason for this being that they constitute the support structure for the internal stone benching along the north-western side of the chapter house. It is obvious that there was originally no door here, and that the passage has been adapted to receive one. The door itself is part of a once-much-larger medieval lattice-braced door that was cut down and reframed in the nineteenth century (fig 248); dendrochronology demonstrated that it dates from Henry III's reign (p 256). It was possibly installed by Scott, but more likely by Lethaby (p 257), and nothing is known of the door that preceded it.

Beyond the door, the passage narrows to 1.1 m and includes a flight of steps (fig 113). The roof too is stepped and slabbed with Purbeck marble.[60] Three steps descend onto what was once a landing (no. 7), but the front of this has been cut away. Then there is a flight of six modern timber steps (nos 8–13), made of deal (figs 17 and 18). At the bottom of these, the passage continues and is paved

Fig 18 Undercroft passage B: detail of scars on the east wall, revealing the original profile of the stone steps. *Photograph*: Warwick Rodwell © Dean and Chapter of Westminster

with Yorkstone (step 14). At its southern end, the passage takes another right-angled turn, into the final section (C). The ceiling at the junction is formed by a quadripartite vault; the ribs are plain chamfered and there is no boss at the intersection (fig 19). Vertical scars and fixings on the walls near the end of the passage ghost the site of a post-medieval doorframe.

The third section of passage (C) is short and contains the final five steps (nos 15–19) descending to floor level in the undercroft, which is 3.25 m below that of the transept (fig 20). Two of the steps are medieval, in Reigate stone, and the others have been renewed. The sloping ceiling above comprises a plastered tunnel-vault. The passage opens into the west side of the undercroft, through a plain, chamfered arch with a two-centred head. No door was intended here, but one had later been fitted to the face of the masonry, without cutting rebates, although the capital and base of an adjacent colonnette in the undercroft were partly hacked away. Two holes have been left by the extracted pintles in the south jamb, and one for the locking device in the north jamb. The door, which does not survive, was probably added in the sixteenth or seventeenth century, when the passage was obstructed and became a store (fig 36). In the eighteenth century it was reported that the undercroft was not accessible from the transept (p 27), and after the Dissolution a blocking wall must have been inserted somewhere within the passage to sever the connection. The most plausible position for this is on the former landing (step 7), where there is a chase in the east wall for a wooden shelf that must have been placed in front of the inserted wall (fig 15).

While the entire passage is clearly primary, the present arrangement of steps within it reflects two phases of modification, one medieval and the other nineteenth century. Understanding these changes has a critical bearing on the interpretation of the original function of the undercroft (pp 87–9). Scar evidence on the walls of the first section of passage (A) shows that it had a level floor throughout,[61] and the steps were all contained within the second and third sections (figs 15, 17, 18 and 20). There were twenty steps in all (as opposed to the existing nineteen) and the primary arrangement provided less headroom than there is at present, a problem that was only slightly eased by bevelling the arrises of the overhead lintels. At original step 4, headroom was a mere 1.42 m (4 ft 9 in).[62] Consequently, it would have been necessary to stoop when descending into the undercroft.

Close examination of the inserted doorway at the head of the modified stairs (section B) shows that its eastern rebate is formed by a fortuitous vertical offset in the masonry of the passage, and its western rebate has been cut

Fig 19 Undercroft passage: detail of the crude quadripartite vault at the junction between sections B and C, viewed from the east. *Photograph*: Warwick Rodwell © Dean and Chapter of Westminster

Fig 20 Undercroft: entrance arch in the west wall, and the steps within section C of the passage, view west. *Photograph*: Warwick Rodwell © Dean and Chapter of Westminster

in situ into the ashlar-work at the right-angled turn in the passage. The door hangs on three Victorian iron pintles set into the eastern rebate, where they must have replaced medieval pintles in the same positions. The masonry adjacent to the west rebate displays evidence for a series of medieval and later fittings (fig 114). There were three large staples leaded into the reveal, indicating a suite of medieval locks. A fourth staple and scar for housing a box-lock are post-medieval and relate to the door that preceded the present one. Two rectangular pockets cut into the reveal indicate that one of the earlier doors had battens on the back. Finally, two more holes in the masonry are probably associated with sliding bolts that allowed the door to be secured from within the undercroft. Towards the base of the jamb are two areas of damage to the arrises. While these injuries could be accidental, they are also consistent with the application of a crowbar or similar implement in an attempt to force the door.

In order for a door to open at the entrance to passage B, there had to be a level area in front of it. Creating that necessitated rearranging the steps in the upper part of the main flight. Consequently, original steps 1 to 6 were completely removed, step 7 was extended to form an intermediate landing (which improved the headroom), another landing (present step 4) was established where the door needed to swing, and four new steps were cut into the floor of passage A. Access to the undercroft was thereby greatly improved.

The newly installed door could only be as high as the lowest of the lintels forming the corbelled roof of the passage: that left an irregular stepped aperture above the door, which was not closed. It is now filled by fixed boards, but small pockets cut into the stone, lead plugs and broken fragments of iron remain where several bars were formerly secured in the masonry above the door, confirming that the aperture was protected with an iron grille. All indications point to the creation of a very secure entrance at this point. Although the modification was certainly medieval, it is not intrinsically datable.

In more recent times, the stairway was modified once again. The seven lowest steps (the original nos 8–14) in passage B were removed to create a flat floor when the passage was closed off, and the southern end adapted for use as a wine cellar (in the seventeenth century?). When that function ceased, and the passage was reopened in the mid-nineteenth century, a short section of timber stair, with only six steps, was constructed (the present nos 8–13).[63] This was probably intended only as a temporary measure, to be replaced with stone steps when the crypt was fully restored. Although that occurred in 1909, the timber stair is still in place (fig 17).[64]

The octagonal chamber

The undercroft is a regular octagon measuring 8.7 m (28 ft 6 in) across the sides (fig 14); the walls are 5.5 m (18 ft) thick and finished with coursed Reigate ashlar internally. At the centre of the chamber stands a stout circular column of Purbeck marble, 1.78 m high (figs 21, 22 and 23). The shaft consists of four drum-sections, 1.08 m in diameter, three of which have been carefully hollowed internally to form circular cavities with rectangular apertures for access; the lowest drum-section is solid. The second drum is hollow for its full depth, and presents a squarish aperture to the south (fig 24).[65] The third drum has also been hollowed, but not for its entire depth, so as to maintain a separating diaphragm between this and the cavity below; the aperture faces east.[66] The fourth (uppermost) drum is the thinnest, and has been hollowed for its full depth (fig 25); it is an integral part of the upper cavity.[67] Both cavities are smoothly finished internally and were certainly cut before the column was assembled. The purpose of these empty compartments has never been explained, and Scott commented on the hollowing of the pillar, 'as if for the concealment of valuables'.[68]

The arrises around the apertures are unmoulded and there is no evidence for doors or fixings of any kind. The openings are wedge-shaped in plan, and if the cavities were secured, that must have been achieved by inserting tapered blocks of stone. If carefully done, the existence of the voids would have been undetectable except by anyone with foreknowledge. Indeed, one is left with the distinct impression that the cavities were meant to be invisibly sealed, after items had been deposited in them. They may not have been intended to receive holy relics, but foundation deposits are a possibility.[69] This column was not merely a structural component of the undercroft, but the foundation upon which the stability of the entire chapter house depended. The nature of the two intended deposits cannot be ascertained; nor can it be assumed that they were even installed. There is no trace of mortar in the reveals, and it seems likely that the mouths of the cavities have never been plugged.

The combined bell-shaped capital and abacus of the column has a simple profile and is formed in two halves.[70] Separate blocks form the moulded base and chamfered plinth.[71] Springing from the capital are sixteen chamfered vault-ribs. Eight of these run radially to the angles of the chamber, where they are met by wall-shafts (figs 20, 26 and 27). Their inverted bell-shaped capitals are crudely cut in Reigate stone, without a moulded abacus or neck-ring.[72] The detached shafts are of Purbeck marble, as are the bases. The latter have plain

Fig 21 The undercroft, before 1909: view north east after the clearance of soil from the interior, showing the altar recess in the east wall. On the right is the handrail to the steps leading to an entrance through the site of the south-east window. *Photograph*: © Dean and Chapter of Westminster; WAM box 10 (15)

Fig 22 The undercroft in 1899: view north west, showing the two apertures in the central column, the original west entrance with steps and the lime-concrete screed to take a tile pavement. *Photograph*: © Dean and Chapter of Westminster, after Feasey 1899, plate 14

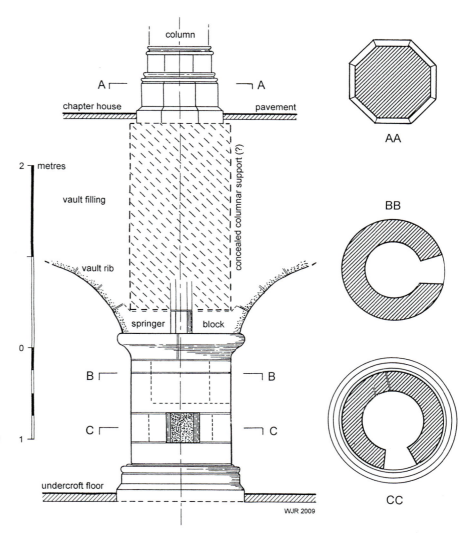

Fig 23 Undercroft: south elevation of the central column, showing its relationship to the column in the chapter house above and the presumed columnar masonry support concealed within the vault structure. Sectional plans are given at three points: (A) octagonal base in the chapter house; (B) upper cavity in the column; (C) lower cavity. *Drawing*: Warwick Rodwell © Dean and Chapter of Westminster

Fig 24 Undercroft: the south-facing aperture to the lower cavity in the central column. *Photograph*: Warwick Rodwell © Dean and Chapter of Westminster

Fig 25 Undercroft: the east-facing aperture to the upper cavity in the central column. *Photograph*: Warwick Rodwell © Dean and Chapter of Westminster

ring-mouldings that are not water-holding, and stand on plinth-blocks which are simply triangular pieces of Reigate stone set in the obtuse angles between adjacent sides of the octagon.[73] The shafts have leaded joints with the capitals and bases, respectively. Intermediate ribs spring from the central column and diagonal ribs from the wall-shafts, and these meet to form a tripartite division in each vaulted bay. Overall, the vault is of stellar plan, without bosses at the junctions of the ribs.

Six of the chamber's sides are pierced by large tunnel-like embrasures containing windows (fig 27). The sides are splayed and lined with coursed ashlar; the sills are canted and in four instances they are still finished with lime plaster.[74] The mildly pointed soffits are also plastered, and each exhibits an upward kick *c* 1.5 m from the inner wall face. The west wall contains only the small, pointed opening through which the undercroft is entered, and the north-west wall is of plain ashlar since it is

externally abutted by solid masonry. The windows are small, rectangular and contained in stone frames that are set back 1.8 m from the outer face of the wall. The lintels are of Purbeck marble, but the jambs and sills are in Reigate stone, much renewed in several of the windows. Only the jambs are chamfered. Externally, the apertures are slightly splayed, with flat rendered sills, and have chamfered two-centred heads and soffits, cutting across the corners of the rectangular frames (figs 28 and 112). The apertures were seemingly unglazed: the present iron frames containing twenty-four small rectangular panes date from *c* 1932.[75] Each window was protected by two iron grilles, one being integral with the outer arch and presumed original.[76] The other was possibly secondary, and attached to the rear of the set-back stone frame. None of the inner grilles now survive.[77]

The eastern side of the chamber is differently treated, there being a full-height recess of rectangular plan

Fig 27 Undercroft: internal window embrasure in the south-east side. *Photograph*: Warwick Rodwell © Dean and Chapter of Westminster

Fig 26 Undercroft: Purbeck marble vaulting-shaft in the angle between the east and north-east sides. *Photograph*: Warwick Rodwell © Dean and Chapter of Westminster

Fig 28 Undercroft: south-west window, splayed external reveal with a replacement iron grille. The window frame itself is deeply recessed. *Photograph*: Warwick Rodwell © Dean and Chapter of Westminster

occupying almost the entire width of the bay, with the window reveal opening from the back of it (fig 21).[78] The recess was filled with built-in vestment cupboards in 1932, and it is not possible to examine the features that are known to exist in its north and south flanks.[79] The former contains an aumbry with a square head and rebated surround to receive a wooden door.[80] The latter is fitted with a simple piscina, having a two-centred head and circular drain.[81] Photographic evidence shows that the east wall, against which an altar would have stood, is of plain ashlar.

The floor of the undercroft is paved with red clay tiles, laid in 1909 (fig 115). Photographs reveal that there is a lime-concrete screed under this, with a level and unbroken surface; it was exposed when the post-medieval soil filling was cleared away by Scott shortly before 1860. A photograph of 1899 shows a pitted surface and remnants of roots (probably from ivy) that had invaded the undercroft when it was derelict (fig 22). Almost certainly the screed was the bed for a medieval tile pavement, as Clayton noted.[82] However, he made the unwarranted assumption that no pavement had ever been laid on it, and then proceeded, very unconvincingly, to reinterpret a surviving medieval account for tiling the floor. A Pipe Roll entry for 1291–2 expressly records that 'the treasury beneath the chapter house' was paved with tiles, and that repairs to the door and other works were carried out at the king's expense.[83] Given the relative inaccessibility of the undercroft, its floor would have received little wear, and after the chamber had been abandoned as a treasury it is logical that the tiles should have been salvaged for reuse elsewhere before partial infilling with soil occurred. The tiles would have been laid on a thin bed of lime mortar, which would have peeled away from the lime-concrete screed when the floor was taken up; and any residual evidence for tile impressions would have been destroyed when the soil was shovelled out of the chamber in the mid-nineteenth century.[84]

Constructional sequence

In common with some other antiquaries, Jewitt attempted to explain the immense thickness of the walls of the undercroft by arguing that they represented two distinct periods of construction. He noted that a vertical break is visible in the masonry in the window splays, *c* 1.6 m behind the external face of the chapter house. He interpreted this as evidence for a smaller and earlier octagonal building having been encased by Henry III's work. In order to sustain this theory he had to assume that the entire interior of the undercroft had been relined with ashlar, and the entrance passage from the transept created:

he represented this on his plan (fig 29). He did not, however, include the inner window splays, which are unquestionably contemporaneous with the internal ashlar skin of the chamber. Jewitt concluded, 'this [sequence] can only be conjecture, as there is no part now visible which is of earlier date than the thirteenth century, the whole having been cased at that time'.[85] Scott took a similar view, finding the straight joint in the masonry 'perplexing'.[86] However, he failed to consider the logistics of building the chapter house complex.

That there is a physical break in the walls is not in doubt, but it can easily be explained as a constructional feature. Significantly, at floor level inside the chapter house, the break coincides with the interface between the two lower steps or benches in front of the wall arcading. If there had been no undercroft, this is where one would have expected the inner face of the foundation for the main wall. When the plan of the chapter house was laid out on the ground, it would have been easier to excavate the trenches for the perimeter wall and buttresses, and to construct the masonry in them, working from a level surface rather than in a large hole. While the outer face of the chapter house was ashlar, the core was of rubble, and a temporary inner face (of rubblework) was created by building in a trench: this expedient also saved on shuttering.

By leaving the soil core inside the octagon, a firm base was maintained for the masons to work off. The height of the walls and the huge size of the windows demanded prodigious quantities of scaffolding and timber centring. That, and the volume of stone that had to be craned onto the scaffolding, imposed a load of many tons on the ground inside the chapter house. Had the podium containing the vaulted undercroft been constructed first, it would have been incapable of sustaining this sort of loading for at least two years (that is, until the immense volume of lime mortar contained within it had cured sufficiently). With no restriction on weight, the walls could be taken up to their full height. At the same time, a pit could be dug in the centre of the floor, and the column installed for the undercroft vault. Although it cannot be seen on account of the surrounding vault, there must be another section of column standing directly on top of the capital, rising up to chapter house floor level, and there carrying the base of its central column (fig 23).[87]

The slender Purbeck marble column would next have been erected, the eight radiating iron tie bars installed at capital level, and the chapter house vault constructed. The purpose of the iron 'spider' was to provide stability for the column during construction, and not to contain the thrust of the vault (fig 106). The entire weight of the skeletal

Crypt of Chapter-house.

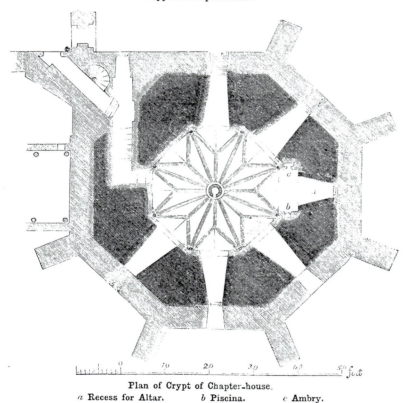

Plan of Crypt of Chapter-house.
a Recess for Altar.   *b* Piscina.   *c* Ambry.

Fig 29 Undercroft: plan and interior view looking west, after the removal of a considerable accumulation of soil. All the windows were still blocked, except that on the south. The south-east window had been enlarged to form a doorway, and a flight of steps introduced. *Drawing*: Orlando Jewitt c 1859; after Jewitt 1863, plate 29

components of the vault had to be borne by the centring and scaffolding until all the ribs were in place and structural stability was achieved. Again, this operation could not have been carried out successfully on top of a recently erected vault over the undercroft. Once the chapter house itself was vaulted, the centring could be removed and the scaffold struck. That is the moment when

canvas was required for hanging in the unglazed window openings. The purchase of the canvas in 1253 is recorded.[88]

With the interior of the chapter house clear of scaffolding, the remaining plug of soil inside would have been dug out and carted away via one or more 'barrow doors' (which were doubtless the window apertures for the undercroft, already formed in the outer wall). Then the inner skin and window embrasures in the undercroft would have been built in ashlar, and the large intervening spaces packed with rubble and mortar. At that stage, the vertical interface in the masonry that Jewitt, Scott and others have commented upon would have been created. Finally, the vault was installed over the undercroft and the lime-concrete bed laid in the chapter house, ready to receive the tile pavement. However, before that was done, light-weight scaffolds would have been erected to install the window glass and sculptures, and carry out decoration. Having accomplished all these tasks, it remained only to lay the tile pavement, and the chapter house was ready for use. The year was probably 1255.

The antiquarian record

The chapter house today presents an air of completeness and architectural perfection: the principal spaces are neither subdivided nor cluttered by secondary intrusions, and the external elevations are unmarred by subsidiary abutments. But this situation has only obtained since the 1860s. Prior to Scott's restoration, the interior was so fragmented and packed with the impedimenta of offices and archive storage that hardly any medieval fabric could be seen. Moreover, the exterior was hemmed in by a miscellany of domestic structures: the roof and parapets had been changed, the flying buttresses had been modified (one demolished) and their arches infilled and all the medieval windows had either been bricked up or superseded by small round-headed openings. Essentially, the chapter house was both unrecognizable and inaccessible to scholars. This was a consequence of its complete secularization since the Dissolution of the abbey. The major period of change was between the closing years of the seventeenth century and the opening of the nineteenth. The progression of these works and the effect they had on the medieval fabric is poorly recorded, and can only be reconstructed through studying official documents, antiquarian records and the archaeology of the structure.

Representations of the chapter house in its medieval form are few and cannot be relied upon as entirely accurate. The earliest is a sketch depicting the 1303 robbery of the royal treasury (fig 118); despite its simplicity, the three pointed arches bear a striking resemblance to the windows of the undercroft (fig 112), and the canted outline to the upper part of the drawing is surely meant to indicate the angular form of the building. Some early maps of Westminster include views of the abbey in which the chapter house is readily recognizable. Thus Agas's map of c 1562 depicts the four southern and eastern sides, each

with a large window and a decorated parapet.[89] Morgan's map of 1682 contains a view showing the south window and three of the flying buttresses (fig 31). On both maps the chapter house appears with a 'flat' roof. An early seventeenth-century elevation drawing of a single bay provides another representation of a large window and decorated parapet (fig 30). Later maps illustrate, in plan only, the accumulation of minor structures around the external walls. They were all outbuildings associated with the adjacent prebendal houses (fig 126).

The compartmentation of the outer vestibule – forming on the north a store-room and staircase leading to the chapter library, and on the south a passage to the inner vestibule – probably occurred in, or soon after, 1591. Plans of 1804 and 1820 recorded the layout (fig 32),[90] and several views of the portal in the cloister reveal how one arch was infilled and fitted with a window to light the stair, while the other was converted into a Tudor doorway with a grilled opening above (fig 149).[91] On account of its accessibility, descriptions and illustrations of the decoration on the outer portal are numerous.[92]

The long-term use of the inner vestibule and chapter house itself as a record office gave rise to various surveys and descriptions in the eighteenth and early nineteenth centuries, some accompanied by good plans and sections, now preserved in The National Archives (chapter 8).[93] They show that a mezzanine floor and staircase were inserted in the inner vestibule, and the main chamber was divided into three levels: ground floor, a continuous gallery around the outer walls at mid-height and a complete attic floor beneath a new and somewhat raised roof (figs 120 to 122). The small office at mezzanine level, on the south side of the vestibule, was almost certainly created for the use of Thomas Rymer, the historiographer, c 1694; it was here that he wrote his Foedera.[94] Rymer (c 1643–1713) was granted permission to study any documents that he wished, but not to remove them from the Treasury. Consequently, it was determined to separate a special study area, 'by boards, doors and locks, from the other part of the Treasury'. The location was described as being 'at the entrance and going into the Chapter House in the Abbey, before coming into the round building'.[95] That can only refer to the inner vestibule.

In addition, two single-storeyed offices were constructed in 1801 between the flying buttresses on the eastern and north-eastern sides of the building. Doorways were cut through the medieval walls to access these spaces, and a new external entrance was also created in the north wall (fig 33).

The earliest account of the chapter house appeared in 1799, by John Carter,[96] who had already drawn and

Fig 30 Early seventeenth-century external elevation of three bays of the chapter house, omitting the buttresses. The heraldry in the glazing is shown as though viewed from the interior. The legend reads: 'The forme of the place wherein the recordes are kapte in Westm^r Abbey called nowe the Threasury. It is a round place like the Temple Church with 6 or 7 longe windowes of greate height, 8 square within and vauted over and a piller of stone in the middst'. *Photograph*: © The Bodleian Library, University of Oxford; Bodleian Library MS Rawlinson C. 704, fol ii

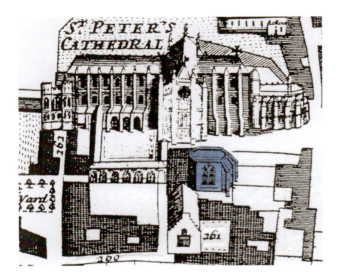

Fig 31 William Morgan's map of London of 1682, showing the chapter house with a 'flat' roof and the medieval south window still intact

described the outer portal in 1782 (fig 149).[97] He also prepared measured drawings of the outer vestibule, including moulding profiles.[98] Antiquaries were certainly aware of the artistic treasures concealed beneath the inserted timber floor and behind the presses, and opportunities for access occasionally presented themselves. The existence of the tile pavement was known well before Scott investigated it in 1859, and it seems first to have been described in 1823: 'There is reason to believe that the joists of the present flooring are laid upon the original pavement; which appears to consist of figured tiles, each six inches square, ornamentally disposed, and wrought with Leopards or Lions, Flowers, Foliage, and other subjects'.[99] In 1835 and 1841 floorboards were lifted so that specimens of medieval tiling could be inspected and drawn

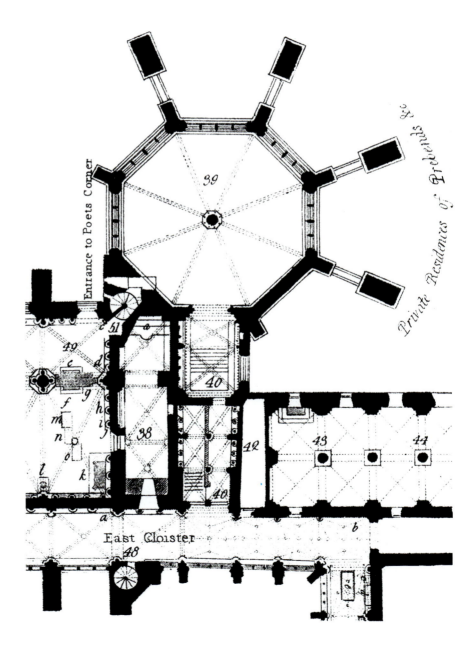

Fig 32 Extract from a plan of 1820, showing the subdivision of the outer vestibule (40) and the inserted staircase to the library in its north-west bay. The vestibule office (42), where the original stairs lay, is shown with its entrance from the cloister walk, although that had long been blocked. Also, the dividing wall between the Pyx chamber (43) and the remainder of the dorter undercroft (44) has been omitted. Curiously, the chapter house windows are given in their pre-1750 form (except for the blocked one on the south west), and the various low-level structures built between the buttresses have been omitted. Drawing: after Brayley 1823, II, plate 60

Fig 33 The chapter house from the north east before 1801, showing the crenellated brick parapet, reduced windows and inserted doorway in the north face. Note also the infilling of the arch under the flying buttress. *Drawing*: pencil sketch by John Carter; *photograph*: © Dean and Chapter of Westminster; WAM Langley Coll I.4 (7)

(p 209), and the first published illustration of a group of tiles appeared in the former year.[100] Referring to the chapter house, a popular handbook to the abbey (1842) mentioned sculptures, paintings and tiles, 'heraldic and otherwise', adding that 'portions [of the floor] are shewn'.[101] This implies that public access was available to the record office, as confirmed by figure 129.[102] Several floorboards were loose and could be lifted, and the first plan of the eastern half of the floor was drawn in 1858 (fig 210).[103] In 1859, following the removal of the public records, Scott investigated the pavement more thoroughly, and further illustrations of tile designs began to appear in publications.[104] At the same time Jewitt engraved views of the interior just before it was stripped of its record office fixtures (figs 129, 133 and 212).[105]

Although the blind arcading and wall paintings were entirely concealed by presses, they had not been obliterated with limewash. The paintings on the east wall (fig 34) were rediscovered in 1801, when the presses were removed to make breaches for new doorways in the first and fifth bays.[106] A very intricate watercolour drawing by Carter[107] shows the Judgement scene at that time (fig 173). He recorded much fine detail that is no longer visible. The interior was described in 1823: 'It would seem, (as far as can be ascertained through the intervals of the presses, &c.) that the walls are surrounded, at different heights, by two distinct tiers of trefoil-headed arches, supported by small columns. The lower tier, in the east side, rises from a basement-seat; and the wall immediately behind is beautifully gilt and painted in Oil, on an absorbent ground, with a series of Angels, who appear to be receiving the Good and Faithful into the Celestial Regions, and rewarding them with Crowns of Glory; the wings of the Angels are partly expanded, and the feathers are inscribed with texts of Scripture, in black letter, closely written' (fig 177).[108] The Apocalypse scenes on the north-west wall were discovered in 1841 by Frederick Devon, the record office clerk at the chapter house, and a description of the paintings was published in 1847.[109] The first illustration in colour of the decoration on one of the arches of the east wall was published in 1842.[110]

Antiquarian accounts of the undercroft are few and terse. When Thomas Pennant saw it, shortly before 1790, he described it as 'a very singular crypt', recording that the ground level had risen considerably about the building and the windows were blocked: entry was possible only through 'Mr Barrow's' house.[111] Evidently, access from within the abbey had been severed (p 18). A similar picture was painted by Neale and Brayley in 1823, when they noted that all six windows were 'closed by the accession of earth on the outside: they were guarded by strong iron bars …. There is, at present, no other entrance than through an enlargement of one of these windows, from an adjoining garden; but the original entrance was on the north-west side, by a narrow passage opening from the Church … The Crypt is now used as a wine and store cellar: the ground has accumulated greatly above the ancient floor.'[112] The earliest known illustrations comprise a measured plan and a colour-washed sketch looking south-west inside the undercroft, both probably made by John Carter around the beginning of the nineteenth century.[113] The plan contains an orientation error,[114] but establishes that an external entrance had been broken through the south-east window and stone steps added inside the chamber, to descend from sill to floor level (figs 35, 36 and 37). Another watercolour by Carter, shows the exterior of the chapter house, as seen from the garden of 2 Little Cloister, revealing that the head of the window had been squared to form a doorway (fig 38). The view is complemented by the disposition of features shown on Dickinson's plan of 1719 (fig 39).[115]

Carter's internal watercolour appears to be an accurate depiction of the conditions obtaining at the time. It confirms that a considerable depth of soil had been dumped inside the undercroft, up to about the mid-height

Fig 34 Surviving polychromy and gilding on the arcade mouldings of the east wall (bay 20). Note also Scott's skilful repair of the stiff-leaf capitals. *Photograph*: Warwick Rodwell © Dean and Chapter of Westminster

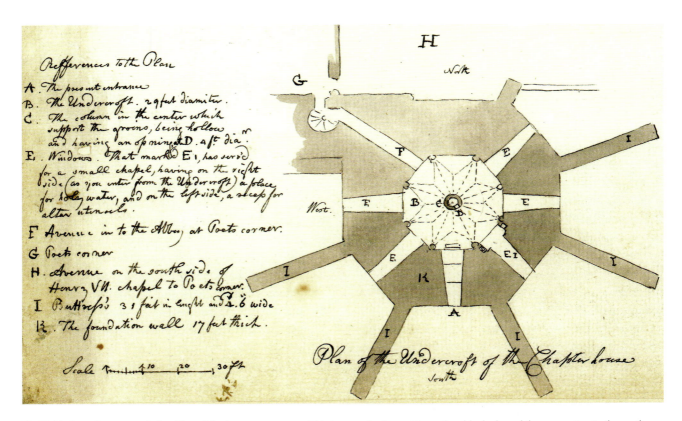

Fig 35 Undercroft: annotated plan. The original entrance passage 'F' is incorrectly shown (it was then blocked), and the connection to the south transept misunderstood. The windowless side labelled 'north' is actually the north-west face, and the external entrance labelled 'A' is the south-east face. *Drawing*: John Carter *c* 1800; *photograph*: © Dean and Chapter of Westminster; WAM CN 7.II.B.6b

Fig 36 Undercroft: the interior, looking south west. The figure is shown entering via the external opening on the site of the south-east window. The original west entrance (converted into a wine cellar) is behind the door seen to the right of the central column. *Drawing*: in pen and wash by John Carter *c* 1800; *photograph*: © Dean and Chapter of Westminster; WAM CN 7.II.B.7

Fig 37 Undercroft: interior view, showing the partial infilling of soil and the entrance created through the former window in the south-east side. *Drawing*: F Nash, 1810; *photograph*: © Dean and Chapter of Westminster; WAM Langley Coll VI.21(2)

Fig 38   The south-east face of the chapter house, seen from the garden of No. 2 Little Cloister, showing the entrance to the undercroft created by enlarging an original window opening. *Drawing*: in pen and wash by John Carter *c* 1800; *photograph*: © Dean and Chapter of Westminster; WAM CN 7.II.B.6a

of the central column. It also shows the secondary entrance through the south-east window embrasure, together with cupboard doors enclosing the recess in the eastern bay,[116] and the door on the end of the passage (then a wine cellar) in the west bay. The undercroft had clearly been assigned to domestic use associated with one of the properties adjoining the chapter house. Access to the undercroft in the later nineteenth century was not only re-established through the south transept passage, but was also maintained via the enlarged south-east window: the

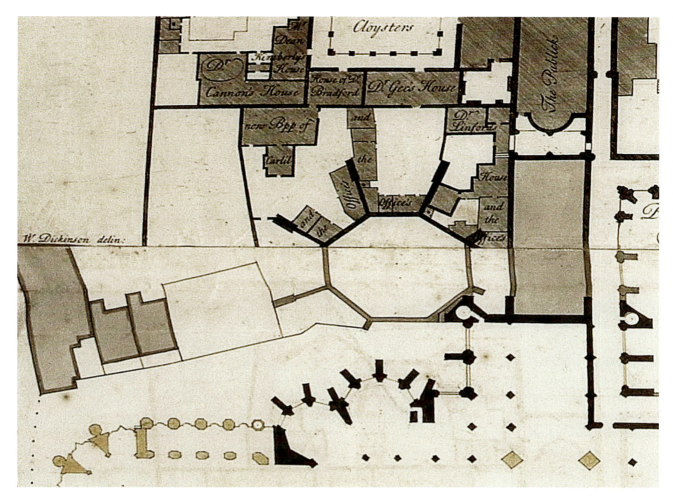

Fig 39 Extract from a composite plan of the abbey precinct (north at the bottom). The upper part shows domestic structures abutting the chapter house on the south. *Drawing*: William Dickinson 1719; the lower part was added to the plan by Nicholas Hawksmoor in 1731; *photograph*: © Dean and Chapter of Westminster; WAM Hawksmoor no. 14

internal stone steps were replaced with a timber staircase, which was finally removed when the crypt was 'cleaned out' in 1909.[117]

The principal account of the undercroft was provided by Jewitt in 1863.[118] He illustrated the interior, looking west, after the partial filling of earth had been removed, to reveal the bases of the central column and vaulting shafts.[119] Jewitt also drew a plan in 1859, upon which he differentiated the masonry to represent the two periods of construction, as he supposed them to be (fig 29). Both illustrations show the secondary entrance through the south-east window and the internal steps fully exposed. He recorded that only the intruded doorway and the south window admitted light, the other four having been blocked.[120]

King Henry III and the chapter house of Westminster Abbey

2

David Carpenter

Ut rosa flos florum sic est domus ista domorum

As the rose is the flower of flowers, so is this the house of houses

So runs the inscription on the tiled floor of the chapter house of Westminster Abbey (fig 40). The claim to pre-eminence is, and always has been, absolutely justified. Matthew Paris, who saw the chapter house in its first beauty, rightly described it as 'incomparable'. The comment was not lightly made. It comes, as is well known, in a summary of the notable events of the fifty years between 1200 and 1250, and is thus eloquent testimony to the chapter house's fame. But there is something more about the testimony which has not been appreciated. When Paris first wrote his account of those events, probably early in 1251 (in his *Chronica Majora*), he mentioned the rebuilding of the abbey, and the new feretory for the Confessor, but said nothing about the chapter house.[1] The same was true when Paris wrote out

the list again in his *Historia Anglorum*, probably between 1250 and 1255.[2] It was only when Paris had a third stab at the list, 'very likely after 1255' in his *Abbreviatio Chronicorum*, that the chapter house features.[3] Clearly he had now seen the finished building and been moved to include it in the roll of honour. Paris also did something else. He stressed that the chapter house was the work of the king: 'and the lord king built there the incomparable chapter house'. It is this statement which is the point of departure for this paper. There has perhaps been a tendency to regard the building of the chapter house as merely an adjunct to the building of the abbey. It says little about the king, being simply the room where the monks would hold their daily meetings. There was far more to it than that. Henry had built a house for the monks,

Fig 40 Chapter house floor: inscription I in the tile pavement: *'Ut rosa flos florum sic est domus ista domorum'*. *Photograph*: © Dean and Chapter of Westminster 2008

certainly, but he had also built a house for the realm, and, even more, a house for himself. Put another way, Henry saw the chapter house from the first as a place where he and his spokesmen would address the realm surrounded by architecture which at every turn proclaimed and enhanced the dignity and splendour of his kingship.[4] Once this is appreciated, much about the design and decoration of the chapter house falls into place.

Before developing this theme, it may be helpful to put the chapter house in context by saying a little about the king and his age.[5] Henry III succeeded his father King John at the age of nine, in 1216, and he reigned for fifty-six years until his death in 1272. Henry's reign was a period of momentous change. The spiritual life of the country was transformed by the arrival of the friars and by the work of pastorally minded bishops. The population increased rapidly so that, according to some calculations, it neared six million by the end of the century, three times its size at the time of the Domesday Book. The population of London around 1300 approached perhaps 80,000.[6] Meanwhile, the money supply rocketed, and a new network of markets and fairs came into place.[7] The wealth of England was displayed in the sumptuous rebuilding of great churches: Salisbury Cathedral and the angel choir at Lincoln stand beside Westminster as testimonies to this vibrant age. Henry III left England more beautiful than he found it.[8]

Yet if these are 'good' things, there was another side. The English had a far stronger sense of their national identity by the end of the reign, but it was an identity often expressed in virulent hatred of foreigners. Indeed in 1263, during Simon de Montfort's period of power, a 'statute' expelled all foreigners from the country.[9] The rise in the population, meanwhile, was outrunning the ability of the land to sustain it, creating growing numbers of peasant smallholders living on the edge of subsistence and starving to death in years of bad harvest. There were other sufferers. The king both broke the financial back of the Jews through heavy taxation and sanctioned the belief that they crucified Christian boys in macabre parody of the crucifixion of Christ. The way was thus prepared for the eventual expulsion of the Jews in 1290. At Lincoln the angel choir was being planned in 1256 at the very time that the city's Jews were being persecuted for the supposed murder of 'Little Saint Hugh'.[10] The sculpture in Westminster Abbey encapsulates the extremes of the age: on the one hand, the censing angels in the south transept are graceful, confident, humane; on the other, the heads in St Faith's chapel have pinched cheeks and bared teeth, as though grimacing in agony.[11]

Politically, it was Henry's reign that saw the establishment of Magna Carta, with Henry's version of 1225, not John's of 1215, becoming the definitive text.[12] It saw too the emergence of what was, in important respects, a new type of national assembly to which a new name indeed was given: 'Parliament'. The first Parliament so named in an official record met in 1237.[13] Its central place in the constitution was affirmed in 1258 when the Provisions of Oxford laid down that three Parliaments should meet each year 'to treat of the common business of the realm and of the king together'.[14] With this development of Parliament, as we will see, the chapter house was intimately connected.

In the first phase of his reign, Henry, though possessing a will of his own, ruled with the great ministers inherited from his father by his side. What historians have sometimes called his personal rule began in 1234 and lasted down to the great revolution of 1258.[15] It was a rule in which an increasing part was played by Henry's queen consort, Eleanor of Provence.[16] At the time of her marriage in 1236, no queen had been involved in English domestic affairs since Eleanor of Aquitaine in the 1160s. Eleanor of Provence changed all that. Indeed, her place beside her husband was proclaimed in the large parallel heads of king and queen, Henry and Eleanor, sculpted and painted in the muniment room at the abbey, a room which Christopher Wilson has argued was intended as a royal pew.[17] Henry's personal rule was a period of peace for England (though not for Wales) and it was that which made the rebuilding of the abbey possible, allowing him to devote both time and resources to it. Beginning in 1245, the eastern part of the church, the transepts and the chapter house were all completed, or nearly so, by 1258. Thereafter, as England plunged into the period of revolution, reform, rebellion and civil war that lasted down to 1267, progress was much slower, although it was still made, thanks in part to the way the baronial reformers were prepared to sustain the work.[18]

Both the calm and the conflict of Henry's reign owed much to his personality. *Vir simplex erat et timens Deum*, he was a '*simplex* and God-fearing man', opined the Osney Abbey chronicler, picking up two of Henry's most pronounced characteristics.[19] The term *simplex* – frequently used of holy men, in the sense of honest, uncomplicated and pure of heart – is intended here as a compliment, but the word could also be used to mean naïve or, indeed, plain stupid, and of simplicity in that sense Henry was often accused. Certainly – product perhaps of his long minority – he found it very difficult to judge the effects of his actions and calculate how to get from A to B. Other characteristics served both to aggravate and ameliorate this failing. Henry was warm-hearted, and passionate about things he wished to achieve. Thank heavens, contemporaries might have said, when it came to the building of Westminster Abbey. They were less appreciative of other cherished objectives, like the establishment of his foreign relatives in England and the making of his second son king of Sicily. Henry was quick to anger, and in his rage could accuse and threaten like the best of his Angevin predecessors. But, as was often noted, his anger was short lived, and his basic temperament was generous and conciliatory. He also liked an easy life. Instead of his father's hectic gyrations round the country, he spent his time at his favourite palaces in the south, improving their comforts and enhancing their splendour. All this helped Henry's relations with leading nobles, whom he was often ready to appease, but hindered reform of the realm, which, unlike his brother-in-law, Louis IX of France, he lacked the will to drive through in the face of vested interests.[20] Hence reform had to be forced on him in 1258.[21] In the end, a king who at heart wished to create harmony, dispense justice, and uphold the rights of the crown lacked the skill and determination to achieve these objectives, given the competing factions at court, the demands of the Sicilian project and the difficulties of reforming local government. The king who wanted peace ultimately created war, or, to put it more fairly, created conditions in which Simon de Montfort could make war.[22]

In all his trials and tribulations Henry had one pre-eminent saving grace. As the Osney Abbey chronicler – and virtually everyone else – noted, he was indeed God-fearing.[23] In all the turmoil after 1258, there was no attempt to murder or depose Henry as there had been to murder and depose John. Matthew Paris quoted both Llywelyn the Great and Louis IX as saying that Henry's alms-giving and masses would preserve him from all shames and dangers.[24] Henry was indeed assiduous at attending mass, and fed 150 paupers at court every day, increasing the number to thousands on the feast days of his patron, Saint Edward the Confessor.[25] Henry's devotion to the Confessor was, of course, absolutely central to his piety, and to it we owe Westminster Abbey. I have argued elsewhere that it developed between 1233 and 1238, at the start, that is, of his personal rule.[26] Essentially, during a period of political disaster Henry embraced the Confessor as a saint of mighty power who would succour him in this life and conduct him to the next. He also hoped to imitate the lawful and conciliatory rule for which the Confessor was famed.[27] The abbey, begun in 1245, was a gigantic offering to the saint, designed to win his favour and persuade him to intercede with God on Henry's behalf. It was also a gigantic public statement. The great church, the church of Henry and Edward, was growing up

at the centre of the realm, where, more than anywhere else, Henry lived and Parliament met. It dwarfed the surrounding buildings and was visible from far and wide, visible indeed as soon as the travellers from Dover came over the top of Shooters Hill and saw London spread before them. The abbey proclaimed that the Confessor stood behind Henry and his dynasty. It also proclaimed Henry's care for the community, for the last thing he wanted was to keep the Confessor just to himself. Rather the abbey was an offering to the realm, inviting everyone to enter and be helped by the Confessor's miraculous power, while, of course thanking Henry in the process.

The chapter house was very much part of the first build at the abbey and was evidently nearing at least structural completion in 1253 when canvas was ordered for its windows and the six steps from the vestibule to the entrance were being built.[28] It was certainly in use by 1257 when the first recorded meeting within it took place. The chapter house was, of course, built for the monks, but it was also, as I have suggested, planned from the start as a place where king and councils might meet to discuss the business of the realm. To understand why this was, we need to look at the previous history of the abbey buildings.

By the time Henry decided to rebuild the abbey church in 1245, the conventual buildings had long been used for royal meetings. In 1244 itself, a great council of lay and ecclesiastical magnates met in the abbey's refectory alongside the south cloister.[29] Later, during the same assembly, the bishops alone assembled in the infirmary chapel of St Catherine where they were joined by the king.[30] A few years earlier, during the Parliament of 1237, it had again been in the infirmary chapel, in the presence of the king (and, doubtless, assembled magnates) that the bishops excommunicated all violators of Magna Carta, Henry having just confirmed the charter in return for taxation.[31] Either on this, or on another occasion, in 'a certain *colloquium* of the king in the chapel of the blessed Catherine at Westminster', king and barons had sought absolution from an earlier sentence of excommunication.[32] The king had been in the same chapel in June 1222, discharging purely secular business, for it was there that he ordered William de Ferrers, earl of Derby, to surrender the castle of the Peak.[33] This use of St Catherine's chapel for council meetings goes back to the twelfth century, as indeed does the use of the old chapter house. It was thus in the chapter house in 1184, 'many clergy and people having been congregated', that Henry II accepted, after much debate, the right of the monks of Canterbury to elect the new archbishop.[34]

Kings, therefore, had used abbey buildings for meetings long before 1245, but the need to do so intensified during Henry's personal rule. This was because assemblies of the good and great met at Westminster more frequently (and probably for longer periods) than they had ever done before. Such assemblies were also far more significant than before in negotiating relations between the king and his subjects, which made it all the more desirable that they should meet in what the king would think an appropriate setting, which meant, of course, a setting likely to be helpful to himself. Westminster, home of the Exchequer and the Court of Common Pleas, had long been the administrative capital of the realm. But Henry lived at Westminster far more than any previous king. Part of this was due to the loss of Normandy in 1204, which meant that he spent most of his time in England, whereas his predecessors had spent half of theirs shuttling round the continent. It was also because of his attachment to his sainted predecessor, Edward the Confessor, which meant he wished to spend as much time as possible beside his patron's shrine. Westminster thus became easily Henry's favourite residence. If we take the years between 1234 and 1258, then he was there for roughly 30 per cent of his time, as against 11 per cent at Windsor and 7 per cent at Woodstock, his next most visited homes.[35] This makes a startling contrast to John who, even when in England, spent a mere 3 per cent of his time at Westminster. Even if we add in the Tower of London, the Temple and Lambeth (places in which Henry never lived during his personal rule) the figure only rises to 9 per cent.[36]

Where the king was, so too were great councils and parliaments. Between 1235 and 1257 there is evidence for some fifty-four parliamentary-type assemblies, of which around forty met at Westminster, some for considerable periods of time.[37] The frequency and length of such sessions was not surprising because great assemblies now enjoyed a power they had never before possessed: control of the purse strings. Henry's predecessors had been able to do without general taxation. Henry – if he was to be mighty in war and magnificent in peace (or as magnificent as he would like) – could not: the gradual alienation of the great landed estate which the king of England had gained at the Conquest, together with the restrictions of Magna Carta, saw to that. It was also clearer than ever before that such taxation needed the sanction of an assembly that was representative in some way of the realm. Magna Carta in 1215 had laid down that taxation could only be levied 'by the common counsel' of the realm, and although the clause was omitted from Henry III's versions of the charter, in effect it remained in force. Both the need for taxation and the need for consent thus gave such assemblies a new power. During his personal rule, Henry came to them again and again, begging for supply. After 1237 the reply

again and again was that he could have it only if he allowed the assemblies to choose his chief ministers, conditions which, denuding him of power, he refused to accept. So there was deadlock. The importance of these assemblies may also have meant they were larger than ever before. The first known occasion when knights from the shires were summoned to Parliament (in the vain hope that they would consent to taxation) was in 1254.[38] It is also likely that the issue of taxation encouraged many of the lesser tenants in chief to attend on an unprecedented scale.[39] On his ability to get his way at these gatherings, to which increasingly the name of Parliament was given, Henry must have felt the whole future of his kingship depended, as indeed it did. His ultimate failure to manage the Westminster Parliament of April 1258 brought his personal rule crashing to the ground.

Against this background, it seems highly likely that Henry conceived the chapter house from the outset as being for the business of the realm as well as for the business of the monks. Certainly that was a function it came to play, not merely in the fourteenth century when, as is well known, it was a chamber where the Commons sometimes met, but also in the reign of Henry III.[40] Thus the first evidence for the chapter house being in use comes from April 1257 when 'before prelates, clergy and people congregated in a great multitude', the archbishop of Messina, on Henry's behalf, solicited support for the Sicilian enterprise.[41] The second known use of the chapter house took place during Simon de Montfort's great parliament of 1265, the first to which knights from the shires and burgesses from the towns were both summoned. It was thus in the chapter house on St Valentine's day that the king's oath not to revenge himself on his opponents, and his confirmation of both Magna Carta and the Montfortian constitution of June 1264, were announced.[42] These are, of course, only two instances, but given that we have no official record of when and where assemblies met in this period, and are almost totally dependent on exiguous and erratic references in chronicles, we may well think that there were many more.

Neither the Burton Abbey annalist, the source for the meeting of 1257, nor the London alderman, Arnold fitzThedmar, the source for that of 1265, say anything about the king being present, let alone of his speaking. But that Henry expected to speak in the chapter house, and did so, is suggested by a good deal of circumstantial evidence. As Michael Clanchy was the first to appreciate, Henry was indeed a speech maker. In 1250 and 1256 his speeches at the Exchequer were recorded officially in the Exchequer records.[43] He also addressed great assemblies. In 1244, at Westminster, according to Matthew Paris, Henry begged the assembled magnates for financial aid 'ore proprio' ('in his own voice'), and then went on to make an impromptu speech to the bishops, a speech also recorded verbatim in a newsletter.[44] Four years later Paris himself quoted verbatim from Henry's speech to a 'great parliament' at Westminster where he defended his right to choose his own ministers.[45] Certain episodes take us a little closer to Henry speaking in the chapter house itself. Henry certainly *did* speak to assemblies within the abbey precincts because his 1244 efforts were made in the abbey's refectory and the infirmary chapel of St Catherine.[46] Henry also spoke in chapter houses, because in 1250 it was in the chapter house of Winchester that he delivered a *sermo* to the monks 'as if preaching', urging them to elect his half-brother, Aymer de Lusignan, as their bishop.[47]

A final pointer in the same direction is provided by Henry's remarkable interest in the lecterns to be placed in the Westminster chapter house. The first of these he commissioned from the carpenter, Master John of St Omer, in September 1249, instructing him to make it 'similar to the one in the chapter house at St Albans, and, if possible, even more handsome and beautiful.'[48] Accordingly, John and his assistants actually worked at St Albans where they are found receiving their wages in 1253.[49] By May 1256 they were evidently finished, for in that month (a piece of evidence that seems to have escaped even Colvin's eagle eye) Henry ordered the lectern 'which he had caused to be made at St Albans' to be transported safely in chests to Westminster, which may well mark the moment when the floor and glazing were finished and the chapter house was ready for use.[50] In the same order, Henry also said he wanted a cloth and cope of samite to be ready for his arrival at Westminster at the feast of Pentecost; doubtless he inspected the lectern at the same time. Whether he actually used it, is another matter. The lectern (from which the readings took place at the monks' daily meetings) was probably placed somewhere in the middle of the chapter house facing the president's seat in the centre of the eastern bay.[51] Thus when the knight, Peter de la Mare, made his speech at the Good Parliament of 1376 he 'arose and went to the lectern in the middle of the chapter house so that all could hear and, leaning on the lectern, began to speak.'[52] Would, however, Henry have spoken from the same place, and thus looked up at the president's seat? Surely not. He would have spoken from the president's seat itself, as indeed he did at Winchester in 1250.[53]

If, however, Henry spoke from this position at Westminster, did he find something unsatisfactory about it? For the fact is that he went on to install a *second* lectern in the chapter house, one specifically described as

lectrinium regis, 'a lectern of the king'. This was under manufacture in March 1259 when the king ordered John [of Gloucester], his master mason at the Abbey, 'without delay to cause to be made the iron work of the lectern of the king at Westminster according to the ordination of Master William, painter of the king'.[54] Presumably, then, the lectern that William designed was composed of wrought-iron leaves, scrolls and spirals like those found on contemporary doors, grilles and gates.[55] If, moreover, as seems likely, it is this lectern that the king's goldsmith, William of Gloucester was working on between 1258 and 1261, then it may also have been gilded.[56] Although still in separate pieces, the iron lectern was evidently ready by September 1260 when Henry ordered it to be assembled 'without delay in the new chapter house at Westminster so that it is ready and prepared for the next arrival of the king there'.[57] This time, therefore, one can be almost sure that Henry went into the chapter house to see his new lectern. It is hard to believe that he did not also intend to speak from it. Whether this was because Henry liked to read his speeches we do not know, although those he gave at the Exchequer were detailed and would have been helped by a text.[58] There was, in any case, more to it than that. Henry surely felt that standing before a lectern, especially the regal one he had commissioned, accorded far more with his dignity than standing exposed to his audience. This, after all, was a king who had ordered a new porch to his palace at Westminster so that he could dismount from his palfrey 'with befitting dignity'.[59] Perhaps, too, if the lectern was to be placed on a platform in front of the president's seat, thus projecting further into the middle of the chapter house, Henry hoped the acoustics would be better than at the seat itself, in the same way as the knights evidently thought they would be better heard from the central lectern than from the benches around the side.[60]

In 1260, having ordered the installation of his lectern, Henry arrived at Westminster on 11 October, just in time for the anniversary of the Confessor's translation two days later when he fed 5,016 paupers, spent most of £229 on a great feast, and listened to water music played on the Thames by an orchestra sent by the Cinque Ports.[61] It was the opening of one of the most important parliaments of the reign, one in which Henry hoped desperately to break free from the restrictions placed on him by the Provisions of Oxford. All his eloquence at his new lectern in the wonderful setting of the Westminster chapter house would be required to do that.[62]

If the arguments developed above are accepted, then much about the chapter house's structure and decoration falls into place, as we have said.[63] The great four-light windows which, in Lethaby's words, made the house 'a vast vessel of light' have often excited comment, being double in their design those found in the abbey.[64] The latter were modelled on those at Reims and may thus have been thought appropriate, as Christopher Wilson has suggested, for what was also a coronation church.[65] Free from this imitative restriction, the decision to go for much grander and more up to date tracery in the chapter house becomes all the more explicable if it was to be a house for the king as well as for the monks.[66] The same is true of the complex vaulting of the cloister bay opposite the entrance, the scrolls of foliage in the tympanum of the doorway, and the exquisitely carved roses in some of the wall arcade diaper, all of it without parallel in the actual church.[67] Naturally, in the eastern bay the upper bench was higher than in the other bays, thus setting king as well as senior monks above those below and around them.[68] And how appropriate and inspiring for Henry, as he spoke, either from his lectern or the president's seat, to look up at the Annunciation statues either side of the inner doorway, with the Archangel Gabriel delivering to an awestruck Virgin the most famous speech in history.

None of this work specifically announced Henry himself; but the chapter house certainly did that, and in emphatic fashion, which brings us to its most famous feature, its tiled floor.[69] As Clayton observed, the tiles run in bands east to west 'so as to lead the eye up to the eastern row of seats' where the abbot and, as we have suggested, the king would sit.[70] By far the grandest and most strategically placed of these bands are the two depicting the king's coat of arms, which start to the left and right of the entrance and run right across the floor, either side of the central column, to terminate at each end of the eastern row, thus marking it out (fig 41 and Plan 2). The three leopards of the royal arms, splendidly virile and fearsome, are placed within a shield supported by centaurs, each coat measuring 500 mm by 500 mm and being made up of four tiles, so that 248 tiles in all were needed to make up the sixty-two shields in the two columns, thirty-one in each.[71] The next largest of the floor designs (including that with the rose window) only measure 360 mm by 360 mm, so the coat of arms is easily the largest. Henry had long been in the habit of placing his arms on objects with which he wished to be associated.[72] But here he was doing so on an extraordinary and unprecedented scale. The contrast with the nave of the abbey – where Henry's arms featured once (the leopards turgid in comparison with those in the chapter house) alongside the shields of the king of France, the emperor and assorted English barons – was striking indeed. The nave of the abbey was for the community.[73] The chapter house, although he might address the community there, was the king's.[74] Whether Henry spoke

Fig 41 Chapter house floor: the arms of England, composed of four tiles (designs 10–13, band 11). The arms, which occur sixty-two times in the floor, are arranged in two parallel lines running east to west. *Photograph*: © Dean and Chapter of Westminster 2008

from the president's seat or his lectern, he was supported on either side by his coats of arms, the light reflected from the shimmering glaze of the tiles rising up in protective and empowering rays around him. Who could resist the king's eloquence in such a setting? And who in such a setting would dare to question the royal word?

To all this, Henry added one final touch. After its first lines declaring the chapter house to be the house of houses, the inscription went on to associate 'King Henry' directly with it.[75] Proclaiming his responsibility in this way was absolutely typical.[76] Few kings were more sensitive to their name and fame. When Henry came to St Albans in August 1251 he asked how many silken cloths he had given to the church and was told thirty-one. He then asked whether they had all been inscribed as he had ordered and was told that 'yes they had'; all bore 'indelibly' the name 'King of the English Henry III', *Rex Anglorum Henricus III*.[77] Likewise in the Abbey itself the inscription on the new shrine of the Confessor declared 'man if you want to know the cause [of the shrine], it was King Henry, friend of this present saint' ('*homo causam noscere si vis / rex fuit Henricus, sancti presentis amicus*').[78] On the chapter house floor the precise wording of the inscription is lost and subject to debate, but one thing is clear: namely that Henry described himself as 'the friend of Holy Trinity' (fig 42). If one asks why he appeared thus, rather than as 'the friend of the Confessor',[79] the answer might lie in the passage from the

Fig 42 Chapter house floor: inscription II in the tile pavement: ' *Rex Henricus Sancti Trinitatis amicus'. Photograph*: © Dean and Chapter of Westminster 2008

Book of Revelation (iv: 1–11) that was read on Trinity Sunday. This conjures up a remarkable vision of the throne of God and, '*in circuitu*' around it, twenty-four seats with twenty-four elders (*seniores*), who fall down and worship before him 'sitting on the throne'.[80] How Henry must have wished his councils were like that!

At Westminster, then, in the reign of Henry III, councils and parliaments had a variety of settings: the great and lesser halls and the king's chamber in the palace, the chapel of St Catherine, the refectory and the chapter house within the precincts of the abbey. Such a range of options was helpful given the frequency, length, size and importance of the meetings. It was up to the king to decide whom he met and where, playing what I have called 'the ritual of the rooms', and suiting session to setting.[81] Here, there may even have been a relationship between the chapter house and the 'royal pew' in what is now the muniment room. Wilson has suggested that, having appeared in the chapter house, Henry may have used the pew 'as a kind of "retiring room"', and perhaps it is not altogether fanciful to go further than that.[82] It was frequently Henry's practice, during his long parliaments, to combine large well-attended sessions with a series of individual meetings.[83] Can one then imagine him, after a *colloquium* in the chapter house, leading individuals up the roomy and well-lit turret stair from the cloister,[84] out through the doorway beneath the great heads of himself and his queen, and thence into the 'pew' itself, where the

intimacy of a royal chamber was combined with a unique and magical view across his abbey?[85] What better setting in which to bend individuals to his will?

With such a variety of halls and chambers to choose from, what then was the especial role of the chapter house? One problem here is that we have very little evidence as to the size and composition of the various meetings which took place during Henry's parliaments. How large was the 'great multitude' which heard the archbishop of Messina speak in the chapter house in 1257? Clearly the chapter house did not have anything like the several-thousand capacity of Rufus's great hall where, before 'innumerable people', Henry commanded the Provisions of Westminster to be read in October 1259.[86] Its capacity must also have been less than the abbey's refectory, which measured some 45.7 m by 11.5 m (150 by 38 ft).[87] Nonetheless the chapter house could still hold a sizeable gathering; the commons that met there in 1376 seems to have been over 250 strong, in which case many must have stood or squatted.[88] If, on the other hand, we think of people seated with space and comfort, then the capacity, given the seven bays with two tiers of seating, would have been around sixty-three, quite sufficient to embrace the leading lay and ecclesiastical magnates upon whom, above all, Henry's future depended.[89] If the magnates (or some of them) did not mind sitting close together, the seating capacity would have been over a hundred. Henry had specially designed the chapter house as a building in which he would speak.

Nowhere else at Westminster had that distinction. It was, I suspect, in the chapter house, more than anywhere else, that Henry wished to address the realm.

And did it work? The answer to that question, as with so much about Henry III (at least in the realm of politics) is both 'yes' and 'no'. Matthew Paris, as we have seen, was bowled over by the chapter house and appreciated that Henry had built it. He also sometimes described 'the Westminster effect' very much as Henry would have wanted. Thus he recorded how the magnates attended the feast of Edward the Confessor on 5 January 1249 'out of devotion and love of the saint, out of veneration for the holy blood of Christ recently obtained and for gaining the indulgence conceded there, and out of reverence for the lord king who had called them.'[90] Yet, alarmingly, far from being impressed by the alms Henry gave to the poor, and the candles with which he illuminated churches, Paris could also record the complaint (made in the parliament of 1248) that Henry's 'unwise and immoderate' expenditure in these areas meant he had to seize goods from merchants.[91] When it comes to the chapter house itself, the irony is that it was hardly completed before Henry's personal rule collapsed, which meant he had far fewer opportunities to use it than he would have liked. If it was indeed in the chapter house that Henry, in October 1260, urged the appointment of his own candidates for justiciar, chancellor and treasurer, then he was completely unsuccessful, for the new appointees were foisted on him against his will, the new justiciar, indeed, being effectively the nominee of Simon de Montfort.[92] Neither of the recorded occasions when the chapter house was used fitted the bill either. The arguments of the archbishop of Messina in 1257 about the Sicilian affair fell on deaf ears. The proclamation of 1265, in which Henry accepted the Montfortian constitution, was deeply humiliating and the complete opposite of what he really thought. Indeed, one wonders whether de Montfort's use of the chapter house on this occasion was deeply symbolic, the building that Henry had designed to adorn his kingship now witnessing its virtual suppression. Yet, in the end, Henry won through. The abbey was consecrated and the Confessor translated to his new shrine. On Henry's death, England was secure and Edward I, returning from his crusade, made no effort to hurry back to his kingdom. If, in the last years of his reign, Henry had entered the magnificent doorway in the cloister, walked along the vestibule, climbed up the steps into the chapter house, and approached his lectern, looking down at the gleaming floor with his coat of arms, and up at the Annunciation statues, the great windows and the high pitched vault, he must surely have felt amply justified. The chapter house was indeed 'incomparable'.[93]

The chapter house of Westminster Abbey:
harbinger of a new dispensation in English architecture?

3

Christopher Wilson

In a chronicle entry for the year 1250 Matthew Paris hailed Westminster's chapter house as an 'incomparable' work and by implication the finest part of Henry III's reconstruction of the abbey (frontispiece).[1] In more recent times, the brilliance of this structurally daring and aesthetically compelling building seems to have dazzled most of the scholars who have had occasion to write about it, for hardly any of them have ventured comments which go much beyond the laudatory or the descriptive. The aim in the present paper is to advance the discussion by showing that the Westminster chapter house represents a uniquely ambitious fusion of contemporary English and French ideas, and by suggesting that it foreshadows the emergence in the 1280s and 1290s of the Decorated style, a phase of English Gothic whose emphasis on innovation and experiment was initiated by buildings other than the great churches which had previously possessed a near-monopoly of the most creative thinking.

The obvious way to begin defining the architectural context of Westminster's chapter house is by considering its relation to the succession of English capitular meeting places that had been built to centralized plans from *c* 1100. The example most familiar to the patron, King Henry III, will have been that adjoining Worcester Cathedral, the church where his father lay buried and which he visited often on that account.[2] But the outdated Romanesque architecture of Worcester's circular-plan chapter house, the earliest of the series, must have made it seem far less relevant as a model than the grandest of the early thirteenth-century examples, the ten-sided structure built next to Lincoln Cathedral around 1220–25 (fig 43).[3] Henry III's two visits to Lincoln between 1225 and the start of work at Westminster

twenty years later were fleeting, and for that reason it is unsafe to assume that he was thoroughly acquainted with the cathedral's architecture.[4] By contrast, Master Henry, the architect whom the king put in charge of the rebuilding of Westminster, can hardly have failed to be aware that during his lifetime Lincoln Cathedral had been the single most powerful influence on major English church architecture. Moreover, Lincoln's splendour and inventiveness made it a very obvious exemplar for an architect in Henry's situation of working for the most ambitious patron of the time. Two other early thirteenth-century centralized chapter houses are likely to have been known to Henry, despite being remotely situated: the twelve-sided example at the Cistercian monastery of Abbey Dore, in Herefordshire, the earliest to incorporate a low vaulted vestibule resembling that at Westminster; and the much smaller chapter house at Beverley Minster, in the East Riding of Yorkshire, which anticipated Westminster's octagonal plan and the raising of its main room above an undercroft (figs 74 and 134).[5] The decision that Westminster should follow Beverley's octagonal plan, rather than Lincoln's decagon or Dore's dodecagon, might well have been due to the desire to minimize the disruption caused by the insertion of a large new building into a pre-existing monastic precinct. Making the north-western side of the octagon coincide with one side of the large triangular-plan buttress at the south-eastern corner of the south transept was certainly a very effective way of siting the chapter house as far north as possible and thereby ensuring that the building of the vestibule required the minimum amount of demolition at the north end of the dormitory (Plan 1).[6] The obvious drawback to this solution was that it blinds the north-west wall of the main chamber

Fig 43 Lincoln Cathedral chapter house: interior looking east. *Photograph*: © English Heritage. NMR

(fig 50), and before adopting it Henry will have discussed the problem with the king, and perhaps with the abbot also. In the space between the buttress at the south-west corner of the transept and the east side of the dormitory Henry contrived a high inner vestibule, a unique feature whose purpose was to house the flight of steps necessitated by the unprecedented combination of an outer vestibule running under the dormitory with a main room whose floor level is higher by 1.68 m (5 ft 6 in).[7]

Comparison of the main room with its Lincoln counterpart reveals at once the radical nature of the updating to which Henry subjected the basic format inherited from earlier examples of the centralized chapter house genre (frontispiece and fig 43). The height-to-width ratio of each side of the enclosing walls is virtually the same – 2.34:1 at Westminster and 2.36:1 at Lincoln – but the effect of the two designs could hardly be more different. Instead of the narrow pairs of lancets that occupy barely half of the width of each side at Lincoln, Westminster is dominated by huge traceried windows of French Rayonnant derivation which take up practically the full width of each side. The high-springing arches of these windows require that the vault itself spring from a far higher level than it does in Lincoln or any other earlier centralized chapter house, where all the vault conoids – that at the centre particularly – are a major obstruction to one's view of the windows.[8] Comparison with Lincoln also reveals how the decagonal plan presents to the viewer relatively frontal views of relatively many of the room's sides whereas Westminster's octagonal plan displays not only fewer sides but sides that are mostly angled more sharply in relation to the line of vision. The effect of this, in combination with the tall proportioning of the space, is to emphasize the vertical in a way which is not anticipated at Lincoln but which is entirely consonant with the French-style verticality of the interior of the abbey church at Westminster (fig 51). Pursuit of this aesthetic goal could well have been as important a factor in the choice of the octagonal plan as the pragmatic consideration mentioned in the previous paragraph.

A further design choice of Henry's that promotes vertical emphasis is the use of vault responds extending down to the wall benches, rather than Lincoln's short shafts borne on brackets in the spandrels of the wall arcade. The form of the Westminster vault responds is not what one would expect in a strongly French-influenced building, for despite the fact that they each receive five ribs they consist of no more than single shafts. Single-shaft vault responds had been an option available to English architects for the best part of a century when Westminster Abbey was begun in 1245, but it seems likely that what prompted Henry to choose this form was a concern to make the responds at the periphery of the room echo the form of the analogous shafts on the pier at the centre of the room.[9] The desire to restrict to eight the number of shafts surrounding the load-bearing core of the pier must in turn have been prompted by a wish to keep the bulk of the pier to a minimum, for one of the most spectacular strokes in Henry's design is the slenderness of the 10.71-m (35-ft) high central support, whose octagonal core is only 330 mm (13 in) across. The outdoing of Lincoln's chapter house, where the central pier is around 910 mm (3 ft) thick and 7.62 m (25 ft) high, will doubtless have been deliberate, although it is possible that the spur to such structural virtuosity had been another ancillary space

at Lincoln, in this case the chapel at the north-west corner of the nave, whose four compartments of quadripartite vaulting are borne on an astonishingly slight pier formed of eight shafts and built, like the core of the Westminster pier, from shallow blocks of Purbeck marble (fig 44).[10]

Flanking the peripheral vault shafts are very narrow vertical strips of plain walling. These represent a small but significant deviation from the concept of maximum glazing which was one of the fundamental premises of thirteenth-century French church architecture at its more ambitious levels. It would have been easy enough to conceal the residual walls behind multiple vault shafts, but since the clearstorey in the abbey church at Westminster includes similar, though broader, panels of solid masonry it is probably safe to assume that Henry incorporated this feature into the chapter house for similar reasons, reasons that are likely to have included conformity to established English usage and concern for the stability of a tall structure.[11] In the French building that most obviously paves the way for Westminster's almost continuous circuit of tracery and glass – the main upper chapel of the Sainte-Chapelle built in the Palais de la Cité in Paris from *c* 1240 (figs 45 and 52) – there is, of course, no residual walling between the windows and the vault shafts, and the architect's determination to avoid any such thing is apparent from the manner in which the outermost shafts on the external window jambs are suppressed in order to accommodate buttresses that have to be wider than the vault shafts within (figs 52 and 55). Clearly Henry felt no such imperative, for the exterior jambs at Westminster are equipped with their full complement of shafts and there are substantial strips of wall between them and the buttresses at the angles (fig 63). The Sainte-Chapelle's upper chapel was, in essence, a vertically elongated version of the cage-like clearstoreys that crowned the most ambitious Gothic great churches raised in northern France in the 1220s and 1230s – Amiens Cathedral, the abbey of Saint-Denis (fig 46), and Troyes Cathedral – and it seems likely that awareness of some or all of those buildings informed Henry's decision to treat the Westminster chapter house as a wholehearted exposition of the 'glazed cage' concept. However, as an exercise in fenestration-focused Gothic, Westminster goes beyond its models in one important respect, for whereas at the Sainte-Chapelle and in the clearstoreys of recent French great churches the traceried heads of the windows, the most decorative parts, are greatly obstructed by low-springing vaults when seen from the majority of viewpoints (fig 45), Henry took great care to make the chapter house windows perfectly visible from any viewpoint. This he did by causing the vault and the window heads to spring at exactly the same level (fig 47), an arrangement which was only made feasible

Fig 44 Lincoln Cathedral: central pier of the chapel north of the west end of the nave. *Photograph*: © Conway Library, Courtauld Institute of Art, London

Fig 45 Paris, Sainte-Chapelle: interior of upper chapel looking south east. *Photograph*: © AKG-Images / Erich Lessing

Fig 46 Saint-Denis abbey church: nave, upper storeys, north side. *Photograph*: © Christopher Wilson

Fig 47 Westminster Abbey chapter house: main chamber, vault looking east. *Photograph*: © Christopher Wilson

by the fact that the long sides of the vault's eight triangular-plan compartments exceed the short sides at the periphery by a comparatively small amount. In the rectangular-plan compartments of high vaults, by contrast, the transverse ribs that are the counterparts to the radial ribs in the chapter house vault usually have at least twice the span of the short sides, and for that reason they normally spring from the sides of the main vessel at a level far below the springings of the window heads (figs 46, 49 and 52). In his pursuit of perfect visibility for the window heads, it is clear that Henry was taking absolutely no chances, as he made the ascent of the radial and diagonal ribs as steep – that is, as nearly vertical – as he possibly could. To achieve this he had to give the radial ridges a marked upwards slope towards the centre of the room (fig 134). The general sense of lightness and buoyancy resulting from the rejection of the horizontal ridges normally found in thirteenth-century English vaults is very evident when one compares this vault with that in the Lincoln chapter house (figs 43 and 47).[12]

Although Westminster's maximized fenestration was obviously influenced by the Sainte-Chapelle, the device that was a prerequisite for the uniquely complete realization of the concept here – the concentricity of window heads and wall ribs – had almost certainly been encountered by Henry in another Parisian work, one which will have been brand new when he saw it. The group of three lateral chapels built out from the easternmost bays of the north nave aisle of the cathedral of Notre-Dame in the early 1240s are distinct from all the nave's earlier lateral chapels in that they are the first to have window heads and vaults struck from arcs that are perfectly concentric (fig 48).[13] It seems to have been only a few years later that French architects began to grasp the potential of this concept, for its earliest systematic application to side aisles is in the easternmost bays of the nave of the cathedral of Châlons-en-Champagne, begun around 1250 (fig 49). The tracery pattern used for some of the aisle windows at Châlons provides the clearest possible confirmation of the source of the idea of concentricity, for it is effectively identical to that shown in figure 48. The first architect of the collegiate church of Saint-Urbain at Troyes, begun in 1262, who ranks as the most independently minded French designer of his generation, went so far as to apply the concept to the clearstorey windows and the high vault, but that was a unique experiment which had no successors.[14]

Fig 48 Paris, Cathedral of Notre-Dame: second northern lateral nave chapel from the east, part of north window and vault. *Photograph*: © Christopher Wilson

Fig 49 Châlons-en-Champagne Cathedral: east bays of nave looking north east. *Photograph*: © Christopher Wilson

The four-light windows of the Westminster chapter house are of a kind which, until around 1240, will have been thought of as proper to the clearstoreys of major northern French churches (fig 50). The absence of such windows from the clearstorey of the abbey church at Westminster (fig 51), and their inclusion in the chapter house, means that Henry's work will not fit neatly into the essentially linear formal development of French High and

Fig 50 Westminster Abbey chapter house: main chamber, blind tracery on north-west side. *Photograph*: © Christopher Wilson

Fig 51 Westminster Abbey: eastern arm and transepts looking east. *Photograph*: © Christopher Wilson

Rayonnant Gothic. This phenomenon was found so perplexing by Jean Bony that it led him to speak of 'a muddled stylistic set-up' at Westminster.[15] It seems not to have occurred to Bony that the presence in the clearstorey of two-light windows modelled on those of Reims Cathedral, and the absence of the key Rayonnant motif of shafts linking the clearstorey to the middle storey, might represent not so much a failure to be up-to-date in mid-thirteenth-century French terms as a bid to assert parity with the French coronation church and, by implication, with the French monarchy itself.[16] This decision that the church at Westminster Abbey should imitate a thirty-year-old design and should eschew the most obvious modern exemplars left the way open for Henry to give the chapter house large windows like those of a French great church clearstorey without any risk of seeming to over-exploit a single motif. Of course we cannot know whether Henry or his royal namesake thought it in any way unsatisfactory that Westminster Abbey's second most important building was lit by windows far more impressive than those employed in the lateral elevations of the abbey church itself. Perhaps they considered that hierarchical decorum had been adequately served by endowing the church with

two large and very up-to-date rose windows set in the terminal walls of the transept. Master Henry at least will have realized that in using radically different architectural modes for the church and the chapter house he had broken completely new ground, for he must have known that at Lincoln Cathedral and Beverley Minster – the only other institutions where polygonal chapter houses had been built concurrently with major phases of work on the adjoining church – just a single style had been employed.[17]

From the viewpoint of Henry III an important factor in the selection of the four-light window for use in the chapter house was probably its appearance in the upper chapel of the Sainte-Chapelle (fig 52), a building that the king will have learned about before 1245 and which he is known to have been particularly keen to see for himself on his first visit to Paris in 1254.[18] Master Henry's first use of the four-light window is likely to have been at the chapel of St Edward built in the lower ward of Windsor Castle from 1240, where the fenestration of the west front is known to have included a large foiled circle, yet there can be no certainty in the matter, for the chapel was almost totally demolished in the late fifteenth century. The oldest four-light bar tracery window still surviving in England

Fig 52 Paris, Sainte-Chapelle: interior of upper chapel, detail of north windows and vault. *Photograph*: © Christopher Wilson

occupies the central section of the west front of Binham Priory in Norfolk (fig 53), which was completed in or before 1244. As a minor monastic house, Binham is not where one would expect to find extremely advanced architecture during the mid-thirteenth century, but the stylistic evidence confirms that the front was a private work of Henry's, contemporary with the building of St Edward's Chapel at Windsor Castle.[19] The central window of the Binham front is extraordinarily up-to-date in many respects, yet it asserts its independence from French precedent in a rather surprising way, for its head is formed

from arcs that are struck from centres well below springing level and are therefore not tangential to the jambs. Since the arcs within the tracery conform to convention in being tangential to the jambs, the result is that the outermost parts of the tracery seem to be cut away by the window head. The source of this very mannered detail must be the plate tracery in the false galleries of Salisbury Cathedral, where the outer parts of all the subordinate arches are cropped by the larger arches, which would normally enclose them without impinging upon them in any way (fig 54). That Henry possessed a detailed knowledge of this

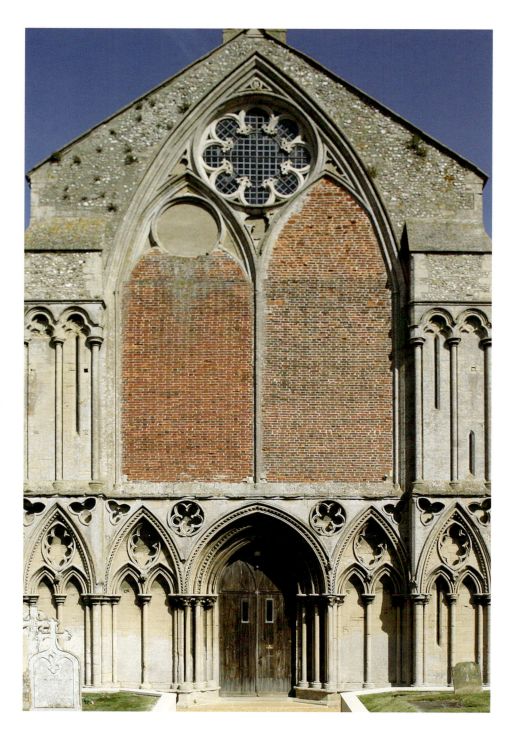

Fig 53 Binham Priory west front: head of central window.
Photograph: © Christopher Wilson

Fig 54 Salisbury Cathedral: nave, false gallery. *Photograph*: © Christopher Wilson

most important work of early thirteenth-century cathedral architecture in southern England is evident from several features of the church at Westminster, and there must be a good chance that he had worked at Salisbury before his employment by the king.[20]

The advent of the four-light window in French High Gothic architecture brought with it the idea of major and minor 'orders' of tracery, according to which the masonry bars forming the constituent uprights, arches and circles are made larger or smaller in gauge depending on the size of the unit to which they belong. The rather simple application of this concept – which is to be seen in the earliest four-light windows, those in the clearstorey at Amiens Cathedral – was subjected to a process of refinement at the hands of other designers, and by around 1240 the architect of the Sainte-Chapelle in Paris was using the systematically hierarchized version that remained in use until the end of the Middle Ages.[21] The smaller order in the lateral windows of the upper chapel there (fig 55), which encompasses the smaller circles and the pairs of lights below those circles, has the standard cross-section consisting of a chamfered part next to the glazing groove and a more prominent roll-moulded front part. The larger order, which encompasses the large central circle and the

arches below it (which also enclose the smaller circles and pairs of lights) has a section consisting of a magnification of the roll moulding of the smaller order flanked on each side by repetitions of the smaller order which are complete except for one chamfer (fig 60). The larger and smaller rolls are separated by deep undercut hollows. The largest arches in the tracery, which may be termed the enclosing arches, have exactly the same section as the large circles and the arches below them. The actual window aperture is a further arch whose jambs are endowed internally, though not externally, with shafts comparable to those pertaining to the tracery proper (fig 52). The head of this arch is constructed from small voussoirs, as was normal until the late thirteenth century, when the use of very large components in window tracery began to be imitated in the design of masonry jointing in general. Just as in the Sainte-Chapelle, the tracery of each window of the Westminster chapter house is organized in two orders whose roll mouldings are separated by deep hollows, the whole set within an arch forming the structural window aperture, the head of which is also made up of small voussoirs. Westminster's single most remarkable departure from the design that clearly served as the main model for its tracery orders is the way in which the springings of the enclosing

Fig 55 Paris, Sainte-Chapelle: head of north window of easternmost rectangular-plan bay. *Photograph*: © Christopher Wilson

arches are allowed to crop the outer edges of the larger order (fig 56). The cropping is achieved simply by extending the intradoses inwards so that they encroach on only the largest of the enclosed elements, and it does not entail, as it had done at Salisbury and Binham, the use of radii whose centres are well below the springing level. Curiously, the enclosing arches do not impinge on the large circles; on the contrary, the mouldings of the circles overlap the very elements of the enclosing arches whose lower parts cut across the outer springings of the larger order. The intention behind all these rather inconspicuous subtleties is not altogether clear. The gentle sense of lateral compression at the base of the window head and of expansion at its crown combine to generate a slight sense of upward movement which was perhaps meant to offset the rather static effect of the square scheme underlying the vertical parts of the windows and the equilateral triangles that govern the springings and apexes of their heads. Other instances of continuity with early thirteenth-century English usage are the modest elaboration of the mouldings, including fillet-decorated rolls in the enclosing arches and the smaller tracery order, the moulded bell capitals to the mullions, and the Salisbury-derived motif of

mouldings dying into cylindrical springer blocks over the capitals of the smaller mullions (fig 56).[22] Yet all of these anglicizations are ultimately minor matters by comparison with Henry's very evident concern to ensure that the interior as a whole should retain the strongly French inflection imparted by its great windows. Henry even went so far as to banish from the remainder of the interior elevations the kind of complex arch mouldings that he retained in the church at Westminster, and which in England were generally *de rigueur* in ecclesiastical buildings put up for patrons of exalted rank.

As Robert Branner showed many years ago, the pattern of the tracery in the chapter house windows reproduces one of the patterns used in Notre-Dame's lateral nave chapels and is therefore to be counted among the pieces of evidence indicating that Henry had journeyed to Paris immediately before 1245 so as to familiarize himself with the important new buildings under construction there.[23] In fact Branner did not make his point quite as effectively as he might have done, for he compared the Westminster tracery to that used in some of the chapels on the south side of Notre-Dame, whereas it is clear that Henry had studied a specific chapel on the north side, namely the

Fig 56 Westminster Abbey chapter house: main chamber, springings of tracery and ribs. *Photograph*: © Christopher Wilson

central one of the three that were built out from the easternmost bays of the north nave aisle in the early 1240s and which were identified earlier as the source of the concentric relationship between the chapter house's window heads and vaults. What makes it possible to be sure that the chapter house tracery pattern is based on that of the second chapel from the east is that this is the only window in Notre-Dame's lateral chapels which has the same overall design and an enclosing arch which is not stilted (fig 57). This window can also be seen as the source of Westminster's strange trick of omitting the topmost part of each of the two un-encircled quatrefoils surmounting the two pairs of lights (figs 50 and 56).[24] In fact the tops of the Notre-Dame quatrefoils do incorporate conventional semicircular lobes, but because their roll mouldings are not separated from the rolls on the arches enclosing them by deeply undercut hollows comparable to those in the lateral windows of the Sainte-Chapelle, the lobes appear somewhat obscured and overshadowed by the parts of the arches directly above them. For this reason it would have been very easy while making an on-the-spot

drawing to misinterpret the top lobes of the quatrefoils as small four-centred pointed arches such as were soon to be incorporated into the chapter house windows at Westminster. Perhaps that is what actually happened during Henry's doubtless rapid study trip to Paris in 1245, or shortly before; but however hurried his inspection had been, he would have had no difficulty seeing that the chamfered moulding immediately adjacent to the glazing defines normal lobes at the tops of the quatrefoils, and it is therefore not very surprising that he should have correctly reproduced that detail in the chapter house windows. The Westminster quatrefoils' juxtaposition of four-centred top lobes formed by the mouldings of the smaller tracery order with semicircular lobes formed by the mouldings nearest the glazing was probably seen by Henry's contemporaries as an eccentricity and not something worthy of being imitated.

The dado below the windows owes its relatively great height and its incorporation of five-unit arcades to the Lincoln chapter house (fig 58). The arches take the form of horizontally halved quatrefoils that find no parallel at

Fig 57 Paris, Cathedral of Notre-Dame: head of window lighting second northern lateral nave chapel from east. *Photograph*: © Christopher Wilson

Lincoln, and since the obvious English parallels all belong to the opening decades of the thirteenth century, this would appear at first sight a rather old-fashioned choice.[25] But wall arcades with halved-quatrefoil arches are among a number of features present in the earlier work at Amiens Cathedral which have the look of English borrowings, and at least one other of those features was imitated in the abbey church at Westminster.[26] The plain spandrels of the Amiens wall arcading (fig 59) are rejected in favour of diapering similar to that in the spandrels of the wall arcading in the part of the abbey church which is contemporary with the chapter house, namely the east side of the south transept. The detailing of the arches themselves is thoroughly (re-)anglicized, partly by the addition of hood-moulds and partly by the moderate

enriching of what will have been, to English eyes, the over-simple and dry profiling of the prototype. Pairs of halved-quatrefoil arches endowed with hood-moulds had been used a year or two earlier on the fronts of the buttresses flanking the central window of the west front of Binham Priory (fig 53), and it is clear that Henry already had a marked penchant for rounded, rather than pointed, cusped forms. They make a further appearance beside the head of the arch to the entrance portal, where statues of the Archangel Gabriel and the Virgin Annunciate are set in shallow niches closely akin to the constituent arches of the wall arcading on the other seven sides, and figures of censing angels occupy trefoils whose rims impinge on the heads of the niches and of the portal itself (figs 58 and 142). The source of the trefoils was probably the pair in the

Fig 58 Westminster Abbey chapter house: main chamber, wall arcade, north-east side. *Photograph*: © Christopher Wilson

Fig 59 Amiens Cathedral: outer south aisle of choir, wall arcade.
Drawing: after Durand 1901, fig 81

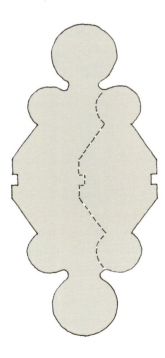

Fig 60 Horizontal section through the major mullion and arches of a four-light window incorporating hierarchized tracery orders. The dotted lines indicate the profile of the minor mullions and arches.
Drawing: © Christopher Wilson

upper spandrels of the rose window on the west front at Amiens, and although those differ in being surrounded by much plain walling they are similar in that their designers both seem to have been unconcerned about the less-than-perfectly resolved relationship between these assertive forms and their settings.[27] The treatment of the entrance portal as an unglazed two-light window should perhaps be bracketed with the concentricity of the vault and the arches of the actual windows overhead as instancing Henry's ability to go beyond even the most up-to-date French exemplars, for its only antecedent in full-scale French Gothic architecture would appear to have been the west portals of the early or mid-1240s at Saint-Nicaise in Reims, where, however, the tracery heads are treated as sculptured tympana. The portal zone at Saint-Nicaise was probably modelled on choir screens, such as that of Chartres Cathedral, in which the space below the loft was screened by freestanding and unglazed two-light tracery units.[28] Only in the choir screen of Strasbourg Cathedral, which dated from *c* 1260 or later and so could not have been known to Henry, did such tracery function as a doorway (fig 61). The probability is that the Strasbourg arrangement occurred in some earlier screen of which no visual records survive, but, even if that was where Henry encountered the idea, its use in the Westminster chapter

house entrance bears witness to his ability to make use of French ideas in ways which could never be classified as mere copying. In the early 1870s the original conception of the portal was vitiated by the intrusion into the oculus of its open tracery of a two-sided slab bearing carvings in high relief, and the undoing of this major error remains a desideratum.[29]

So far the vault of the chapter house has been discussed mostly in terms of its negative capacity – its avoidance of the window-obstructing properties of earlier vaults – and that is not entirely inappropriate, for there can be no doubt that Henry was consciously giving precedence to the extremely up-to-date traceried windows that make up the greater part of the enclosing wall. Comparison with the vault of the Lincoln chapter house reveals the diminution in prominence of the central conoid resulting from the rejection of the ten-sided plan in favour of the octagon. It also highlights how Henry has simplified this region of the design by eliminating Lincoln's ridge ribs and tiercerons and by using ribs of only a single gauge and profile. There is, however, an extremely important measure of continuity, for Lincoln and Westminster share a little-noticed feature which was to prove prophetic of late medieval English vault design. This is the treatment of the series of ridges that define the upper boundary of the central conoid. If

Fig 61 Strasbourg Cathedral choir screen. *Engraving:* Johann Jakob Arhardt *c* 1660; after Reinhardt 1951, p 23, fig 4

this polygonal configuration of ridges had been set parallel to the sides of the enclosing wall at Lincoln and Westminster, the obvious reading of the vaults would be as a series of clearly identifiable triangular-plan compartments. But since the ridges are set so that each angle of the octagon they form is opposite the centre of one side, they run straight through the boundaries between the compartments in a way which greatly diminishes the impact of those boundaries (fig 47). The main effect of this softening of the linear, compartmentalized quality characteristic of most Gothic vaulting is to emphasize the three-dimensional integrity of each vault conoid – the central ones most obviously but also those at the periphery. This aspect of the Lincoln and Westminster vaults is one of the essential preconditions for the emergence in late medieval England of a kind of vault which gives primacy to the conoid rather than to the rib – in other words the Perpendicular fan vault.[30]

In 1861, G G Scott, the future restorer of the chapter house, noted that above the capitals of the central pier and the responds between the windows there were large iron hooks which had been linked by eight radiating tie bars while the works were in progress.[31] In 1925 W R Lethaby argued that the iron ties were intended to be permanent rather than temporary (fig 144). As evidence supporting his thesis he cited the inadequacy of the external buttresses to counter the outwards thrusts exerted by the vault, and the fact that a radial arrangement of iron ties existed until around 1800 in the chapter house of Salisbury Cathedral, a near-replica of Westminster.[32] Lethaby – who will doubtless have been well aware of the clear evidence indicating that in French Gothic churches such iron ties were merely temporary aids to stabilization and were invariably taken out after the structure had been completed[33] – was presumably influenced in his opinion by the fact that some of the timber and iron ties in the abbey church remained in place and were not removed as they would have been in France. Lethaby did not question whether it will have been the original intention of Henry and the Salisbury architect to leave the ties in place permanently, and he also neglected to ask what might have been their motives in declining to provide adequate masonry abutments and in opting for a method of countering the vault thrusts which was unconventional, untried and unsightly. If Henry had really entertained serious concerns about the long-term stability of the vault, and in particular its tendency to spread outwards, there were several possible solutions available to him, none of which would have violated contemporary aesthetic norms to anything like the extent that Lethaby's umbrella-like reconstruction would have done. The most obvious approach would have been to provide boldly projecting buttresses, along the lines of those on the aisles of the abbey church. Another solution would have been to imitate the circuits of iron ties which run through the upper walls of the main chapel of the Sainte-Chapelle and are successfully camouflaged as glazing bars (fig 52). Without referring to the Sainte-Chapelle, Lethaby opined that 'one may assume' that three levels of the glazing bars in the windows of the chapter house link up inside the piers between the windows (where of course one cannot see them) to form bands running round the whole of the octagon. Since this cannot be verified, and since Scott did not mention anything of the kind in the comments he made on the window bars following his thorough-going restoration of the chapter house, it seems safest to discount Lethaby's assertion, at least provisionally.[34] Other techniques that might have been used to reduce the horizontal component of the vault's thrusts are the employment of tufa for the cells between the ribs and the filling up of at least the lower parts of the peripheral conoids with solid masonry.[35] The demolition of nearly all of the original vault in the mid-eighteenth century means that we shall never know how Henry attempted to ensure its stability, but the addition of flying buttresses in the late fourteenth century suggests very strongly that whatever precautions he had taken proved to be inadequate eventually. The plentiful evidence of delayed outwards spread in the Lincoln chapter house, a building which has never been fitted with iron ties, provides confirmation that the underlying problem in both buildings was simply that they were inadequately buttressed from the outset. In all probability the Lincoln designer and Henry were assuming that the outwards thrusts generated by the vaults would be comparatively small because the clear spans involved were fairly modest and because the regular pointed profile of the wall ribs meant that the thrusts were less concentrated on the piers between the windows than they usually were in the vaults over the main vessel of basilican churches, where stilted wall ribs were the norm (figs 46 and 47).

Alongside its skimped buttressing, the most remarkable trait of the exterior was its virtually flat outer roof.[36] The earliest extant view of Westminster to include the chapter house, an anonymous pen and ink drawing datable on internal evidence to the mid-sixteenth century, shows that the roof was concealed behind battlements like those on the abbey church (fig 62). This drawing was not known to Scott, who installed a steeply pitched pyramidal roof like that covering the Lincoln chapter house and also an elaborate and anachronistically detailed parapet.[37] In the mid-thirteenth century steeply pitched roofs were the norm, but for pragmatic reasons it was necessary to install

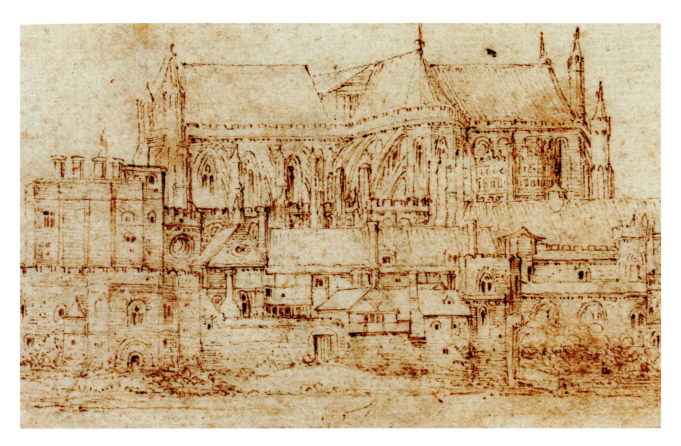

Fig 62 Westminster Palace and Abbey from the south east. The oculus of the window shown in fig 63 appears directly below the high pinnacle buttress at the east corner of the south transept facade. *Drawing*: mid-sixteenth century, anonymous; *photograph*: © Victoria and Albert Museum E.128–1924

roofs on the galleries of the abbey church at Westminster which are of very low pitch, and it is not impossible that those roofs were what gave Henry the idea of extending the same kind of covering to the chapter house. After all, the chapter house is actually joined to the south transept's east gallery and the latter's outer wall rises to a height only marginally more than that of the chapter house's walls (fig 63). Nevertheless, the use of a low-pitched roof on so important a building as the chapter house was a far more significant decision than the choice of such a covering for a subordinate part of a great church's exterior, not least because the galleries of two other recent and major English cathedrals, Canterbury and Lincoln, had already been equipped with very low-pitched roofs. The chapter house of Salisbury Cathedral reproduced Westminster's low roof and probably gave rise to the series of such roofs in south-west England: the Lady chapel of Exeter Cathedral (early 1270s), the eastern arm of St Augustine's Abbey, Bristol (begun 1298), and the presbytery of St Peter's Abbey, Gloucester (begun 1340s). Their use at Gloucester will have helped establish low-pitched roofs as the norm in Perpendicular architecture.

The interiors of the inner and outer vestibules are very different in character from the space to which they lead

Fig 63 Westminster Abbey chapter house from the north east.
Photograph: © Christopher Wilson

57

and also from one another. The inner vestibule has two bays of markedly unequal size, the division between them being fixed so as to coincide with the responds for the sexpartite vault covering the eastern bay of the space which adjoins to the north, St Faith's chapel (Plan 1; fig 81). The decision to make the vault responds in St Faith's chapel and the inner vestibule coincide in this way must have arisen from the need to provide the chapel with borrowed lighting from the main room of the chapter house, for to have covered the eastern bay of the chapel with the kind of quadripartite vault normally used at this period and to have centred a single south window within that bay would have made it impossible to find a site for the north respond of the inner vestibule's vault. The stair up from the outer vestibule is made to occupy the longer western bay, and the landing in front of the entrance to the main room takes up the small eastern bay, a functional division which gives a purposeful air to the unequal sizes of the bays generated by the eccentric planting of the central responds. The presence of a great mass of masonry connected to one of the bulky buttresses on the end wall of the south transept severely limits the space available for the western of the two windows providing borrowed lighting to St Faith's, and, in order to achieve symmetry, the eastern window is made to echo the way in which its western companion is placed hard up against the vault respond. The perfunctory character of the tracery here, which consists of nothing more than two chamfered arches surmounted by single lozenge-shaped openings, possesses a certain curiosity value in that it combines the attributes of plate tracery and bar tracery (fig 64).[38] The windows of the south wall differ from those in the north wall and from one another, their only feature in common being their richly moulded rear arches (fig 65). The rear arch over the lancet lighting the east bay is an almost triangular obtuse arch, a type employed prominently in the outer vestibule and elsewhere by Henry. The window in the west bay is a unique plate tracery design consisting of three trefoil-headed lancets and spandrels voided by a pair of trefoils with pointed cusps.[39] The inconsequential treatment of the north and south walls is offset to some degree by the placing of their window sills at the same level and linking them with a string course running over the double entrance in the west wall. The greatest effort has been lavished on the end walls, those most likely to have been noticed by users of the chapter house. The east wall is entirely taken up by the outside face of the entrance portal, almost a mirror image of its inner face. The west wall was clearly meant to echo both the portal opposite and the treatment of the west side of the main chamber (fig 66).

Fig 64 Westminster Abbey chapter house: inner vestibule, north side. *Photograph*: © Christopher Wilson

Fig 65 Westminster Abbey chapter house: inner vestibule, south side. *Photograph*: © Christopher Wilson

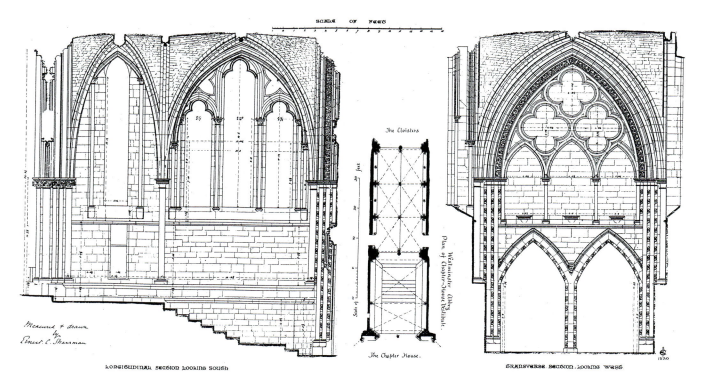

Fig 66 Westminster Abbey chapter house: inner vestibule south and west walls. *Drawing*: E C Shearman, 1880; after *The Builder*, 14 March 1885

Fig 67 Nogent-sur-Oise, priory church: choir, south side. *Photograph*: © Christopher Wilson

The three lights of the blind tracery, which is now the dominant motif, originally enclosed life-sized figures standing on brackets – presumably the Virgin and Child flanked by angels – as on the frontispiece facing the east cloister walk, and the whole composition was framed by leaf carving and voussoirs with foliage-embowered figures comparable to those on the main portal. The tracery here is blind of necessity because the wall that it decorates is part of the east wall of the dormitory. As Robert Branner noted in 1964, the only contemporary parallel for its pattern of 'piled-up' quatrefoils is to be found in the modest but very elegant hall-choir of the Benedictine nunnery at Nogent-sur-Oise, whose construction in the early 1240s was patronized by Louis IX (fig 67).[40] The design of Nogent's tracery would probably have been available 'on paper' to Henry if, as is all but certain, he had visited Paris shortly before the start of construction at Westminster.

Opening through the base of the west wall of the inner vestibule are twin doors which take their obtusely pointed and near-triangular profile from the vault of the outer vestibule (fig 68). The reasoning behind the choice of this particular arch form is easy enough to reconstruct, although it seems not to have been rehearsed in print. Essentially it is a way of avoiding springing the vaults from capitals set at, or below, eye-level, something which would have resulted quite inevitably if conventional pointed arches formed of arcs tangential to the vertical had been

Fig 68 Westminster Abbey chapter house: outer vestibule looking north east. *Photograph*: © Christopher Wilson

employed in the very limited height allowed by the floor of the dormitory overhead.[41] During the first half of the thirteenth century obtusely pointed arches had been used extensively in such workaday contexts as undercrofts (including that below the main chapter house), but the reduction of their curvature here to the point where they became virtually straight takes them out of the functional domain and transforms them into something stylish and sophisticated. The lack of competition from the slender and simple supports, together with the decoration of the windowless lateral elevations with pairs of such arches, further serves to underscore their status as the *leitmotiv* of the design and their important role in the dramatization of the user's experience of the chapter house as a succession of three progressively higher and lighter spaces. Near-triangular arches were to enjoy a certain limited vogue in English architecture during the 1250s and 1260s. The *locus classicus* of the form is the north transept of Hereford Cathedral, begun in the late 1250s, where it is used in contexts ranging from tracery lights to main arcades.[42]

The legacy of ideas bequeathed by the Westminster chapter house to English architects of later generations was not restricted to a single motif. That the design as a whole was greatly admired in the decade or so following its structural completion is placed beyond all doubt by the existence of the chapter house of Salisbury Cathedral, whose main chamber replicates its Westminster counterpart with a degree of fidelity that brings it closer than any other major work of English medieval architecture to being a line-for-line copy of an earlier building (fig 69). The influence of the most original idea embodied in the Westminster chapter house – its seamless continuum of window heads and vault conoids – was felt only once within the ambit of the great church.[43] The nave of Lichfield Cathedral (fig 70), arguably the most accomplished English building of *c* 1260, is the design of an architect utterly determined that the clearstorey windows should occupy all available space under the vault and be as prominent as possible.[44] In pursuit of these goals the Lichfield architect endowed the high vault with the unorthodox upwards-sloping lateral ridges that he must have seen for himself in the Westminster chapter house, and he was even prepared to abandon the upright format conventionally employed for clearstorey windows in favour of convex-sided triangular openings of the kind that light the galleries of the church at Westminster. That these departures from contemporary norms were too radical for the liking of most late thirteenth-century architects or patrons is evident from the fact that they found no imitators.

Earlier in this paper it was noted that the vault conoids of the Westminster chapter house adumbrated fan vaulting and that its virtually flat roof was the first important example of another of the key features of the Perpendicular style. Both of these relationships are interesting as parts of the genealogies of forms which eventually passed into the standard repertory current during the final phase of English Gothic, but in neither case is there any certainty that their adoption by the earliest exponents of Perpendicular was due to influences emanating from Westminster rather than from later buildings which made use of the same forms. What is in all probability the latest major instance of direct influence exerted specifically by the Westminster chapter house occurs in the chapter house of York Minster, begun at some time in the early 1280s.[45] That this was the first in the post-Westminster series of centralized chapter houses to surpass Westminster in both size and richness of treatment was something that those involved in its creation wanted posterity to know, for painted on the wall to the right of its entrance is an inscription which reiterates verbatim the boastful words incorporated into Westminster's tiled pavement: *Ut rosa flos florum sic est domus ista domorum* ('As the rose is the flower of flowers, so is this the house of houses').[46] The urge to compete with Westminster must have underlain the whole of the grandiose rebuilding project conceived at York in the 1280s, for the other component of that project, the nave, was given an internal height of 30.8 m (101 ft), an almost exact match for the main vessels of Westminster Abbey.[47] We have no means of knowing whether it was the clergy of York Minster or their architect, Master Simon, who originated the idea of treating the building of the chapter house and nave as a sequel to Henry III's simultaneous construction of Westminster's church and the adjacent parts of the monastic precinct.[48] The chapter house and the nave each incorporate just a single Westminster-derived element. The former takes the prominent splays and wall passages in the window level of its main room from the aisle windows at Westminster (figs 71 and 72), and the latter's aisle tracery incorporates England's only late thirteenth-century imitation of the three-quatrefoil pattern used at Westminster for the blind tracery on the west wall of the inner vestibule of the chapter house (fig 66) and on the rear wall of the north cloister walk.

The effects of York's rivalry with Westminster almost certainly amounted to much more than the appropriation of motifs and the matching or outstripping of dimensions. There must be a very strong possibility that an understanding of Henry's aims in designing Westminster's chapter house lay behind the powerful contrast which

Fig 69 Salisbury Cathedral chapter house: interior of main chamber looking north west. *Photograph*: English Heritage. NMR

Fig 70 Lichfield Cathedral: nave, north side. *Photograph*: © Christopher Wilson

Simon contrived at York between the relatively flat, tracery-sheathed internal elevations of the vestibule and the complex and varied explorations of thick-wall structure in the main chamber, for this contrast was foreshadowed in the main chamber at Westminster and its two vestibules. As I have argued elsewhere, the York chapter house was probably the building which pioneered

the architecture of dramatized contrasts that was to flourish mightily in early fourteenth-century England, producing one-offs such as the octagon at Ely, the ambulatory and Lady chapel at Wells Cathedral, and the hall-choir at St Augustine's, Bristol,[49] and it would obviously be highly significant if the Westminster chapter house could be shown to have been the ultimate ancestor

Fig 71 York Minster chapter house: main chamber, south side. *Photograph*: © Christopher Wilson

of this most innovatory strand of Decorated architecture. However, at the risk of underestimating the resourcefulness and subtlety of Simon's response to Westminster, one should probably be cautious about making the connection, for the vestibules built by Henry are far more obviously subordinate spaces than is the tall and elegant anteroom which Simon provided at York, where of course there was no monastic dormitory to limit height and lighting.[50] The innovatory aspect of the Westminster chapter house which I think we can be

Fig 72 Westminster Abbey north transept: southernmost window of the west aisle. *Photograph*: © Christopher Wilson

his transformation of the microarchitecture of French cathedral portals into the circuit of enriched stalls that seems to dissolve the very substance of the main room's enclosing wall.[51] The conceptual parallelism between Westminster and York is surely just too close not to have been consciously contrived. What Simon could not have known was that his chapter house was destined to inaugurate a fundamental shift in the imaginative focus of English architecture, when the most inventive thinking would no longer be lavished on great churches of basilican format but on building types hitherto seen as infinitely less important: mendicant and parish churches, the chapels of royal and seigneurial residences, such adjuncts to great churches as screens, funerary monuments, Lady chapels and porches, and such components of monastic precincts as gatehouses, cloisters and, of course, chapter houses.[52] There must be a real possibility that the extraordinary surge of creativity unleashed by this shift would never have occurred at all if Simon had not elected to take up the challenge posed by the hierarchy-defying ambition of Westminster's 'incomparable' chapter house.[53]

Addendum

After this paper had been completed a publication appeared which brought into the public domain new evidence corroborating the testimony of Matthew Paris that the chapter house was the most admired part of Henry III's work at Westminster. This evidence consists of notes representing the final third of a sequence of jottings on London and Westminster that appear to have been made around 1400, or slightly later, by an anonymous Bohemian traveller to France and England.[54] Translated into English these say: 'At the aforesaid monastery there are marble columns and a vault of marble severies [lit. canopies] and very beautiful carving within and there is a very large circular vault which has a very slender clustered [lit. grouped] marble column in the middle [word illegible] the like of which was never seen a vault of such great circumference upon one column and it is their chapter house.' The initial observations about columns, vaults and carving clearly apply to the abbey church. The reference to vaults of marble suggests that the writer had been misled by the striped effect created by the use of alternating bands of Caen and Reigate stone.

confident that Simon took on board is its superior imaginative boldness vis-à-vis the church it adjoined. It is probably not making too much of an architectural historian out of Simon to assume that he will have understood that Westminster's church, though a uniquely sumptuous building and a landmark in the English reception of French ideas of the great church, represented a rejection of the 'glazed cage' concept central to Rayonnant architecture, while the chapter house not only incorporated that concept but developed it in a highly original way. Simon will undoubtedly have known that the Minster's nave resembled the royal abbey church in being the most heavily French-influenced and richly decorated English work of its time, and he more than anyone else will have been aware that in designing the nave he had allowed himself no strokes of imagination that could bear comparison either with the contrasting modes he employed in the two rooms of the chapter house or with

Westminster and other two-storeyed chapter houses and treasuries

Warwick Rodwell

4

Centrally planned chapter houses, mainly of polygonal form, are a peculiarly British phenomenon, and are associated with a significant number of monastic and collegiate foundations. The known occurrences have been listed by Bilson[1] and the ancestry of the type has been briefly discussed by Harvey.[2] In excess of twenty-five structures are either extant or recorded through documentation or excavation, while further examples doubtless await discovery on unexcavated locations. Centrally planned chapter houses were not especially favoured by any one group of religious: they are associated with at least four monastic orders, as well as with churches of secular canons. Nor are they geographically restricted: although the majority of examples are found in England, a few also occur in Wales and Scotland.

There are considerable variations in plan forms: circular at Worcester,[3] circular-dodecagonal at Margam,[4] dodecagonal at Abbey Dore,[5] decagonal at Lincoln (fig 43) and Hereford and octagonal at most of the other locations.[6] The occasional square plan, as at Glasgow and Llandaff, may also be considered as part of the group, although their architectural form is somewhat different. In addition to these fully symmetrical layouts, there are occasional variants, as at Lichfield, where the plan does not conform to a regular octagon, but has two of its opposing sides elongated.

The majority of these polygonal structures are assignable to the thirteenth century, but several belong to the fourteenth and fifteenth centuries. The earliest is the chapter house at Worcester, erected in the first quarter of the twelfth century.[7] While the overwhelming majority of chapter houses of all types and periods are single-storeyed

buildings, designed essentially to serve one function, a small number were intended from the outset to be dual-purpose, or even multi-purpose, structures. These are the two-storeyed, centrally planned chapter houses, of which three are extant in England, one in Wales and one in Scotland – at Westminster Abbey and the cathedrals of Wells, Lichfield, Llandaff and Glasgow. Two others are known but are no longer extant, at Beverley Minster and St Paul's Cathedral, London. We shall examine this group in chronological order.

Some great churches also developed two-storeyed (or occasionally three-storeyed) sacristy-chapel complexes, incorporating functions such as treasury, library and muniment room. These were almost invariably rectangular appendages, except in the case of Salisbury, where a two-storeyed, centrally planned octagonal building was erected. It is relevant to the present discussion and will be considered below as a special case.

Beverley Minster

Of all the places where the novel concept of the two-storeyed chapter house could have been conceived in the early thirteenth century, the college of secular canons at Beverley might be considered one of the least likely. Nevertheless, the minster here provides the earliest known occurrence of the phenomenon. Had the church been built on steeply sloping terrain, it might have been argued that the creation of an undercroft beneath the chapter house was a pragmatic response to awkward topography. Although ground on the north side of the church has been raised, there is no evidence to indicate a sizeable differential in the thirteenth century, and Bilson overstated the case when he asserted that the ground was 'formerly at a considerably lower level than at present, and this may conceivably have suggested the idea of an undercroft.'[8] But he missed the point: it was not the creation of an undercroft that was specially remarkable, but the elevation of the chapter house well above the floor level of the church. That was a novelty.

The chapter house was designed as a two-storeyed, dual-function building, attached to the third bay of the north quire aisle (fig 73). The aisle wall is embellished with blind arcading in the form of trefoiled arches carried on shafts of Purbeck marble. Between the north transept and the north-east transept, the arcading was ingeniously adapted to incorporate a staircase arranged in two flights, one rising from the east and the other from the west (fig 74).[9] They meet at a common landing, where twin doorways once opened into an elevated chapter house. The entrance, now blocked, comprises two sharply pointed arches with a central *trumeau*. Piercing the solid masonry of the aisle wall beneath the landing is a second, smaller doorway with a semicircular head; it now opens into a modern vestry. The evidence points to these being the entrances to two chambers, one located above the other. Unfortunately, no medieval structure beyond the doorways has survived, but excavation in 1890 revealed the foundations of an octagonal building which was clearly a two-storeyed chapter house.[10] Moreover in the centre of the floor lay an octagonal base designed to receive a sixteen-sided pillar, which must have supported vaulting. That in turn carried the floor of the upper chamber. Although no physical evidence survives, it seems likely that the upper chamber was also vaulted and radial support for this would have been provided by eight external buttresses. The chapter house, which was linked to the aisle by a short vestibule at each level, was demolished at the Reformation.

The architectural detailing of the stairs and doorways in the quire aisle harmonizes with that of the eastern arm generally, and there are no grounds for suspecting that the chapter house was other than part of the original design. The construction of the presbytery and transepts may be assigned to c 1225–45, and the same date-bracket should therefore be applicable to the chapter house.[11] Bilson also

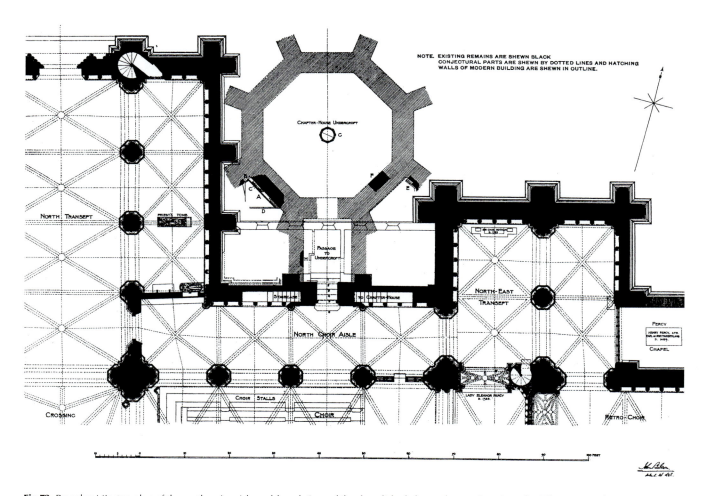

Fig 73 Beverley Minster: plan of the north quire aisle and foundations of the demolished chapter house. *Drawing*: after Bilson 1895, plate 41

Fig 74 Beverley Minster: the entrances to the undercroft and chapter house from the north quire aisle. *Drawing*: F Mackenzie, 1846; after Rickman 1848, opposite page 130

noted that the plinth moulding of the chapter house matched that of the eastern arm.[12] However, a glance at the plan is sufficient to sow a seed of doubt. The dimensions of the chapter house and its vestibule were clearly conditioned by the configuration of the site, so much so that the buttresses interlocked with those of the quire aisle and transepts. It is inconceivable that such an awkward juxtapositioning and aesthetically unpleasing arrangement would have been designed around 1225. The chapter house was clearly squeezed into an available space, at the same time making it as large as possible. The plan of the minster is otherwise impressively regular.

Two alternative explanations may be offered. First, the two-tiered entrance could have been intended to give access to a chapter house of rectangular plan, which would have fitted comfortably. Since it is unlikely that construction of the chapter house proper would have begun until the envelope of the quire and transepts had been completed, and the scaffolding struck, there could easily have been a delay of one or two decades, during which time the design was modified: the chapter house was most likely not built before the 1240s. A second option might be that a polygonal chapter house was a component of the original design, but was intended to be approached via a longer, cranked vestibule, as at Wells, Southwell, York or Lichfield. That would have permitted the chapter house to be sited a little to the north-east of its present position,

and thus enjoy a more elegant relationship to the minster.

At plinth level the overall dimension of the chapter house was 12.2 m (40 ft) across the faces. The lower chamber was sunk into the ground, and its floor level lay 1.7 m below the aisle paving. The short vestibule contained a flight of six steps, at the bottom of which lay a decorated tile floor that sloped towards the north, until it reached the stone paving of the undercroft. The threshold of the upper doorway is 2.37 m above the aisle floor, and while this could equate with floor level in the upper chamber, it is likely that there were several further steps incorporated within the vestibule. The floor of the upper chamber was thus at least 4.07 m (and possibly up to 4.5 m) above that of the undercroft.

It can safely be assumed that the lower chamber and the short passage leading to it were vaulted, and a single section of rib was recovered during excavation. The undercroft must have been relatively squat in its proportions and, architecturally speaking, was of secondary importance. What was its function? Lying so close to the sanctuary, there can be little doubt that it was conceived as a sacristy-cum-treasury. The provision of one was essential and there was no other structure conveniently close to the high altar which could have served that purpose. Indeed, the requirement for a sacristy is itself compelling evidence that the original design envisaged a structural appendage on this site, although that need not have included a chapter house.

The elevated doorway and the two flights of steps leading to the upper chamber confirm that it was the more important space, and its identification as a chapter house is not in doubt. Most likely, both the chamber and the vestibule had vaulted ceilings. Bilson argued that the chapter house did not have a central pillar, and that the space could have been spanned by a single vault. That is indeed the case at Southwell Minster,[13] where the chapter house is of identical diameter to that at Beverley. On the other hand, Cockersand abbey has a slightly smaller chapter house of octagonal plan with a central stone pillar.[14]

Lichfield Cathedral

Like Beverley, Lichfield was non-monastic and had no cloister to which a chapter house could conveniently be appended. Again, it was contrived as an adjunct to the north quire aisle, with its entrance off the third bay (fig 75). The chapter house, which has variously been described as an elongated octagon, or a flattened decagon, measures 11.3 m (37 ft) across at plinth level in the

narrower dimension, and 15.0 m (49 ft) in the longer (fig 76). Internally, the arrangement of the wall arcades and vaulting occupies ten bays. The chapter house, which is assignable to *c* 1240, is two storeyed, including the vestibule (fig 77), and is built in the local red sandstone. The principal floor is at the same level as the quire aisle. The vestibule is a rectangular structure of three vaulted bays, entered via a single arch, broken through the earlier wall-arcading of the aisle. Within, on the west side is an arcade of thirteen bays, each of which comprises a tiny stall with a vaulted ceiling (fig 78). On the east is a plain wall-bench with a blind arcade above, and two doorways. The first opens into a small lobby at the base of a generous newel stair which gives access to the upper floor. The second doorway comprises the elaborate twin portal to the chapter house (fig 79). The vestibule is cranked.

Internally, the chapter house has wall-arcading and two-light windows in each face, except on the west, where the entrance lies, and on the south-west, where a triangular mass of masonry containing the newel stair occupies the re-entrant angle between the chapter house and the vestibule. The same occurs at Southwell.[15] The portal and interior of the chapter house are heavily decorated with

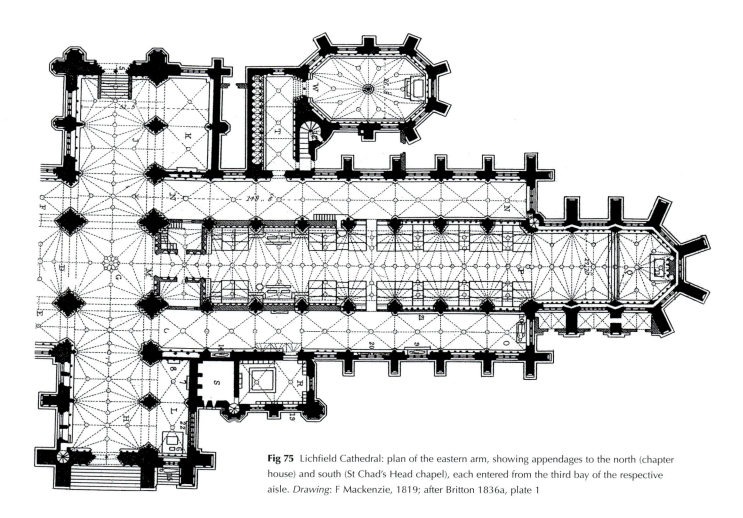

Fig 75 Lichfield Cathedral: plan of the eastern arm, showing appendages to the north (chapter house) and south (St Chad's Head chapel), each entered from the third bay of the respective aisle. *Drawing*: F Mackenzie, 1819; after Britton 1836a, plate 1

Fig 76 Lichfield Cathedral: the chapter house from the east. *Photograph*: © Warwick Rodwell 2008

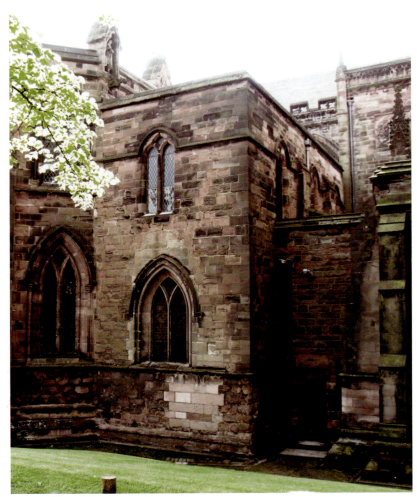

Fig 77 Lichfield Cathedral: the chapter house vestibule from the north west. The buttresses on the right mark the angle of the north transept aisle; the infilling of the gap between it and the vestibule is modern. *Photograph*: © Warwick Rodwell 2008

Fig 78 Lichfield Cathedral: interior of the chapter house vestibule, looking north. *Drawing*: F Mackenzie, 1819; after Britton 1836a, plate 12

canopy-work, detached shafts, stiff-leaf capitals and dogtooth carving. Remnants of the once-extensive polychromatic decoration also survive. Rising in the centre of the floor is a composite pillar supporting the stone vault. The pillar has a decagonal base, a circular core ringed by ten shafts, and a capital encrusted with stiff-leaf decoration.[16]

The entrance to the stairs is utterly plain, contrasting markedly with the richness of the remainder of the vestibule. At the head of the stairs are two doorways, one opening into a rectangular, vaulted chamber above the vestibule, and the other into an octagonal room over the chapter house, now used as the library. Their floors are at different levels and a secondary opening has been cut

Fig 79 Lichfield Cathedral: entrance to the chapter house from the vestibule, looking east. *Drawing*: F Mackenzie, 1819; after Britton 1836a, plate 15

through the wall between them. The rectangular room serves as an annexe to the library. The octagonal chamber has two-light windows in each external face, and at the centre is a plain circular column with a moulded capital and base, supporting a stone vault (fig 80). Although the library is not as lofty as the chapter house, and is less elaborate, it is nevertheless an impressive space of high quality, with moulded detail and sculptured corbels and bosses. The rectangular chamber is much plainer. Both rooms were embellished with decorated tile pavements,

laid *c* 1290–1300, and that in the library is still in remarkably fine condition.[17]

Although some structural anomalies are not easy to explain, it seems likely that the vestibule and chapter house were constructed contemporaneously. Nevertheless, the possibility that the two-storeyed rectangular building was erected first cannot be eliminated without detailed archaeological investigation.[18] The uses to which the spaces were put, apart from the ground-level chapter house, have given rise to much speculation. Lichfield has

Fig 80 Lichfield Cathedral: the interior of the library, looking east, in the early nineteenth century. *Drawing*: in pen and wash, unsigned, private collection; *photograph*: © Warwick Rodwell

the only chapter house vestibule fitted with an elaborate series of canopied wall-seats, a feature generally described as a *pedilavium*. No other convincing explanation has been forthcoming. The two upper chambers contain no intrinsic evidence to identify their functions. There are no lockers, aumbries, piscinae or other indications that either room might have been designed expressly as a chapel, sacristy or treasury.

Unlike Beverley, in this instance there was no call for a sacristy here, since there was already a three-storeyed sacristy, treasury and chapel complex attached to the third bay of the south quire aisle (fig 75).[19] Rebuilt in the 1220s, on the site of a yet earlier rectangular structure, this building comprised a subterranean treasury, a sacristy and chapel dedicated to St Peter at ground level, and an upper chapel devoted to the cult of St Chad's Head. There was also another, single-storeyed treasury added slightly later as an adjunct to the lower chapel.[20]

The most plausible interpretation for the chambers above the chapter house and vestibule is as a library and muniment room, respectively.[21] It may be no coincidence that books were being acquired for the 'new library' in 1260.[22] A rectangular disruption in the tile pavement against the east wall of the library could mark the site of an altar, the presence of which would not conflict with this suggested use.

Westminster Abbey

The chapter house at Westminster occupies the conventional position adjacent to the east side of the cloister, and a description of the complex has been given in chapter 1 (fig 1; Plan 1). In common with the overwhelming majority of chapter houses, it could have been built with its floor at the same level as the cloister, but instead it was raised on a podium, which was approached by ten steps. Built into the core of that podium was a relatively small, octagonal chamber devoid of sculptural decoration (figs 22 and 29), which was clearly designed to be utilitarian, and not decorative. Access was remote, moreover, demonstrating that the chapter house and undercroft were not functionally connected; if desired, it would have been a simple matter to contrive an entrance to the undercroft from one of the chambers flanking the vestibule, instead of the tortuous passage leading out of Poets' Corner (fig 14).

The original function of the undercroft is not easy to

determine, and the evidence is conflicting. The presence of an altar recess, piscina and aumbry clearly indicates its chapel status. Equally self-evident is the fact that, seen from the exterior, this was a highly secure space, with immensely thick walls and small windows, heavily protected with ferramenta. Moreover, the presence of two places for the presumed concealment of precious objects in the central pillar is suggestive of its intended function as a sacristy or treasury. But two major problems render these interpretations untenable. Although the undercroft's location to the south of the quire could be consistent with a sacristy, in terms of daily use the access is so tortuous as to be unworkable. The doglegged passage had multiple steps, low headroom and hardly any daylight.[23] Also, there was a much more convenient sacristy, no longer used as such and now simply called St Faith's chapel. This lofty, rectangular chamber lies between the south transept and the chapter house vestibule, and was constructed contemporaneously with the latter. Its floor is at the same level as that in the transept. The chamber, which is divided into two distinct parts by a transverse arch, is oddly asymmetrical in plan and has the appearance of being primarily a utilitarian space, rather than liturgical or for display. The eastern element comprises one vaulted bay, the north-east corner of which is truncated to accommodate the diagonal passage leading from the transept to the undercroft of the chapter house (fig 81; Plan 1). There is a recess in the east wall for an altar, which is perforce displaced well to the south of the chapel's axis. This is the altar of St Faith, above which remains the fine wall painting that comprised its reredos.[24] In the wall to the south is a piscina.

The larger western compartment is of two bays, also vaulted, and has doorways in its side walls: on the north providing access from the adjoining transept, and on the south connecting with the chapter house vestibule. Traversing the west end of the chamber is a high-level stone gallery, which formed part of the monastic night-stair arrangement (fig 82). Features in the walls confirm the intended use of the western chamber, in particular the series of recesses in the south and west walls. These were evidently cupboards for storing valuable objects. Antiquarian writers refer to this chamber as the 'old revestry', and there is no reason to doubt that it was conceived as a sacristy with an altar. It was constructed as part of the chapter house complex and is far better disposed to serve as the principal sacristy for the quire than the undercroft.[25]

If the chapter house undercroft was not a sacristy, was it a treasury? Superficially, the idea is attractive, until it is recalled that the serious external security was not matched

Fig 81 Westminster Abbey St Faith's chapel: view east, showing the asymmetrical layout and canted north-east corner. *Photograph*: © Dean and Chapter of Westminster 2009

internally (p 16). The door in the south transept opened not only into the undercroft passage, but also gave access to the major newel stair in the eastern arm of the abbey. That was the route by which one reached the internal wall-passages, the triforium and the roofs. Initially, there was no separating door to the undercroft, and thus for all practical purposes the latter was fully accessible from the interior of the abbey. It cannot therefore have been designed as a treasury, and from the monastic point of view the 'revestry' (St Faith's chapel) was more convenient for that purpose. It is also worth noting that it would have been impossible to negotiate the great oak chests of the twelfth and thirteenth centuries that the abbey possesses into the undercroft. The passage and steps, before they were altered, were sufficient only for one person to progress at a time, and even then one had to stoop on account of the low headroom.

Fig 82 Westminster Abbey St Faith's chapel: interior of the sacristy, looking west. *Drawing*: Orlando Jewitt, *c* 1859; after Scott 1861, plate 47

That said, a change in the function and security of the undercroft clearly occurred in the Middle Ages, and access was improved. The steps were rearranged to provide adequate headroom to avoid stooping, and a door with multiple locks was fitted at the top of the stair-passage (figs 114 and 246; pp 17–18). The undercroft was now a secure place, and it is argued that the chamber thereafter assumed the role of treasury. But when did this happen, and whose treasury was it?

Unfortunately, there is no documentary or art historical evidence that allows the improvements to be closely dated, and the newly introduced door does not survive. However, we can be certain that a royal treasury had been established in the undercroft by or during the reign of Edward I (pp 112–13), and it is tempting to associate the improvements with the Pipe Roll entry for 1290–1 recording the laying of a tile floor and work to a door (p 22). The original mid-thirteenth century door from the transept to the stair passage was replaced in the following century, an event dated by dendrochronology to after 1338 (p 259). In all probability it was not made before *c* 1350,

and that is too late for associating the replacement of the outer door with the separation of the undercroft. Moreover, this is not the type of heavy-duty, secure door that was usually fitted to treasuries. It is more likely that the door was renewed because of damage through constant use.

We return then to the question: what was the primary function of the undercroft? The simplest answer is that it was a chapel, but the extreme plainness of its interior contrasts with everything else in Henry III's church, including the triforium galleries. In all respects, except its unusual plan, the architecture of the undercroft resembles a medieval burial crypt: the narrow access passage, the crudely blocked-out capitals to the wall-shafts (without even a moulded abacus), the absence of mouldings on the arches of the passage and the lack of any form of decoration, such as vault-bosses, are consistent with interpretation as a crypt.

Benedictine chapter houses were invariably used as burial places for abbots, as excavations have demonstrated at St Albans.[26] It is unlikely that the crypt at Westminster was constructed for the interment of future abbots: if that had been intended, it would have been provided with greater embellishment and a more dignified entrance. From the early thirteenth century onwards, the abbots were mostly buried inside the church.[27] However, an uncertain number of abbatial interments had previously been made in the Confessor's chapter house, and the demolition of that building, followed by the excavation of the foundations for Henry III's replacement, will have necessitated the exhumation of these burials (see p 108). The construction of a mortuary chapel within the foundation raft of the new chapter house would have provided a suitably dignified place to re-inter the remains, as well as a focus where their names and deeds could continue to be revered. But pious intentions are often not followed to conclusion.

Although firm evidence is lacking, it seems likely that there would have been much less interest in the corporeal remains of a few long-deceased abbots after the death of Henry III, and the potential for adapting the crypt to create the most secure space in the abbey must have been obvious. It had only one, narrow entrance, and, if that were to be made secure, a near-impregnable treasury could be created. The installation of a heavy door with an iron grille achieved that goal. Consequently, the early abbots' remains were never transferred to the crypt (see pp 87–8).

Wells Cathedral

Wells is a cathedral of the 'old foundation', having been a college of secular canons throughout the Middle Ages.

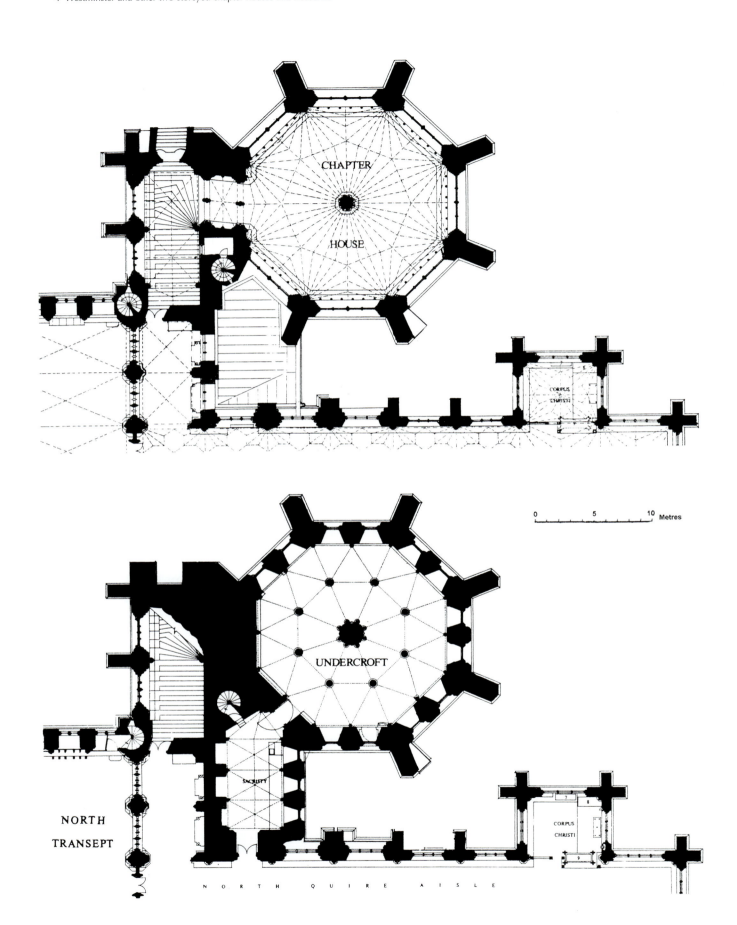

Fig 83 Wells Cathedral: plans of the chapter house, undercroft and their vestibules, 1978. *Drawing*: courtesy of the Dean and Chapter of Wells

However, unlike Beverley and Lichfield, it had a cloister, and, when the foundations for the east walk were being laid out, *c* 1195–1200, there would appear to have been an intention to erect a chapter house in the conventional position. In the event that was abandoned in favour of retaining the ancient Lady chapel that already occupied the site.[28] Instead, a chapter house was subsequently erected in the angle between the north transept and the quire aisle (fig 83). It comprises a two-storeyed, octagonal building with separate entrances and cranked vestibules to both the upper and the lower chambers. Other rooms, including a sacristy, formed part of the construction. The doorway to the sacristy and lower chamber opens off the second bay of the north quire aisle, while the chapter house itself is approached from the eastern aisle of the transept. The

chapter house complex is an addition to the eastern arm of the early Gothic church (fig 84), which was completed in Doulting limestone in the 1190s.[29]

The overall dimension of the octagon at plinth level is 19.8 m (65 ft) across the faces, precisely the same as at Westminster. This and other points of close similarity indicate that Wells was the *protégé* of Westminster, with only a short time-lapse (see p 89). Unfortunately, there is no documented evidence for the beginning of the work at Wells, but the waterholding bases, mouldings and sculpture in the undercroft and its vestibule all argue for a date no later than the middle decades of the thirteenth century. The detail of the doorway leading into the undercroft vestibule suggests *c* 1260; the door itself does not survive. However, the quire aisle wall will not have

Fig 84 Wells Cathedral: the chapter house from the north east. *Photograph*: © Warwick Rodwell 2009

been breached, and the doorway inserted, until the vestibule and undercroft had been completed.

The original door opening from the vestibule into the undercroft survives, and the last tree-ring present on its boards was dated by dendrochronology to 1265.[30] No sapwood remained and the construction of the door could easily have been two decades later, but that still does not provide close dating for the building, because the door would only have been supplied and hung at the end of the contract, and that itself was long drawn out. All indications are that the construction of the chapter house at Wells was most likely initiated in the later 1250s. Its design represents an advance on that seen at Westminster, but that may be more a reflection of the functions of the respective undercrofts than of their chronology.

The Wells undercroft is not approached via a narrow passage, but through a vaulted and well lit vestibule, which appears to have been designed to accommodate a sacristy, a function that it still performs today. It is three-and-a-half bays in length, and fine sculptures decorate the vault bosses and the corbels from which the wall-shafts rise. The northern end of the vestibule is cranked by forty-five degrees, and here lies a large, pointed doorway that opens into the octagonal undercroft. The original door still hangs in its rebate, and is richly decorated with ferramenta on the front and with portcullis framing on the rear (fig 85).[31] The door was well secured with locks and bolts, and there are pockets in the reveals of the opening for the insertion of a drawbar. Interestingly, this could only be applied internally, which must indicate that a watchman barricaded himself into the undercroft. Also at the north end of the sacristy is a narrow door opening onto a newel stair, which not only gives access to the chapter house roof but also to small chambers contained within the mass of masonry in the angle between the chapter house and its vestibules; one of these chambers appears to be a watching-place, having a view over the great stair.

The undercroft chamber is the same size as the chapter house above. It has a robust central pillar, encircled by eight engaged shafts. Concentric with the pillar are eight freestanding columns with moulded bases and capitals; these provide intermediate support for the two concentric rings of vaulting (fig 86). The vault ribs spring from these columns, from the central pillar and from the capitals of the shafts set in the angles of the outer wall. All the capitals and bases are moulded, and the abaci of the octet of columns additionally have dog-tooth ornament. The capital of one freestanding column is also similarly treated.

The floor of the undercroft is at the same level as that in the quire aisle, but since external ground level rises gently towards the north, the lower storey appears to be partially sunk. Six of the faces of the undercroft have pointed windows, each with two sets of iron grillage (fig 87). Since there are two windows per bay, the undercroft is well lit but, at the same time, it is highly secure. There can be little doubt that it was built as a treasury, which was approached through a sacristy. In the fifteenth century the security of the treasury was enhanced by adding a second,

Fig 85 Wells Cathedral: the two heavy doors protecting the entrance to the undercroft treasury. Note the outer door (left) has bolts enabling it to be secured from the inside. *Photograph*: Richard Neale © Wells Cathedral Chapter

heavy door outside the original one (fig 85).[32]

As at Westminster, the main chamber of Wells chapter house is impressively elevated, and approached through two vestibules. The outer vestibule, which is entered via a small door in the north transept aisle,[33] is of two-and-a-half vaulted bays and is entirely filled with a broad flight of steps which turns eastwards towards the top (fig 88). There, a double portal without doors leads into a short inner vestibule of one vaulted bay. From that another twin entrance opens into the octagonal chamber. The ornate wall-arcading defines fifty-one seats. There are large four-light windows in seven of the sides, and a shorter one in the eighth (above the entrance). Although the doorway and abutment of the stairs obstructed two sides at undercroft level, the architect contrived an arrangement here that allowed all sides to be glazed at chapter house level: this marks an advance on the situation obtaining at Lichfield and Westminster.

In the centre of the chamber stands a slender, sixteen-shafted pillar on an octagonal base which supports the elaborate vault. The floor is paved with limestone. The chapter house is demonstrably later in style than the undercroft, and was completed by 1306.[34] Nevertheless, the design of the chamber has much in common with Westminster. Whether there was simply a hiatus in construction at Wells, or the upper chamber suffered damage and had to be rebuilt, remains an enigma. At least half a century elapsed between the initiation and completion of the chapter house project. In 1286 reference was made to 'completing the new building begun long since', and this can only refer to the chapter house complex.[35] Setting aside the decorative detailing, which clearly belongs to the late thirteenth century, there is much in the architectural frame that would be unexceptional in the mid-century, and a case may be argued for at least partial adherence to the original design. Indeed, it remains to be established archaeologically just how much of the shell of the upper chamber is contemporary with the undercroft. It has been discovered that the parapets, buttress-tops and pinnacles are all secondary,[36] but the open arcading beneath the roof carries no 'late' detailing and could be relict from the original design (fig 84). Surely,

Fig 86 Wells Cathedral: south-east view of the interior of the undercroft. *Photograph*: © Warwick Rodwell 2008

Fig 87 Wells Cathedral: basement of the
chapter house, showing the barred windows
on the east side of the undercroft.
Photograph: © Warwick Rodwell 2009

Fig 88 Wells Cathedral: vestibule and stairs leading to the
chapter house, 1824. *Drawing*: after Britton 1836b, plate 18

Fig 89 Wells Cathedral: the interior of the roof of the chapter house. *Drawing*: pastel, Albert Goodwin, *c* 1865–70, private collection; *photograph*: © Warwick Rodwell

it suggests that a gallery was intended at this level?

Above the chapter house vault is another half-storey of unused space, beneath the flat lead roof. This space is lit by a continuous arcade of narrow, pointed openings on all sides (fig 89). Rising from the central vault-pocket is a stub of masonry that carries a heavy oak post, clasped by eight curved braces, which together support the roof framing; they are assisted in this task by a concentric octet of posts rising from the ridges of the vaulting below. The roof structure is an impressively complex piece of carpentry, without parallel (fig 107),[37] and its design must surely have been inspired by the stone vault in the undercroft. Although half a century later than the Westminster chapter house, this roof, together with Salisbury's (p 98), may well provide clues to the form of the lost structure there.

Glasgow Cathedral

Glasgow Cathedral is unusual in that the entire eastern arm is two-storeyed, a feature doubtless suggested by the terrain. The presbytery occupies the upper floor, with the crypt (or 'lower church') beneath. The chapter house is attached to the north-east corner of the presbytery, which it overlaps by one bay (figs 90 and 91).[38] The structure is square in plan, with clasping buttresses at the angles and additional buttressing midway along each side. It measures 12.8 m (42 ft) across at plinth level, and is two-storeyed; both are vaulted and have a supporting central pillar. The entrance in each case is via a short flight of steps from the northernmost chapel of the row of four that closes the east end. A spiral stair set within the wall junctions also connects the two levels.

The chapter house was constructed in the 1240s with the new eastern arm, and was partly rebuilt in the early fifteenth century, following lightning damage in *c* 1406.[39] The chambers are lit by pairs of lancet windows in each bay, which are larger on the upper floor than on the lower. Although the upper chamber is loftier and seemingly the more important, it has a plain doorway, whereas the lower chamber is entered through an elaborate portal. Today, this is regarded as the chapter house and the upper as the sacristy, but this is not a reliable indication of medieval usage. In the thirteenth century there was another structure attached to the first

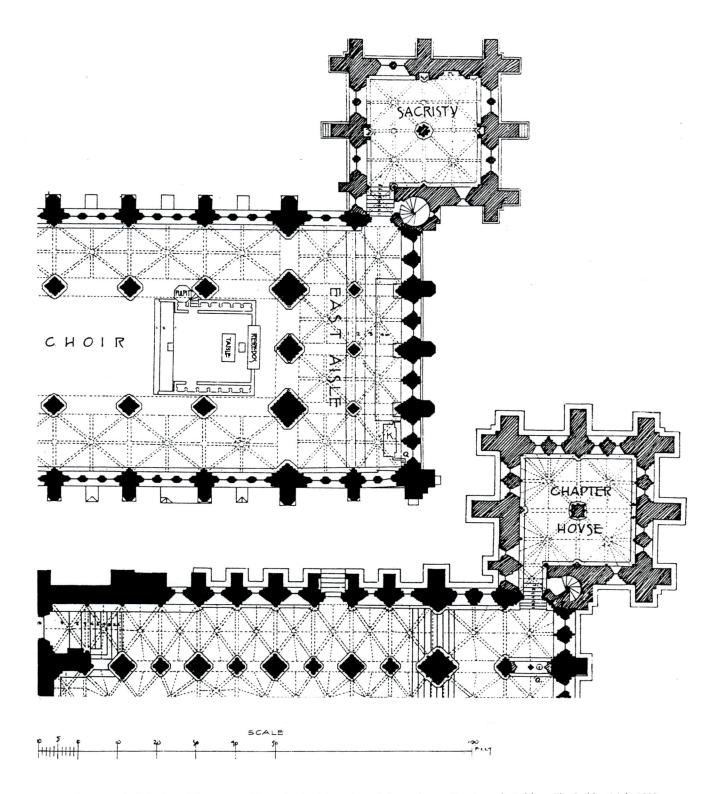

Fig 90 Glasgow Cathedral: plans of the upper and lower levels of the quire and chapter house. *Drawing*: adapted from *The Builder*, 1 July 1893

bay of the north quire aisle that was rectangular and also two-storeyed. The upper level contained the sacristy and the lower housed the treasury. Consequently, the chapter house appendage did not need to accommodate either of these functions.

Curiously, the chapter house seems to have been in the lower chamber, where a new president's seat was installed against the east wall in the early fifteenth century. In all probability, the upper chamber contained the medieval library, which may explain the larger windows.

Fig 91 Glasgow Cathedral: the chapter house from the north west. *Drawing*: D Small; after Eyre-Todd 1898, page 214

Llandaff Cathedral

Llandaff has a two-storeyed chapter house of square plan, 8.5 m (28 ft) across. It is attached to the first bay of the south quire aisle, and has clasping buttresses at the angles (fig 92).[40] The principal chamber is on the ground floor; it has a quadripartite vault and a circular central pillar with a moulded capital and waterholding base. The room is lit by single lancets in each bay on the three external sides. The entrance from the aisle is through an almost insignificant doorway, in the west reveal of which is the opening to a small newel stair that rises to the chamber above. The treatment of the first quire aisle bay is unusual, in that it alone is vaulted and serves as a vestibule to the chapter house. Although now absorbed in an east–west thoroughfare, the vestibule was constructed as an enclosed space, which was almost certainly designed to serve as a sacristy.[41] It has been argued that the vestibule dates from the early thirteenth century, with the chapter house added in the middle of the century.[42]

The upper chamber has been reconstructed in modern times, and there is no evidence to show whether it initially had a central pillar and stone vault. It serves as a library, which may have been its medieval function. There is also a small chamber above the vestibule, which was probably a muniment room.

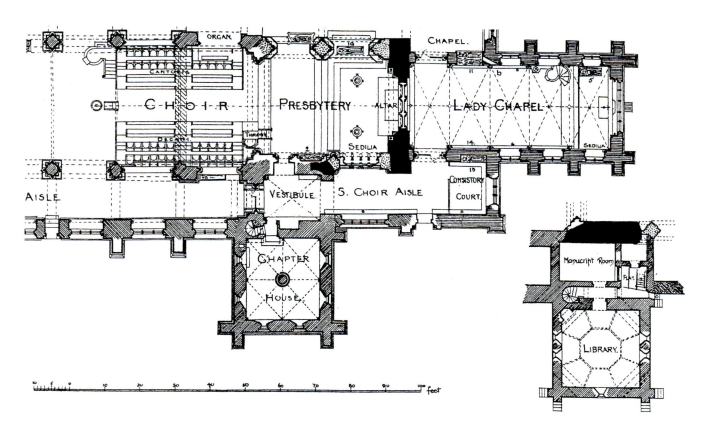

Fig 92 Llandaff Cathedral: plans of the eastern arm and library above the chapter house. *Drawing*: adapted from *The Builder*, 7 May 1892

St Paul's Cathedral, London

In terms of location, this was the most unconventional of all chapter houses: it lay in the middle of the small, two-storeyed cloister, which it completely dominated. Construction was begun in 1332.[43] The form of the chapter house is known only from a small number of illustrations of uncertain reliability, and several ambiguous descriptions.[44] The structure was already ruinous before the Great Fire of 1666, following which it was demolished.[45] Hollar's ground plan of St Paul's (1657) and his partially reconstructed view of the cloister and chapter house from the south provide the principal evidence (figs 93 and 94).[46] The building was octagonal in plan, heavily buttressed, and measured *c* 13.8 m (45 ft) across the faces.[47] The undercroft was connected by a short vestibule on the east to the lower cloister walk. The floor levels were the same in the cloister and undercroft but, owing to a gentle southward fall in ground level, they were five steps below the floor of the nave. Inside the undercroft was a quartet of pillars supporting vaulting and the floor of the chapter house above.[48] Curiously, the undercroft was open on all sides, and the four-centred arch on the south appears in Hollar's engraving. The responds had complex mouldings, confirming that there were no rebates for doors or settings for windows.[49]

The upper chamber was probably vaulted, although it is not known whether it had a central pillar. It was approached, uniquely, from the west aisle of the transept, through the upper cloister walk and a vestibule of two vaulted bays. Floor level was well above that in the transept, and Hollar's plan shows a broad flight of steps projecting into the west aisle of the transept. While the upper chamber was clearly the chapter house, the function of the open-sided undercroft is unknown. Superficially, it would appear to be a wasted space. Conceivably, it fulfilled a mortuary function, in which case the inspiration may have come from the crypt at Westminster, but there are no records of interments in the chapter house or cloister.[50]

For the sake of completeness, it may be mentioned that the arrangement at St Paul's probably inspired an equally unconventional structure associated with the college of canons serving St Stephen's Chapel in the palace of Westminster. There, in the angle between the great hall and

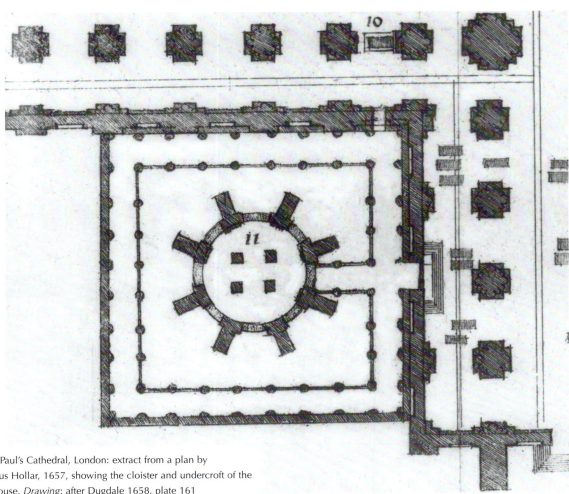

Fig 93 St Paul's Cathedral, London: extract from a plan by Wenceslaus Hollar, 1657, showing the cloister and undercroft of the chapter house. *Drawing*: after Dugdale 1658, plate 161

Fig 94 St Paul's Cathedral, London: the chapter house and the interior of the cloister from the south, by Hollar *c* 1657. *Drawing*: after Dugdale 1658, plate 127

the chapel, is a rectangular cloister which, like St Paul's, is constructed on two levels. Projecting into the cloister garth – from the west walk in this instance – is a two-storeyed chapter house (now known as the Oratory). This is not centrally planned, but is a squat, rectangular structure with a semi-octagonal eastern termination. The cloister and chapter house were constructed *c* 1535, and the lower levels of both retain much late medieval fabric, but the upper levels have been very substantially rebuilt.[51]

Salisbury Cathedral: a special case

Although the chapter house at Salisbury is single-storeyed, it has close design links with both Westminster and Wells, and once again the overall dimension of the structure at plinth level is 19.8 m (65 ft). The building is now dated to the 1260s (fig 99 and see chapter 5).[52] The local water-table at Salisbury precluded any semi-subterranean construction, and the chapter house floor is at cloister level. Also, since Salisbury was a secular cathedral and its chapter house stands in isolation, mid-way along the east cloister, no direct connection between it and the interior of

the church was feasible (fig 100). Hence, this was not a suitable location for combining functions such as sacristy or treasury.

Consequently, at Salisbury we find a parallel development of a second centrally planned octagonal building to cater for those essential functions (fig 95). Attached to the south-east transept, and entered through its southern chapel, is a compact two-storeyed sacristy, treasury and muniment room (fig 100).[53] The structure is an early addition to the transept (probably 1260s), and without it there would have been no sacristy provision.[54] The overall dimension of the octagon at plinth level is 11.25 m (37 ft), which is only a little less than that of the chapter house at Beverley. The sacristy, complete with a fireplace, occupies the single-bay vestibule, beyond which is the octagonal treasury.[55] The windows are small and secured by copious ferramenta (fig 96), and there are two sets of double doors, the first protecting the entrance to the sacristy from the transept, and second at the entrance to the treasury (fig 97).[56] A central oak post with radiating braces supports the heavy floor structure of the muniment room above. Access to that room is via a steep narrow

Fig 95 Salisbury Cathedral: two-storeyed sacristy, treasury and muniment room, viewed from the south west, from the roof of the chapter house. *Photograph*: © Warwick Rodwell 2009

Fig 96 Salisbury Cathedral sacristy: the heavily barred south-east window of the treasury. The outer ferramenta have been removed, but the infilled pockets are clearly visible where the ends of the bars were leaded into the masonry. *Photograph*: © Warwick Rodwell 2009

Fig 97 Salisbury Cathedral sacristy: view south from the transept, through the first set of double doors to the second set at the entrance to the treasury. *Photograph*: © Warwick Rodwell 2009

staircase leading off the west side of the sacristy.

Again, the thirteenth-century security arrangements are impressive: there is a door with a full-height rack-bolt at the bottom of the stairs, and two further doors on the landing outside the muniment room.[57] Although the substructure of the floor to the upper chamber is timber, it nevertheless carries a complete and well preserved late thirteenth-century tile pavement.[58] A central oak post with eight radiating braces supports the low-pitched roof (fig 98). Numerous parallels may be drawn between Salisbury, Wells and Lichfield.

Discussion

In order to understand certain aspects of Henry III's chapter house at Westminster, we need first to look back to what preceded it. The earliest reference to a chapter house is found in a set of verses composed *c* 1245, describing Edward the Confessor's church. The writer tells us that there was a cloister and 'a chapter house with a vaulted front and round towards the east'.[59] This confirms that the chapter house was apsidal-ended, and suggests that either the body of the structure was vaulted, or there was a separate vaulted vestibule. The term 'vaulted front' points towards the latter. In all probability, the vestibule was a low structure, roofed with two bays of groined vaulting similar to that surviving in the Pyx chamber. The Norman vestibule cannot have been coincident with the present

chapter house entrance, since at least half of the site was occupied by the dormitory undercroft. The Confessor's chapter house must therefore have lain a little to the north of the present structure, with its vestibule probably on the site of St Faith's chapel. The mid-eleventh-century door now hanging in the vestibule may well have come from the Confessor's chapter house, although that cannot be proved (pp 252–5).

Chapter houses were popular places for the burial of abbots and other senior figures in the community, and at St Albans the full complement of interments has been excavated: by the early thirteenth century there had been nine burials, and more followed.[60] We know that several abbots of Westminster were interred in the chapter house, or its vestibule, and their monuments were necessarily displaced during the rebuilding by Henry III. Moreover, interments could not take place there in future, since the new chapter house had its floor raised above a crypt; and no burials are recorded in the vestibule (but see pp 108–10). It is not possible to be certain how many abbots were buried in the old chapter house, but according to John Flete, a monk of Westminster (1420–65), there were eight abbatial tombs in the south cloister walk, three of which survive today.[61] The south cloister is an unlikely site for the burial of a succession of eleventh- and twelfth-century abbots, and it is reasonable to conclude that these tombs, and presumably their accompanying corporeal remains, had been moved there. The context for that relocation can

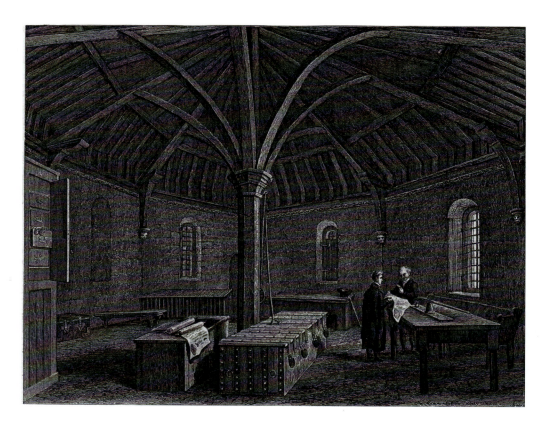

Fig 98 Salisbury Cathedral sacristy: interior of the muniment room on the upper floor. *Drawing*: after Hall 1834, opposite page 18

hardly have been other than the demolition of the old chapter house in the later 1240s. There is nothing new in this suggestion, but was it really Henry's intention permanently to obstruct free passage along the south cloister walk with at least eight tombs, or was this merely a temporary measure, pending the creation of a suitable new setting for them? Reconsideration of the design and construction of the new chapter house undercroft suggests a potential answer to this question.

Hitherto, there has been a general assumption that, because the undercroft was in use as a royal treasury before the end of the thirteenth century, it must have been built expressly for that purpose. However, archaeological evidence demonstrates unequivocally that the chamber could not have been constructed as a treasury, principally because it had no doors and could not be made secure (p 75). On the other hand, the altar recess, aumbry and piscina confirm its intended use as a chapel, with direct access, albeit via a tortuous passage, from the south transept. Add to this the fact that the architectural detailing is basic and unadorned, and the chamber presents the classic aspect of a mortuary chapel. It is therefore entirely plausible that Henry created this crypt as an integral part of his new chapter house, expressly to receive the displaced monuments and remains of the early abbots.

Either inertia or a conscious change of plan left the undercroft empty, and the abbatial monuments remained in the south cloister. The decision to house part of the royal wardrobe within the abbey may have been Henry's, or that of his son, Edward I (pp 112–13). Possibly the works recorded in 1291, which included laying a tile floor and repairing a door, signalled the change of use. At the very least, they confirm that the undercroft had been appropriated as a royal treasury by that date. There is no reliable evidence to show when that function ceased, although it had probably done so by the close of the Middle Ages (see chapter 7). The undercroft briefly resumed the role of treasury during the First World War, when the Coronation chair and other items of exceptional importance were stored there for safety.

We must now summarize the evidence from the sites discussed and attempt to set Westminster in context. The earliest centrally planned chapter house in Britain is at Worcester. After this came Alnwick, Margam, Abbey Dore and Lincoln: these structures, dating from the twelfth and early thirteenth centuries, were all single storeyed, vaulted in stone, and arranged around a central pillar. In each instance the chapter house was attached to the east cloister walk, and was not only a single-storeyed but also a single-purpose structure. Then, quite suddenly, a new phenomenon appeared in the second quarter of the thirteenth century: the two-storeyed chapter house complex. As the term I have adopted implies, these structures could, and mostly did, comprise more than just two chambers, one above the other. Six of the two-storeyed chapter houses discussed here, together with the centrally planned sacristy-treasury at Salisbury, were all built within the middle three decades of the thirteenth century; only the enigmatic structure at St Paul's belongs to the following century.

It is clear from the foregoing descriptions that Westminster, in common with certain other major churches, built adjuncts to cater for several needs. In addition to the capitular chamber, the provisions could include one or more vestibules, stairs, sacristy, treasury, library, muniment room and mortuary chapel. Additional to their use as 'waiting rooms', there may have been special functions attached to some vestibules, such as the presumed *pedilavium* at Lichfield. The second provision most frequently encountered in the design of chapter house complexes was the sacristy: we find this combination at Westminster, Beverley and Wells (with the addition of a treasury); and in those instances where a separate structure already housed the sacristy and treasury – as at Lichfield and Glasgow – a library was integrated with the chapter house instead. In the case of Llandaff, all these functions were compressed into a single complex. Additionally, at Westminster, a doorway in the south side of the vestibule suggests that an adjoining chamber in the dorter undercroft was also intimately connected with the chapter house complex.[62]

Prima facie, the earliest two-storeyed chapter house would appear to be Beverley, and the idea of combining a chapter house and a sacristy in a single, elegantly designed and centrally planned structure may have originated there, although that is contingent upon accepting that when the chapter house was erected towards the end of the building sequence in the eastern arm (perhaps in the 1240s) it did not represent a modification, but followed the original design. The possibility that a two-storeyed, rectangular building was initially intended cannot be discounted, since such structures were already known elsewhere: at Lichfield, for example, where a three-storey block combining the functions of sacristy, treasury and chapel had been erected *c* 1230 on the south side of the quire. While the lower chamber at Beverley was clearly a stone-vaulted sacristy, with a central pillar, the chapter house above may or may not have been similarly constructed. It could have been stone vaulted without a pillar (*cf* Southwell), or vaulted in timber (*cf* York).

Next in sequence must come Lichfield's chapter house,

which is remarkable on several accounts. As at Beverley, it was an addition to the north side of a church with no cloister, and it provides the earliest occurrence of a long, L-shaped vestibule, no later than the 1240s. The chapter house is located at ground level, is modest in scale and unique in its elongated octagonal/decagonal plan. The upper storey is clearly the subsidiary chamber, but is well appointed and may always have been a library. The separate chamber above the vestibule was most likely a muniment room.

More-or-less contemporary with Lichfield is Westminster's chapter house, the construction of which was begun c 1246. In terms of size, it ranks amongst the largest, and is certainly the most lavishly decorated. In part, it follows the conventional Benedictine arrangement by being accessed from the east cloister. The unconventional element is the fact that the floor of the chapter house is not at cloister level, but is reached by a broad flight of steps contained within the inner vestibule. Elevation at once imparted both greater *gravitas* to the chamber, and facilitated the construction of a semi-subterranean undercroft.

King Henry could see the chapter house from his palace to the east, and access to the abbey for royal officials was easy. A path ran from the palace, through a gate in the precinct wall, to the east door of the transept, which was used as a royal entrance (fig 116). Immediately inside the transept door, on the left, is the door leading to the undercroft passage. Also in the transept formerly lay the night-stair to the dormitory and the great gallery above the east cloister walk that now serves as the Muniment Room. The gallery, it has been argued by Wilson, was constructed by Henry III as a royal pew.[63] It is not surprising that somebody hit upon the idea of commandeering the undercroft for a treasury: by modifying the arrangement of steps within the entrance passage, and installing a heavy door at the first right-angled turn, a secure chamber was expeditiously created. As we have seen, treasuries at or below ground level were being established in other great churches (for example, at Lichfield, Glasgow, Salisbury and Wells).

Similarities between the chapter houses at Westminster and Wells are striking, and it cannot be doubted that the latter drew inspiration from the former. First, the two are dimensionally similar in plan, which is unlikely to be coincidental. Second, the spacious and well-lit undercroft at Wells represents a development from the smaller, dimly lit crypt at Westminster. By introducing an octet of columns it was possible to support two concentric rings of vaulting and thus make use of the entire space contained within the walls. Third, the Wells undercroft was designed

as a treasury from the outset, albeit not a royal one. Its vestibule also served as a sacristy.

The sceptic might dismiss the dimensional similarity of Westminster and Wells as fortuitous, but when one adds to the equation a third chapter house – at Salisbury – which is also of the same size, the idea of coincidence has to be set aside. Many architectural details at Salisbury bear comparison with Westminster, and in date the former is a precise contemporary of Wells (see chapter 5). There are several indicators of architectural rivalry in the Middle Ages between the chapters of Salisbury and Wells, and it is entirely plausible that both simultaneously strove to emulate Henry III's 'chapter house beyond compare'. At Wells, massive effort was devoted to creating an impressive treasury-undercroft which itself was unparalleled in contemporary England. We can only guess at the intended detailing of the chapter room above: either funding ran out and it was not built, or a mishap occurred and the upper storey had to be taken down and reconstructed.

However, it is to Salisbury that we must turn for a roof and parapet that is only a decade later than those at Westminster. Although the space above the vault is less voluminous than at Wells, and can never have been floored, the carpentry is well finished and the central oak column has a finely moulded capital (figs 107 and 108). Although not outwardly apparent, the roof space is quite well lit by a multiplicity of small quatrefoil openings which are incorporated in the corbel-arcade that supports the parapet (figs 99 and 109).[64] The parapet too is enriched with a blind arcade, and was formerly crenellated.

Not only do pictorial sources indicate that Westminster's chapter house had a flattish roof, but the structural evidence supplied by Wells and Salisbury (both the chapter house and sacristy in the case of the latter) weighs heavily in its favour too. These three surviving roofs, although differing in detail, have much in common: most notably, they are centrally planned structures, low-pitched, and each supported by a post from which springs an array of curved braces, like the ribs of a vault. All have low-pitched, pyramidal roofs, concealed by parapets. The seventeenth-century drawing of the Westminster chapter house shows a continuous frieze of quatrefoils in the parapet, and these were most likely pierced and thereby admitting light to the roof space (fig 30). The original drawing did not include crenellations, but these have been roughly sketched in, perhaps indicating that they were known to have existed once.

Before leaving the Westminster, Wells and Salisbury trio, it is worth noting that the inspiration for the chapter house at York appears to have been drawn from them. It is slightly later, the roof having been dated to 1288 by dendrochronology,[65] and clearly represents an attempt to provide the minster with a chapter house that outshone its predecessors. Hence, the external dimension was marginally greater than that of any other chapter house (21.3 m; 70 ft across the faces) and the central pillar was omitted, creating a vaulted space which must have been a source of wonderment. This was made possible by building a timber vault in imitation of stone. If any further proof is needed that York drew inspiration from Westminster, it can be found in the 'rose' inscription. The York version, which is painted on the north wall near the entrance to the chapter house,[66] follows the wording of one of Westminster's tile inscriptions (no. I; p 32) and reads: *Ut rosa flos florum sic est domus ista domorum* ('As the rose is the flower of flowers, so is this the house of houses').[67]

The fabric of the Westminster chapter house:
filling in the gaps from Salisbury

5

Tim Tatton-Brown

As is now well known, almost the whole of the external fabric of the chapter house at Westminster dates from George Gilbert Scott's great restoration of 1866–72. Right down to modern ground level, the use of Chilmark stone shows that even at the lower levels (below the great traceried windows) the masonry-facing is all later nineteenth-century work,[1] although there is still a medieval core behind it (pp 146–50). The only exception to this is on the north-west side of the chapter house, where much of the wall, with its great blind window, is original thirteenth-century work, because behind the face is an area of solid medieval masonry, which contains the south transept staircase and passages and also serves as the east wall of St Faith's chapel. As Plan 1 shows, this chapel was built contemporaneously between the south wall of the new south transept and the two vestibules of the chapter house. The work was rapidly executed between 1246 and *c* 1252, and much of the original Reigate stone and Purbeck marble can still be seen within St Faith's chapel and the staircase (figs 81–2). Purbeck marble was used not only for the decorative work in the chapter house string-courses, shafts, capitals, abaci and bases, but also for some of the structural work (lintels, ties and corbelling: p 16), and it can still be seen in various places in the passages and stairs in this area, albeit mostly now covered in whitewash (fig 16).

This means, alas, that more than half of the main chamber of the medieval chapter house at Westminster has been destroyed, including all the original vaulting and the roof. To reconstruct these missing parts, there is a very limited amount of earlier pictorial evidence (p 146) and, rather remarkably, another chapter house at Salisbury Cathedral, which must have been very close in form to that at Westminster (figs 99 and 100). The Salisbury chapter house has also been heavily restored but, unlike Westminster, the original vault and much of the timber and lead-covered roof still survive. At Salisbury the restoration was directed by the cathedral architect, Henry Clutton (assisted by William Burges), and carried out in 1855–56.[2] Clutton, however, became a Roman Catholic in 1856, and had to resign his position, so that the last stages of the work were overseen by the new architect, G G Scott. Hence Scott already knew both chapter houses well when he came to start his restoration at Westminster in 1866.

Writing in his *Gleanings from Westminster Abbey*, Scott agreed with Matthew Paris that at Westminster Henry III had built an 'incomparable' chapter house. He continued: 'That at Salisbury was not yet commenced, and though evidently built in imitation of this, and having some features of greater richness, it still would have yielded the palm to its prototype at Westminster.'[3] Scott went on to bemoan the then current state (in 1860) of the Westminster chapter house, and described the 'careful investigation' of the surviving details which he undertook 'some years back', including his observation that the window over the west entrance, which he found walled up with pieces of the original ribs from the vault, was, 'from the bases visible on its sill … of five instead of four lights'. He later changed his mind, when further evidence came to light, and restored this window with four main lights, like all the others (p 150). Scott also described the central pillar, about 35 ft high, which was made entirely of Purbeck marble, adding, 'I may mention that on the top of the capital is a systematically constructed set of eight hooks of iron, for as many cross-ties. The same was the case at

Fig 99 Salisbury Cathedral: the chapter house and sacristy from the south east in 1948. *Photograph*: English Heritage. NMR

Salisbury, and I have no doubt that the hooks on the columns in the church are many of them original, and were intended for security during the progress of the works.'[4] We will return to these later.

The octagonal chapter house at Westminster was clearly planned from the very beginning of Henry III's rebuilding,

and the foundations of its undercroft must have been started in 1246.[5] By that date, the ten-sided chapter house at Lincoln had probably just been completed, as may have been the smaller octagonal sacristy, treasury and muniment room at Salisbury (fig 99; p 85).[6] Westminster's chapter house is only slightly larger than Lincoln's, with internal

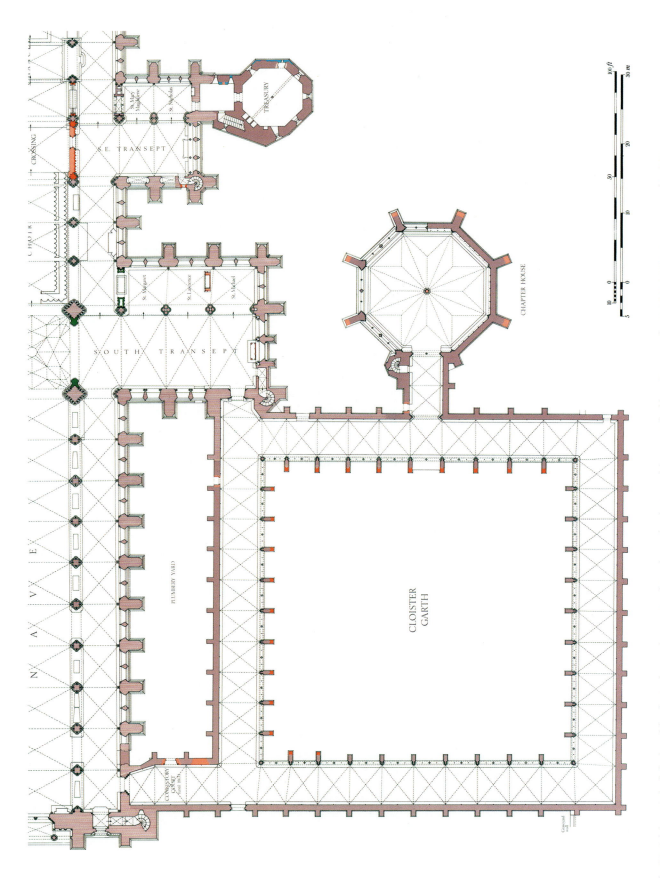

Fig 100 Salisbury Cathedral: plan of the chapter house, showing its relationship to the cloister and the sacristy building. *Drawing*: after RCHME 1993 © Crown copyright. NMR

diameters of 18.0 m and 17.7 m, respectively. Lincoln's and Salisbury's chapter houses, however, have exactly the same internal dimension.

For many years, it has been conventional to date the chapter house at Salisbury to the late thirteenth century because of the finding of 'sundry pennies of Edward I' in those parts of the foundations that required underpinning.[7] The coins have now disappeared and in 1855, when they were found, no accurate record was made to show that they were archaeologically stratified beneath the building. Indeed, at that date the principles of archaeological stratification were not yet understood. A fuller discussion of the dating of the Salisbury chapter house will be published elsewhere, but it seems likely that it was started, perhaps in the later 1250s, very soon after Westminster's was completed. The Salisbury chapter house was probably finished by 1266,[8] and was certainly in use by 1269–70.[9] This is most obviously suggested by the great similarity of the design (particularly in the window tracery) of both buildings.

If we compare the plans of the Westminster and Salisbury chapter houses, at first sight they appear to be very similar (Plan 1; fig 100).[10] They both even have recessed seats in their east face. However, at Westminster each face has only five seats (with just one on either side of the doorway in the west wall), and two steps down in front of each seat, while at Salisbury there are seven seats per face (and a larger one on either side of the west doorway), but only a single step down below them. This gives Westminster thirty-seven principal seats (presumably for the abbot and senior monks), and Salisbury fifty-one principal seats. In the case of the latter, this number was no doubt carefully planned so that every canon had a designated seat,[11] and the seven recessed seats in the east wall were for the bishop (uniquely, a canon and prebendary at Salisbury), dean, precentor, and the four archdeacons. The two larger seats flanking the doorway may have been for the chancellor and treasurer, mirroring the arrangement in the choir stalls (figs 100 and 101). A similar arrangement is encountered at Wells Cathedral, where there are again fifty-one principal seats, and a single step below them (fig 83). It is possible, but perhaps unlikely, that the vicars sat on the step below the seats. At Westminster, with its additional steps, it is more likely that the lowest step was used by junior members of the monastic community. However, it is almost certain that at both Westminster and Salisbury (and later York), the chapter house was, from the beginning, intended also to be used as a place for official secular assemblies, including Parliament:[12] hence their magnificent carved decoration (especially the superb sculpted frieze in the spandrels

above the seats at Salisbury) and very large windows filled with stained glass. The windows at Westminster, Salisbury and York are all notable for having contained early heraldic shields, as well as grisaille patterns and religious imagery (figs 30 and 102).[13]

All the original window tracery at Westminster has been destroyed, and only in the Salisbury chapter house windows can we see how the masonry was originally secured, with molten lead poured into the joints.[14] There are also integral ferramenta, to stiffen the tracery. In the lower quatrefoils, simple iron rings were fitted at the centre of each, while in the upper octofoils, a more elaborate system was used, comprising two concentric iron rings, held in place by eight radial bars (fig 103). The arrangement is carefully depicted in Buckler's view of 1810.[15] No doubt a similar arrangement obtained in the windows at Westminster.

As well as the bars that ran across the window openings, another series of eight iron bars, each c 8.8 m (29 ft) long, spanned the interior of the chapter house radially at the same level. These ran from the internal angles to the large octagonal Purbeck marble abacus block on top of the compound capital of the central pier (fig 104). Each bar had a rectangular cross-section and had an eye forged on both ends. The eyes dropped onto iron hooks, which projected from just above the abacus of the central pier and from the tops of the corresponding shafts in the angles of the outer walls. The complete arrangement thus had a spider-like appearance (fig 144). Each hook had a shank that ran horizontally into the masonry, the inner end terminating in a T-bar: one arm pointed downwards and engaged with a pocket cut into the top of the Purbeck marble abacus, while the other end pointed upwards and was housed in the underside of the limestone *tas-de-charge* (fig 105).

The radiating iron bars are described by Sir Christopher Wren in his well-known survey of Salisbury Cathedral, made for Bishop Seth Ward in 1668.[16] He states that:

> The Chapter House is an Octagone or 8 sided Figure with a Pillar in ye Center, it wants butment and therefore ye Vault is secured by 8 Irons that tie ye center to ye Walls, they are fastened like curtaine rods upon hookes, ye hooks are yeoted into ye Walls with lead, but the force of ye Vault hath broken ye Stones into which they are yeoted and drawn out 5 of the 8, by which meanes the walls and Vaults are spread, and cleft with many great cracks. It seems the hookes were too short and they should have been yoated into hardstone not freestone; the remedy will be to take out those Hooks and to bore cleane through ye Coines and to put in hooks with long stemms and anchor them on ye outside and this can never faile.

Fig 101 Salisbury Cathedral chapter house: the interior looking west in 1852. *Watercolour*: G F Sargent © Salisbury and South Wiltshire Museum

Wren's advice was perhaps not taken until just after the mid-eighteenth century,[17] because on the south-west buttress (the only one not to be enlarged in 1855–56, since it adjoined the south wall of the vestibule) a large iron plate, with a screw-threaded bolt in it, can still be seen projecting from the centre of the buttress at the level of the

95

Fig 102 Salisbury Cathedral chapter house: the interior in 1820, showing the grisaille and heraldic glazing in the east window. *Drawing*: after Britton 1835, plate 49

vault-springing. Screw-threaded bolts do not seem to have been used at Salisbury until after the death of Francis Price (Surveyor, 1737–53),[18] although Wren used them at an earlier date in the dome of St Paul's Cathedral, for example.

The radial bars seem to have been removed around the end of the eighteenth century, shortly after they were noted by John Carter.[19] The hooks remained *in situ* in both the central pier and the walls. When the pier was

taken down and replaced in its entirety with new Purbeck marble, Clutton arranged for the original plinth and base, a section of the shaft, the foliated capitals and the abacus to be reconstructed as an archaeological exhibit, and he placed it in the south-west corner of the cloister. He preserved the ends of the iron bars where they were attached to the hooks in the abacus block, and a ring of masonry at the base of the *tas-de-charge*. He also retained

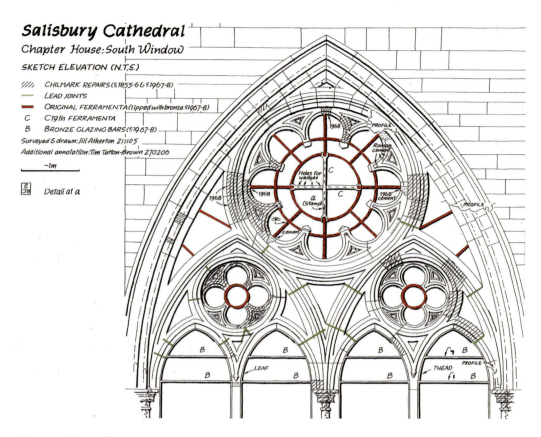

Salisbury Cathedral

Chapter House: South Window

SKETCH ELEVATION (N.T.S.)

////   CHILMARK REPAIRS (c1855-6 & c1967-8)
—   LEAD JOINTS
▬   ORIGINAL FERRAMENTA (tipped with bronze c1967-8)
C   C19th FERRAMENTA
B   BRONZE GLAZING BARS (c1967-8)
Surveyed & drawn: Jill Atherton 211105
Additional annotation: Tim Tatton-Brown 270206

~1m

Detail at a

Fig 103 Salisbury Cathedral chapter house: arrangement of the ferramenta in the tracery of the windows. *Drawing*: Jill Atherton, after Tim Tatton-Brown

Fig 105 Salisbury Cathedral chapter house: detail of the masonry at the top of the column, showing the embedded T-shaped ends of the anchors onto which the tie-bars were hooked. *Photograph*: © Tim Tatton-Brown 2009

Fig 104 Salisbury Cathedral chapter house: the remains of the original central column, now displayed in the cloister. The sawn-off ends of the radiating tie-bars can be seen between two later iron girdles that were clamped around the thirteenth-century ironwork to restrain it from fragmenting the capital. The girdles are in turn held together with more ironwork employing screw-threaded bolts. *Photograph*: © Warwick Rodwell 2009

a series of later iron repair bands around this masonry, jointed with forelock-bolts; the final ties of the late eighteenth century used screw-threaded bolts. All this evidence can still be studied in the cloister at Salisbury (figs 104 and 105). Clutton did not reinstate iron hooks in his new central pillar.

Considering the outward thrust exercised by the vault, the buttresses supporting the piers of masonry between the windows were remarkably slight before they were increased in depth in the 1850s. Internally, the piers have clusters of Purbeck marble shafts around them, and these form the principal jambs to the windows.[20] Very slender stone mullions, with Purbeck marble shafts along their inside faces, were then made to divide each window into four lights. On top of all these jambs and mullions, Purbeck marble capitals and abacus blocks were fitted, which were then ingeniously linked to each other with a series of iron bars with hooks on their ends. A single bar spanned the four lights in each window, and evidence for an exactly similar arrangement can conveniently be studied in the east cloister arcade at Salisbury. The hooked ends of the bars fitted into pockets cut into the tops of the abacus blocks, and molten lead was poured around them, to secure and waterproof the joint. At Westminster, when Scott unblocked the west window of the chapter house, he found the bar that spanned the four lights was still *in situ* (p 150).[21]

Precisely the same arrangement of radiating iron bars and embedded hooks formerly existed at Westminster.[22] Although the date at which the bars themselves were discarded is uncertain, the hooks remain in the central pillar and in the angles of the outer walls (figs 50 and 106). We must, therefore, conclude that at Westminster, as well as at Salisbury, all the masonry just below the springing-point for the vaults was tied together by wrought iron bars across the window heads and radially spanning the interior of the chamber, from the central pier to the angles of the walls. Once the masonry structure had been 'locked up' at this level, the centring for the vaults could be erected, and the bar-tracery for the upper parts of the windows constructed. A similar arrangement of tying-bars was employed at Westminster to secure the tops of the pillars of the main arcades in the abbey church, and the complete system remains intact (figs 51 and 72).[23]

The great pyramidal roof on Scott's restored chapter house at Westminster was clearly based on that at York Minster but, as Lethaby pointed out, this was a mistake (fig 4; p 147).[24] As is well-known, the later chapter house at York has no central pier, and the vault above is only made from timber which 'hangs up' to the exceptionally complicated roof above.[25] Lethaby goes on to say that the

Fig 106 Westminster Abbey chapter house: Purbeck marble capital of the central pillar with radiating iron hooks for the attachment of tying-bars. *Photograph: Warwick Rodwell © Dean and Chapter of Westminster*

chapter house at Wells 'still retains a flat roof; the one at Salisbury is a capricious alteration against, I believe, the evidence'.[26] Unfortunately, Lethaby does not appear to have examined the roofs very carefully at either Wells or Salisbury, as both are clearly original, and they are not flat, but simply low pitched (fig 107). The roof at Salisbury was heavily restored in 1973, with many new principal rafters being put in, but as Cecil Hewett has shown, the primary framework was rapidly built on top of a central timber pier that 'could have had no vertical stability, indicating an almost simultaneous assembly of the whole complex'.[27] Exactly the same applies to the roof at Wells which, although somewhat later in date, has many similarities in design (for further discussion of the significance of the Wells roof, see p 81). On top of the central post at Salisbury is an elaborately moulded capital, and all the original braces had finely carved stopped-chamfers on their lower sides (figs 108 and 109).[28] The addition of later supports has considerably cluttered the space, detracting from the original elegance of the framing.

Pictorial indications and the comparative evidence provided by Salisbury and Wells therefore render it highly likely that the original chapter house roof at Westminster Abbey was also shallow pitched. Scott claimed to have found evidence that the angles between the sides of the chapter house at Westminster were punctuated by pinnacles rising from the buttresses (p 147). Consequently,

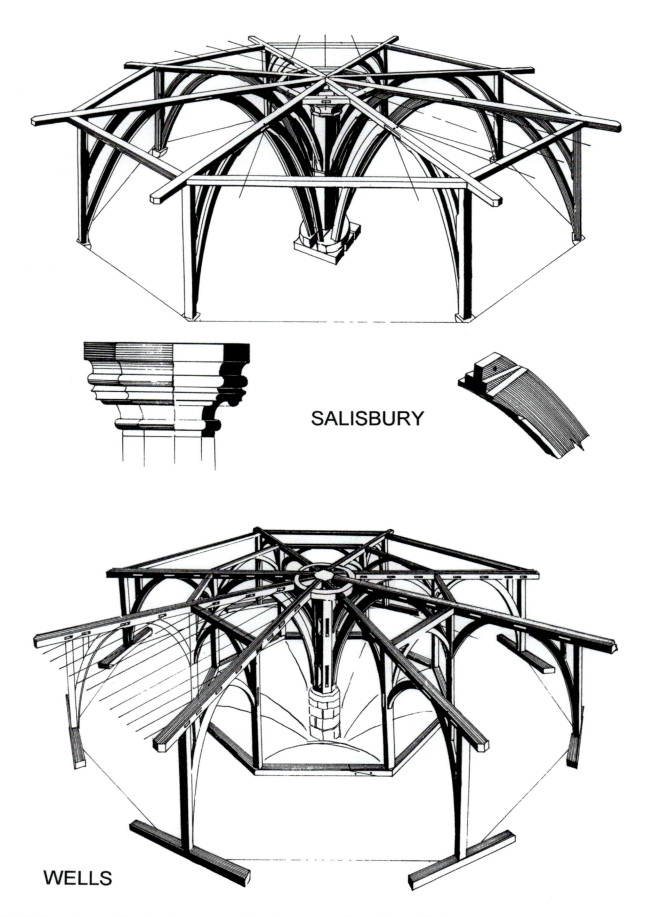

Fig 107 Perspective views illustrating the construction of the chapter house roofs at Salisbury and Wells cathedrals. *Drawing*: after Hewett 1985, figs 102 and 106

Fig 108 Salisbury Cathedral chapter house: the roof structure, supported by a central post with a moulded capital and curved braces (primary and secondary). *Photograph*: © Warwick Rodwell 2009

Fig 109 Salisbury Cathedral chapter house: detail inside the roof, showing one of the chamfered arched-braces and the continuous series of small quatrefoil openings immediately below parapet level. *Photograph*: © Warwick Rodwell 2009

he designed and installed the present needle-like pinnacles, for which he may have drawn inspiration from Lincoln. If there ever were pinnacles at Westminster, it is likely that they were added along with the flying buttresses in the late fourteenth century (p 10), and had been removed by the seventeenth. There is no pictorial evidence to support the notion of pinnacles: Morgan's map of 1682 simply shows a plain parapet (fig 31), and the earlier seventeenth-century view indicates a continuous quatrefoil frieze (fig 30). Interestingly, the latter also has crenellations sketched in as an afterthought. This perhaps indicates an awareness by a later artist that crenellations had been removed from the parapet, but is more likely a representation of the brick crenellations added in the eighteenth century. However, it is relevant to note that a seventeenth-century view of Salisbury Cathedral also shows crenellations on its chapter house;[29] they were removed before the end of the eighteenth century,[30] and a moulded coping was placed directly on top of the arcaded frieze, with the result that the roof-line of the chapter house has a markedly truncated appearance. At both Salisbury and Westminster it is highly unlikely that crenellations constituted part of the original parapet, and they were probably added in the fourteenth century, replacing a moulded coping.

Decoration is another field in which Salisbury can potentially shed light on Westminster. A considerable amount of evidence survives in the cloister, chapter house and vestibule for the thirteenth-century treatment of the walls and vaults. Although the walls of the cloister and vestibule were faced internally with medium-sized ashlar, as at Westminster, they were nevertheless given a thick coat of limewash to mask the jointing pattern. Over that was then painted, in single red lines, a pseudo-ashlar pattern, the scale of which was remarkably small: the visual effect was to produce a pattern that more closely resembled brickwork than masonry (fig 110A). The rubble-filled webs of the vaults in the vestibule and chapter house were plastered and similarly decorated with a small-scale pseudo-ashlar pattern. Polychromatic scrollwork was painted around the bosses and on the creases of the vaults. A good deal of this decoration still survives in the vestibule (fig 110B), and it was also preserved on the vault of the chapter house until the mid-nineteenth century (fig 101). Unfortunately, the vault was completely repainted in imitation of the medieval scheme in 1856 (fig 69).[31] Considerable remains of red and green paint survived on the ribs too. In his initial scheme for the restoration of Westminster, Scott proposed to replicate the decoration on the vault at Salisbury (fig 132), but in the end he created an inauthentic striped pattern in the masonry itself (frontispiece and fig 106).

In conclusion, comparison with Salisbury suggests that much of the masonry of the upper walls and windows of the Westminster chapter house was held together by ironwork and poured-lead jointing which, as Lethaby observed, was put in to hold the whole structure together in perpetuity.[32] Some of these tie bars had presumably pulled out by the fourteenth century, when flying-buttresses started to be erected around the outside of the chapter house (p 10). Westminster very probably had a shallow-pitched roof, surrounded by a moulded coping perhaps later replaced by crenellations. Internal decoration could well have consisted of painted imitation stonework on the walls and on the vault, with scrollwork round the bosses and in the vault creases.[33]

A

B

Fig 110 Salisbury Cathedral: fictive ashlar painting; *above*: on a layer of limewash, over true ashlar masonry in the north cloister walk; *below*: on the plastered vault in the chapter house vestibule, which also carries stencilled patterns. *Photographs*: © Warwick Rodwell 2009

The monks of Westminster and their chapter house

6

Barbara Harvey

Monastic chapter houses served many purposes. Some of these were an integral part of monastic life; others more distantly related to it, if related at all. Some were chosen by the monks; others imposed on them, willy-nilly. The latter might be expensive, as the monks of Durham Cathedral Priory were reminded in 1424, when their chapter house was, for two weeks, the scene of negotiations between English and Scottish lords for an Anglo-Scottish treaty. This intrusion cost the priory £100, a sum representing about 5 per cent of its net annual income.[1] But chapter houses were built principally to accommodate the chapters from which they took their name, and especially the daily chapter that was, for several centuries, a normal feature of Benedictine life. Although, as David Carpenter has persuasively argued in this volume,[2] Henry III built the chapter house for his own use as well as that of the monks, its fundamental design reflects its monastic purpose. This paper is concerned mainly with the daily chapter at Westminster Abbey in the thirteenth century, a century divided into two nearly equal parts by the dismantling of the Confessor's chapter house and the erection of Henry III's. At a later point, however, it will discuss the use of the old chapter house and the new for burials, and the brief role of the new chapter house in the later fourteenth century as a meeting place of the Commons in Parliament.[3]

Chapters: their origin and purpose

A Benedictine chapter was, in principle, a meeting of the entire community of monks in the monastery in question, including, for part of the meeting, novices who were professed but still in custody.[4] It took place within a liturgical office known as the capitular office, but derived its name from the portion, or chapter, of the rule of St Benedict read at the beginning of the meeting.[5] The reading and the correction of faults, following spontaneous confession, or naming by other monks present, were essential components of the latter. 'Fault' in this context is a word with a wide application, from grumbling at a set task to the apostasy committed by any monk who ran away and thus broke the vows from which there could be no release. By the thirteenth century, many offences existed between these extremes, but underlying every monastery's written or unwritten code, and its tariff of punishments, was St Benedict's distinction between lesser and graver offences.[6] Punishments ranged from a rebuke addressed by the president to the offender prostrating before him, to beating, loss of seniority, and, most dreaded of all, exile to another monastery. Most punishments were performed in public, and the main thrust of the system was towards humiliation.[7] The only plea by an accused monk that seems to have been acceptable was '*mea culpa*', and for contumacious monks accused of a serious offence who withheld this plea a period of imprisonment might follow.[8] Nor were faults corrected only in chapter. The sentence of fettering and imprisonment for a day imposed by Abbot Samson (1182–1211) on a troublesome monk of Bury St Edmunds – apparently without reference to the chapter or to senior monks, the abbot's traditional advisers – alerts us to the fact that, in the years around 1200, a Benedictine abbot might still take draconian measures without consultation.[9] But we must also remember that monastic customaries, our principal source for procedures when faults were corrected in chapter, have little to say about the many preliminary enquiries that no doubt took place outside the meeting, or about the personal animosities that may explain many accusations, wherever they were made.

Despite the demands on time made by the correction of faults, a normal chapter also dealt with other items, summarized by David Knowles in his classic account of the subject, as 'business'.[10] These ranged from announcements, probably by the succentor, of liturgical arrangements for the next day, and possibly for a longer period, to matters that were not of a routine character and might be confidential. Such were the reception of novices to profession and admission of seculars to confraternity; and, by the end of the twelfth century, chapters might legitimately expect to witness the sealing of documents to which the common seal was applied, for these normally related to long-term commitments for the monastery in question. The chapter at Bury St Edmunds had established a formal right of this kind before the death of Abbot Samson.[11]

In common with the capitular office, the chapter is not mentioned in the rule of St Benedict, but St Benedict's insistence that the abbot should consult the whole congregation of monks before reaching a decision on any serious matter and ensure that monks listened frequently to the rule, anticipates in two respects meetings that would later be called chapters.[12] In the Carolingian church, daily chapters existed by the end of the eighth century.[13] In England they were regarded by the tenth-century reformers and by reformers in the Anglo-Norman church as a necessary feature of monastic life.[14] When, therefore, the monks of Westminster took possession of their new chapter house in the mid-1250s, such meetings had almost certainly been a feature of life in their monastery for nearly two centuries, and, if we reckon from St Dunstan's foundation of a small monastery here in the mid-tenth century, quite possibly for longer.[15] For at least two centuries they had possessed a chapter house, a room dedicated to this purpose.

The chapter at Westminster Abbey: procedure

During this long period, large Benedictine communities – and Westminster, with some eighty monks at the end of the eleventh century and between fifty and sixty a century later, was large – were profoundly affected by the withdrawal of the abbot from the common life, and, somewhat later, by the formal division of the properties of each monastery between the abbot and the convent.[16] These developments gave momentum to a widespread

desire – which came to the surface of events in the second half of the twelfth century – to infer from the duty of an abbot to consult his chapter in serious matters a right on the chapter's part, in certain areas of monastic life and especially in appointments to major offices, to give or withhold actual consent to the course of action he proposed. Such demands reflected unease not only about the remoteness of the abbot, but also about the independent way of life now enjoyed by many of the obedientiaries, or office-holders, who administered much of the property and therefore much of the income of their monasteries. Above all, the constitutional claims of chapters in this period reflect dissatisfaction with the seniors as an adequate source of advice for the abbot in serious matters. In this context, 'seniors' is a term denoting a defined group consisting mainly of those who were senior in profession in the community in question, but also including some whose outstanding qualities won for them promotion above others professed at an earlier date. We should envisage a group including both cloister monks and obedientiaries. At Westminster, in the mid-thirteenth century, it numbered fourteen or sixteen, a number representing about one quarter of the monastic body of that period, and in chapter its members were seated on either side of the president.[17] Since both cloister monks and obedientiaries had many other duties to perform, the accepted quorum when the seniors were needed may have been quite small.

On feasts, chapter met after prime – the office said or sung when daylight was full – but on private or ordinary days they met after the so-called morrow mass – a low mass celebrated later in the morning; and this was in each case the common practice.[18] Among the obedientiaries, those with forinsec cares taking them outside the monastery may have been on the road before the hour of the meeting and occasionally absent for several days or more. But, since anyone with administrative responsibilities was vulnerable to accusations of faults in carrying out his duties, even the most important may have found it politic to be present whenever possible.

Abbots were expected to attend chapter and preside if 'at home', a phrase covering residence at La Neyte, their house in present-day Pimlico, as well as their chamber or apartment in the precinct.[19] The chapter at which Abbot Arundel (1200–14) accused all holding administrative office of a fault, and deprived them of such preferential places in chapter as they had been given, was remembered for more than fifty years. Its memorable feature, however, was not the abbot's presence but the mistake of the rather naive prior who thought that the abbot expected him to accept the public humiliation now meted out to the rest.[20]

Yet it is unlikely that the abbots of this period, who followed an itinerant mode of life, were frequently in chapter or easily recalled if needed. Walter de Wenlok (1283–1307) was, to our knowledge, frequently absent for long periods and, in 1291, spent several months in France.[21] The prior too, the abbot's deputy, now lived privately, but he did not possess the country retreat at Belsize, in Hampstead, enjoyed by his late-medieval successors, and his only apartment was in the precinct.[22] Despite his occasional absences, the daily chapter was, in a real sense, his chapter, and we can assume that he frequently occupied the abbot's or president's seat.

By custom, the prior, his assistants, the claustral priors, and a small number of seniors met before each chapter to review matters likely to arise and ensure that only those that were, in Lanfranc's influential words, 'of utility and pertaining to the religious life' were considered.[23] Careful management of the kind implied in this preliminary meeting does much to explain how it was that at Westminster, as in other monasteries leaving some record of these matters, little that was controversial was actually decided in chapter, although final decisions might well be formalized here.[24]

When the moment came, other monks were summoned by bell or clapper and all entered the chapter house in procession and in order of seniority. In the chapter house, as in the abbey church, there were two sides, sometimes called 'choirs', and in the new chapter house these met at the president's seat, situated in the centre of the eastern wall. Seniority alternated from side to side, and this meant that a monk's immediate senior and junior in profession, if present, were normally seated, not next to him on either side, but opposite.[25] In the new chapter house, there were three tiers, including the step from which the wall arcading springs, but four in the president's bay. The monks probably sat on the step and on the tier immediately below, but not on the bottom tier. Monks abhorred 'crowding', but if, as seems likely, the places of absentees were left vacant, there would normally have been a sense of space to spare.[26] Mats were provided at the sacrist's expense and renewed, if necessary, once a year.[27] Elsewhere in the monastery, this item of furnishing served several purposes: mats were used in the dormitory, for example, to minimize the noise made by those walking on any paved area, but on the benches in the cloister no doubt to provide a little warmth for those sitting there.[28] It is unlikely that they were used in the chapter house to cover the remarkable tiled floor where the dominant motif was, and is, the royal arms. In the case of the chapter house, the customary refers to their use on the *scanna*, a word that, in this context, probably denotes the benches

or tiered seats on which the monks sat day by day, and on the penitential step before the president's seat, which had a role in the correction of faults.[29] If these suggestions are correct, the wear and tear on the mats that the sacrist paid for each year may have been caused by the movement of monks along or up and down the tiers to take their places at each meeting, stand at the penitential step when required to do so, or move for another reason. *A fortiori*, on later occasions when the Commons in Parliament met in the chapter house, their boots, being heavier than the footwear of the monks, may well have caused some at least of the exceptional damage to the chapter house mats noted by the sacrist in his accounts.[30]

The reading from the rule of St Benedict took place early in the proceedings, after the conclusion of the brief capitular office. The martyrology, now forming part of this office, was read by a monk of junior status, and he may also have read the passage from the rule. In the new chapter house, the reader stood at the lectern which, as we are later told by the Anonimalle chronicler, was in the middle of the room.[31] If so, he was near the crucifix, itself reverenced by every monk on entering or leaving the room, and also centrally placed.[32] On feasts, the reading may have been followed by a passage from the Gospels, and, occasionally, against the wishes of many of the monks, additional texts were read. Thus in 1234, the visitors sent by Gregory IX required the monks of Westminster to listen twice a year in their own chapter to the decrees of the general chapter of the English Black Monks, a body meeting triennially and concerned to halt the growing irregularity of Benedictine life. When, however, in 1251, Abbot Richard Crokesley (1246–58) insisted that the latest statutes of the general chapter, enacted two years previously, should be read, he encountered stiff opposition which was overcome by the intervention of the abbot of Bury St Edmunds, the president of that body.[33]

During the correction of faults, most accusations were probably made by the obedientiaries *ex officio*, or so it would appear from the carefully ordered precedence given to them whenever one of their number wished to speak. The precentor and succentor, who were particularly charged with responsibility for the fitting performance of the Divine Office, were given precedence after the abbot and prior and the prior's deputies for this very purpose.[34] Whatever the source of the accusation, the accused went to the so-called '*gradus*' or penitential step, and, standing before it and pleading '*mea culpa*', indicated his readiness – if this was so – to accept the punishment now handed down.[35] This step was in front of the president's seat, and was probably identical with that on the bottom tier at this point. In the case of all except light offences, the accused, in principle at least, was required to prostrate when asking for mercy. It seems likely that he did so on the pavement in front of the penitential step and that the mat provided by the sacrist for the step was in fact used for the comfort of those prostrating in this way.[36]

Virtually no evidence survives enabling us to identify the offences committed, as distinct from the wide range of possibilities, and actual penalties are recorded as rarely as offences. Only two cases of the exile of a monk of Westminster have come to light in this century. In 1251 Abbot Crokesley is said, by an evidently hostile witness writing on the fly-leaf of an abbey book, to have imposed the penalties of fettering and beating on Richard de Slowtre, a runaway monk recaptured at Rochester, before sending him to Gloucester abbey and then to Hurley priory, one of Westminster abbey's dependent houses.[37] In July 1307, Abbot Wenlok sent Roger de Aldenham, one of his leading opponents in a bitter controversy between the abbot and Prior Reginald Hadham at this time, to Hurley.[38] It is, however, known that severe forms of punishment were used until a late date in other monasteries in this period, and a little evidence to this effect survives from later periods at Westminster. In 1359–60, the infirmarer's provision of two privies and some stone steps in the house of the keeper of delinquent monks implies that from time to time such monks were incarcerated in a prison in or near the infirmary.[39] In 1395, Robert Barton, a monk of some twelve years' standing, who, though already suspended by the abbot for another offence, spent six nights outside the monastery, was deprived of his wages, his voice in chapter, his seniority at table and in choir and chapter, and he was, for a time, excommunicated.[40]

The difficult years

In the early fifteenth century, the daily chapter at Durham Cathedral Priory lasted about an hour.[41] In the thirteenth century, the Divine Office in a Benedictine monastery, and the timetable in general, were more crowded than they later became, and it is unlikely that more than an hour, if as much, was then available for the chapter at Westminster. Much of the time available – more than it has been possible to discuss in this account – was consumed in the practice of an elaborate decorum. Clearly, an abbot wishing to fulfil his obligation to consult the whole congregation of monks on serious matters by using the daily chapter for this purpose would find it necessary to postpone much other business. At this point, however, much depends on the current interpretation at Westminster of the abbot's obligation. Were the prior and

convent, meeting in chapter, to be consulted on all such matters, or was it sometimes sufficient for the abbot to consult the seniors or some of them – the system to some extent legitimized by John of Ferentino, the papal legate, in decrees for St Mary's Abbey, York, in 1206, which also had a wider reference?[42] And did consultation, when it took place, imply an obligation on the part of the abbot to accept the advice of the chapter – the radical view by now gathering some support in the wider Benedictine world?

The convent's constitutional claims at Westminster grew with its success in acquiring its own portion of lands or other forms of property. Its first successes of the latter kind belong to the second half of the twelfth century, when Abbot Laurence (1156–73) and his immediate successors, Walter of Winchester (1175–90) and William Postard (1191–1200), were persuaded to make grants of manors or appropriated churches, or simply an annual payment in perpetuity, to the convent which, in return, undertook to observe anniversaries: in Laurence's case, for his parents, but in the other two for the grantor himself.[43] For a comprehensive separation of their goods from those of the abbot, the convent waited until 1225. In this year, Abbot Richard de Berking executed a formal and wide-ranging deed of this kind in which he surrendered to the convent a large measure of control, defined with great particularity, over about two thirds of the abbey's vast estates.[44]

Given the difficulties to be overcome in dividing possessions as numerous and varied as those of Westminster Abbey, it is not surprising that the agreement of 1225, soon known as the first composition between the abbot and convent, was quickly followed by a supplement, providing for situations not envisaged in the former, and in July 1227 by arbitration conducted by the bishops of Bath, Salisbury and Chichester on matters now in dispute between the abbot and convent.[45] Neither of these acts touched constitutional issues except in so far as every formal agreement between abbot and convent did so. But the original agreement of 1225 included clauses of this kind that were evidently disputed by Richard Crokesley, Berking's successor, and raised issues that were in contention for the rest of the century. First in importance among these were questions relating to the appointment and dismissal of obedientiaries. In 1225, Abbot Berking surrendered, though not in the clearest of terms, the customary rights of the abbot both to appoint and to dismiss.[46] In 1252, however, during Crokesley's abbacy, mediators, acting with Henry III's approval and quite possibly on his initiative, won acceptance for the decision that in future the abbot should choose the two cellarers and two hostellers from short-lists nominated by the convent. In so doing they set aside the larger promise made by Berking. They also restored to the abbot the right of dismissal, always the more sensitive of the two issues.[47] It was only in two ordinances enacted by the prior and convent during vacancies in the abbacy, the one in 1283–4, and the other in 1307–8, that the convent was able to reclaim even a limited voice in such dismissals.[48] By the end of the century, they also had the right, conceded by Abbot Wenlok after strenuous resistance, to divide among themselves the surplus issues of the wealthy foundation supporting the anniversary of Eleanor of Castile – a spectacular violation of St Benedict's absolute prohibition of private property among his monks – and the right to nominate a short-list of two from which the abbot would choose the warden of this fund.[49]

The disputes summarized above spanned four abbacies: from Berking's election in 1222, to Wenlok's death in 1307. From Richard Ware's abbacy (1258–83), no addition to the compositions regulating the division of goods between the abbot and convent survives, but the timing of the ordinance of 1283, agreed in chapter on 31 December, less than a month after Ware's death, suggests that he may have resisted some of the demands which it expresses, and our sources contain other hints that this was so.[50] Behind the disputes, and forming part of their pre-history, lay the first grants in perpetuity to the convent by Laurence, Walter of Winchester and William Postard, and the new note of confidence on the convent's part discernible in these charters. The disputes themselves culminated in the bitter quarrel between Wenlok and Prior Reginald Hadham, who, in 1307, appealed to Rome against Wenlok's alleged violation of the compositions. Hadham was himself then charged by Wenlok with serious offences of a disciplinary kind and by Wenlok suspended from office and excommunicated.[51] In fact, the dismantling of the old chapter house and the erection and coming into daily use of the new took place in a period in the history of the community at Westminster that would have astonished earlier generations of monks by its challenge to the authority of the abbot, the rock on which Benedictine life rested.

The monastic chapter was involved at many points in these events, from the sealing of the grants in perpetuity to the convent executed by Laurence and Walter of Winchester, and very likely that executed by William Postard, to the ordinance of 1283, which testifies to its own grant 'in pleno capitulo' ('in full chapter'). By the latter phrase we should probably understand an open and formal chapter, and the need to state this may be explained by the fact that the chapter had been especially summoned to approve the ordinance. But whatever kind of chapter we have in mind, it seems clear that much of the detailed,

time-consuming, and, to some extent, controversial drafting needed at every revision of the compositions must have taken place under different and less formal conditions. Discussion of the most appropriate way of dismissing obedientiaries, who controlled day by day so much of the life of the monastery, was hardly suited to a room without doors; yet the new chapter house at Westminster had none. And although serious divisions among the monks have left no trace in our sources until 1307, when only sixteen, representing fewer than one third of the community, were willing to act as compurgators for Hadham as he faced Wenlok's charges, we should not assume that the monks in chapter had always, or indeed often, been of one mind earlier, as the compositions were made or revised.[52] But how and when parties were formed is normally hidden from view.

The later medieval chapter

In the later Middle Ages, the chapter acquired new business, and notably that of consenting to the deposit of funds in the common chest. This institution is first mentioned in the accounts of the abbey treasurers in the years around 1500 but may have been introduced at an earlier date.[53] In this period, moreover, use of the abbey's common seal, for so long a cause of concern to the convent, was for a time subject to a real measure of control by the chapter, and the chapter's consent was now normally recorded in the grants to which it was applied. Among these were a considerable number relating to corrodies, a form of life-pension that the prior and convent tried to subject to their consent during the vacancy after Richard Ware's death.[54] Yet, by the mid-fifteenth century, the chapter's control over the common seal was so weak that George Norwych, a spendthrift abbot (1463–69), was able to contract debts amounting to more than £2,000, a sum equivalent to some 80 per cent of the monastery's net annual income, by means of bonds under the common seal: this he apparently used without consultation with anyone other than a few favourites.[55] In fact, references to the chapter's or convent's consent normally found in grants of corrodies and in long leases of property in the later Middle Ages quickly became formulaic. Without them, in the case of corrodies, grantees would not be able to prove a legal interest extending beyond the life of the abbot who made the grant; but in the case of corrodies, and in that of leases, references to the consent of the chapter tell us little or nothing about the actual circumstances in which the seal was applied.[56]

From the mid-fourteenth century, at Westminster and in Benedictine houses more generally, circumstances combined to reduce the importance of the daily chapter in monastic life and remove occasions of belligerence. Among the new circumstances at Westminster, and in the long term the most important, was the acceptance as a normal feature of monastic life of the irregularities, including wages for each monk, for which the chapter had contended in the thirteenth century.[57] These circumstances, together with a generous use of private chambers, weakened the common life on which all chapters depended for their own vitality. Whether fortuitously or not, an increasing concern for the privacy of chapters, and the exclusion of seculars from their proceedings, accompanied their actual decline. Hence the decree of the general chapter of English Black Monks in 1343 that if chapter house doors could not be locked while meetings were in progress, entrance to the cloister must be secured.[58] We can assume that the number of monks normally attending the daily chapter fell in this period, and, if so, many chapters may have been held in a smaller room than the chapter house. Indeed, on many occasions in the second half of the fifteenth century, the sacrist's accounts reveal a state of affairs in the chapter house itself that would have made temporary moves to a different room necessary. The two carpenters, for example, who worked for fifty-one days in the chapter house in 1466–67, and the scaffolding mentioned in 1483–84 and 1485–86, would have posed a challenge to normal procedures.[59] But these cannot have been new experiences in the history of the chapter, which, indeed, had no dedicated room at its disposal for several years in the thirteenth century, as the new chapter house was built. If, however, numbers fell and meetings were often held in a less imposing room than that used by earlier generations of monks, the daily chapter itself retained considerable importance in the life of the monastery. In his definitive decrees for Black Monks, published in 1336, Benedict XII emphasized the unique importance of the reading of the rule and the correction of faults in the religious life.[60] On a lower plane, we may admire the chapter's role in disseminating information, and especially vital information about liturgical arrangements for the day, the morrow, and the days immediately ahead. The succentor, the warden of the Lady chapel, and others with rotas relating to duties at the Divine Office or at the many altars in the abbey where post-obit masses were now celebrated, no doubt hoped that monks currently within the monastic walls would diligently read the copies that were now displayed in the cloister and for which the sacrist apparently provided the raw materials.[61] But it is questionable whether any obedientiary in this position, or his deputy, in such a monastery, could safely dispense with the spoken word and some face-to-face discussion of duties.

Although its association with chapter meetings was less regular in the later Middle Ages than previously, the chapter house remained the only possible setting for solemn events of a different order of importance in the life of the community. Among these, from 1504 onwards, was the annual reading of the obligations undertaken by the abbot and convent of Westminster in accepting the endowment of Henry VII's munificent foundation, centering on the new Lady Chapel now in process of construction. The historiated initial letter illustrating this annual event occurs in the so-called indenture of abstract, in which the obligations were fully set out, and this miniature is the earliest known representation of the interior of the chapter house (fig 111).[62]

From a point between the entry to the chapter house and the lectern, said in the late fourteenth century to be in the middle of the room (and, as far as we know, still in that place in the early sixteenth century) the miniature looks eastwards across a floor, which is tiled, but with plain tiles, to two tiers of benches and wall arcading springing from these. The benches apparently have decorated tops, and it is possible that these were, in fact, mats provided for the comfort of monks sitting on the benches at chapter meetings. The abbot stands on the lower tier, holding his pastoral staff. Six monks are visible in the side – or so-called choir – on his left, and a seventh can be glimpsed. In

Fig 111 Historiated initial letter from an indenture dated 1504, showing the annual reading of that indenture on the lectern in the chapter house at Westminster Abbey. *Photograph*: © The National Archives; TNA: PRO E 33/1, fol 83

the side on the abbot's right, however, instead of monks – and in addition to the steward of the abbot's lands – are three law officers of the crown, although, as we know from the indenture, only one of the three need attend a reading. In the foreground, a monk reads the indenture – which is in codex form – to the assembled company. His small stature ensures that he does not obscure any part of the lectern, large though it is, or any part of the opening in the indenture from which he is reading – and reading perhaps with some difficulty, for the text lies well above his eye-level. Moreover, the gold tassels hanging from the corners and seam of the volume are conspicuous. In fact the indenture itself, including its outward physical features, is the focus of the miniature, and this may explain the absence from the latter of features of the chapter house with which the artist may well have been familiar and which now appear remarkable. This applies supremely to the royal arms on the actual tiles in this room. He had one point to make above all others, and he did not clutter the scene in making it.

Burials in the old and new chapter houses

It is safe to assume that, down to the early thirteenth century, the abbots of the Confessor's foundation at Westminster were normally buried in the old chapter house (see pp 87–8). Edwin, however, whose death, probably in 1068, may have occurred before the completion of this room, is an exception. Although John Flete, writing in the mid-fifteenth century, and our principal written source for abbatial burials, does not record, and may not have known, in which cloister Edwin was buried, we need not doubt that he was buried in one or other of the cloisters before his later translation to a more prestigious site.[63] Moreover, the short abbacy of Geoffrey, his Norman successor, ended in his deposition and return to Normandy.[64] But from Vitalis (d 1085?) to William Humez (d 1222), burial in the old chapter house is likely. If so, we may assume that when this room was dismantled, probably in the late 1240s, in preparation for the construction of the new chapter house, abbots buried in the former were moved to the south cloister, for it was here that Flete located the burials of eight abbots, excluding Edwin, and described their tombs.[65]

The promotion of abbatial burials from chapter house or cloister to the monastic church was a common development among Benedictines from the thirteenth century onwards. The timing of this change, however, varied from monastery to monastery and may reflect fortuitous circumstances as well as changes in burial fashions. At Westminster, in 1223, only a year after the burial of William Humez in the old chapter house, Ralph

Arundel was buried in the nave of the abbey church.[66] If an abbot was to be buried in the abbey church at this time, the choice of the nave as the site was probably inevitable, since the eastern arm of the church was affected by new work recently begun in the Lady Chapel. But the choice of Arundel as the first abbot to be buried in any part of the church, and thus to come nearer in death to the shrine of the abbey's saint than any of his predecessors, is arresting. He was, in fact, the predecessor of Humez, but had been deposed nine years previously by a papal legate, after a lengthy enquiry into his conduct of matters both spiritual and temporal.[67] The choice of Arundel may point to the conclusion that, when Humez was buried, the old chapter house accommodated the last abbatial tomb slab for which it had an appropriate space. When Richard de Berking died, in 1246, the construction of Henry III's church, and with it the new chapter house, was under way, and the design of the latter, which included an undercroft, made burials of a normal kind impossible.[68] Berking, like Arundel, was buried in the Abbey's new Lady Chapel, completed in the previous year.[69]

Secular burials in the old chapter house were, it appears, rare, if indeed any took place at all. At Westminster the privileges of confraternity did not include burial within the precinct, but the latter privilege might be the subject of a separate grant.[70] Although the old chapter house may not have been finished at the time of the Confessor's death in January 1066, long delay is unlikely since the room was built as an extension of the eastern arm of his church.[71] From an early date, therefore, we might expect to find that burial here was a privilege enjoyed, though exceptionally, by benefactors to the abbey; and if a historian had existed at Westminster in the twelfth century as much concerned to record burials there as, for example, Orderic Vitalis was to record those occurring at St Évroul in Normandy in the decades around 1100, we might discover that this was so.[72] So far, however, I have found no explicit reference to a secular burial here. It is, moreover, of interest in this context that Alice, first wife of Geoffrey de Mandeville I, who was himself a notable benefactor to the abbey, was buried in the cloister, probably in or before 1085, and that her husband later expressed a wish to be buried beside her: not for either of them a tomb in the chapter house.[73]

Flete, our principal written source for burials in the new chapter house, as in the old, mentions only four, and these are of an unusal kind. When Henry III's new work at the abbey was complete, the remains of Abbot Edwin and those of three others were translated from their previous place of burial and placed in a marble tomb at the entrance to the chapter house on the south side;[74] there, the tomb could still be seen when Flete wrote. The three in addition to Edwin were Ethelgota, queen of Sebert, ruler of the East Saxons (d 616/617), the putative founder of the first church at Westminster, Hugh, the Confessor's principal chamberlain and, as Flete tells us, the most loyal knight among all his nobles, and Sulcard, the chronicler, whose account of the abbey's first foundation and miraculous consecration by St Peter is cited verbatim earlier in Flete's work.[75] The following epitaph for the four was written on a lead slab and placed below the tomb:[76]

Iste locellus habet bis bina cadavera clausa:
uxor Seberti prima, tamen minima:
defracta capitis testa clarens Hugolinus,
a claustro noviter huc translatus erat:
abbas Edwinus, et Sulcardus cenobita:
Sulcardus major est: deus assit eis.

This chest contains, enclosed within it, the remains of four persons.
In the first place, but very small, is Saebert's wife.
The famous Hugh, with the broken crown of his head, was recently translated hither from the cloister.
Abbot Edwin and Sulcard the monk:
Sulcard is the larger; God is with them.

But Flete also cites an epitaph for Hugh alone which, he says, is on the wall above his tomb:

Qui ruis injuste, capit hic, Hugoline, locus te;
laude tua clares, quia martyribus nece par es.

This place holds you, O Hugolin, who fell unjustly;
You are distinguished by your merits, for in your death you equal the martyrs.[77]

We should probably understand that this epitaph was written above Hugh's first tomb, in the cloister, and, much later, painted in a similar position above the tomb for the four at the entrance to the chapter house, and so preserved to be read by monks of Flete's generation.

Ethelgota is a mythical figure, whose putative remains had been buried with those of Saebert in the sanctuary of the Confessor's church, but were now, it appears, separated from his, which awaited translation to the ambulatory of Henry III's church.[78] For Edwin, the first abbot of the Confessor's foundation at Westminster, and for Hugh and Sulcard, varying degrees of service to the Confessor or his memory can be claimed. Hugh's services to the Confessor may have exceeded those of the able administrator and loyal noble, since the unjust death and quasi-martyrdom

imputed to him in the epitaph composed for his first tomb in the monastery may have been incurred, as Barlow suggested, in defence of Edward the Confessor's will or of his memory.[79] Sulcard wrote before the monks of Westminster were pursuing the cult of Edward the Confessor vigorously, but those at Westminster who read his work in the mid-thirteenth century will not have failed to notice that it ends on a high note, celebrating the peace that Edward the Confessor brought to England, his restoration of the abbey church, and his decision to be buried there.[80] Links with the Confessor are a sufficient explanation of the choice of these three for translation to the new chapter house. Although we have no evidence that Henry III, whose devotion to the Confessor was now in the ascendant,[81] took the initiative in this matter, his good will for such an embellishment to the new chapter would certainly have been necessary. As for Ethelgota, if she was not to be in the church, she was scarcely disparaged by the place to which she was now moved.

Edwin's remains are described by Flete in his narrative of the translation as bones; and the epitaph provided for the new tomb draws attention to the broken crown of Hugh's head. It seems likely that the remains of all four were unarticulated and that the marble tomb was, in fact, an ossuary. Above, the epitaph first composed for Hugh's first tomb may have been painted; below, on a lead slab, was the epitaph composed for the four. Where, then, was the marble tomb?

The design of the chapter house proper, which included an undercroft, made encoffined burials there, whether of wood or stone, impossible.[82] But the design was compatible with the burial of unarticulated remains in ossuaries, if these were set into the masonry filling above the crypt vault. A small, triangular, area (1.60 m × 1.60 m × 2.12 m) near the entrance, and on the south side when viewed from within the chapter house, was tiled over later than the rest of the floor. Though an awkward shape for a tomb of the normal kind, it may have been used for ossuaries of an appropriate size in the interim period.[83] Even so, this area was tiled by 1300, more than a century before Flete observed that the tomb was still visible, and for this reason it must be ruled out of consideration.
The inner vestibule of the chapter house, the second possible site, has a ledge on the south side that is wide enough to accommodate a small tomb chest; and the outer vestibule, the third possibility, has not only a ledge on the south side with a similar capacity, but also the capacity to accommodate such a chest in its south wall. By 1600, when Camden noted that the places of burial of Edwin, Hugh and Sulcard were unknown, all traces of the actual site of their burial had evidently disappeared.[84] Flete, however,

writing while the site was still visible, may himself provide the vital clue. The phrase that he uses to locate this site – *ad introitum domus praedictae* [*sc capitularis*] *ex parte australi* – invites comparison with his description later in his *History* of the place of burial of Abbot Simon Bircheston in the east cloister. This was opposite the door of the monks' dormitory, which was itself next to the entrance to the outer vestibule of the chapter house, and he describes the tomb as being *ante introitum locutorii domus capitularis, juxta ostium dormitorii*.[85] To Flete, the outer vestibule was the *locutorium*, or parlour, of the chapter house: a place where conversation was permitted free of the constraints applying to proceedings in the chapter house itself. Such a relaxation of earlier conventions applying to this space is well suited to what we know of the prevailing trends in monastic life at Westminster in the late Middle Ages. If Flete used different phrases in these two passages advisedly, we may perhaps conclude that, to a fifteenth-century observer, the entrance to the chapter house proper was not the outer but the inner vestibule. If this is so, it seems likely the inner vestibule was the site to which Flete referred in his description of the translation of Ethelgota, Edwin, Hugh and Sulcard.

The 'ancient place' of meeting of the Commons?

For many years, the belief that the chapter house of Westminster Abbey became the habitual place of assembly of the medieval Commons in Parliament rested securely, as it seemed, on references to it in the official record of the Parliament of 1376 and the first of the two Parliaments of 1377 as '*lour auncienne place*'.[86] Translated as 'ancient place' this description, however, is difficult to reconcile with the evidence as a whole, and for this reason the suggestion made by Sir Goronwy Edwards many years ago that 'ancient' may be used in the official record in the sense of 'formerly' and without the implication of 'long ago' has been widely accepted.[87]

The Commons met in the chapter house in 1352, and although Parliament met here on occasion in the thirteenth century, this is the earliest reference to the use of the chapter house by the Commons for their separate deliberations.[88] To our knowledge, they also met here on three occasions in the 1370s and 1380s; and they may have done so on three or four other occasions, of which the latest was in 1395.[89] But their normal place of meeting down to the 1380s was the Painted Chamber in the palace of Westminster; on each occasion when they met in the abbey, they were sent there because other claims on this chamber, themselves related to the business of Parliament, were given priority. In and after 1397, the Commons'

regular place of assembly was the abbey refectory, a much larger room, better suited than the chapter house, we may think, to the needs of the Commons now numbering some 250, and one having its main door conveniently near the main entry to the cloisters. If, when the chapter house was one of their meeting places, the Commons ever felt disconcerted at moving from the rectangular Painted Chamber to the octagonal chapter house, or from a very large room to a significantly smaller one, we do not hear their complaints. Such matters were features of what David Carpenter has identified in an earlier period of government as 'a kind of ritual of the rooms'.[90]

Among the occasions when the Commons met in the chapter house, the Good Parliament in 1376, immortalized in the vivid, near contemporary account preserved in the Anonimalle chronicle, eclipses all others in interest.[91] Its fame has obscured the interest of the dates when the Commons met in the chapter house as a set meriting consideration as a whole, and, in particular, the interest of the long gap between the meetings of 1352 and 1376. In 1349, the abbot and twenty-six monks, probably a little more than half the community, died in the Black Death – a catastrophe without parallel in the monastery's history.[92] As monks sometimes did in bad times, the monks of Westminster began to build, and they were fortunate in having in Nicholas Litlyngton, who became prior in 1349 and abbot in 1362, one of their number who could afford to contribute munificently from private resources to this enterprise. The new work embraced the south cloister, where work began around 1350, the main entry from the precinct and the abbot's chamber above, where work was in progress in the 1360s, and the west cloister; adjacent to this cloister, a spacious new house for the abbot was begun in 1370 and took some nine years to complete.[93] As Armitage Robinson pointed out, however, the Jerusalem chamber in the abbot's new house was ready for its windows by 1375–76.[94]

Like all new work, the abbey's in this period was probably much interrupted, but there is a striking similarity between the period of the new work in the main cloister area at Westminster and the period in which no meetings of the Commons in the abbey are recorded. Moreover, although an alternative, if essentially private, route normally existed from the palace of Westminster to the main cloister area through the abbey infirmary (fig 116), ambitious new work began on the infirmary itself in the mid-1360s and took more than twenty years to complete.[95] For many years in this period when, as far as we know, the Commons did not meet in the abbey, it would not have been practicable for them to use either the chapter house or the refectory. But when, in 1376, it became possible to do so again, the official memory was of the former room as their ancient, or former, place of meeting. If it had been difficult or impossible for the Commons to use this room for nearly twenty-five years, the use of the phrase '*lour auncienne place*' by the king's spokesman, and by those who instructed them was, to say the least, a noteworthy feat of memory. It may shed light on another puzzling feature of this parliament and any later parliaments when the Commons used the chapter house, namely the very fact that they were sent there despite the practical advantage to both the Commons and the monks of Westminster in their using the refectory instead. In addition to a ritual of rooms in government, there was perhaps also a hierarchy of rooms, and, it may be suggested, some of those now deliberating on this matter in the palace of Westminster saw the chapter house as the superior room. In describing it as the Commons' 'ancient place' of meeting, they expressed a preference for it.[96]

The royal wardrobe and the chapter house of Westminster Abbey

Jeremy Ashbee

One of the first appearances of the chapter house in the documentary record occurs in the work of the monastic chronicler Matthew Paris, giving the building the epithet 'incomparable', and establishing from the outset a place for it in the written record, as well as in the history of British and European architecture. The chapter house has since been the subject of researches by many of the most eminent scholars in Britain: antiquaries, architects, historians and even clerics and record-keepers.[1] In the early twentieth century, it briefly attracted the attention of Thomas Frederick Tout (1855–1929), author of the most detailed survey of the institutions of medieval English government, *Chapters in the Administrative History of Medieval England*.[2] Tout was briefly addressing a side-issue to his main theme: the evolution of the King's Wardrobe 'as the chief administrative, directive, financial, secretarial and sealing department of the household', effectively as an embryonic form of the Home Civil Service. Tout was generally less concerned with the non-administrative operations of the Wardrobe, one of which was its earliest function – the acquisition and storage of royal property – but naturally he found it impossible to separate this topic entirely from subjects at the heart of his thesis. The question of where the various repositories of the wardrobe were located required Tout to discuss Westminster Abbey, and particularly two small rooms off the monastic cloister on the south side of the abbey church: the basement or undercroft of the chapter house, and the northern portion of the dormitory undercroft, conventionally known to modern writers as the Pyx chamber (Plan 1).[3] Contemporary administrative documents occasionally referred to these rooms as storehouses, not for the monks

of Westminster Abbey, but for the secular apparatus of the royal household. Tout was in fact already familiar with this use of the abbey: in 1911, he had given a lecture entitled 'a medieval burglary', in which he delivered a scholarly and entertaining account of a celebrated event there, a raid on a royal treasure-house inside the abbey, in the spring of 1303.[4] Tout had ample experience of highly complex subjects, yet clearly he found this particular topic especially troublesome, acknowledging 'I cannot profess to have given a satisfactory solution to the intricate problems involved. A detailed study of all the evidence might still be worth working out.'[5]

Neither can this paper resolve all the issues that caused Tout difficulty; instead it will largely restrict itself to one: tracing precisely which rooms were used for which purpose, at which date. This question itself has a long pedigree in published works of the nineteenth and twentieth centuries.

The earliest use of Westminster Abbey as a royal treasury

The earliest period for which there exists firm documentary evidence that an English king was depositing parts of the royal treasury in Westminster Abbey is the reign of Edward I (1272–1307). However, several strands of investigation strongly suggest that this was not the origin of the practice, and that Henry III (1216–72) had also used the monastic buildings in this way.

The most direct evidence for an early use of parts of the abbey for secure storage lies in the fabric itself, particularly the basement of the chapter house. There has historically been some debate as to whether the design of the building changed during construction, but the accepted consensus is now that the structure finished in the mid-to-late 1250s was the building originally intended. The basement – obviously the earliest part to be laid out and built – contains several features which, if they were not designed in connection with use as a strong-room, are difficult to explain (but see further, pp 17–18 and 88). Foremost among these, and still obvious to anyone trying to enter the basement, are the heavily barred windows (fig 112) and the tightly restricted access to the interior. Unlike the upper floor, reached by a grand processional route from the east cloister walk, the basement can only be entered through a narrow and unobtrusive door in the south wall of the south transept in the abbey church itself; this door also gives access to the spiral stair up to the triforium. From a narrow and dark passage (behind the north-east wall of St Faith's chapel), the route turns southward, running down a short flight of steps, before turning eastward at the bottom and entering the basement itself through its west wall (figs 14 and 113).

Although the passage variously incorporated up to four doors – at the entrance from the transept (fig 250), at the head of the stairs (fig 246), at the foot of the stairs, and at the opening into the basement itself (fig 36) – the history of these is complex, and the last two have no relevance here since they were post-medieval additions (p 18). A further point on which several writers have remarked is that the stone stair incorporated a break halfway down, now filled by six wooden steps (fig 17): it has been suggested that there was perhaps originally a pit here, bridged by some kind of temporary structure that

could be removed at need.[6] Recent archaeological study of the passage has, however, demonstrated that there was initially a continuous flight of stone steps in the passage, without a door at the head (fig 15). Alterations to the arrangement of steps and the installation of a secure door at the first turn in the passage represents an early modification to convert the basement into a secure place (fig 114). Thus the Victorian timber steps are now seen to be the result of a much later change, and do not conceal a pit (p 18).

Within the basement itself, the most obvious feature of interest is the central pillar supporting the vault (and, indirectly, the column of the upper storey), but hollowed out in two places to create small cavities opening southward and eastward (figs 22 to 25 and 115): Scott interpreted these as built 'for the concealment of valuables', a statement that most subsequent writers have accepted without comment.[7] 'Concealment' is an emotive term, but seems to be justified in this instance: neither compartment shows any sign of fixings or rebates for doors, in the nature

Fig 113 Chapter house undercroft: central section of the narrow passage and steps leading down from the south transept. *Photograph:* Warwick Rodwell © Dean and Chapter of Westminster

Fig 112 Chapter house undercroft: south-east window with ferramenta in the outer arch. *Photograph:* Warwick Rodwell © Dean and Chapter of Westminster

of typical medieval aumbries, and it seems most likely that the cupboards were sometimes closed, perhaps with thin pieces of Purbeck marble, to match the surrounding stones of the column drum.[8]

The completion of the chapter house by the end of the 1250s need not mark the beginning of treasury occupation at the abbey, for there was a second space, considerably older, close at hand, which was certainly used for this purpose in the fourteenth century and very plausibly might have served as a treasury much earlier: namely the Pyx chamber (fig 117). This room was formed within the northern end of the dormitory undercroft, built in the mid-to-late eleventh century.[9] The undercroft underwent numerous physical alterations, notably the insertion, in the twelfth century, of a series of stone cross-walls dividing the formerly vast space into smaller compartments; and, in the mid-thirteenth century, a re-configuration at its northern end to accommodate the new outer vestibule, which was to give access to the chapter house. The vestibule now provided the means of entry into the Pyx chamber, through a door in its south

Fig 114 Undercroft passage: closing-rebate for the inner door (no 2) at the head of the main flight of steps. The scars reveal a history of medieval and later locking devices. *Photograph*: Warwick Rodwell © Dean and Chapter of Westminster

Fig 115 Chapter house undercroft: view south west, showing the tile floor laid in 1909 (*cf* fig 22). *Photograph*: English Heritage. NMR c 1920

wall: the present access from the east walk of the cloister is believed to date to the early fourteenth century and no earlier (Plan 1). The Pyx chamber might well have been used as a treasury long before the chapter house basement was adopted for this purpose.

The documentary record for this period is suggestive but not sufficiently precise to determine the question.[10] An early reference, which indicates the problem, is recorded on the Close Roll as a writ of 13 October 1254, instructing various officials, including the abbot of Westminster and the king's treasurer, to visit the New Temple and 'Westminster', to view the king's 'jewels' ('jocalia') there, held under the control of the keeper of the royal wardrobe.[11] The involvement of the abbot in this matter certainly suggests that a location inside the abbey, rather than in the king's palace immediately adjacent, was indicated.

There are several precedents from earlier in the thirteenth century for the use of monastic buildings by the secular authority of the royal wardrobe. The best known is the New Temple mentioned above where, from 1225 onwards, the formula 'the lord king's wardrobe at the New Temple' was used in royal documentation.[12] The Templars provided a remarkably varied set of services – effectively acting as bankers – and the Crown was not their only customer. It is also notable that the wording of writs makes it clear that the royal clerks were not authorized to view the royal treasure in the Temple without the permission of the Master of the Temple. This procedure was cumbersome and, unsurprisingly as the reign of Henry III wore on and pressures from warfare required the king to raise funds rapidly by pawning some of his jewels, an administrative change is detectable whereby the Keeper of the Wardrobe was granted unfettered access to the treasury.[13] It clearly became desirable to find further locations from which material could be abstracted when needed without reference to some other authority. This could easily be achieved in the king's fortress, the Tower of London, under the exclusive command of royal officials, or in the Palace of Westminster; but if the abbot of Westminster could be persuaded (or pressured) to release space inside the abbey to the Keeper of the Wardrobe and his clerks, this would serve just as well. Writs for the abstraction of such jewels from storage at Westminster became increasingly frequent during the late 1250s and 1260s, the period of Civil War in which the king's need for funds had to be satisfied instantly.

Another case, from Edward I's reign, and closer to the experience of Westminster, comes from the documentation for Edward's second campaign against the Welsh, in 1283. In mid March, when the royal party had advanced

westward along the coast to the Cistercian abbey of Aberconwy, Exchequer documents show that some of the monastic buildings were immediately requisitioned as storage for the royal wardrobe, both cash and materials; the abbey became a centre for distribution throughout the north Wales theatre of operations. Thus, among the very earliest entries mentioning Aberconwy one concerns the abstraction of 2,000 marks, bound for Anglesey, from 'the wardrobe in Conwy Abbey', while other clauses mention the stockpiling of timber for a stockade, iron for the new castle and the safe storage of cash, as well as numerous works on the wardrobe buildings themselves.[14] There is no reason to doubt that the king intended from the first that the Cistercian monks should be removed to a new location; by the autumn, he had secured the provisional consent of the Chapter General of Cîteaux, and had sent the mason James of Saint George to secure a new location, some eight miles away.[15] Nevertheless, it appears that the monks were forced into a co-existence with the English royal household, doubtless an uneasy one, including for a considerable time with the king and queen in person, from March 1283 until October 1284, when the new abbey site was ready for the monks to occupy.

In addition to references in the Close and Patent Rolls mentioned above, there are a few hints in other sources from the 1260s that a similarly difficult arrangement of cohabitation was taking place at Westminster. There is a series of complaints – including one in 1268 from the papal legate Ottobuono – about the practice of royal clerks entering the cloister from the royal palace, sometimes taking a short cut through the buildings of the old infirmary (fig 116).[16] The most likely context for such clerks to need access to the monastic cloister is in connection with a royal treasury in the vicinity – no other office for secular administrators is known to have existed inside the abbey precinct.[17]

Locations of the Westminster treasury in the reign of Edward I

Despite the suggestion made above that the abbey contained a royal treasury during the lifetime of Henry III, it is during the reign of his son Edward I that the documentation for this is placed on a more secure footing, and moreover that the volume of material held in the abbey greatly increased, particularly in the final decade of the thirteenth century. Tout interpreted this as part of a general phenomenon, in which itinerant institutions become more static: the Exchequer became a fixture in the Palace of Westminster and the Wardrobe in the Tower of London.[18] Westminster Abbey became an outstation of the

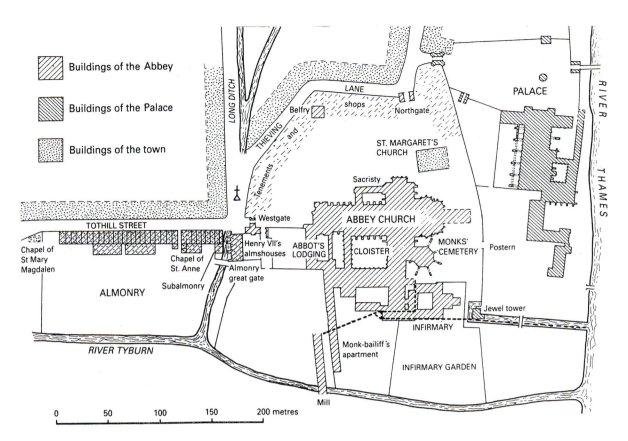

Fig 116 Plan showing the relationship between the palace of Westminster and the abbey in the later Middle Ages. *Drawing*: John and Sarah Blair; after Harvey 1993, map 1

Wardrobe, and thus of the Tower, and several inventories of the period confirm that substantial amounts of the material held in the abbey had been brought there from the Tower.[19] The reason for this transfer can only be conjectured, but pressure of space is likely to have played an important part. The latter part of Edward I's reign saw massive expansion of several institutions inside the Tower of London, including the royal mint and exchange, together with the manufacture and storage of arms and ammunition, to be rationalized in the following century under the umbrella of the Privy Wardrobe. The wars with Wales and Scotland also entailed the dispatch of a number of important political prisoners to the Tower. Moreover, the Tower Wardrobe itself, always subject to internal reorganization, became increasingly specialized as a storehouse for materials in bulk – principally cloth, spices and armaments. In such circumstances, it is entirely understandable that the precious and delicate jewels and plate would seem out of place, and that an alternative storehouse should be chosen.

The most informative documentary reference to the location of a treasury inside the abbey comes from the Pipe Roll of the thirty-second year of Edward I's reign, but concerning a payment of £5 7s 10d made to John le Convers in 1290–91, thirteen years earlier, for 'paving the treasure house of the king's wardrobe underneath the chapter house at Westminster, repairing the door and other things, in year 19'.[20] This wording is unequivocal and for several writers, notably Harrod and Tout, it has been taken as conclusive proof that this was the location (fig 22). Unfortunately, the situation is complicated rather than clarified by a second document, an inventory taken in the twenty-seventh year of the reign (1299), in which are described 'all the jewels of the same king and other things found in the treasury of the king's wardrobe under the monks' chapel there'.[21] The formulation 'monks' chapel' is fairly meaningless; there is no precedent for labelling this or any other monastic chapter house as a chapel, but neither is it possible to apply this wording to any known space in the abbey: for example, the only other candidate for a royal treasury lay below the dormitory in the east range of the cloister, but there is no suggestion that the dormitory contained a chapel or oratory that might explain the reference. Though the manuscript is badly rubbed, the word '*capellam*' (chapel) is unmistakable, and the most plausible explanation is that a clerk mistranscribed '*capitulum*' (chapter house) as '*capellam*' when making a fair copy of the inventory, perhaps working from

Fig 117 Pyx chamber: view of the interior, looking south east from the entrance in the cloister. *Photograph:* © Dean and Chapter of Westminster

a contracted form, such as '*caplm*'.

Partly because of this documentary confusion, the arguments favouring the chapter house basement have failed to convince several scholars, who have preferred to see the royal treasury in the Pyx chamber (fig 117).[22] As will be described below, one piece of documentation for the robbery of 1303 is easier to reconcile with the location of the Pyx chamber than with the chapter house, and there is incontrovertible evidence, both physical and documentary, that the former was used as a royal treasury later in the fourteenth century. The arguments for and against each space have been various, including discussion of the precise topographical import of the preposition '*subtus*',[23] which can, in fact, accommodate a location to the side of something, as well as directly below,[24] and an analysis of the architecture in a crude sketch of a burglar in the treasury, produced several years after the robbery by a monk of Rochester who had in all probability never seen the room.[25] The documentary evidence is admittedly slight, but the contradictions between the different versions can be removed by suggesting that both the chapter house and Pyx chamber were used for this purpose during the late thirteenth century. Neither room is

enormous in its own right, and if the '*vetus thesauraria*' in the Tower of London was being entirely transferred to the abbey,[26] it is plausible that more than one space would have been needed to accommodate it.

The inventory of the treasury 'under the monks' chapel' in 1299 gives an excellent indication of the range of materials held there, and the appearance of the room itself.[27] The goods are listed within individual containers – some of them wooden chests bearing labelling on the outside (usually a letter of the alphabet) – and each item is given an approximate value. Some entries bear an additional note of an individual item's provenance, or a change in affairs since the inventory was first made. Thus, in 'a large chest F', the first item encountered was a gold coronet missing two stones, valued at £125, with an addendum that the item had since been removed from the treasury by Sir Otto de Grandson. Even a cursory examination of inventories of this kind reveals important points about the operation of the wardrobe. First, some of the items kept at Westminster Abbey were of extraordinary individual value. The coronet's value is equivalent to precisely half the weekly sum estimated to pay a workforce of around 3,000 men engaged on building the new

Beaumaris castle,[28] whereas the 'great gold crown with precious stones', brought from the Tower to Westminster in 1297, valued at £4,000,[29] would alone have paid for the whole of the castle at Aberystwyth.[30] Second, the items in storage were not always rigidly grouped by category: 'chest F' was not restricted to items of personal jewellery, but also contained, among other things, a jasper cup, an ivory chess set and a horn formerly belonging to Saint Thomas Cantilupe, late bishop of Hereford. Occasionally it is clear that a chest held principally or exclusively items of one type, such as a green painted chest containing items for the king's daughter's chapel, or 'the jewels that belonged to the lady Blanche', but many others contained an unsorted mixture of personal ornaments, items of plate, sacred relics, textiles, and occasional books and documents.[31] The inventory does not mention coin, but, in normal circumstances, this would be expected to comprise a significant part of the Wardrobe store; however, in the late 1290s and early 1300s, the cost of wars in Scotland had depleted this element of the treasury.[32] Third, the wardrobe treasury was subject to the addition and subtraction of items, under the scrutiny of the Keeper of the Wardrobe and his subordinates, as the king took possession of other people's property, or as he chose to sell or give away items of his own treasure.

The robbery of 1303

On 6 June 1303, while Edward I was at Linlithgow, engaged in a military campaign against William Wallace, his chancery ordered Ralph of Sandwich, constable of the Tower of London, Walter of Gloucester, John of Bakewell and Roger of Southcote to institute proceedings in London over a matter of the utmost gravity:

> Since we have heard from the testimony of trusted men that certain malefactors and disturbers of our peace have by force of arms broken into our treasury within Westminster Abbey, and have seized and carried off a large part of our treasure found in the same treasury, and committed other enormities against us there, to our manifest contempt, to our inestimable harm, and against our peace. We, wishing for an appropriate and immediate remedy, appoint you to make inquiry, on the oath of knights and other honest and law-worthy men of our city of London and in our counties of Middlesex and Surrey, from whom the truth of the matter may best be ascertained, who were the malefactors, who else knew about them … and any treasure which is found in the hands of such malefactors you are to place in a hidden and secure place.[33]

The findings of the inquiry have been discussed many times before, and need no extensive treatment here, but for two details relevant to Westminster Abbey itself. The first is that a common thread in the declarations of several juries in London was that some of the monks of Westminster were complicit in the plot to steal the royal treasure, and, as a consequence of this, Abbot Walter de Wenlok, forty-eight monks and thirty-two servants of the abbey were taken as prisoners to the Tower of London, from which they petitioned their gaolers for false imprisonment.[34] The justice or injustice of this accusation against the monks exercised a clear influence on contemporary commentators and has been of great interest to modern historians. The second is that some of the jury declarations and confessions of the accused, exacted by Ralph of Sandwich and his colleagues, contain information about the location of the treasury in which the robbery had taken place, and about the use of other buildings in the abbey and palace.[35]

On 20 June, the Keeper of the Wardrobe, John of Droxford, arrived at Westminster with the unhappy task of inspecting the burgled treasury and assessing the level of the king's losses. This inspection was carried out with some ceremony in the presence of the constable of the Tower, the mayor of London, the justiciar of England, and the prior of Westminster, among others. In the memorandum that followed, the procedure for entering the treasury was set out in full. Walter of Bedwyn, coffrer of the Wardrobe, held the keys with him (the keys to the treasury doors: it is not stated whether he also carried the keys to individual chests and hutches) and now presented them in a canvas bag with a wax seal; the seal was found to be unbroken. Droxford broke the seal, removed the keys and unlocked the treasury. On entering, he found that 'chests and coffers had been destroyed and many of their goods carried off by thieves.'[36] This detail is of significance, in that it goes some way to exonerating the monks from one of the charges that have been levelled at them: that having easy access to the royal treasury within their convent, they simply let the thieves in.[37] Unless there was another set of keys, in the possession of the monks, this memorandum would suggest that however the thieves entered the treasury, it was not by the door. Unlike the earlier arrangements in the New Temple, at Westminster, the monks evidently provided only a room as a repository.[38]

This memorandum contains no specific information to settle the question of where the burgled treasury had lain. Slightly more information, suggestive rather than conclusive, is provided by the confession of the figure generally taken to have been the ring-leader of the thieves, Richard Pudlicote.

Eight days before Christmas he came there to break in with tools acquired for the job, namely two chisels, large and small, a knife and some smaller iron 'engines', and he worked at night until a fortnight after Easter, and on the night of Wednesday, the eve of St Mark, he got into the treasury, stayed inside through St Mark's day sorting out the things he wanted to carry off, and on the following night he got out, leaving part of the treasure under the bush, to recover it the next night, and the rest he carried away with him, getting away through a gate behind St Margaret's church.[39]

Taken at face value, Pudlicote's confession suggests that he took more than three months, working at night, to break through the masonry wall of the treasury from the outside; his text is not specific about the location, although it may be noted that, if the room under the chapter house is intended, this would mean breaking through a wall around 18 feet thick, clearly an absurd proposition. What seems more plausible is that the thief or thieves forced an entry from outside the cloister by loosening the masonry around a window. An earlier passage from the same confession explains that Pudlicote was already familiar with the layout of the monastic buildings, because he had successfully committed another burglary there in the previous year.

On the evening following the day that the king left (Westminster) for Barnes, the said Richard had noticed a ladder on a house being roofed near the gate from the palace to the abbey, and he placed this ladder against a window of the chapter house, which opened and shut with a cord: using this cord he opened the window. From there he went to the refectory door, which he found locked, but opened it with his knife and went inside. He found 6 hanapers in a cupboard behind the door, and in another cupboard more than thirty silver dishes and under a bench hanapers of drinking cups all gathered up. He took all these away with him and shut the door behind him, but left it unlocked… This is how he knew the layout of the abbey, where the treasury was and how he could get in.[40]

Like much of Pudlicote's confession, this excerpt sounds far-fetched and unreliable. Some element of collusion with the monks seems a more likely version of how the refectory came to be robbed in late 1302. Yet if taken again at face value, this anecdote might favour the identification of the Pyx chamber as the royal treasury. Pudlicote's route from the chapter house to the refectory would take him past the Pyx chamber door, but nowhere near the entrance to the chapter house crypt, access to which lay inside the body of the abbey church. If the treasury were in the crypt, Pudlicote's only way of 'learning where the treasury was and how he could get in' would be by peering in through one of the crypt's six windows, which were at ground level (fig 112).

The proceedings which the royal officers instituted in the city of London provided one further piece of topographical evidence. This is the testimony of the jurors of Walbrook towards Ludgate, in which the treasury of 1303 is identified with reference to yet another previous burglary, in 1299: 'Moreover the jurors have a great suspicion against the aforesaid monks because four years ago, this same treasury was broken into from inside their cloister, namely under the door of the said treasury towards the cloister.'[41] There is an obvious uncertainty about how reliable the knowledge of the Walbrook jurors would be on the detailed topography of the monastic complex, and how literally we should take the statement that the 1303 robbery occurred in the 'same treasury' as that of 1299. The expression could refer generally to the institution just as well as to a particular room, but it is notable that the argument is based on the layout of the complex, and the question of who would have access to the door into the treasure room. For this reason, the reference only makes sense as referring to the Pyx chamber.

Even the 1299 robbery was not the first burglary of the royal treasury in Westminster Abbey: in or before 1296, at least one further attempt had been carried out. On 6 June 1296, a letter patent was issued for the delivery from Newgate gaol of 'John le Keu le Lechesman, in custody there for trespasses committed at the king's treasury within the abbey of Westminster.'[42] Unfortunately no further detail is available about this robbery or its location, though its date is worth noting: evidently the shortcomings of the abbey treasury as a repository for valuables had become apparent in the mid-1290s, soon after works had been carried out to improve the treasury buildings, but this did not deter the wardrobe administrators from relocating more and more goods there from the Tower of London.

One final piece of evidence, sometimes cited by modern historians, is a sketch showing the robbery in progress. It occurs as a marginal illustration in a manuscript of the *Flores Historiarum*, drawn up in Rochester Cathedral Priory, probably only a few years after the events.[43] The picture, a rough sketch in pen, shows a single male thief holding a goblet above a pile of round objects, perhaps plates or bags of coin, against a background of three pointed arches (fig 118). The image has a greater similarity to the chapter house basement than to the Pyx chamber, whose architecture is Romanesque, but there are obvious objections to the use of this image as

Fig 118 This medieval drawing shows Richard Pudlicote in the process of robbing the royal treasury at Westminster Abbey. *Photograph*: © The British Library Board; BL Cotton MS Nero Dii, fol 194r

evidence for the location of the robbery, particularly in the poor quality of the drawing, and the matter of how a Rochester monk could have detailed knowledge of where a robbery took place, or what an extremely private room in Westminster Abbey should look like. The conceptual content of the picture, if it has any, lies much more in its depiction of a lone thief, not tonsured, acting alone: it may well have been in the interests of the monks at Rochester to exonerate their Benedictine brothers at Westminster from accusations of collusion in the crime. Perhaps the most sensible comment is a rather gruff sentence from Lethaby: 'I only see an indication of a vaulted structure'.[44] The prudent course would be to treat the picture as a historical curiosity with more than a little amusement value, but to dismiss it entirely as a piece of historical evidence.[45]

On the basis of evidence presently available, the most likely explanation of the robbery is that it was carried out by a party of laymen and from outside the abbey, rather than from inside the cloister. Taking advantage of extremely lax security in the Palace of Westminster, and probably with the collusion of officials in the palace, the thieves broke into the treasury from the little-visited cemetery area to the south-east of the abbey church. This area gave access not only to the basement windows of the chapter house (still visible), but also to the east windows of the Pyx chamber (now blocked and obscured by a nineteenth-century building). To a potential thief, the chapter house basement windows might have a slight advantage, as being further removed than the Pyx chamber

from the dormitory windows of the abbey, from which the noise of breaking and entering might be detected.[46] But the evidence for the robbery itself does not settle the question between the two possible locations.

The revival of royal treasury occupation at Westminster Abbey

Accounts of the Exchequer during the fourteenth century show unequivocally that the use of Westminster Abbey for the storage of the royal treasury was not abandoned after the series of burglaries between 1296 and 1303. Nevertheless, the commission which Edward I gave to John of Droxford and the other officials charged them with placing the remaining and recovered treasure on a more secure footing,[47] which required new arrangements to be made in the short term. The treasure was divided into three lots and given into the care of three individuals: Droxford himself, to be kept in an unspecified wardrobe store, Ralph of Sandwich, constable of the Tower, to be taken into the fortress, and John le Blund, mayor of London, to be secured in the chamber of the Guildhall.[48] This appears to have been a stop-gap measure, while arrangements were being made to transport all the treasury into the Tower of London, and the indenture concludes with a statement that all the treasury was in the Tower, though within the custody of the Keeper of the Wardrobe.

The accommodation of the treasury in the fortress

seems to have been somewhat improvised, but the location chosen for it did at least have the advantage of allowing dual control of access between the authorities of the Treasury and those of the Wardrobe. Some of the detail about the location comes from two decades after the transfer, though it seems likely that they describe an arrangement from the time of the transfer in 1303.[49] The treasury was moved into 'a tower near the east gable of the great chapel' (St Peter ad Vincula), the tower now known as the Flint Tower.[50] The present structure is a rebuilding of the nineteenth century, but like most of the fortress's mural towers, it probably contained single rooms at ground and wall-walk level with no direct connection between the floors, and only narrow slit windows, overlooking a drop into the outer ward. The inventory states that the keys opening the door into the tower were held by the Treasurer and Chamberlains of the Exchequer, but, once inside, only the Keeper of the Wardrobe could open the cupboards containing the objects themselves.[51]

The Flint Tower provided a more secure store than the abbey had ever done, and was evidently kept in use through the 1320s and 1330s, when jewels, plate and documents were repeatedly moved within the Tower of London, in successive attempts to impose order on a chaotic situation.[52] Nevertheless, it is clear that items of different types were as intermixed in the treasuries as they had ever been, and, furthermore, that it was considered perfectly usual for material of the same type to be divided between the various repositories. Most important for this present study is that the treasury once again contained at least one storehouse inside Westminster Abbey and, fortunately, the wording used is often sufficiently precise to identify the space as the Pyx chamber, rather than the chapter house basement.

The Pyx chamber had evidently been subjected to a number of physical changes soon after the 1303 robbery and the removal of the treasure to the Tower of London. The archaeology of the room itself (and the whole dorter undercroft) is extremely complex and worthy of further discussion in its own right, but the most invasive changes can be summarized here. Most drastic was an internal compartmentalization of the space by the reconstruction or insertion of a cross-wall dividing the northernmost half-bay of the undercroft (under the day stairs) from the main body of the Pyx chamber.[53] This rendered the original door into the Pyx chamber (in the south wall of the outer vestibule of the chapter house) redundant, and required the creation of a new doorway, entering directly from the east walk of the cloister. This entrance was protected by two wooden doors – an inner and an outer. Apparently at the same time, the east windows were heavily

barred with iron. The fine tile pavement and the dendrochronological dating of the doors are discussed elsewhere: a date early in the fourteenth century seems likely for both.[54] The most probable interpretation of this evidence is that Edward I's administrators had never abandoned the idea of keeping a treasury inside the abbey, and that these physical works were carried out as part of an improvement of security, before storage could resume. From the second quarter of the fourteenth century, there is documentary confirmation that this was once again taking place.

For example, in 1331, the outgoing Treasurer, Robert Wodehouse, archdeacon of Richmond, presented his successor, the Archbishop of York, with the keys, among other places, of 'the treasury of Westminster underneath the dormitory'.[55] This is very unlikely to mark the date at which treasury use of the Pyx chamber began or resumed, but earlier documents tend to be less precise – a 1327 document speaks only of 'the treasury of Westminster'.[56] However, this use continued through the reign of Edward III, a period in which the financial demands of war required items of the treasury to be pawned and redeemed as occasion demanded, leaving a number of records. Thus, for example, on 16 June 1345 the great crown, together with several lesser crowns, was placed 'in a chest in the king's treasury in the cloister of Westminster next to the chapter house'.[57] This second document contains the additional detail that the keys of this treasury were held in the Exchequer of Receipt, beside the door into St Stephen's Chapel in the Palace of Westminster, and a third, from ten years later, mentions that the keys of individual chests might be held in the accountant's chamber, immediately above.[58] Variants of this wording, mentioning the cloister of the abbey, were collected by Francis Palgrave, running through the remainder of the fourteenth century and beyond, often citing this treasury in conjunction with the treasury in 'the High Tower of London', as seen, for example, in the Wardrobe inventory of 1356 (fig 119).[59]

It seems likely that continuity of treasury use of the Pyx chamber was maintained through the fifteenth and sixteenth centuries, to the time in 1610 when Arthur Agarde, making a survey of record repositories, found in the Exchequer of Receipt 'the auncyent keys of the treasury of leagues in the cloyster of Westminster Abay', and finally was able to enter the Pyx chamber itself: 'in the fourth threasaurie, beinge in the cloyster of the said abbay of Westminster locked with 5 stronge keyes and within two stronge double dores are kept the records with others which I cannot now name at large, because I tooke notes but on a suddaine, by reason I could not make any stay there, but as I remember in parte.'[60]

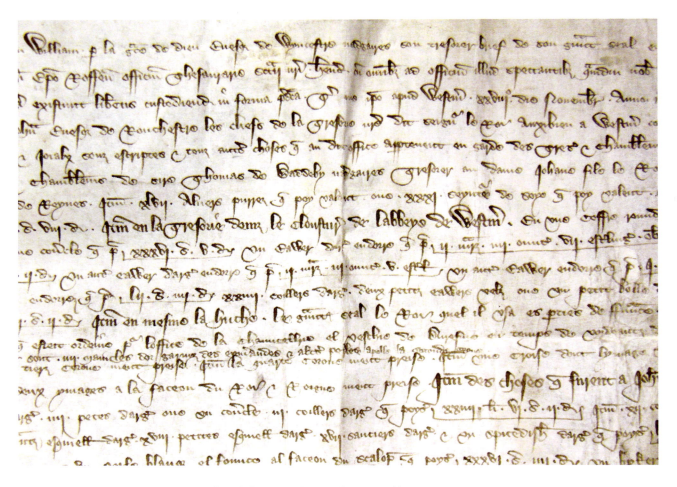

Fig 119 Extract from the inventory of the royal wardrobe, 1356. *Photograph*: Jeremy Ashbee; TNA: E 101/333/28

Conclusion

The story outlined above sets out the place of the abbey in the wider matter of the use of precious goods by the medieval English monarchy, a salutary reminder that, in David Carpenter's evocative phrase, 'the Plantagenets, like their Anglo-Saxon predecessors, were very much the givers of rings.'[61] The current presentation of the rooms, either full of the modern accoutrements of a functioning ecclesiastical vestry, like the chapter house basement, or like the Pyx chamber, displayed empty as a precious example of Romanesque architecture, can only be improved by the memory that they once housed items of almost inconceivable value, many with great religious or historical significance, and evidently of the highest artistic standards of workmanship. The story of the robbery in 1303 (or more accurately, of four robberies) may have received a disproportionate amount of attention, but it does serve as a clear punctuation mark in a historical story with few such 'events', characterized by the unvarying rhythms of the monastic hours and the ecclesiastical year.

Some of the questions it throws up are unanswerable with the present evidence. Why was the decision first taken to adopt the abbey as a store? Why, when Westminster Abbey had quickly shown itself to be far from burglar proof, and when the royal estate contained so many castles and manors, did Edward I and his successors persist in depositing their most precious possessions there? The answer to the first question may perhaps lie in the way that modern historians have categorized the goods and the institutions of the medieval monarchy. Much of the work of scholars such as Tout was concerned with tracing processes of administrative fission, by which a system of separate administrative departments came into being, with separate responsibilities: thus, for example, a single wardrobe apparatus came over time to be divided into more specialized bodies, such as the Great and Privy Wardrobes. But examination of the inventories shows that the materials kept at the abbey were remarkably diverse, comprising cash, documents, personal jewels and religious relics. It may be that the sacred or quasi-sacral nature of some of the items particularly favoured deposition in the abbey, especially given the close proximity of the shrine of Edward the Confessor, and Henry III's particular attempts to associate himself and the English monarchy with their own royal saint. Elements of regalia used by Henry III were believed, rightly or not, to be the genuine items used by the Confessor, and though occasionally in the keeping of the abbey (as security for a loan, as in 1258), they were more generally held by the Wardrobe organization. For the wardrobe to employ a storehouse within the precinct of the abbey might go some way towards reconciling the anomaly by which sacred relics were under the control of a secular power.[62] It is possible that it was this body of relics that established a precedent for storage in the abbey, and in time attracted a more diverse range of items to accompany it.

The second problem, the persistence of secure storage at the abbey remains almost inexplicable. In the 1290s and 1300s the king was committed to wars in Scotland, and it may have been untimely to look for another storehouse: nevertheless, material continued to move from the Tower to the abbey through the 1290s, and it would hardly have been impossible to cancel this movement. Perhaps as each robbery was discovered, and the perpetrators punished, the administrators felt that they had managed the risk. The 1303 robbery was clearly of such an order that more drastic measures were unavoidable: the abbey treasury was cleared out and removed to the Tower. But within a short period – and after building works had been undertaken at the Pyx chamber – the administrators – this time of the Exchequer treasury – once again felt that it was safe to resume their use of the abbey. As far as the historical record shows, their confidence was justified, and no further robberies from the abbey treasury are known.[63]

The chapter house as a record office

Elizabeth Hallam Smith

8

'Seldom do we see a noble work of art reduced to such a wreck!' fulminated George Gilbert Scott in his *Gleanings from Westminster Abbey* on the subject of the chapter house; 'it was made over to the tender mercies of some barbarian, who fitted it up for the records, with studious regard to concealment or destruction of its architectural beauties.'[1] Like Scott, many contemporaries were very critical of the way in which the chapter house had been fitted out as a record repository, as depicted in plans and a section drawn in 1807 (figs 120 to 123).[2] In 1799, for example, it was decried as 'this once celebrated place. Here observers will find little but modern carpenters' work, vast rolls of parchment, dust and rubbish – and the famous Domesday Book'.[3]

My purpose here is to give the other side of the story, to trace the use of the chapter house as a record office, and to ask what this institution contributed to historical scholarship and record-keeping. I will show how the building housed a substantial and important collection of public records for more than 300 years – from the mid-sixteenth century until 1864 – including, for the last 100 years or so, the most famous record of all, Domesday Book itself.[4] I will look at what records were stored there and how they were managed, preserved and used, and how the record-keepers and the Office of Works themselves – Scott's so-called barbarians – coped with, and modified, their inappropriate building.

The backdrop to this saga are the tides that seem inevitably to occur in the history of state record keeping. There are ebbs and flows, periods of disorder, of chaos and confusion even, followed always by government and parliamentary initiatives, new funds, then recovery and re-

organization, but slipping again slowly into a seemingly ineluctable decline.[5] Like the other great state record offices at the Tower of London[6] and the Rolls chapel, the chapter house was far from immune from these cycles; indeed, its last custodian, Joseph Burtt, excoriated the building for its unsuitability and its keepers for neglecting the precious records in their charge. 'No portion of the public records', he said, 'has been worse off than that formerly in the chapter house at Westminster.'[7] Let us see how fair his verdict was.

The chapter house treasury from the Middle Ages to 1753

In the Middle Ages a number of monasteries in London and elsewhere, including the New Temple and St Bartholomew's Smithfield, were commandeered by the Crown for the storage of royal valuables, including treasure and records.[8] Given Westminster Abbey's status as the principal royal monastery, and its proximity to the royal palace and law courts, there was considerable logic in using its cloisters and chapter house for this purpose. The Pyx chamber was a strong room of the Exchequer of Receipt and was used to store records, as well as bullion, probably from the late thirteenth century onwards; and there is evidence that the undercroft of the chapter house was also used to keep valuables, including records, until the time of the Pudlicote burglary in the early fourteenth century.[9]

Although primarily a space for the monks,[10] the chapter house may also have been used to store records on occasions in the Middle Ages, and was certainly required for 'overflow' sittings of the House of Commons when the abbey's refectory was not available. These uses might have given it the status of a royal property and created the obligation that the Crown should keep it under repair.[11] Sir Christopher Wren later believed this to have been the case,[12] although when the abbey was suppressed in 1540, and re-established as a cathedral with a dean and canons, they, rather than the Crown, seem to have taken responsibility for its upkeep, paying for new windows in 1543.[13]

The chapter house's first properly documented appearance as a repository for the public records, shortly after the abbey's re-foundation by Queen Mary in November 1556, is not auspicious. Early in 1557, when fines and records were moved between the Treasury of Receipt and the king and queen's Treasury within the abbey of Westminster, 2s 2d was spent on 'making clean of both the treasuries within the monastery'. Worse, in 1558 a labourer was paid for two days' work in 'washing and drying of the chests of records in their majesties treasury,

the pavements and other places of the same being foul with doves' dung'.[14] These references suggest that the use was well-established by that time, not least because the chapter house was, sadly, already a neglected and filthy building. Perhaps the records were first moved in during the 1540s. The abbey had demolished its refectory, used previously for meetings of the Commons, in 1542, and in 1548 the House of Commons chamber moved to a permanent home in the former St Stephen's chapel. For the record-keepers to fill the chapter house with records, as an overflow from the Pyx chamber, in response to these changes, could have been a way of making a firm claim to the space for the Crown, although the need for extra space must also have been a key consideration.[15]

In 1559 the Marian foundation was dissolved in its turn, to be replaced in the following year by a new collegiate establishment. The Crown appears to have retained the chapter house: a decade later, in 1569, Lewis Stockett, surveyor of works, was granted funds for repairs

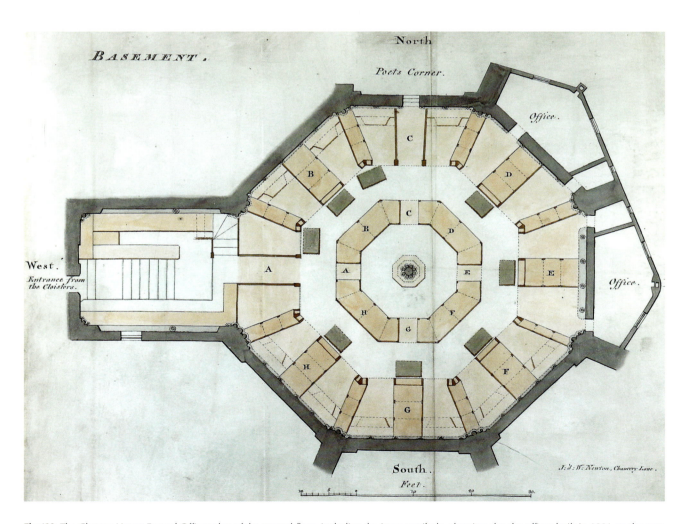

Fig 120 The Chapter House Record Office: plan of the ground floor, including the inner vestibule, showing also the offices built in 1801 on the east and north-east sides. Although labelled 'basement', this does not relate to the chapter house undercroft. *Drawing*: J and W Newton, 1807; *photograph*: © The National Archives; TNA: PRO MPB 1/2

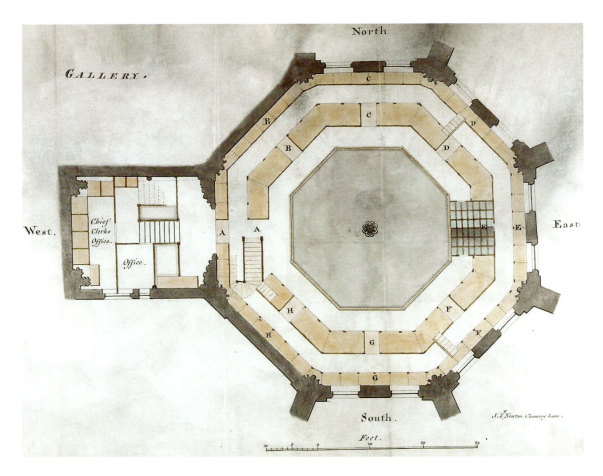

Fig 121 The Chapter House Record Office: plan of the gallery floor, including also the mezzanine floor in the inner vestibule. *Drawing*: J and W Newton, 1807; *photograph*: © The National Archives; TNA: PRO MPB 1/2

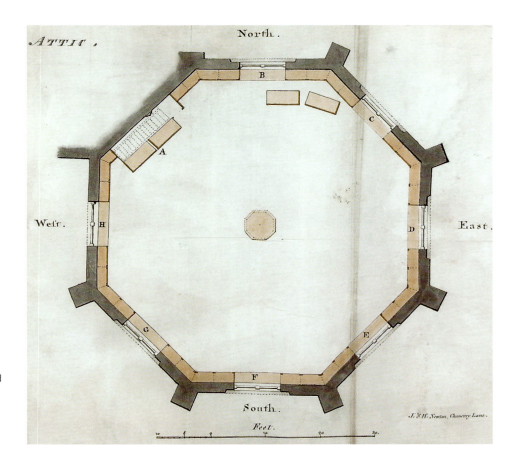

Fig 122 The Chapter House Record Office: plan of the attic floor. *Drawing*: J and W Newton, 1807; *photograph*: © The National Archives; TNA: PRO MPB 1/2

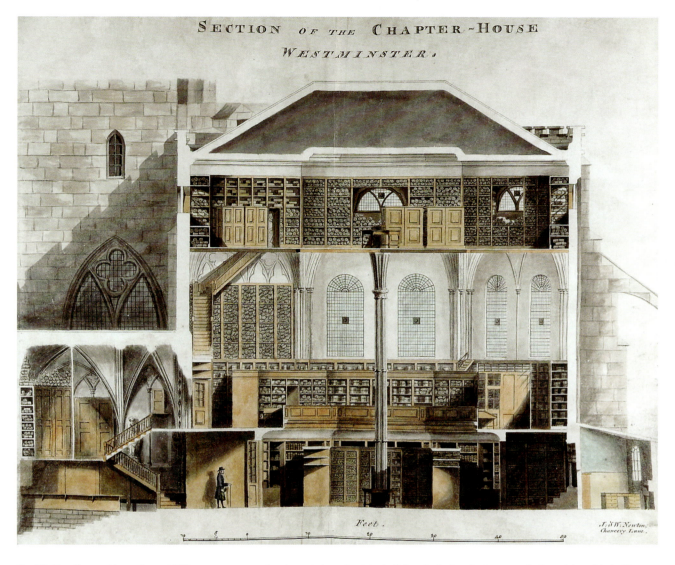

Fig 123 The Chapter House Record Office: east–west section through the axis of the building, including the inner vestibule and the added office on the east side. *Drawing*: J and W Newton, 1807; *photograph*: © The National Archives; TNA: PRO MPB 1/2

to the arches of the 'round house of the records in the Treasury House, Westminster'.[16] By this time the repository seems to have been in better order; in 1573 an anonymous petitioner even proposed to Lord Burleigh a scheme to relocate important Exchequer records to the two treasuries in the abbey, including leagues and treaties, from the Palace of Westminster, where they were kept in unsatisfactory conditions and in danger of fire.[17]

A fine line drawing of the early seventeenth century (fig 30)[18] gives some indication of the appearance of the chapter house at this time, and confirms the impression that its vaulted ceiling supported a low roof, like that at Salisbury. It was drawn some time after 1610 by an anonymous and clearly star-struck antiquary from Pembrokeshire who visited the distinguished principal record-keeper there, Arthur Agarde,[19] and, with his help and advice, transcribed and calendared records relating to

the county of Pembroke in the fourteenth century. The author describes the chapter house as being 'a round place like the Temple Church with 6 or 7 large windowes of greate height, 8 square within and vauted over, and a piller of stone in the middst'. He pays tribute to Agarde's catalogues of the many ancient and diverse records in his charge, and to the quality of his help and advice, attested to also by a number of the antiquaries and scholars of the age.[20]

A records scholar of distinction and a member of the Elizabethan Society of Antiquaries, Agarde is today regarded as the founder of modern archival scholarship. He articulated the principles of good record-keeping that are still followed. Particularly striking is his enumeration of the four enemies of archives: fire, water, vermin and misplacing; and a fifth, taking the records away.[21] In 1570 he was appointed one of the two deputy chamberlains at the Treasury of Receipt, whose tasks were to care for the records in their charge, to make searches and copies and to strike tallies. He became the senior deputy chamberlain in 1574, and from 1609 he was paid an extra £40 a year specifically for sorting and digesting the records, in addition to his existing fees of £17.[22]

In 1610 Agarde completed work on a *Compendium of Records*, describing the contents of various record repositories in London, including the four Treasuries of the Exchequer, for which he was responsible.[23] The third Treasury was, he wrote, in the chapter house of Westminster Abbey, secured by three locks and containing chests with parchment labels indicating their contents. He itemized the contents of each chest, including feet of fines, fine rolls and plea rolls, all arranged by reigns, and he provided a particularly full and excellent list and index to the contents of Chest B, which he had recently sorted and catalogued.[24] Near to the chapter house was, continued Agarde, the fourth Treasury, in the cloister – that is the Pyx chamber. Secured by no less than five locks, this contained golden leagues, papal bulls, assays of gold and silver, Henry VII's chapel indentures and Henry VIII's divorce papers, all stored in chests.[25]

Agarde died in 1615, and his now sadly decayed memorial in the cloisters of the abbey, near the chapter house, is said to have described him as '*diligens scrutator*' of the records.[26] Building on his foundations, the work of the chapter house continued during the rest of the seventeenth century, with records continuing to flow in, even during the Interregnum. In 1656, for example, records (probably of the House of Commons) were moved out from the roof of the parliament building and sent across to the chapter house.[27]

From the Restoration until Queen Anne's reign, the chapter house, still in its original form, came under the uneasy and divided dominion of two able but disputatious scholars, who held the two posts of deputy chamberlain: the competent functionary John Lowe and the colourful herald and antiquary Peter le Neve, the first President of the revived Society of Antiquaries.[28] They were charged by the government to work with Thomas Rymer on his *Foedera*, but, in between wrangling with each other on the fair division of their duties, they quarrelled with Rymer over his access to the records.[29] Le Neve strongly, and correctly, objected to Rymer being allowed to take away the records, and insisted that a room be constructed for him in the cloister, at the entrance to the chapter house (see further, p 24), and that the records should be released to him in batches.[30] Rymer and his band of assistants adhered to this system only in part. In 1709, the antiquary Ralph Thoresby noted that he had visited at the chapter house 'the industrious antiquary and ingenious poet Mr Rymer, whom we found amongst the musty records supervising, his amanuensis transcribing.'[31]

By this time, all was not well with the chapter house building, and over the next half-century, and indeed beyond, a long, complex and repetitive saga unfolded, as the record-keepers battled with a reluctant Treasury to try to get it repaired and fitted out to meet the needs of record storage. Until 1727 the repository was headed, as before, by two deputy chamberlains, replaced from 1727 by a single keeper of the records assisted by three clerks.[32]

From the point of view of the record-keepers, there were three main problems. Most striking was the decayed and increasingly dangerous state of the repository. In 1701, le Neve and Lowe reported to Christopher Wren, who was Surveyor-General of the fabric of the abbey, that in this, the repository for the records of the nation, the rain was beating in, and endangering the records.[33] Partial repairs were undertaken by Wren,[34] but the matter continued to exercise several parliamentary committees from 1705 to 1732.[35] But no action was taken, and, for more than two decades, the chapter house continued its grim saga of decay, its vault eventually reaching the point of no return.

In 1737 the Office of Works found that, because of the removal of one buttress many years earlier and the decay of the rest, the roof was in danger of collapse.[36] By 1740 the state of the roof was so bad that the Office of Works recommended it be taken down to avoid collapse, suggesting that meanwhile it should be shored up to protect the records.[37] Still no action was taken and, in 1744, the canons of Westminster living in the adjoining houses, normally seen as villains by the record-keepers, joined the fray. They petitioned the Treasury 'that the walls and buttresses [of the chapter house] are in so ruinous a condition that great stones are frequently falling down, by which we are exposed to constant danger'. In response the Office of Works informed the Treasury that the walls and buttresses needed shoring up and a new timber roof should be built at a cost of £625 15s.[38] By 1751 the costs had risen to £680, so Richard Morley, the keeper of the records, informed the Treasury.[39] The matter was then at last resolved with the radical reconstruction and Georgianization of the building, including a new flat-topped pyramidal roof, undertaken by William Kent and Thomas Ripley.[40]

A second problem was that the neighbouring buildings posed a fire risk to both the chapter house and the Pyx chamber. In 1686 Lowe reported that a brewhouse and wash-house adjoining the Pyx were 'rotting and boiling many records'.[41] Although an important collection of leagues and treaties was moved into the chapter house in 1696,[42] this solution was only a partial one. Several more canons' houses lay adjacent to the chapter house itself, with their wash-houses and, later, coal stores right up against the walls. This issue caused much bad feeling between the abbey and the record office, compounded, in 1744, by the aforementioned stones falling off the chapter house onto the canons' houses that persisted right up to the 1850s.[43]

A final problem was the need of the record-keepers for space for the never-ending tide of incoming records, for places where they could sort and methodize them, for offices for listing them and making them available to searchers, and for proper and secure presses to keep them in. The chapter house was not a suitable building for the purpose, and its dramatic reconstruction in the 1750s would meet this need only in part. For example, in 1703, le Neve and Lowe complained to the Treasury that they had no place to put a large consignment of records from the time of Charles I. They implored the Lord High Treasurer to order Wren to build a gallery there: 'Sir Christopher Wren having absolutely refused to build any such gallery for such use'.[44] It was perhaps Wren's respect for the integrity of this fine building, which he judged 'no contemptible fabric',[45] that prevented him from carrying out the modification that the record-keepers wanted;[46] although, interestingly, it was reported to a committee of the House of Lords in 1705 that a gallery had recently been built for the fines and *posteas*.[47]

In the endeavour of sorting and digesting the records, the deputy chamberlains, Dudley Downes and John Lawton,[48] proposed to the Treasury in 1719 that fifty great chests be built, as well as presses for sorting records, requesting also additional funding for two men skilled in ancient writing and well-versed in Latin, as well as a further workman to brush and clean the records and sew on covers.[49] This was agreed, as was, in 1755, a new door, shelves and further presses, as requested by Richard Morley, a subsequent keeper of the records.[50]

By now, for the first time for at least a century, the chapter house had been modified into what was, by the standards of the time, a well-appointed and secure record office, fit to hold many of the nation's greatest archival treasures. But the risk of fire from adjoining buildings remained, and the improvements had been made at the expense of much of the original fabric. The crumbling Gothic vaults had been replaced with a low wooden roof; a gallery and presses were attached to the walls; a suspended wooden floor was constructed at ground level; the original windows were blocked and replaced with round-headed lights; and arcading and wall paintings in the north bay were destroyed to make way for a new door.[51]

As the *History of the King's Works* puts it, 'the building which had once been one of the architectural glories of Westminster had been sadly degraded by its adaptation to the utilitarian purposes of a record office' (fig 124).[52] Yet

Fig 124 The Chapter House Record Office in the late 1850s from the south east. *Photograph:* © Dean and Chapter of Westminster WAM

paintings in the low level arcade were preserved by the lowest row of presses, and the celebrated medieval tiles had been saved by the suspended wooden floor.

The chapter house Exchequer record office, 1753 to 1838

All these works allowed Domesday Book and other archival treasures of the Exchequer's Treasury of Receipt to be moved out of their previous home in Tally Court, in the Palace of Westminster, and into the reconstructed chapter house by 1753.[53] Here they were to remain for just over a century. As in the days of le Neve and Rymer, the chapter house now once again became the focus for scholarly work on a major government-funded project to print the records – in this case an edition of Domesday Book.[54] This was proposed by the Society of Antiquaries in 1755 because 'this inestimable remain of antiquity runs every hour the risk of being irretrievably lost, should a fire happen in the neighbourhood of the chapter house.'[55] Government funding was found in 1767, and, after many years of acrimony at the chapter house and obstructive behaviour by some of the record-keepers, an excellent edition by Abraham Farley, keeper of the records, was published in 1783. With its later indexes, it remains the foundation of Domesday scholarship to this day.[56]

We now reach the early nineteenth century, a time when parliament once again started to concern itself with the state of the nation's archival heritage.[57] In 1800 the House of Commons set up the Record Commission,[58] which, renewed five times, was to continue its work until 1838, in the spirit of the utmost acrimony and accusations of incompetence and of squandering much public money.[59] Nevertheless it promoted the notion of a national collection of records and, more practically, probably saved a great many public records that would otherwise have been lost.[60]

Inspecting the state repositories in 1800, the Commissioners found the chapter house to hold 'the largest and most various collection [of records] in the Kingdom.'[61] The keeper of the records, George Rose, held several other offices, including that of clerk of the Parliaments. In reality he spent little time on the records, rather using his skills as a high-profile politician and publicist to seek to provide the impression of competence.[62] In his report to the Commissioners he wrote vaingloriously but haphazardly of the records in his charge: parliament rolls, *quo warranto* rolls, plea and forest rolls, records of the courts of Star Chamber, Wards and Requests, and Domesday Book. His own remuneration was, he told the Commissioners, £400 a year and that of his four clerks totalled £420 a year.[63]

In the same report Rose complacently described the chapter house as being in remarkably good condition and secure from fire except for a risk from two nearby houses. But it was very cold and therefore little work could be done in the winter months; he asked therefore for an office to be built for the clerks.[64] In response, later in 1800, the Commissioners leased a small strip of land next to the chapter house, forming the entrance to a canon's house, from the Dean and Chapter for forty years. Two offices for the clerks were shoehorned into this space under the supervision of James Wyatt.[65] An interesting section from the first part of the nineteenth century (fig 125) gives a sense of the proportions of the building at this time.[66]

The Commissioners also found, however, that one third of the chapter house records was unlisted, and commented that if the clerks were to attend more often this work could be carried out with dispatch.[67] They instructed that a full inventory of the chapter house records be made for them on vellum. Two fair copies of this survive in the public records,[68] with graphic illustrations – such as the coloured section shown in figure 123. It is beautifully produced with colourful illustrations and floor plans, which bring the record office vividly to life, although if examined in detail, many of its contents make disturbing reading. Thanks to it and to other sources, including a later detailed description of the fabric by Francis Palgrave, published in 1848,[69] it is possible to take a virtual tour of the chapter house record office in 1807.

We start in the 'basement' storey (actually the ground floor), with its ranks of presses in the inner and outer octagons housing bills, answers, depositions, writs, inquisitions *post mortem* and its great chests containing deeds and treaties (fig 120). Some of these were said to be in good order, but all too many are described as being 'in great confusion', 'not arranged', or 'partly decayed'. The recently constructed offices for the clerks are tucked in against the walls on the east and north-east, and the separate door in the north wall and the passage from the cloisters are clearly depicted. We know from a plan in Westminster Abbey muniments (fig 126) and another in the Soane Museum that abutting the wall and the two buttresses at the foot of this drawing were Mr Longland's wash-house, and Mrs Deacon's wash-house and coal-hole, but these do not appear here.[70]

In the grand entrance from the cloisters, bills and answers, described as 'an immense mass of miscellaneous records', were to be found 'in a state of great confusion and covered with dust insomuch as it would take several years to arrange them'. Similarly in the main basement area, the contents of the chests, including the foundation documents of Henry VII's Chapel, and are said to be 'quite perished'.[71]

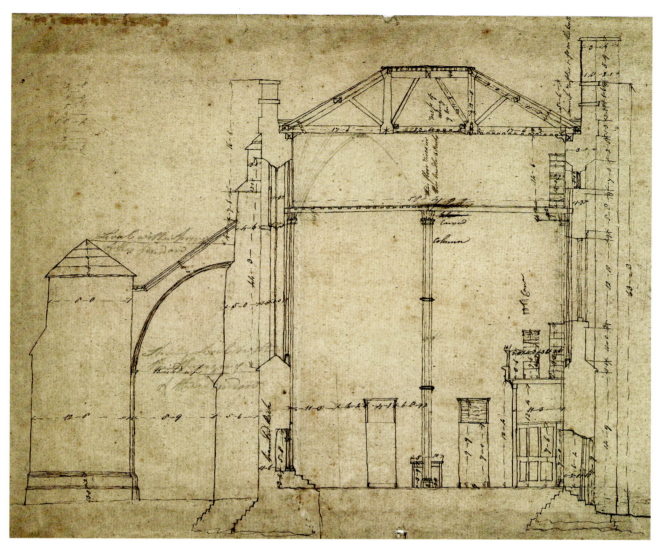

Fig 125 The Chapter House Record Office: east–west section through the building, looking south. *Drawing*: early nineteenth century; © RIBA Drawings Collection, Victoria and Albert Museum; RIBA: SC 82/11, 143A

Moving up a level we reach the gallery (fig 121). Its outer octagon contained presses for plea rolls and feet of fines and the inner presses more of the same, together with some of the county bags of medieval Common Pleas records. These were generally in a better state of preservation than the records at the basement level. On the left is the chief clerk's office, known also as the library, of which the inventory contains an interesting watercolour (fig 127). The inventory itemizes very choice items in the presses of this office, including the medieval parliament rolls, close, patent and pipe rolls, the eyre and forest rolls, the Henry VII chapel inventories and records relating to Ireland, Wales and forfeited estates. The index to the inventory also shows that the foundation indentures of the Henry VII Chapel were in the 'CCO', which is to say the chief clerk's office or library.[72]

But the detailed accuracy of the listings of even these,

the most high-profile records, is seriously questionable. Let us take Domesday as an example. A contemporary 'Catalogue of Books at the Chapter House' in Rose's papers in the British Library states that Domesday was in the chief clerk's office or library, with many other important manuscripts, such as the *Valor Ecclesiasticus*.[73] But by contrast in the inventory, Domesday Book, tantalizingly, appears only in the index section, which states that it is kept in 'a closet on the stairs to the gallery'.[74] The impression is given of great laxity, and we know that this state of affairs continued right up to the 1830s, when, Palgrave later stated, 'even Domesday was allowed to be at large.'[75]

Up the steep stairs to the attic storey (fig 122), we pass closets containing the records of the Court of Augmentations. Reaching the attic level, we find presses storing monastic surrenders, a wealth of wardrobe and

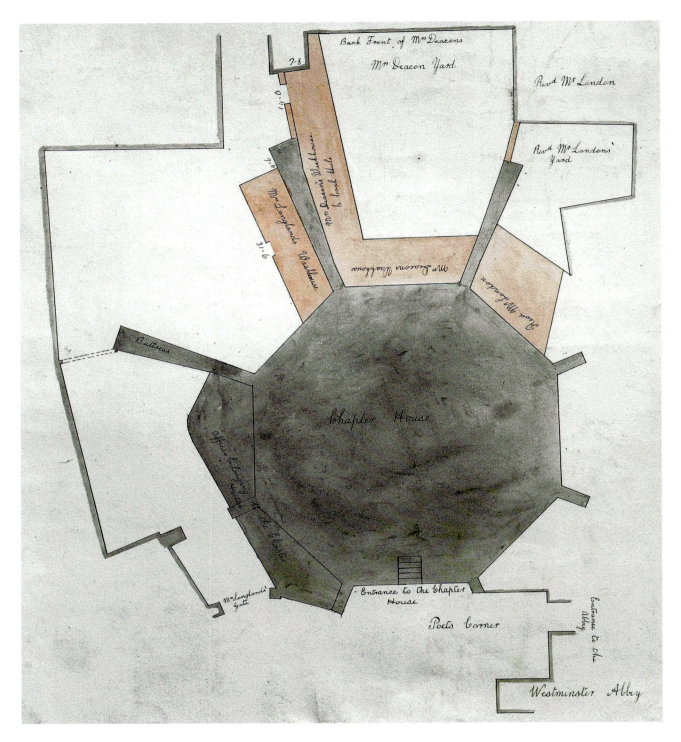

Fig 126 Chapter house: plan showing the domestic structures erected against the southern part of the building, in the gardens of the canons' houses. *Drawing*: © Dean and Chapter of Westminster; WAM (P)377

household and building accounts, and records relating to Scotland, Calais, Montreuil and Ponthieu. All these presses were against the outer walls, and Palgrave's later description of the attic level gives the reason. The old stone vault was, he said 'replaced by a flat of planking … supported by beams radiating from the [central] pillar and abutting on the outer walls … The room formed by the

space between this planking and the roof is usually called the Star Chamber'. From the peculiar construction of the flat, forming the floor of the 'Star Chamber,' he continued 'it has not been thought prudent to place any weighty object in any part towards the centre of the beams. The Records have therefore been arranged as nearly as possible against the walls, and … no danger of giving way is to be

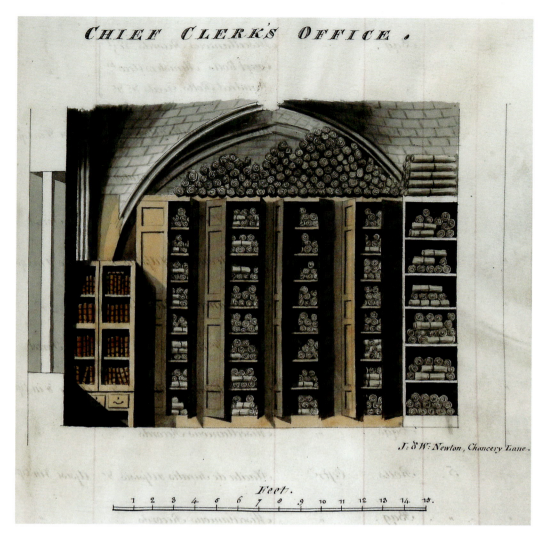

CHIEF CLERK'S OFFICE.

J. & W. Newton, Chancery Lane.

Feet.

Fig 127 The Chapter House Record Office: document presses in the chief clerk's office in the inner vestibule. *Drawing*: J and W Newton, 1807; *photograph*: © The National Archives; TNA: PRO OBS 1/692

apprehended so long as the Records remain as at present.'[76]

The crypt of the chapter house was not included in the inventory, nor in Palgrave's description, but we know from other evidence that it was used as a store and wine cellar at this time (p 27).[77]

Meeting in 1812, the Commissioners reviewed progress since the compilation of the inventory and, somewhat optimistically, congratulated themselves on having had the records arranged and catalogued properly.[78] Their confidence proved short-lived. In 1816 and 1817 Rose asked that urgent repairs be undertaken, adding that the new rooms for the clerks were too damp to be used.[79] The fabric continued and would continue to be a problem, as can be seen in a photograph taken in the late 1850s (fig 124). And after 1818, when Rose died, the Commissioners made arguably an even more disastrous appointment: their own secretary, John Caley.

Caley instituted arrangements for sorting, repairing and binding some of the records that look decidedly haphazard to modern eyes. These included an inappropriately tight rebinding of Domesday Book, undertaken in 1819.[80] He also unravelled Rose's system as described in the inventory, such as it was, by re-arranging more of the records under counties, greatly extending the much earlier system of 'county bags'. This was a dreadful archival sin which would have to be completely disentangled again later in the nineteenth century. Caley also took great exception to Rose's belief in keeping records in chests, which he said, caused them to moulder. He barred the chapter house to researchers as far as possible, and took many choice items home to his house in Clerkenwell, from where the fortunate few amongst his friends might have them delivered via his footman.[81]

On Caley's death in 1834, somewhat surprisingly, the Commissioners appointed a competent successor in the shape of Francis Palgrave, a Record Commission sub-commissioner and a noted records scholar.[82] Palgrave arrived with a reforming agenda, but the clerks already at the chapter house had other ideas. Charles and Frederick Devon, brothers who had been appointed by Caley in 1821, were particularly difficult characters, who clearly took an instant dislike to Palgrave.[83] With their principal, J W Clarke,[84] they 'severally refused,' Palgrave later wrote, 'to give me any information as to the content [of the chapter house] and I found several important documents in places where they must have been intentionally concealed.'[85]

At the same time they also criticized Caley and his régime to Palgrave. Caley, they told Palgrave, had insisted that the main task of the clerks was to make themselves 'generally acquainted with the nature of the records'. This was so that they could interpret and explain them to searchers, to lawyers in the law courts, and to parliamentary committees. Any time left over could be used in compiling calendars or indexes, but these were far less important because 'a mere index-maker must of necessity from the nature of his occupation become a dolt, being to the exclusion of more important knowledge'. The records were unlabelled as a matter of policy and had to be found by local knowledge. They were kept in open cupboards or on the open shelves and – apart from the golden papal *bulla* – were not on any account to be locked up, so that they could be accessed quickly. Palgrave summed up the state of the chapter house in scathing terms: 'the Office [is] almost wholly unprovided with Calendars, and the Records wholly unprotected and exposed to damage and decay.'[86]

Palgrave did his best to galvanize his recalcitrant and unproductive clerks into action,[87] insisting that they attended at their contracted times, starting a programme of sorting, cleaning, re-binding, boxing and listing the records, and compiling and publishing inventories, including the still invaluable *Kalendars and Inventories of the Exchequer*. The central octagon was cleared of its untidy heaps of assorted common law records, which were confined to sacks, to make space for the plea rolls of the King's Bench and Common Pleas.[88] Perhaps for the first time since the days of Agarde, two centuries earlier, what today we would see as a sense of real purpose and professionalism had returned to the chapter house record office.

Sporadic attempts to improve the chapter house's fabric had continued over the previous decade:[89] in 1826 a neighbouring wash-house was removed and iron shutters were put in, but this left a further two wash-houses and a coal-hole directly abutting its walls.[90] Only a fortunate change in wind direction saved the chapter house and its contents from the conflagration which consumed much of

the Palace of Westminster in 1834, destroying almost all of the House of Commons records in the process.

Palgrave watched the conflagration from the roof of the chapter house,[91] and his fervent determination to clear the records from the building must surely date from this event, though it remained unachieved in his lifetime. 'If any of the materials of the [Chapter House]' he later wrote, 'were once kindled, the flames would rage with great intensity and communicate with every part, all being connected with wooden floors and wooden staircases … The whole interior would be a mass of ruins, [and] it is most probable that the whole would collapse.'[92]

The chapter house as a branch of the Public Record Office, 1838–64

In 1838, following the Public Record Office Act, the chapter house became a branch of the new Public Record Office (PRO), along with other offices, such as the Tower of London and the Rolls chapel. Francis Palgrave, appointed to the post of Deputy Keeper, the executive head of the PRO,[93] now became preoccupied with office politics on the grand scale, and with the long search for a suitable site for the new single record repository. Not until 1851 was building work on the PRO in Chancery Lane started.[94]

Where did the chapter house fit into this picture? The very brief entries in the published annual *Reports of the Deputy Keepers of Public Records* give the impression of a quiet backwater, run by Frederick Devon, left as the most senior clerk after the death of J W Clarke in 1840 and the departure of Charles Devon to pursue his work as a record agent. The staff, including the able Joseph Burtt, continued to care for, store and list the records,[95] and routine transfers out of documents are noted, such as, in 1842, the removal of the papal bulls to Rolls House.[96] Documents were arriving there too, such as, in 1853, the recently completed enumerators' books from the 1851 census.[97] Searches and copies continued to be made for the public,[98] and fees continued to be levied for research, bringing in nearly £110 in 1838, £42 in 1848, but sinking to under £9 in 1858, all of which was solemnly documented in the *Reports*.[99]

But the printed *Reports* were a facade: behind the scenes, the reality was very different. Most of the senior record-keepers at the PRO were difficult and obstructive to Palgrave at times, but Frederick Devon was in a different league from the others. He displayed consistently uncooperative and unpleasant behaviour towards Palgrave for over twenty years.[100] In his manuscript annual returns to Palgrave and Lord Langdale, the Master of the Rolls and

Palgrave's superior, Devon penned hundreds of pages of vituperative criticism of Palgrave. He revelled in his own disloyalty, depicting it as a force for good aimed at improving the public service.[101] In 1843 he was forced by Palgrave to apologize to the Master of the Rolls, Lord Langdale, for his disrespectful language,[102] but to no lasting effect. Because of his continuing erratic and difficult behaviour, he was never given the status of Assistant Keeper Grade I to which he aspired, unlike his colleagues in the other branch repositories.[103]

From his very first report, written in 1840, Devon made it clear that he was a passionate and uncritical proponent of the chapter house record office and wanted to keep it exactly as it was (an endeavour which was almost entirely successful: Caley's legacy was to persist to the end). In response to Palgrave's stated wish to close down the chapter house as soon as possible, Devon hampered Henry Cole's team of workmen, who were cleaning and packing up common law records prior to removing them to Carlton Ride (near Pall Mall), instructing them to unpack and place mis-shelved records back in the dirt and dust.[104] He praised dry dust as a preservation medium, writing that 'experience teaches me that nothing more is wanted for the preservation of records than open shelves, slight covers, dry places and fresh air.'[105]

In his continuing attempts to undermine Palgrave, he went on to castigate the new boxes and presses into which some of the records had been placed and which he said – with some justification – had caused them to mildew: in the early 1850s he was to give Lord Langdale, the Master of the Rolls, what he called an 'ocular demonstration' of the effects of mould and managed to obtain a warrant from him over-ruling Palgrave's instructions to box up the records. Throughout the 1850s he continued to oppose the idea of removing any records at all to any other repository, describing Carlton Ride as 'damp and injurious' and Rolls House as 'some crazy old building'.[106] The new Record Office at Chancery Lane was by this time under construction, but Devon saw it as altogether inferior to the chapter house, alleging that the slate shelves – widely regarded then and now as state-of-the-art for the time – were sweating and thus damaging the records.[107]

Devon was particularly obsessed with Domesday Book, as all its keepers tend to be. He wrote about it in his reports at length, saying that it was like a miracle-working relic.[108] When, in 1846, Palgrave asked him to arrange for it to be kept in an iron chest or box for security, he protested furiously, saying that he would rather even it were transferred to Henry Cole at Carlton Ride than be shut away, at risk of damp and mildew.[109] He was almost as passionate about sharing his knowledge of all the records

in his care with the public, and here he was in some ways ahead of his time. He saw himself as an antiquary rather than a record-keeper, arguing that he was there above all to help searchers with their historical and genealogical research. Critics of antiquarianism see it as 'neither history nor wisdom', he wrote in 1856, 'and *The Times* calls it learned twaddle – yet these records do contain most valuable public and private information.'[110]

But despite his antiquarian enthusiasms, Devon was very unhelpful to George Gilbert Scott, who was working on the abbey's restoration. In 1841, Devon stated that the records were of little value and that 'there can be no absolute necessity for interfering with the records on their account.'[111] And when, in 1849, Scott found a large heap of parchments, writs and skippets in the small office adjoining the outer vestibule of the chapter house, Devon described them as 'debris and rubbish' and simply left them there.[112] By the 1850s, Palgrave clearly had ceased any attempts to remove Devon from the chapter house. In 1851 he promoted him to Assistant Keeper Grade II, although this did not buy him any extra loyalty. Right up to the year of his death, in 1859, Devon continued to criticize Palgrave, even though Palgrave organized the re-painting and re-carpeting of his office when Devon became very ill during 1858.[113]

But, as time went on, the restorers were moving ever closer. During the 1850s, as Devon plotted ever more feverishly to keep his little world just as it was, the abbey was 'indurating' the stonework (that is, cleaning it and attempting to stabilize it with shellac solution) at the entrance of the chapter house and trying to manoeuvre for its return to its own use, while Scott was discussing with Gladstone his schemes to fund the restoration of this 'dismantled' and 'mutilated' building.[114]

Within two weeks of Devon's death in December 1859, work on clearing out the chapter house (fig 212) began in earnest, under the aegis of his longsuffering and more able deputy, and now successor, Joseph Burtt.[115] The moves were substantially completed by mid-July 1859,[116] by when the Pyx chamber, according to Scott, contained only empty chests and cases, apart from the Pyx chest,[117] although an engraving (fig 128) depicts several chests that were subsequently moved to the PRO,[118] possibly not until later in the nineteenth century.[119]

The clearance of the chapter house in six months was no mean feat, but was clearly not without problems. In his first report to Palgrave, Burtt continued with the chapter house tradition of criticizing and blaming his superiors and predecessors for his problems. Little work, he said, had ever taken place to manage the records properly; even the most valuable had been allowed to fall into a state of decay.

Fig 128 The Pyx chamber: interior showing the chests during the process of emptying the building. *Drawing*: Orlando Jewitt, 1859; after Scott 1863, page 9

Such lists as had been compiled, he said, showed 'how small an extent any correct principle of classification has guided their formation.' He singled out the county bags and historical collections in the library for particular obloquy, as these had removed the records from their original series. 'No portion of the public records', he ended, 'has been worse off than that formerly in the Chapter House at Westminster.'[120] He noted that the haste with which the move had been undertaken had caused further confusion and disorder.[121]

An engraving of the chapter house published in 1860 confirms his graphic picture of a muddled and chaotic repository (fig 129).[122] Indeed, so confused were the common law writs that they had to be kept in the chapter house for a further two years, until August 1861, so that they could be sorted.[123] However, once in their new home in Chancery Lane, most of the records, including the county bags and historical collections, were carefully and incrementally sorted, re-ordered, repaired and boxed according to the best archival principles of the Victorian age.

Palgrave was not to see the chapter house in its final empty and melancholy state: he died in July 1861.[124] In 1862, his successor, Thomas Duffus Hardy, the new Deputy Keeper of the Records, used it as a hostage in his battle with the Treasury for a new building on the Rolls Estate, such was the pressure on the PRO to accept new and accruing records. 'The Chapter House can hardly be called in a dilapidated state' he wrote, with scant regard for the facts. 'It is not in ornamental repair, but sufficiently in repair for a depository of Records as regards security.'[125] This threat clearly worked well: the Treasury found funds for a new block at the PRO, started in 1863. But it was not until June 1864 that the keys to the chapter house were finally handed over.[126]

By this time, pressure to restore the chapter house was mounting. In 1862 Dean Stanley had organized a meeting of key politicians there;[127] this was followed, in 1865, by a meeting of the Society of Antiquaries. This, Stanley reported, 'was held in its dirty and disfigured walls, to urge the duty of restoring it to its pristine beauty. Under

Fig 129 Chapter house: view of the interior looking west, just before it ceased to be used as a record office. *Drawing*: published in the *Illustrated Times*, 25 February 1860; *photograph*: © The National Archives; TNA: PRO 8/61, p 98

the auspices of Mr Gladstone, then Chancellor of the Exchequer, and Mr Cowper, First Commissioner of Works, the adequate sum was granted by Parliament and the venerable building will become a trophy of the archaeological and architectural triumphs of the nineteenth century.'[128] The Society's Minute Book reports the meeting and details the resolutions passed, including one urging Parliament to fund the restoration of the

chapter house, 'without delay, to its architectural beauty'.[129]

And so it was that the chapter house fell into Scott's clutches, and lost all of its Georgian accretions. Despite its manifest shortcomings as a record office, and its often haphazard management, it did also have some good and competent keepers, some of whom – such as Agarde, le Neve, Farley and Palgrave – were fine scholars. Less happily, it was also overseen by certain keepers – in particular Rose and Caley – whose archival aspirations exceeded their competence by a considerable degree. Their unfortunate experiments subjected the records in their care to needless damage and risk, which considerably outstripped the threats to the records kept in a state of somewhat more benign neglect in the other great state repositories at the Tower of London and the Rolls chapel.[130] All this would go a long way to support Joseph Burtt's view that the chapter house record office was the worst-managed record repository of all.

Yet against such odds, the chapter house record office did allow for the survival of some of this country's greatest historical documents for three centuries. Like the PRO at Chancery Lane, which supplanted it, it can now be revisited as a working archive only in the imagination.[131] But is it fanciful to trace something of its spirit in James Pennethorne's wonderful Round Room at the PRO, still there in its original form, and completed as part of Hardy's extension, in 1868 (fig 130)?[132]

Fig 130 The Public Record Office, Chancery Lane: the Round Room c 1998. *Photograph*: Crispin Rose Innes © The National Archives

Sir George Gilbert Scott and the restoration of the chapter house, 1849–72

9

Steven Brindle

Westminster Abbey has long been the object of intense interest and study by Britain's antiquaries, and the history of the restorations and repairs of the abbey buildings since the Reformation is a major subject in itself. However, the chapter house languished in its mutilated Georgian form right through the first century of the Gothic revival. As long as it was occupied by the Exchequer's record office and filled with presses and galleries, any change seemed unlikely (figs 123 and 129).

The story of the chapter house's restoration began with the appointment, in 1849, of George Gilbert Scott (1811–78) as surveyor of the fabric to the Dean and Chapter, in succession to Edward Blore (fig 131). Scott had been in practice with W B Moffatt in 1835–46, but by 1849 he was working on his own as an up-and-coming church architect. In his twenties he had been converted by the writings of A W N Pugin to a passionate belief in the Gothic style, and had developed a serious interest in the study of medieval architecture, which informed his own work.[1] He adopted a much more regular and professional approach to the role than Blore, making annual reports setting out those works that were essential and those that were desirable. The reports were supplemented with long letters to the sub-dean, Lord John Thynne, a cultivated aristocrat of conservative outlook with whom Scott enjoyed a close, if deeply respectful, working relationship.[2]

One important theme of Scott's surveyorship was a reduction in the crowds of Georgian monuments obscuring the abbey's architecture.[3] Another was his pioneering concern for historic fabric, in particular for the large areas of decaying Caen and Reigate stone. Any other early Victorian architect would have replaced them, but

Scott's instincts were quite different: he sought advice from a number of sources, and from 1853 he began to have the surfaces treated with a solution of shellac in 'spirits of wine' (probably ethyl alcohol), a process he termed 'induration' (see chapter 10, appendix B). Scott's favoured mason-contractor, Henry Poole, gradually applied this treatment around the abbey through the 1850s and 1860s, eventually treating most of the historic surfaces. Poole said

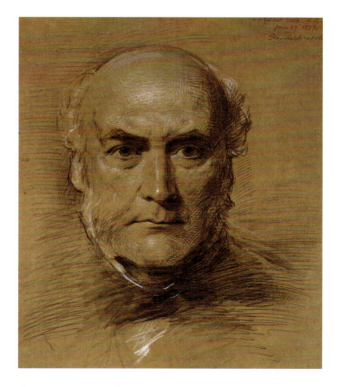

Fig 131 Sir George Gilbert Scott. *Drawing*: in crayon by George Richmond 1877 © National Portrait Gallery, London

that indurations were always 'begun in the presence and with the personal aid of Mr Scott, who afterwards frequently visited the work'. In 1858 they reached the outer portal of the chapter house, and the fabric vouchers include a payment of £50 to Poole for indurating it.[4]

However, Scott went well beyond merely patching and repairing the surfaces: he became one of the most scholarly architects of the Gothic revival, and his work at the abbey became a matter of profound personal interest. He made a detailed study of its buildings over many years, which he put on permanent record in 1861 with the publication of his *Gleanings from Westminster Abbey*, a landmark in the scholarly understanding of the place.[5]

Scott put this understanding to good use. Previous surveyors, from Wren to Blore, had repaired the abbey as found, occasionally re-designing areas in what they deemed an appropriate manner, but Scott was the first to aim at archaeological exactness in his work. His approach was typified by his report on the restoration of two bays of the cloister in 1868, when he claimed that 'these have been carried out with great exactness and may be confidently said to be a precise restoration of the original to its minutest details.'[6]

As Scott's knowledge of the abbey grew, he hoped to carry out more ambitious projects. In 1853, Thynne commissioned him to produce a design for a new cloister or 'campo santo', east of the chapter house, to receive the burials of eminent men, and also to serve as a repository for some of the monuments that they planned to remove from the abbey church.[7] This was never executed, but Scott did a great deal inside the church: in the 1860s he re-ordered the sanctuary, installed a new screen and clergy seating and rebuilt the high altar and the screen behind it.

As Scott's reputation grew he became the busiest architect in Britain, with numerous assistants and projects in progress all over the country.[8] His involvement at the abbey was probably a factor in his being appointed as architect to several cathedrals, including Lichfield (from 1857), Chichester, where he rebuilt the collapsed central tower (1861–66), Salisbury (from 1863) and Hereford, where he replaced James Wyatt's west front. At the same time he carried out a wide range of secular commissions, including the Foreign Office (1862–73), the Albert Memorial (1864–68) and St Pancras station (1869–72).

Scott died, still in office as surveyor, in 1878. His last great aim at Westminster had been to restore the north transept facade.[9] Funds were short, but, by the time he died, he had rebuilt the lowest stage with the portals. The upper part of the facade was 'restored' with significant changes to its design by his successor, J L Pearson, a work that aroused great controversy even at the time.[10]

Nevertheless, Scott probably did more at the abbey in his twenty-nine years as surveyor than anyone else, and his most important single commission there was the restoration of the chapter house. He published three accounts of his work.[11]

Scott began his investigations of the chapter house soon after his appointment. At an early stage he discovered the medieval entrance to the library, originally the monks' dormitory, in the cloister bay immediately to the south of the chapter house portal (Plan 1). This had been blocked, and a new wooden staircase to the library built within the outer vestibule of the chapter house (fig 32). Scott recommended to the Dean and Chapter that the original stairs should be restored as the access to the library, and that the chapter house portal, 'which is perhaps one of the most beautiful features of its kind', should be restored. This was done in 1852–53. The blocking of the northern arch of the entrance was removed (fig 149), and the mason Samuel Cundy was paid £186 to clean and repair the stonework, though the hole in the vestibule vault does not seem to have been made good properly.[12]

The progress of the restoration

Work began on the new Public Record Office in Chancery Lane in 1851. In 1854, the chapter house was already being emptied of its records, and the Dean and Chapter were beginning to think about its future, even though they did not own it: the government did. The Sub-Dean wrote to Scott in March 1854: 'I presume that when it has served this purpose they will restore it to the Dean and Chapter, and I cannot suppose that they will offer it in the mutilated condition to which it has been reduced.'[13] As we shall see, Thynne was being over-optimistic on the issue of ownership.

Scott had apparently already produced a design for its restoration, for on 18 March 1854, Canon Repton of the abbey wrote a minute of a conference he had had with the Chancellor of the Exchequer, William Ewart Gladstone, on the subject of the abbey buildings:

> I then alluded first to the state of the Chapter House, its dismantled condition, and the claim of the Chapter to it in a restored condition. I suggested the possibility of attaching to it Cloisters in the direction of College Street – part of College Garden – as a receptacle of the Monuments and appropriate vaults for the burial of men of eminence in the state.

Gladstone had said that the abbey was a matter of national importance, but responded very cautiously to the possibility that parliament might authorize a contribution to this project: 'Mr Gladstone wished to see Mr Scott's design for restoration of the Chapter House, and also to know his opinion of the cost of the same.'[14] This was not a propitious moment for such a project, for nine days later (on 27 March 1854), Britain declared war on Russia. Nevertheless, the incident shows that the abbey was canvassing support for the cloister or 'campo santo' idea at a high level, and was also hoping to get the chapter house back, and restored, into the bargain. Around this time Scott produced a fine reconstruction drawing of the interior, which he exhibited at the Paris International Exhibition of 1855, where it won a gold medal (fig 132); three further drawings showed the proposed restoration of the vestibules.[15]

Any real progress, though, had to wait on the completion of the new Public Record Office in 1859. Eventually, on 18 June 1864 the Rolls Office handed its keys over to the Office of Works. The little extensions added for the record-keepers in 1801 had been built on the abbey's property, and were to have their doors bricked up before being surrendered to the Dean and Chapter.[16] The chapter house stood empty and desolate, and the *Illustrated London News* published an engraving, showing it in this state (fig 133).

For Scott, having studied the building and produced his reconstruction drawings, there was no doubt that the chapter house was a key monument in the history of English architecture, albeit in a tragically mutilated state. In 1861 he wrote:

Matthew Paris, under the date of 1250, after stating that the king had rebuilt the church, *Dominus Rex aedificavit capitulum incomparabile* … It was, indeed, an

Fig 132 Chapter house interior: Scott's proposed reconstruction. *Drawing*: part of a set prepared *c* 1855; after Scott 1861, plate 13

Fig 133 The chapter house emptied of records in 1859, with Scott making an inspection; view looking north east. *Drawing*: Orlando Jewitt, after Thornbury 1878, III, page 451

incomparable chapter-house. That at Salisbury was not yet commenced, and though evidently built in imitation of this, and having some features of greater richness, it still would have yielded the palm to its prototype at Westminster.

Its beauties, however, are unhappily now for the most part to be judged rather by imagination than by sight, for seldom do we see a noble work of art reduced to such a wreck!

... I undertook some years back, the careful investigation of its details, and such was the difficulty presented by the fittings and other impediments, that, though every possible facility was afforded me by the gentlemen in charge of the records, it occupied me on (and off) for several months. I believe, however, that I succeeded in getting at nearly every part of the design. The internal view which I exhibit was founded on the result of my examination, and I think you will agree with me that a more elegant interior could scarcely be found.

After a fairly detailed consideration of the evidence that he had found (of which more below), Scott concluded:

> The records are now in great measure removed, and soon will be entirely so. Let us hope that the Government will recollect the condition of five centuries back – that they should keep the building in repair, and that they will give it up to the Chapter, with a restoration fund proportioned both to the extent of the dilapidations and the merits of the building.[17]

Scott gained a valuable ally when Arthur Penrhyn Stanley (1815–81), was appointed dean in 1863. Dean Stanley chaired a meeting of the Society of Antiquaries in 'the degraded Chapter House' on 2 December 1864. The meeting, attended by 'men of eminence in art and literature without distinction of party', petitioned William Ewart Gladstone to fund its restoration. Gladstone was famed for his devotion to economy in public spending, but he was also a devout and cultivated high church Anglican and had already, as we have seen, expressed an interest in Scott's design for the chapter house as Chancellor of the Exchequer back in 1854. Now, as Prime Minister, he agreed to the request. However, there was no suggestion that the building would be handed back to the abbey: the chapter house would be restored, but by the Office of Works. There was never any doubt, though, that Scott would be the architect.

The Office of Works' file begins in January 1866, when Scott was asked for an estimate of the cost of work, which was to include replacing the missing buttress, rebuilding the vault and roof, 'restoring the central shaft to the perpendicular', replacing the windows, filling them with stained glass, and 'restoring as far as possible the original lines of the building.'[18] Scott responded on 3 February with a broad estimate of £25,000, but also a cautionary note about the difficulty of producing an estimate given the nature of the work and the unsettled state of the building trades.[19] The Office of Works obtained a parliamentary vote of £25,000, and, on 1 May, asked Scott for 'a plan for the works': it was presumably in the summer that his office prepared the extant contract drawings (figs 134 and 135). In June 1866, John Taylor of the Office of Works engaged a firm of builders, Messrs Pullen and Horne, to dismantle the cases and galleries.[20] A surveyor, John Lee of Craven Street, Charing Cross, produced a detailed estimate based on Scott's plans: it provides much information about the work, but the overall total of £20,008 15s 7d, was to prove over-optimistic.[21]

Next, Scott wrote to the Office of Works on 2 July 1866, recommending that the firm of Henry Poole and Sons be engaged to carry out the work, rather than opening it to competitive tender. Knowing that this would fly in the face of all usual practice, he set out his argument with great care, laying special emphasis on the importance of conserving historic fabric:

It is a work partly of restoration and of an antiquarian character, and one in which the utmost care and vigilance are required in preventing the destruction of old details and in watching for minute evidences of the old details as they arise; and partly of work of renovation in exact conformity with the spirit of the work in the adjoining Abbey.[22]

Scott vouched for the firm personally in the most emphatic terms. He must have primed them to be ready to tender for the work, for on the same day (2 July 1866), they wrote to the First Commissioner of Works, offering to carry it out for £20,000.[23]

Scott's recommendation was questioned, but ultimately accepted.[24] However, a Mr Hunt of the Office commented on the 'wide uncertainties' of the job and expressed concern that the government might end up being overcharged. He therefore recommended that, instead of Messrs Poole being awarded a lump-sum contract, they should perform it according to a schedule of prices. The First Commissioner and the Treasury agreed.[25] This delayed matters for a couple of months, but, on 19 December 1866, the Office of Works accepted Poole's tender, on the basis of a schedule of prices agreed by Hunt and Scott, and with the proviso that it should be completed within the parliamentary vote of £25,000.[26] Hunt was justified in his concerns: the work cost a good deal more than £25,000, and it was as well for all parties that Poole's tender of £20,000 was not accepted.

Work began early in 1867, and Scott sent a certificate for the first £2,700 worth of work in March.[27] In June, he wrote to the Office recommending, in view of the unusual form of the contract, that a clerk of works be appointed, and suggesting John Kaberry for the role.[28] Again, the Office accepted his advice.[29]

The project evidently proceeded slowly and painstakingly, but once it had begun Scott was oddly dilatory in his dealings with the Office of Works. By September 1868, £15,172 had been spent, and they asked him for a statement of how much would be spent in that financial year (to March 1869). No reply came, and, on 12 December, they asked again. On 16 December Scott replied in a letter that gave the first signs that the costs might over-run. He alluded to the budget figure of £25,000, which was supposed to include stained glass for the windows. He said that the building had turned out to need much more repair than he had anticipated, and while he thought it could be completed for this sum, stained glass would require an additional £6,000. Amongst other things, he had found evidence that the building originally had pinnacles, and had felt obliged to introduce them into the design.[30]

Restoration proceeded through 1868 and 1869, though there is no correspondence about it on the Office of Works' file. A single photograph, probably taken in 1868, recorded progress (fig 136). Scott's apparent dilatoriness in reporting to his clients is puzzling, given that at the same time he was working on the government offices in Whitehall and the Albert Memorial. It may be that he and his office were over-stretched, but this was in marked contrast to his relations with the Dean and Chapter, to whom he sent detailed annual reports. At the end of one of these reports to the abbey, on 24 February 1868, he added:

Though not strictly within the range of my Report, I will mention that the restoration of the Chapter House

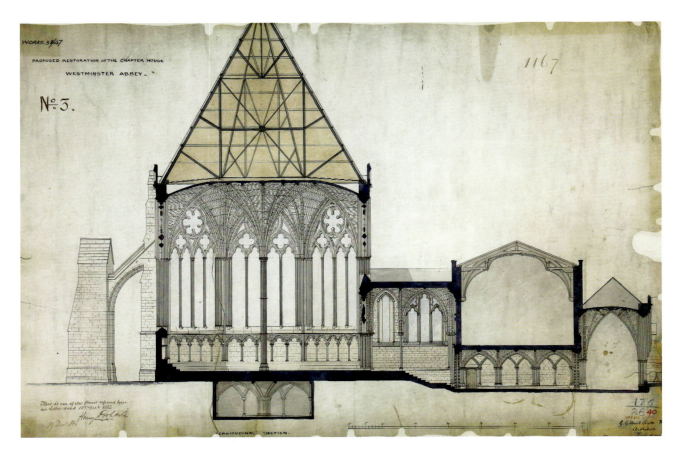

Fig 134 Cross-section looking south through the chapter house, vestibules and undercroft, including also the library (above the outer vestibule) and east cloister. This shows the proposed restoration and was one of Scott's contract drawings of 1866, signed at the foot by the architect and the contractor. Note the early version of the roof frame and the absence of pinnacles. *Drawing:* © The National Archives; TNA: WORK 38/47

is progressing very favourably. Two of the windows are now completed so far as relates to stonework, and a third is in rapid progress. I have hitherto been able to recover with perfect certainty of every detail which has been restored of the main building, though some belonging to the flying buttresses have been left to conjecture, and the same will, I fear, be the case with the cornice and parapet of the Chapter House, though with no other features.[31]

There are no other references to the chapter house in Scott's reports to the Dean and Chapter, and there is no evidence that he made regular reports to the Office of Works at all. Indeed, he seems positively to have kept them in the dark, until problems intervened and he was forced to explain himself.

In the autumn of 1869, Scott forwarded another two certificates for payment. Mr Bedder of the Office of Works sounded a note of caution, pointing out that only £830 of the vote would be left, and on 4 October the Office resolved that Scott should not be permitted to spend any money beyond the budget of £25,000, and be asked to

present accounts.[32] On 12 October, Scott sent a long and rather anguished explanation. The letter starts by circling around the issue: the job had always been a difficult one to estimate; he had hoped that the budget would have a margin of error; recently, he had begun to hear 'rumours of indefinite doubts' from the contractors. At last, on page 4, he gritted his teeth and owned up: 'I find, much to my chagrin, that the grant is already consumed, and that much work remains to be done.' Scott then went into some detail about what had gone wrong:

The piers between the windows, for instance, proved so shattered in their internal structure as to necessitate rebuilding, rather than reparation. The internal mass of the walls generally proved to be such mere rubble as to suggest a greater thickness of new ashlar than was at first thought necessary.

I found among the debris buried in the late work evidence of large octagonal pinnacles at the angles which, when once discovered, the true principles of restoration demanded to be reproduced.

Many expedients, also, from time to time, suggested

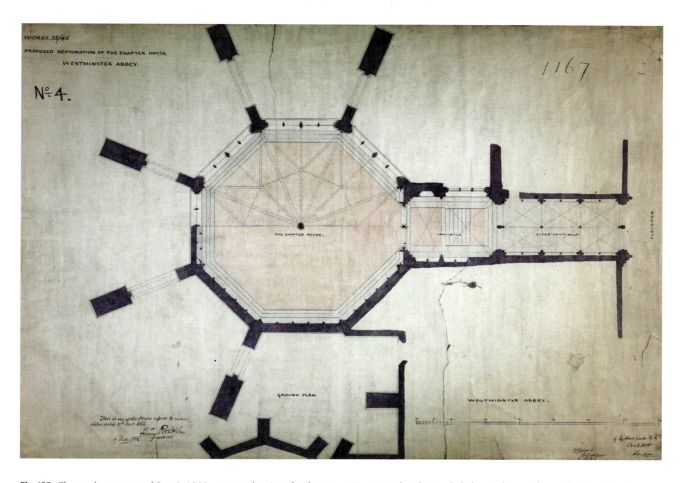

Fig 135 Chapter house: one of Scott's 1866 contract drawings for the restoration. Note that the single-light window on the south side of the inner vestibule is not shown as restored; nor is the adjacent buttress shown on this plan. *Drawing*: © The National Archives; TNA: WORK 38/46

Fig 136 Chapter house: reconstruction work in progress *c* 1869. Note the large voids to either side of the completed section of wall on the south-east side. *Photograph*: © Dean and Chapter of Westminster; WAM (Wright Coll), photo no. 6

themselves, for rendering a structure in its own nature so light more substantial.[33]

In fact, the increase in cost was not as bad as all that. Scott estimated that the builders' work would now come to nearly £28,000. Adding his own charges and expenses, and the clerk of works' salary, the total would amount to £30,000.

It seems that all this had arisen from genuinely unforeseeable circumstances, and that Scott and Kaberry appear to have been supervising the work with meticulous care. Nevertheless, the restoration ground to a halt for over a year while the paperwork was sorted out between the Treasury, the Office of Works, Scott and the contractors.[34] It took until February 1870 for Poole and Scott to get estimates together: when they did, it emerged that completing the project would cost £4,795 for the contractors, with another £250 to Scott and £215 to Kaberry. This would raise the total cost to £30,840. On 19 February, the Treasury approved a new vote of £6,395. The Office of Works was clearly determined to finish the job, but questioned a number of points in the account, and was not ready to approve a new contract.[35]

Matters languished until July 1870, when the Office asked Scott to explain a number of items, including rent for No. 3 Poets' Corner, insurance payments, a payment of £140 to an engineer, R M Ordish, for designing the roof, and £4 10s for erecting scaffolding in the chapter house at Salisbury. Scott explained, but the board declined to pay for any of them. Scott replied in detail, stating that he had originally designed a timber roof, and that it was the First Commissioner who had requested it be of iron. The contract for the outstanding works was finally signed by Poole and Sons in November 1870. Work resumed after an interval of over a year.[36]

On 15 December, the Office wrote to Scott to ask if the work would be finished in time for the account to be signed off before 31 March 1871. He replied that it would. However, when March came, about £500-worth of work remained to be done, the main unfinished areas being the tiled floor ('the tiles are in progress of preparation'), and the restoration of the 'Great Doorway' (the inner portal) and of the outer doorways. The Office of Works went back to the Treasury, explaining the need to make provision for up to £1,500 for the work in the year 1871–72.[37]

There was a final series of exchanges between Scott, the Office of Works and the Treasury over his commission. Scott had asked for an additional £157 10s for the investigative works that he had undertaken at the outset. Mr Hunt of the Office of Works thought that it was an unusual case, and that Scott's request was 'fair and reasonable'. However, Scott seems to have used up whatever credit he had with Hunt's superiors. On 27 March 1871 the Office wrote referring to their letter of 29 January 1866 in which they had asked him to give a total estimate for his services, and declining to pay the £157 10s. Worse was to follow: on 31 March 1871, the Office wrote to him again, declining to reimburse him the £140 that he had paid Ordish for designing the iron roof and deducting the sum from his account.[38] Scott had spent his own time and money on the chapter house in good faith, and was the loser thereby to the tune of £297.

Progress on the chapter house moved towards completion. There is nothing more on the file until 7 August 1871, when Scott wrote to the Office of Works to inform them that there had been no practical necessity for a Clerk of Works since the beginning of July except for an 'occasional eye to the very trifling works which have been going on'. He recommended that Kaberry be regarded as paid off as of that date.

The Office of Works took no further notice of the case until 28 November, when it wrote to Scott to ask if the work was completed. There was no reply. On 7 January 1872 the Office wrote again. On 8 January, Scott replied that 'The work is now virtually complete. There is a little induration of stonework to do and some trifles which I have pointed out to the contractor, which can hardly take a week to effect.'

On 11 January 1872 the Office of Works confirmed to the Treasury that the restoration was complete for a final cost of £30,840. On 7 February Scott's office wrote to the Office of Works, to hand over the keys and confirm that the contract had been satisfactorily completed.[39] Scott and Poole had carried out a slow and meticulous restoration, lasting five years, probably longer than it had taken to build the chapter house in the first place.

The exterior

So far as the exterior of the building is concerned, what we see today is entirely nineteenth-century restoration, with extensive areas of twentieth-century re-facing. As Scott wrote,[40] little of the medieval design remained by the 1840s: 'Of the external details, scarcely a trace remains; decay and mutilation have brought their work to a final completion. Nor am I aware of any old prints or description which would aid in the rediscovery of the design. But I have recently spied out from the window of a neighbouring house a small portion of external tracery, which I had not seen before'[41] (fig 124). The building had probably originally been faced in Reigate stone, possibly with some dressings in Caen stone. Scott had chosen

Chilmark stone from near Salisbury, which he had used at Salisbury Cathedral, and specified in the estimates. The mullions and flanking shafts of the windows were originally of Purbeck marble, which Scott replaced with a mixture of Devonshire marble and grey Carboniferous limestone (probably Kilkenny marble). During the work he discovered evidence to suggest that the building once had pinnacles, which he reinstated conjecturally: 'I found among the debris buried in the late work evidence of large octagonal pinnacles at the angles which, when once discovered, the true principles of restoration demanded to be reproduced.'[42] If there were pinnacles they are likely to have been fourteenth-century additions to the structure, contemporary with the flying buttresses (p 10). However, Scott subsequently acknowledged that he had been obliged, for lack of evidence, to introduce elements of conjectural restoration: 'I know of no parts which are conjecturally restored but the following: the external parapet, the pinnacles, the gables of the buttresses, and the roof.'[43]

The buttresses

The chapter house's flying buttresses are such a prominent feature that it is surprising to find that Scott makes no reference to them in either of his books. Lethaby, writing in the 1920s, noted that although the Salisbury chapter house internally follows the model of Westminster quite closely, it is without flying buttresses. He noted the irregularities in the layout of the Westminster chapter house buttresses, that the arches differ in their spans, and their plinths do not range with that of the main building. Lethaby concluded that the chapter house had been constructed without flying buttresses, and depended for the stability of its vault on the 'chainage' of iron bars, spanning between the top of the central pillar and vault-springers.[44] The fliers were added in 1377 (p 10).

When Scott arrived, he found one of the buttresses was missing, having been removed in 1707 by Wren (fig 33). He reinstated this, and re-faced the others. The buttresses had been given pyramidal caps in the eighteenth century: Scott replaced these with the present steep gables, acknowledging that they were among the elements that he had restored conjecturally.[45]

The roof

Scott's steeply pitched roof is a prominent feature of the abbey, but it has been much criticized. Scholars have tended to think that Scott was mistaken, and that the building originally had a low-pitched roof. The closest medieval exemplar, the Salisbury chapter house, which was evidently modelled on Westminster, has always had a low-pitched roof (figs 99 and 107). Furthermore, one of the earliest known views of the Westminster chapter house, on Agas's map of 1633, shows a low-pitched roof (p 24). There is no archaeological evidence either way, and the flying buttresses do not constitute evidence, as they are evidently conceived to pick up the loads generated by the vault, not by any roof structure. Surprisingly, Scott did not refer to the matter, and so we cannot be sure why he opted for a steep roof, but it should be remembered that, at this date, the chapter house was almost hidden behind the Georgian houses of Old Palace Yard, with only an oblique view of it open. Maybe he thought a high roof would help the chapter house to 'read' effectively, and hold its own against the much higher abbey church (see also p 98).

The design of the roof was the subject of some dispute between Scott and the Office of Works, and, in August 1870, he wrote to the Office explaining how matters had developed.[46] His drawings initially showed a timber roof, but the First Commissioner had asked for the frame to be of iron. Scott did not feel capable of designing this himself and approached an engineer. This was Rowland Mason Ordish (1824–86), a highly regarded structural engineer with great expertise in designing iron structures. He had worked for the celebrated firm of Fox, Henderson and Company while they were building the Crystal Palace, both the first version in Hyde Park and the rebuilt version at Sydenham, and on Birmingham New Street station. Since 1858 he had been in independent practice, and, in 1866–68, he was assisting W H Barlow with the detailing of the great roof of St Pancras station, then the widest clear-span roof in existence. Scott had been confirmed as the architect for St Pancras early in 1866, and would have met Ordish on that project. From then on, Ordish became Scott's favoured consulting engineer for iron structures.[47] Ordish made a drawing for Scott, 'of which I did not fully approve.' He then produced a second design, which Scott said would have been too costly. This was probably the design shown in the surviving contract drawing (fig 134). Scott asked him for a third design, 'the principal object being to relieve the central pillar from the weight of the vaulting. This was most effectively carried out.'[48]

No evidence has been found for the actual construction of the iron roof, or of the foundry which produced the ironwork: no foundry marks are visible on it. In July 1870, with the roof complete, the Office of Works questioned a number of items in Scott's account, including the £140 fee to Ordish for 'design & estimate for iron roofing.' Scott gave the explanation of Ordish's fee summarized above. In March 1871, the Office of Works cited legal precedents and ruled that the fee should be paid

Fig 137 Chapter house roof void: vertical view towards the apex. *Photograph*: © English Heritage Photo Library

from the architect's commission. So Ordish's £140 was deducted from Scott's account with the Office.[49]

The roof void is an impressive space, though not a trace of medieval masonry is visible. The roof frame essentially consists of eight very long, raking principals of cast iron (17.5 m), made up of three sections bolted together. Each sits on a fine cast-iron base. The uprights are tied together by six tiers of iron purlins, heavy castings with thick flanges, and holes cast into the webs to reduce their weight. This framework carries long timber rafters, which in turn carry the boards over which the lead is laid (figs 137 and 138).

As we have seen, Scott asked Ordish to 'relieve the central pillar of the weight of the vaulting', and his means of doing this was to suspend eight wrought-iron hangers from his cast-iron principal rafters, running down to an iron shoe or plate, hidden under a layer of concrete above the central pillar. Lethaby wrote that 'his engineer [Ordish] has hung up the vault to the iron roof,'[50] and this is what it looks like, though we cannot be certain whether these tie rods are actually taking any of the weight of the vault (fig 139).

Fig 138 Chapter house roof: detail of the iron frame at wall-top level. *Photograph*: © English Heritage Photo Library

Fig 139 Chapter house roof: the top of the vault, iron frame and suspension rods, which disappear into a layer of concrete above the central pillar. The ring-shaped concrete feature is there to brace the vaulting ribs, and is not really part of the suspension system, despite the rods passing through it. *Photograph*: © English Heritage Photo Library

The windows

The chapter house's windows, magnificent in scale and design, are of great significance in the history of Gothic architecture in England (figs 50 and 63). They are huge in scale, being 5.95 m wide and 11.6 m high, the main lights being 1.3 m wide and the circular lights 3.0 m in diameter. During the renovation of the record office in 1751 they had been horribly mutilated. Five windows had had their tracery partly removed, the central mullion apparently being left *in situ*, and filled with brickwork to form two small arched windows: some of the historic views record what remained *in situ* (figs 33 and 38). In two sides the tracery had been cut away. On the eighth side, though, the blind window remained visible, and Scott wrote:

> The windows are almost entirely walled up, though a considerable part of the tracery, no doubt, remains imbedded. Their design is, however, readily ascertainable, one of them being a blank, owing to one face of the octagon being in contact with the transept of the church: a nobler four-light window could hardly be found.[51]

One might have thought that some of the moulded jambs of the windows would have survived for re-use, but Scott's remarks, in his letter of October 1869, show that that was not the case.[52]

The only known photograph of the restoration in progress shows the south-east face of the chapter house with its window and flanking buttresses standing as rebuilt, with what seem to be great voids on either side, suggesting that the whole of the window-arches had been rebuilt (fig 136). We cannot be sure how much medieval masonry remains in the window-jambs, but Scott's restoration was certainly very extensive.

Scott found the window on the west side over the door blocked up, and made an interesting discovery: from its sill it could be seen to have had five, rather than four, lights, 'no doubt to avoid the stumped look it might have had from being so much shortened'. On taking out the blocking stones, Scott found that they were the moulded ribs of the lost vaulting, 'carefully packed, like wine-bottles in a bin, with their moulded sides inwards.'[53] Subsequently, further evidence emerged for the original design of the west window: it turned out that the ferramenta had been made for a four-, not a five-light window (see further, p 94). They had been retained when it was rebuilt, and then walled up. Scott attributed the window's reconstruction with five lights to Abbot Bircheston in the fourteenth century, but he restored the window to its presumed original form, with four lights, which maintains the overall rhythm of the wall-design better (compare figs 132 and 140).[54] The glazing of the windows with pictorial scenes, long urged by Scott, was carried out in stages from 1882 onwards to designs by Clayton and Bell (fig 230). Initially, the windows were all filled with clear glass.

The outer portal

Scott seems to have found the outer entrance in the east cloister walk in a more legible condition than it is today, but in a sad state of decay: 'The tympanum is exquisitely decorated with scroll-work, and formerly contained a sitting statue (probably of the Virgin and infant Saviour) under a niche, and supported on either side by angels, which yet remain, and the more perfect of which is very beautiful. This doorway was magnificently decorated with colour and gold, traces of which are still clearly visible'.[55]

This is one of the instances that demonstrates Scott's concern to preserve original fabric. He did not replace a single stone, but had Poole indurate the portal, with great care, claiming that the operation had been 'perfectly successful', leaving a hard, sound surface. Nevertheless, the tympanum has since been covered in whitewash. Little of the detail visible in John Carter's engraving of 1782 is now visible, nor that of a drawing of 1873 (fig 141), and it is hard to be sure how much survives beneath the limewash.

The outer vestibule

As we have noted, Scott reinstated the medieval day stair as the access to the library in 1853, enabling him to remove the stairs and partition walls from the outer vestibule. The space was restored and the missing area of vaulting was reconstructed with such care that one has to look carefully to pick out the nineteenth-century work.

The inner vestibule

At the far end of the outer vestibule, a double portal leads to the higher inner vestibule. This had suffered relatively little, but had had a timber staircase and mezzanine inserted into it (fig 123). When these were removed, the medieval masonry was found to be well-preserved, and this is probably the least altered area of the whole chapter house. The three-light window to the south had been destroyed, but Scott reconstructed the design from archaeological evidence.

Fig 140 Chapter house: the interior, as rebuilt. Note that the west window was reconstructed with four lights, rather than the five shown in the 1855 proposal (fig 132). *Drawing*: by 'F W', and published by the *Illustrated London News*, 29 March 1873, page 296

Fig 141 Chapter house: the outer portal, seen from the east cloister. The masonry above the central pedestal was replaced when a memorial tablet was removed. *Drawing*: F G Knight, 1873; after Lethaby 1906, fig 13

The inner portal

Scott particularly admired the great double archway leading from the inner vestibule to the chapter house proper, but, when he first visited in 1849, the central column had been lost and parts of the jambs were encased in panelling. The investigations were laborious and difficult, 'giving one more the look of a master chimney-sweeper than an architect.'[56] On the inner side of the archway, Scott found the figure of the Virgin from the Annunciation, sealed behind the panelling, and realized that it belonged with the figure of the Archangel Gabriel, which was already standing in the vestibule (see further, pp 174–5). Recognizing their great importance, he reinstated the figures in their correct positions on the west wall (fig 142).

Scott pronounced himself 'unable to ascertain'

whether the portal had open tracery or a central sculpture. However, the antiquary John Carter, writing in 1799, suggested otherwise: 'This double archway has had its dividing column in the centre with nearly all its open tracery (in the manner of the Chapter Houses at Wells and Southwell) cut away.'[57] Nevertheless, Scott allowed himself to make his own aesthetic judgement here. In his reconstruction drawing of 1855 he drew a figure of Christ in Majesty over the dividing column, and this is what he built when it came to the actual restoration (fig 132). Probably no other feature of his work has been so much criticized: almost all the comparative architectural evidence suggests that the circle should have been left open (fig 144). Iconographically, the resulting design makes little sense. As Lethaby pointed out, the figure of Christ bears no relationship to the Annunciation composition. The censing angels in the spandrels, part of

Fig 142 Chapter house: the inner portal, seen from the main chamber. Scott's incorporation of the figure of Christ in the quatrefoil is generally agreed to be a mistake. There would almost certainly have been no figure here in the original design, and it makes nonsense of the iconography because the thirteenth-century angels, censing the figures of the Archangel Gabriel and the Virgin Mary, have their backs turned towards Christ. *Photograph*: © Dean and Chapter of Westminster

the original design, turn their backs on Christ, as they are censing the Annunciation figures. The figure of Christ is finely carved, but looks inescapably Victorian, especially given its proximity to Gabriel and the Virgin Mary to either side (fig 142).

The central pillar

When the chapter house's vault was removed in 1751, the central pillar of Purbeck marble was left in place, and the new floor added above, resting radial beams, which sat

Fig 143 Chapter house: detail of the Purbeck marble capital of the central pillar in 1950, showing the stiff-leaf foliage, the subtle piecing-in of repairs to the abacus moulding by Scott's craftsmen, and the original iron hooks installed in the thirteenth century to carry tie bars. *Photograph*: English Heritage. NMR

upon it (fig 123). Scott found the pillar to be out of true, and the estimates made specific provision for it being righted for the modest-seeming sum of £9. He referred to the pillar and the eight hooks at its capital, hypothesizing that they were a temporary arrangement, 'intended for security during the progress of the works.'[58] The central core of the pillar is only 33 cm (13 in) in diameter, and the eight minor shafts 107 mm (4¼ in) in diameter.

Despite suggestions to the contrary, Scott did not replace the central pillar, although it had apparently developed a lean and had to be straightened. Lethaby thought that the existing capital was 'probably a copy of the original', but it, too, is original and was carefully repaired by Scott (fig 143; p 11). He also retained the iron hooks (p 98). Lethaby thought that Scott had been mistaken about the iron bars being temporary, pointing out that eight bars of forged iron 30 feet long would have been very costly. He believed that they would have been a permanent part of the structure, citing Salisbury, where the original tie bars remained *in situ* into the nineteenth century (fig 144).[59]

The vault

The original vault had been completely removed in 1751, but Scott had ample evidence for its design, as the vault springers survived both on the outer walls and at the top of the central column. A major design element of Scott's vault was the banding in the webs, made with contrasting colours of stone (frontispiece). He probably did not have any direct evidence of this, and may have extrapolated this element of the design from the vaults in the inner vestibule and the cloister. At any rate, he showed hints of banding in his 1855 drawing (fig 132), as well as stencilling, and it was allowed for in his specification, where he prescribed '6″ filling of beds', meaning that the webs are 6 inches thick, in 'hard grey block chalk and firestone properly worked in voussoirs and set in cement.' He also erected scaffolding in Salisbury Cathedral chapter house specifically in order to 'guide us in the construction of the lost vaulting' – presumably to check angles and dimensions.[60]

Seen from above, the vault is a very substantial piece of

Fig 144 Chapter house interior: the completed restoration, including the stained glass. This drawing, originally by W S Weatherley, was amended by Lethaby to correct what he considered to be Scott's mistakes. Lethaby has added the eight radiating tie-bars at the springing of the vault, and blacked out Scott's figure of Christ in Majesty in the quatrefoil of the inner portal. *Drawing*: after Lethaby 1925, fig 58

masonry, with a curious detail on the upper side of the springers, where small internal flying buttresses help to support the bases upon which the pinnacles stand. Those bases partly project into the conoids and have no direct support from below (fig 145). In the centre, over the pillar, there is a layer of concrete: eight iron hangers, suspended from the roof frame, disappear into it. It seems, as Lethaby noted, that Scott wanted some added security and has hung the vault from the roof-frame. It would be interesting to know whether there are any tensile forces passing through the tie-rods.

The wall arcading

The wall arcading around the chapter house is an important element of its design, with parallels in most of the other surviving polygonal chapter houses in the British Isles. Prior to 1860, the arcading was entirely concealed

Fig 145 Chapter house roof: detail of a vault pocket, showing one of the eight trapezoidal projections inside the angle between the outer walls. This carries the foot of a cast iron principal (see fig 138). Note the support given by the three diminutive flying buttresses which press against the groins of the vault. *Photograph*: Warwick Rodwell © Dean and Chapter of Westminster

behind presses and panelling, though Scott must have secured access to portions of it in order to have made his drawing of 1855. Scott found most of the arcading preserved behind the panelling:

> The walls below the windows are occupied by arcaded stalls with trefoiled heads. The five which occupy the eastern side are of superior richness and more deeply recessed. Their capitals, carved in Purbeck marble, usually with the square diaper so frequent in the church, but, in one instance, with a beautifully executed pattern of roses.[61]

However, four doorways had been cut through the arcading to give access to the little offices added on the outside – two on the east wall, through either end of the 'Judgement' panel, and two in the north-east wall. A fifth door had been made through the north wall to provide a new external entrance from Poets' Corner. Scott and his contractor blocked the doors and made good the walling so carefully that it is difficult to pick out the patches (fig 58).

The survival of the medieval wall paintings might lead one to think that the wall arcading had survived as well, but this was not so. Lethaby recounts a conversation with one of Scott's assistants, W S Weatherley. It seems that the mouldings of the arcade had all been hacked back to allow the seventeenth- and eighteenth-century presses to be fitted, the heads, parts of the arches, and the fronts of the capitals being horribly mutilated. Scott restored the damaged masonry, piecing in new stonework:

> the late Mr S. Weatherley … pointed out to me that only an inch or so of the inner part of most of them was really old, and that the rest had been spliced on with great accuracy. Mr Weatherley gave me a sheet of profiles that had been made in 1868 from the remaining parts by the clerk of works, John Kaberry … Mr Weatherley also wrote that the 'detailing and superintendence' of the work was confided to the younger Gilbert Scott by Sir Gilbert.[62]

If one looks at the mural arcades very closely today, the joints where Scott's new work is spliced onto the old can just be made out. It is exceptionally fine work, emphasizing both Scott's care to preserve every piece of medieval stonework that he could, and his concern that this restoration should be absolutely faithful.

The mural paintings

Although their existence was already known, the wall paintings – like the arcading, the statues and the tile floor

– had been completely concealed and were not fully revealed to view after Scott's investigative work (chapter 11). In *Gleanings*, he gives quite a detailed description of the Judgement scene on the east wall, but makes only a passing reference to the Apocalypse paintings on the southern walls.[63] It is clear that Scott took a profound interest in the Judgement painting, but was not much impressed by the Apocalypse paintings, and did not show them in his 1855 reconstruction. Scott is not known to have carried out any restoration work to the murals: this was done much later, under the auspices of the Ministry of Works (p 196).

The tile pavement

The record office had a timber floor, which concealed the great tile pavement and, although the tiles were being studied and published by antiquaries from 1842, it was Scott who revealed the full extent and beauty of the floor (see chapter 12). He put the large provisional sum of £400 for repair of the floor in his schedule of work of 1866. A number of the tiles were missing, and Scott had them replicated, probably by Herbert Minton and Sons at Stoke-on-Trent, though positive proof of this has not been found. The repair of the floor was the last major element to be completed. On 8 March 1871, Scott reported to the Office of Works that £500-worth of work remained to be done, including restoration of the floor: 'the tiles are in progress of preparation'.[64] The work was executed with remarkable fidelity to the original designs, although the nineteenth-century tiles can easily be distinguished (fig 146).

Summary

Scott said of his work at Westminster Abbey that: 'This is an appointment which has afforded me more pleasure than any other which I have held.'[65] His restoration of the chapter house was the most important element of it. He had been obliged to replace a very high proportion of the stonework – probably more than he expected. Some elements, such as the pinnacles and parapet, may be described as speculative. Others, notably the tall roof and the figure of Christ in Majesty over the inner portal, probably departed from the medieval design and have been much criticized. Nevertheless, taken all in all, Scott's restoration had been a faithful one, undertaken with immense care and a sincere wish to recover the original design (frontispiece). Very few of Scott's contemporaries could have matched this achievement, and it is well to remember that he was a champion for archaeological

Fig 146 Chapter house pavement: detail showing how the nineteenth-century replacement 'griffin' tiles (design 7) stand out because of their bright colour, shinier surface and relatively unworn condition.
Photograph: © Dean and Chapter of Westminster

understanding and recording in an age when clients were not necessarily sympathetic. In a letter of 24 May 1872 to Lord John Thynne, he made an *apologia* for his approach:

> If I am sometimes troublesome in this matter of archaeology, I must plead that it is a duty I owe to the public and to future generations … These antiquities had been less attended to by my predecessors, but I have the pleasant pride of feeling that the manner in which I have been permitted by Providence and by my kind clients to bring them to light during the last 23 years will earn for all, for clients and for their officer, the gratitude of those who follow us.[66]

Posterity has tended to temper gratitude with irritation when contemplating Scott's work here, but that we can appreciate the chapter house as a great work of medieval architecture at all is thanks to him and his excellent contractors. Sir Nikolaus Pevsner provided a notably balanced judgement: 'A last word on Scott and his much attacked restorations. There is one thing at least that ought to be remembered. He found the chapter house full of bookcases, staircases, galleries … If we have an idea today of its noble original beauty, Scott has given it us.'[67]

The sculptural decoration of the Westminster chapter house portals

Richard Foster and Pamela Tudor-Craig

10

This chapter seeks to place the sculptural enrichment of the two main portals in the context of the creation of the chapter house as a place of wise deliberation and judgement: in the words of the 1266 *Customary* commissioned by Abbot Richard de Ware, 'the workshop of the Holy Spirit, in which the sons of God are gathered together in order to be reconciled with him'.[1] Not only was it the centre of government for a great Benedictine monastery but, in the eyes of the monarch who rebuilt the abbey, it also served as the spiritual arm of his palace. David Carpenter has said, and researches everywhere suggest it, that whatever the monks may have thought, Henry III intended this chapter house to be a theatre from which he could 'address the realm'.[2] As such, the king himself must have taken an active part in shaping its iconography.

Every fragmentary clue to the overall scheme is, therefore, of vital importance. Fortunately, written and drawn evidence survives to supplement the present visual record. The fragile carving – and even more ephemeral colour of this originally sumptuous monument – has suffered nearly five hundred years of deterioration (fig 5). Of deliberate defacement at the Reformation or later, there is relatively little. The angels either side of the tympanum of the doorway from the cloister have lost their heads. Enough remains of the southern one to show that it was a clean break. Their first description, cited below, suggests that all the figures here had been beheaded before 1682. On the portal between the vestibule and the chapter house, six heads – one on the outer and five on the inner figurative jambs – have also been surgically removed. The statues of the Virgin and the Archangel Gabriel, the glories

of the interior, miraculously kept their heads, as did their attendant censing angels. However, the impact of London's atmosphere in the seventeenth, eighteenth and early nineteenth centuries upon paintwork and the native Reigate stone – not the most resilient in the first place – has blunted, in particular, the outer cloister doorway. A battery of well-intentioned remedies applied since the mid-nineteenth century to halt decay (for which see appendix B) may have helped indoor surfaces, but was externally disastrous.

The outer portal

From the reign of Edward VI the chapter house was used by the Crown as a repository for records of the Exchequer and other courts, the forerunner of the Public Record Office (chapter 8). The chapter house continued to serve this function until the public records were gradually transferred to their new home in Chancery Lane, from 1859. During this long period, the northernmost of the cloister doorway's twin arches was blocked up and a window punched through to light a new internal staircase. The partly blocked southern arch was provided with another window and a gate, the fastening of which probably protected the sculpture within the chapter house from vandalism. The general disposition is discernible in a view of the cloister's east walk drawn by John Carter in 1779 (fig 147).[3] Once the main figures of the great tympanum had been decapitated, the outer doorway was ignored by both vandals and scholars. The topic of its figured voussoirs – the ancestry of Christ – was inoffensive to both Catholic and Protestant. By 1682, however, with the ailing Charles II hesitating on the

Fig 147 East cloister and outer portal of the chapter house. *Drawing*: in watercolour by John Carter, 1779; *photograph*: © Pamela Tudor-Craig; WAM Langley Coll VI.5(4)

brink of Catholicism, it became politically acceptable to study the remains of the Catholic imagery around the cloister. In an openly nostalgic work, Henry Keepe, a member of the abbey choir, gave us the first description of the outer tympanum: 'Over the entrance to the Chapter House was placed the statue of the Blessed Virgin and Our Saviour in her arms and two angels on each side, all richly enamelled and set forth with gold and blue, some vestigial of all which are still remaining whereby to judge of the former splendour and beauty thereof.'[4] It was before this figure of the Virgin that Abbot Ware's *Customary* of 1266 required the monks to pay homage whenever they passed.[5] The 'former splendour and beauty' of the doorway may be reflected in a payment of £25, noted among the royal outgoings between 22 February and 19 April 1253, for 'task work at the entry to the Chapter House'.[6] This unusually large sum may have covered the whole complex of the doorway and its painting.

A vivid impression of the original colouring of the tympanum comes from the 1802 description by James Peller Malcolm, who could still see 'the arch over the entrance most magnificently adorned with carving, gilding and painting. On either side are three pillars, between them foliage. One range of the mouldings contains circular scrolls which have been gilt and the depths coloured black. Another, scarlet … A plane between them has been painted with white foliage on a red ground, and the outside ones in compartments of golden flowers.'[7] The doorway's gilding seems to have been a particularly impressive feature: the writer of an 1805 guidebook to London recommended a visit to the abbey's east cloister 'on account of the beautiful arched entrance to the chapter-house with which it is adorned. Every part of this magnificent portal is exquisitely carved and gilt, and so enriched by ornament, that its beauties are only to be described by the pencil.'[8] An undated sketch attributed to William Lethaby, surveyor of the fabric from 1906 to 1928, shows the central corbel still with lively indications of colour, which may have been extrapolated from tiny fragments visible only from a scaffold (fig 148).[9] The survival into the twentieth century of the merest trace of colour on this tympanum would be the more remarkable in that it was adhering to crumbling Reigate stone (p 2).

Though some vestige of the central figure of the Virgin and Child was still apparent to Keepe's keen eye in 1682, what little was left of her had to give way, some forty years later, to a monumental plaque. In 1723, John Dart recorded: 'Over the door going to the Library on a white marble table the monument to Elizabeth, d. 3 July 1720 aged 35 by her truly afflicted husband Thomas Moore gent., Librarian to this church.'[10] Elizabeth Moore's monumental plaque was still *in situ* when John Preston Neale wrote his description of the abbey in 1823.[11] Hence, it must have been Edward Blore or George Gilbert Scott who re-sited it at the southern end of the east cloister walk, just beyond the junction of the thirteenth-century cloister and the ancient passage, the 'dark entry', leading to the little (or infirmary) cloister. So it is futile to search for evidence of the lost Virgin in the stones making up the present blank centre of the tympanum since they have been twice disturbed: once in 1723, when the carved

surface was scraped back to insert the monumental plaque, and again when that plaque was removed sometime during the years 1849 to 1878.

Our knowledge of the history of this portal is not confined, though, to notes on colour or records of attempts to halt decay. There is a large and essential portfolio of visual studies, to which the greatest and earliest contribution is that of John Carter (1748–1817), the first and most careful antiquary to record all the best English Gothic sculpture surviving to his time.[12] His position as draughtsman to the Society of Antiquaries, held from March 1784, gave him an authority that was only imperilled when his opposition to the cavalier treatment of Gothic architecture and detail by James Wyatt brought him into disrepute with the establishment in 1795–97.[13] Nonetheless, between 1779 and 1808, Carter spent much time studying the 'superb' outer doorway from the cloister to the chapter house. 'In these cloisters' he wrote, 'I have passed, perhaps, some of the most rational hours of my life.'[14] In his *Ancient Painting and Sculpture in England*, Carter published the first major study, dated 1782, of the outer doorway from the cloister, the key to our understanding of it (fig 149).[15] A discrete 'reconstruction' of the tympanum, printed in 1808,[16] shows that Carter saw beyond the post-Reformation interventions and offered

Fig 148 Outer portal: the Virgin's pedestal, showing the polychromy surviving at the beginning of the twentieth century. *Drawing*: sketch by William Lethaby; *photograph*: © Richard Foster; WAM: CN 4.1.3iii

what is probably the most accurate interpretation of the evidence we have. His ghost of a standing figure of the Virgin and Child is less inadequate than any other (fig 150).

Carter correctly indicated that the corbel on which the Virgin stood had subsidiary supports on either side. He did not, however, infer that these secondary corbels must have supported a pair of colonnettes, which, in their turn, would have held a trefoil canopy above the Virgin's head.

Such a canopy is suggested by the resetting of stonework in a triangular formation reaching the apex of the tympanum, shown clearly in a beautifully detailed measured drawing of 1873 by Frederick Knight (fig 141).[17] Six major sculptures standing on corbels were disposed along the north facade of the abbey. Those needed no canopies, since they stood beneath shallow arched recesses. On the other hand, the figure of St Faith painted on the

Fig 149 Outer portal as it appeared in 1782. *Drawing*: John Carter; after Carter 1786, following page 6

Fig 150 Outer portal: measured elevation omitting secondary intrusions. *Drawing*: John Carter, 1808; after Carter 1795–1814, II, plate 5

east wall of her chapel stands on a corbel and does have a canopy with slender columns. To the objection that St Faith is 'later' – though how much later is still debated – it can be countered that all the major statues of the west front of Wells Cathedral stand in similar tabernacles, and probably date from the years 1220 to 1248. By the convention of the twelfth and thirteenth centuries the figure of the Virgin ought to have been a seated figure: she is the *Sedes Sapientia*. However, the position of the canopy (if we may trust the triangular formation of stones to indicate its position) is sufficiently far above her corbel to

require a life-size standing figure, and the shallowness and plan of her corbel could hardly accommodate such a figure seated on a throne.[18]

More in doubt are the gestures of the standing angels either side of the Virgin. As intrepid as thirteenth-century artists were in swinging censers within inches of the figure venerated,[19] there is scarcely room here for them to do so without knocking into the tabernacle. They might instead have been carrying candlesticks.[20] Lethaby was of this opinion, enlisting the prototype of the Virgin's door at Amiens and the Madonna page by the eponymous master in British Library MS Arundel 83.[21] It is possible that the putative censers or candlesticks, as well as the colonnettes of the tabernacle, were made of gilt metal.

In fact, the whole design of the tympanum, with figures in very high relief set against a background covered in coils of stiff-leaf foliage, strongly recalls the decorative conventions of contemporary metalwork. The reliquary cross of St Andrew in the Cathedral Museum at Regensburg, dated c 1250, furnishes a comparison.[22] Typically Germanic figures, agitated and with angular folds, are set against the background of a curling foliate trail. As this refers to the Cross as the Tree of Life, so the example at Westminster is linked to the Tree of Jesse, which springs in the voussoirs surrounding the tympanum.[23] The idea of naturalistic figures set against colourful foliage sprays may have originated in enamelwork, as demonstrated in the thirteenth-century Rhenish reliquary of St Vincent at Ally in Cantal.[24] Many of the relics listed in the Westminster inventories were once housed in receptacles similar to surviving Continental examples.[25] The assimilation of precious metalwork into the decorative language of Henry III's Westminster Abbey has been observed by scholars from William Lethaby to Paul Binski and Christopher Wilson. This portal was no exception.

Another feature where the facility of metalwork might have led the way is in the suggestion of one element overlapping another. Carter observed that the wings of the tympanum's angels must have invaded the territory of the inner order of the voussoirs.[26] That inner order is composed of stones carved with the most technically ambitious display of stiff-leaf sculpture. Each block – having been shaped to fit its curved position along the arch and given a highly rounded outer surface – was placed on its end and hollowed out. The tunnel through the stone was then painted and the outer surface carved down towards it with an elaborate composition of stiff leaves. Apertures were cut between leaves and background to produce a filigree of foliage with the concave coloured ground showing through. This technique is demonstrated in a single voussoir preserved in the abbey's museum collection (fig 151).[27] Its outer surface has broken away, exposing the tunnel, which is painted red, possibly as a base for gilding. The inner voussoirs still framing the cloister tympanum are in a similar condition, but without the colour. There are further essays in this technique on the north side of the inner doorway, but they are much restored. It appears also in the east cloister at Wells, where it is found on the monumental doorway opening into the south transept, and on the small doorway leading out of the cloister towards the bishop's palace. The former doorway dates from the late 1180s;[28] the latter from c 1220.[29]

The design function of these projecting open-work voussoirs was to ease the transition from the plane of the recessed tympanum background to the foreground of the arch. As Carter surmised, it follows that the furls of the angels' wings must have jutted forward in front of these voussoirs, and that the heads of the angels, between their wing-bearing shoulders, must have come forward further still, indeed have been carved in the round. This is confirmed by the decapitated neck of the southern angel, of which we have the whole cross-section. The heads of both must have leaned forwards and slightly sideways towards the central Virgin.

A previously unpublished drawing of c 1810–13 takes next place after Carter in the sequence of antiquarian studies of this outer doorway (fig 152). It was attributed to John Flaxman by Edward Croft-Murray and may, in fact, stand as the first conjectural 'restoration' looking towards the intention of realization.[30] Flaxman had ample opportunity to study the chapter house doorway: he was a member of the committee overseeing James Wyatt's restoration of Henry VII's chapel and sculptor of two monuments within the abbey.[31] Croft-Murray believed the 'JW' at the bottom of this drawing to be a collector's initials. Since Flaxman praised Wyatt's work in Henry VII's chapel,

Fig 151 Westminster Abbey Museum: hollowed stiff-leaf voussoir in the lapidary collection. *Photograph*: © Richard Foster

it is possible he gave this sketch to Wyatt, and these are James Wyatt's initials. In which case the drawing would have to be no later than 1813, the year Wyatt died. In 1810 Flaxman had been appointed professor of sculpture to the Royal Academy, and, in the following year, he presented the first of a series of lectures, published in 1829. It was his thesis that, in the reign of Henry III, our native sculpture reached the level of classical art and had been further elevated by the spirit of Christianity. This was the context in which his imaginative attempt to visualize the original design of the cloister doorway tympanum was set. However, the relative scale of these tall angels and Flaxman's small Virgin, with two extra little angels kneeling at her feet on what are, in fact, the bases for the colonnettes, is not convincing. Nevertheless, his pen and wash sketch is perhaps the first of many aspirations to reinvent the sculpture.

John Preston Neale's drawing of the portal in 1820 is a slightly re-worked version of Carter's, with heads on the angels, but no further additions.[32] George Gilbert Scott's long regime, from 1849 to 1878, saw several attempts to suggest alternative figures for the tympanum – among them a print of 1855 putting what appears to be a decapitated deacon in the centre,[33] and an elaborately coloured reconstruction, made before Scott opened up the blocked northern arch, which has a giant figure of St Peter on the Virgin's pedestal.[34] Fortunately, none of these suggestions was realized.[35]

The two fragments of carved figures now on the Virgin's pedestal appear in a drawing published in 1881 in *The Graphic*,[36] but are not seen in the earlier nineteenth-

Fig 152 Outer portal: reconstruction of the tympanum sculptures. *Drawing*: in pen and wash, probably by John Flaxman *c* 1810–13; *photograph*: © Richard Foster; Society of Antiquaries Library, Westminster Abbey Red Portfolio, fol 27

century studies. These rather pathetic stones may have been found by Scott in dismantling the staircase to the library, which occupied the outer vestibule until his time. Scott argued enthusiastically that 'when any part of the walls have to be taken down every piece of wrought stone found imbedded therein should be carefully set aside, as from these the most valuable authority for the restoration of earlier parts is often obtained. An original detail (especially in carving) though partially decayed or mutilated is infinitely more valuable than the most skilful attempt at its restoration.'[37] Having removed the monument to Elizabeth Moore, the painful gap above the corbel will have craved a feature. Carved fragments newly found may have conveniently presented themselves as a

temporary expedient. The lower of them seems to be from a figure of the later Middle Ages. However, perched above it are the remains of a possibly twelfth-century figure. They have survived here for more than 120 years.

For the outer voussoirs of this doorway we are, once again, indebted to Carter. On those occasions when we can make the comparison, it is clear that Carter's published engravings are sometimes worked up for public consumption beyond the evidence of the weathered sculpture, recorded more accurately in his preparatory drawings. In this instance, we are fortunate in having his original drawings on tracing paper, probably dating from 1781–82.[38] The first figure above the springing of the arch on each side shows Jesse with the stem of his tree growing from his loins – still discernible in the stonework. Above him, on both sides, is King David playing his harp (figs 153 and 154). The harps are now quite weathered away. Carter suggests another four crowned figures on the south side and three on the north. There might have been more crowns. In 1803, Malcolm wrote of the voussoirs: 'Within them are twenty statues. I recognized the Blessed Virgin &

Fig 153 Outer portal: King David. *Drawing*: pencil on paper by John Carter, probably 1782; *photograph*: © Richard Foster, WAM Langley Coll VI.B.15 (19)

Fig 154 Outer portal: voussoir showing King David. *Photograph*: © Richard Foster

Infant Jesus and King David. Fragments of paint and gilding adhere in parts enough to show their former splendour.'[39] Malcolm was referring to the uppermost voussoir on the south side, which may represent a woman and is still legible on Knight's measured drawing of 1873 (fig 141), which Lethaby considered the last cogent account of the tympanum. So the overall scheme of ten figures either side of the arch conveyed the ancestors of Christ, springing from Jesse and David. This strange arrangement of two Jesse trees, with the Virgin and Christ at the top, derived from the voussoirs of the Virgin portal at Amiens Cathedral, where they enclose a Last Judgement on the tympanum.[40] Direct borrowing from Amiens Cathedral in the design of Westminster, implying comings and goings by Westminster's master mason, Henry of Reims, has been suggested by Binski.[41]

Every cathedral in the Île de France built between St Denis in the 1140s and the later thirteenth century included in the sculptural programme of its portals or in the stained glass around its east end a representation of the Tree of Jesse. In the period up to c 1220, it was usually associated with the Coronation of the Virgin; later, as at Amiens, it might accompany the Last Judgement. At Reims, the coronation church, a single voussoir figure of Jesse, c 1245–55, confirms that the subject was intended for the west-front portals, but its completion was thwarted by long interruptions in building and changes of iconographic programmes. Here at Westminster, however, the subject is not confined to the voussoirs: it reaches its destination in the tympanum, where the Virgin and Child are the genealogical climax. Embowered in the leaves of the tree of life, they represent its flower and its fruit. The origin of the Tree of Jesse and its particular association with the Virgin Mary lies in some of the earliest of Christian exegesis on the prophecy from *Isaiah*: 'There shall come forth a rod out of the stem of Jesse, and a branch shall grow out of his roots: and the spirit of the Lord shall rest upon him, the spirit of wisdom and understanding, the spirit of counsel and might, the spirit of knowledge and the fear of the Lord'.[42] Tertullian (c 160 – c 220) made the connection in his *De Carne Christi*,[43] and the interpretation was followed by all the early Fathers. In his *Commentary on Isaiah* of c 410, St Jerome uses wordplay upon the Latin *virga* ('rod'), and *virgo* ('virgin') to reinforce the point: *nos autem virgam de Iesse sanctam Mariam virginem intelligamus*.[44]

Despite its importance in both Old and New Testaments, the Tree of Jesse was not illustrated before AD 1000.[45] The rising interest in the human descent of Christ during the twelfth century ran parallel to the new enquiry into secular genealogy and the birth of heraldry. The north doorway of the baptistery at Parma, of 1196, shows twelve kings with their names inscribed on scrolls or books. They are taken from the family tree given in the *Gospel of St Matthew*, who lists twenty-eight descendants from David to Joseph.[46] The *Gospel of St Luke* gives forty-one generations and agrees with Matthew only in giving Joseph the same grandfather.[47] Given such unpromising prime material, very few Jesse trees are specific. They range in length from the Hildesheim ceiling, with a hundred ancestors, and abbreviated trees, with just Jesse, David, Mary and Christ. A group of twelfth-century manuscripts with abbreviated trees from Cîteaux or Clairvaux suggest the influence of St Bernard's devotion to the Virgin.[48] In place of Christ's patriarchal and royal progenitors, interest shifted to the Lucan prophets who foretold the coming of the Saviour. A twelfth-century manuscript in the Bibliothèque Municipale de Douai[49] shows the central stem inhabited by Jesse, David and the Virgin and Christ, with Habakkuk, Solomon, a sibyl and Ezekiel to their left, and Daniel, John the Baptist, Isaiah and Jeremiah to their right.[50]

Emphasis on the Tree of Jesse as illustrating the transmission of wisdom through the prophets rather than by physical inheritance is stressed in British Library MS Arundel 44, a twelfth-century copy of the *Speculum Virginum*. The text, attributed to Conrad of Hirsau, provides for the religious instruction of maidens and takes the form of a dialogue between a nun and her spiritual mentor. Sixteen manuscript copies survive, so its popularity is evident.[51] Chapter eleven is devoted to an exposition of the seven gifts of the Holy Spirit. It opens with a Tree of Jesse and is more remarkable for the weight of its symbolic content than the felicity of its composition (fig 155).[52] The tree bursts into seven leaves for the gifts of the Holy Spirit; below stand the seven pillars of wisdom's house.[53] On the open book in the Virgin's hand is the phrase 'The Lord possessed me', an abbreviated quotation from *Proverbs*: 'The Lord possessed me [wisdom] in the beginning of his way, before his works of old'.[54] Since the proclamation of the feast of the Assumption by Pope Sergius in the seventh century, the text of *Ecclesiasticus* 24:3–21 was allotted to Mary. This passage, redolent with imagery of a fruitful plant, firmly linked her to the *virgo* of the *Vulgate*: 'I took root in an honourable people … I was exalted like a cedar in Libanus, and as a cypress tree upon the mountains of Hermon … my branches are the branches of honour and grace … I am the mother of fair love, and fear, and knowledge, and holy hope'. In minds contemporary with the chapter house there was, therefore, an association between the Tree of Jesse and the Virgin Mary, both as channels for holy wisdom – one through prophecy, the other through incarnation. We shall return to this theme. First, however, we must pass through the

Fig 155 Tree of Jesse from a twelfth-century *Speculum Virginum*. *Photograph*: © The British Library Board; BL MS Arundel 44, fol 114v

vestibules and approach the second of the chapter house's sculpted doorways.

The inner portal (western side)

On its vestibule (western) side, this doorway has an arch of two orders supported on three Purbeck shafts with stiff-leaf capitals. The outer of the orders has foliated voussoirs; the inner has voussoirs with a foliate trail inhabited by figures. Both foliage and figures have some well-judged replacement carving from the period of Scott's restoration. Less well-judged is his insertion of the double-sided sculpture of Christ enthroned, which fills the circular quatrefoil supported beneath the arch by a central pillar of Purbeck marble. This large quatrefoil would originally have been void, affording an impressive glimpse of the interior, as can still be seen at the chapter houses in Southwell Minster and Wells Cathedral. Scott's interpolation not only spoils the view and blocks the light into the vestibule, but also interrupts the iconography of the inner side of the doorway, discussed later. The central pillar and the tracery are replacements by Scott: both were almost completely lost by the end of the eighteenth century, according to Carter.[55]

On the northern side of the doorway, both jambs between the three shafts are filled with circles of deeply undercut stiff-leaf foliage. The south side has matching stiff-leaf foliage in the outer jamb, but the inner is more specifically enriched with a column of eleven small sculptured figures embowered in a deeply undercut foliate trail. This asymmetrical arrangement of the jambs – foliate one side and figured the other – has no obvious explanation. It is repeated on the chapter-house side, where the inner southern jamb has another eleven figures while the other jambs have the same conventionalized foliage as the vestibule side. The carving of the figures on both jambs is entirely original thirteenth-century work of extremely high craftsmanship (fig 156). Writing in 1906, Lethaby described them as 'lovely' and suggested the taking of 'large photographs would record much of value and beauty.'[56] Although some heads and attributes were lost well before Lethaby's observation, much sharp carving still remains today. The figures have gentle faces, delicately detailed feet, and hands with long curving fingers in the court style exemplified by the Westminster retable. Their drapery is flowing and deeply carved. Each is individualized to varying degrees by facial features, gestures and small details of costume. Our study of these figures has been helped greatly by the survival of plaster-cast copies of the jambs, now in the Victoria and Albert Museum.[57] These casts were certainly made before 1877,

and may have been taken as early as the 1830s (see appendix A). From them, many valuable details may be deciphered that have been blunted by the passing of a century-and-a-half, or more.

The uppermost figure of the jamb on the vestibule side portrays the Virgin seated beneath what was probably a pointed gable with a crenellated tower on either side. There is the suggestion of a small crown upon her head, though its decay precludes certainty. The fourth figure beneath the Virgin has long been recognized by his horned brow as Moses (fig 157),[58] though there is no suggestion of his other conventional attribute, the stone tablets. Although he is one of the better preserved figures, comparison between the patriarch's appearance now and in the nineteenth-century plaster-cast gives a sad measure of the loss of a powerful face that would once have deserved comparison with the vivid corbel heads in St Faith's chapel and the triforium gallery (fig 158). Indeed, this Moses must have been a

Fig 156 Inner portal, west face: door-jamb figure; plaster cast in the Victoria and Albert Museum. *Photograph*: © Richard Foster

worthy ancestor of Giovanni Pisano's mighty prophets on the west front of Siena Cathedral. The presence of Moses led Lethaby to think all the figures might be patriarchs, though their precise identification eluded him. In 1906 he wrote, 'At the bottom Adam seems to pluck a fruit; a little higher, Tubal Cain or some other holds the symbol of some craft'.[59] Nineteen years later, he was even less certain: 'None of the small figures can be identified, with the exception of one about the middle, which has the horns of Moses. One next below is half clothed and is putting his hose off or on; one near the bottom holds a square block; one near the top is clothed like a friar, or possibly a pilgrim; most are sleeping'.[60] In fact, the sculptures form a group rather more diverse and unusual.

The figure beneath Moses is naked to the waist and displays prominent ribs (fig 159). Closer examination shows him to be scraping his right shin with a curved object. The sharper detail of the Victoria and Albert

Museum plaster-cast reveals the fingers of his left hand splayed down his leg. Here is the figure of Job in his suffering, not adjusting his hose, but scratching his sores with a shard of pottery. At first glance, Job may be an unexpected presence. However, he can be found in another coronation church, and in a prestigious position. At Reims Cathedral, Job sits on his dunghill in the tympanum of the north portal. An association of Job with kingship can be traced, not in the Biblical text, but in *The Testament of Job*, a Hebrew poem written between the first centuries before and after Christ, and known to artists in the medieval period.[61] Here Job is said to have been not merely a rich man, but a king.[62] So his appearance among the mighty in the coronation churches of England and France is no coincidence. French manuscripts sometimes portray Job in royal robes and crowned, illustrating both the *Testament of Job* and his Biblical words: 'I put on righteousness, and it clothed me: my judgement was as a robe and a diadem.'[63] The opening folio of the *Book of Job* in a late-eleventh-century Bible from the Abbaye de la Sauve Majeure underlines this sentiment: Job is dressed as a king, but, instead of a sceptre, he holds the scales of justice (fig 160).[64] It was his dual role, as both penitential man and model of

Fig 157 Inner portal, west face: door-jamb figure of Moses; plaster cast in the Victoria and Albert Museum. *Photograph*: © Richard Foster

Fig 158 Inner portal: detail of the head of Moses; plaster cast in the Victoria and Albert Museum. *Photograph*: © Richard Foster

Fig 159 Inner portal, west face: door-jamb figure of Job; plaster cast in the Victoria and Albert Museum. *Photograph*: © Richard Foster

Fig 160 Job as king, in the *Bible de la Sauve Majeure*. *Photograph*: © Bibliothèque de Bordeaux MS 1, fol 250v

the righteous king, that justified Job's station in the doorway to the chapter house, a place of judgement and punishment. The prophet was, moreover, regarded as a type for Christ the Redeemer. Gregory the Great repeatedly refers to him as such in his sixth-century *Moralia in Job*, the work in which the pope set out the framework of the three levels governing medieval Biblical exegesis. Job was truly a type of Christ, since he prophesied of the Passion, not by words alone, but also by his own sufferings. The clay potsherd with which Job scrapes his sores represents the earthly form taken by Christ in order to scrape away the sins of humanity: 'For what is the potsherd in the hand of the Lord, but the flesh which He took of the clay of our nature? … It is hence that our Redeemer was come, as it were, to scrape the humour from our wounds'.[65] At the end of the twelfth century, Gregory's exegesis on Job was summarized in the *Remediarium Conversorum*, a much shorter work by Peter of Waltham, a London archdeacon.[66] So this way of contemplating the image of Job was accessible to the designers of the chapter house.

The second sculpture beneath the Virgin presents another clearly differentiated figure, recognized by Lethaby as a pilgrim or friar wearing a cowl. Around his waist a knotted cord clearly marks him out as a Franciscan friar (fig 161). From the inception of their order, the Franciscans had enjoyed a harmonious relationship with the Benedictines, who had provided St Francis with his first headquarters at Porziuncula. The friars had been well received in England in 1224. Their order was soon firmly established, thanks in large part to the patronage of Henry III. The king had given gifts and grants to at least seven Franciscan communities around the country. In July 1253, when work at the chapter house was in full swing, he gave the friars of Chichester money to pay their debts and ordered the provision of twenty-six tunics for their use.[67] The presence of a Franciscan image in a Benedictine house may reflect the brief period before relations between the two orders soured.

Given the exalted company this friar keeps on the door jamb, it is likely he is intended to represent St Francis himself. One clue supports this suggestion. With the exception of the Virgin, all the other figures show their bare feet: this figure hides his beneath his habit. The first biographer of St Francis, Thomas de Celano, describes how the saint, following his reception of the stigmata, 'hid those marks carefully from strangers, and concealed them cautiously from people close to him'.[68] This would certainly not be the first representation of St Francis in England, even though he had been canonized only twenty-five years earlier. Matthew Paris, in his entry for the year 1227 in the *Chronica Maiora*, written between 1240 and 1250, had illustrated the two iconic scenes of the saint's life: St Francis

Fig 161 Inner portal, west face: door-jamb figure of St Francis; plaster cast in the Victoria and Albert Museum. *Photograph:* © Richard Foster

feeding the birds and the reception of the stigmata.[69]

Identification of the remaining figures of this door jamb remains open to speculation. The fourth from the bottom is headless and rests his hand on what appears to be a cushion-top casket secured by an interlaced fastening: a reliquary, perhaps. This is the figure Lethaby tentatively called Tubal Cain. His belt is knotted through a circular buckle. Many noble donors had added to the abbey's collection of relics, which were placed on the matins altar on rogation days, following the tradition recorded in Abbot Ware's *Customary*,[70] and venerated again on the feast of relics, kept on 16 July according to the calendars in the Litlyngton missal.[71] A large illuminated letter in this manuscript shows the altar set with relics for the feast day.[72] None of the five reliquaries illustrated is a cushion-top casket, but they represented only a fraction of the abbey's relics. John Flete, writing in the first half of the fifteenth century, records holy relics donated before the time of Henry III by Sebert, Offa, Athelstan, Edgar, Ethelred, Canute, Edward the Confessor

and William the Conqueror.[73] Any of these royal donors might have been intended here.

The differentiation of the remaining six figures is more subtle. They have no attributes to guide us. Two are tonsured and four wear hooded robes, leading to the identification of five of the six figures as monks. Four hold a hand to their face (fig 156). This gesture is likely to indicate contemplation rather than sleep, as Lethaby suggested. Perhaps he was recalling Edward the Confessor's vision of the seven sleepers of Ephesus. There is support for interpreting this gesture as contemplative in James Robinson's account of the twelfth-century Lewis chessmen. He suggests the roles of European chess pieces were descended from Arabic prototypes. The *vizier*, the king's wise counsellor, always at his side, becomes the queen in European chess sets. All eight of the Lewis queens sit with elbows on their knees and hands to their cheeks. According to Robinson, this eloquent pose expresses thoughtfulness and contemplation,[74] qualities pertinent to a monastic chapter house. The hand-to-face gesture also recalls the sorrowful pose often employed in depictions of St John at the foot of the Cross in both Eastern and Western traditions.[75] Some slight variation in the dress of the five monks leads us to speculate whether they may portray different orders, or even, following the example of St Francis, the founders of those orders. The differentiation between them would have been far more obvious before the loss of their painted colour: for example, St Benedict dressed in a black habit; St Dominic in dark brown; and St Bernard in white and black.

The one remaining figure, sitting above Moses and badly decayed, appears to have had neither tonsure nor cowl. It does seem to have some rather feminine features: a waist cinched in more sharply by its belt and suggestions of a necklace and of a female hairstyle or headdress. However, there is no subtle indication of breasts, as there is in the representation of the Virgin at the top of the jamb. If we were to seek a female companion for the two Old Testament men beneath her, we might perhaps look to Esther, whose plea to King Ahasuerus on behalf of the Jews was taken to prefigure the Virgin's intercession between Christian souls and Christ the King.[76]

With only three figures definitely identified, it may seem a foolhardy venture to consider whether any overall programme was intended for the door jamb, given that time and decay have obscured so much of the evidence. However, a theme does seem to emerge. Job, in the midst of his sufferings, made the greatest declaration of faith in the whole Bible: 'I know that my redeemer liveth, and that he shall stand at the latter day upon the earth. And though, after my skin, worms destroy this body, yet in my flesh *shall*

I see God.[77] In *Exodus*, God spoke to Moses *'face to face, as a man speaketh with his friend'*;[78] and St Francis carried with him the physical evidence of his close encounter with God: the stigmata. So perhaps we may see this most unusual grouping as representing the 'special friends of God', with the crowned Virgin presiding over them in a prototype of the *Sacra Conversatione*. Henry III himself certainly wished to be thought of as such a friend of God. When the French king, St Louis, asserted that 'the attention ought not always to be devoted to the hearing of masses but that we ought to hear sermons as often as possible', Henry replied that 'he would rather often *see a friend*, than hear speak of him'.[79] Other evidence of the king's frame of mind is closer at hand. In the fragmentary inscription surviving on the floor tiles of the chapter house it is possible to decipher the phrase *Rex Henricus Sancti Trinitatis amicus*: 'King Henry, friend of the Holy Trinity' (figs 42 and 226; see p 231).

The figure sculpture of the vestibule door jamb is not its only point of interest: the foliage enclosing the figures offers some of the first naturalistic leaves of English Gothic sculpture, coeval with the north-east corner of the abbey's north transept and a year or two later than those in the Windsor cloister. Uncharacteristically, Scott overlooked this naturalistic foliage. The restorer of the chapter house found 'fully developed tracery, but no natural foliage unless it be the roses and rose leaves in a single diaper pattern.'[80] The foliage on the outside door-jamb was described as 'rose leaves' by both Lethaby[81] and Rigold,[82] who referred to the spandrels within the chapter house. Although the branches bear no flowers, they do have five heart-shaped leaves in a pinnate structure, consistent with a briar rose. However, there is also a second leaf form – pinnate again but with longer pointed leaves, each having a deep central vein. These leaves are associated with large pendulous fruits, seen most clearly around the two lowest figures (fig 156). The rounded shape with a prominent calyx of these fruits suggests they are pomegranates. Both roses and pomegranates have iconographic associations with the Virgin and Child. The Virgin's emblem of the rose was a favourite of Henry III, who used four of the flowers on his gold penny issued in 1257, and it famously appears in the chapter house's floor-tile inscription: 'as the rose is the flower of flowers, so is this the house of houses' (pp 230–1).

The pomegranate, a symbol of fertility in the classical world by virtue of its multitude of seeds, came to represent the Resurrection in Christianity. The fruit had been held in high symbolic esteem by Judaism too. In *Exodus*, the Lord instructs Moses to have a priestly robe made for Aaron. Its hem was to be decorated 'with pomegranates of blue, and of purple, and of scarlet.'[83] Christianity inherited the symbolic value of the pomegranate largely through patristic exegesis

of the *Song of Songs*, by which the rather limited view of the Virgin in the *Gospels* was embellished with rich allegories, such as the *hortus conclusus*. The *Song of Songs* mentions the pomegranate six times. 'Your cheeks are like a piece of pomegranate'[84] is glossed in Bede's *In Canto Cantorum* as signifying both the chaste modesty of the Church and its identification with the Passion: 'The church therefore has red colour in her cheeks when she confesses, by her words, the sacrament of the passion of the Lord, and she shows whiteness [the pith of the pomegranate] when, oppressed by persecutions, she demonstrates the chastity of a pure heart, and by her deeds shows forth what saving grace the Cross may have.'[85] The saving grace of the Cross is perhaps the meditative focus of the four contemplative monks. Though exotic fruits, real pomegranates may have been available as models for the sculptor, perhaps as close at hand as the abbey's scriptorium: grated pomegranate peel had long been used in the making of ink. Pomegranates were certainly imported in 1290 for Queen Eleanor of Castile. They may even have come earlier from her native land during the negotiations leading to her marriage with Henry III's son, Edward in 1254.

The inner portal (eastern side)

Moving to the interior of the chapter house, the door jambs show the same asymmetry as the outer ones: foliate to the north and figured to the south. By way of contrast however, the foliate trail of the figured jamb is stiff-leaf rather than naturalistic. The stem is not rounded, but flatter, with a deep groove running its length. Otherwise, the carving of the two figured jambs is broadly consistent. It is tempting to imagine the sculptor cautiously abandoning the security of this familiar conservative style for the daring novelty of the more naturalistic outer jamb.

The topmost figure is an enthroned Christ, identified only by the remains of his cruciform halo, since both head and arms are missing. Five of the eleven figures have lost their heads, but their bodies show they were well-off enough to be able to afford shoes – unlike their barefoot counterparts on the outer jamb – and to sport rich clothing. The carving of the drapery is exceptionally fine, despite some damage, and is comparable with the best contemporary manuscript illumination. A strikingly close match is to be found in the drawing of King Edgar in a copy of Matthew Paris's *Estoire de seint Aedward le rei*, dated between 1250 and 1260.[86] We know that manuscript illumination informed interior decoration. Eleanor of Provence, Henry III's queen, borrowed a book from Roger de Sandford, master of the Knights Templar, to use as inspiration for painting her 'low room' in the king's garden at Westminster Palace.[87]

Although the carved figures of the inner door jamb have lost several heads and any attributes they may have possessed, their poses reveal something of their status. The figure immediately beneath Christ sits with one ankle resting on his other knee (fig 162). This self-confident pose is comparable to contemporary illustrations of Henry I and Henry II in the earliest manuscript of *Flores Historiarum*,[88] produced partly at Westminster and partly at St Albans, where some of its illuminations were likely to have been made under the supervision of Matthew Paris (fig 163). The manuscript illustrates ten coronations, from Arthur to Edward I, all but the last being drawn between 1250 and 1265.[89] Five of the kings share a particular gesture: grasping with curled fingers the band across the lower neck that holds together the edges of the open pallium.[90] This same gesture is repeated in three of the door-jamb figures. Besides these conventional thirteenth-century kingly poses, close examination of the casts in the Victoria and Albert Museum shows that another three had clear traces of crowns around their brows; and the seventh from the bottom, though headless, has the shadow of a sceptre in his left hand and rests the other hand on the remains of what was once the hilt of a sword.

Here then, we have a set of ten enthroned kings. The capital surmounting the jamb has foliage and lions, whereas its counterpart to the north has only foliage,

Fig 162 Inner portal, east face: door-jamb figure of a cross-legged king; plaster cast in the Victoria and Albert Museum. *Photograph*: © Richard Foster

Fig 163 The coronation of Henry I from the *Flores Historiarum*, 1250–65. *Photograph*: © Chetham Library, Manchester; MS 6712, fol 129r, col 486

preserving the asymmetry observed in the door jambs. Like the jambs, the capital is original thirteenth-century work.[91] However, being carved from Purbeck marble, it has survived intact with much sharper detail (fig 164). Stuart Rigold counted only a pair of lions:[92] he missed the third. The three lions of this capital, like the three lions displayed prominently in the tiled floor of the chapter house (fig 41), must refer to the coat of arms of England. So our kings are English, rather than Biblical. The presence of a range of English kings is hardly surprising in a coronation church. Writing in 1753, J Newberry lamented the loss of statues of ancient kings that once stood in niches on the abbey's buttresses;[93] and Lethaby suggested that fragments of thirteenth-century stained-glass crowns in the east windows once belonged to a set of kings at least eight feet tall and probably set in the windows of the apse.[94] Stone kings were a standard of the mason's repertoire: Master John of Gloucester, the king's mason, was instructed to give five images of kings cut in freestone, apparently surplus to requirements, to the keepers of the works at St Martin's, Ludgate.[95]

Since this jamb is presided over by Christ as King of Heaven, we may further infer that our figures were intended to be saintly, or at least pious. Henry III much prized his pedigree of saintly kings: useful moral armour at times of political uncertainty. Matthew Paris extolled the prominence of saintly English kings in the opening to his *Estoire de seint Aedward le rei*, dedicated to Queen Eleanor and probably presented to her shortly after her marriage to Henry in 1236: 'There is no country, realm or empire in the world, I dare say, where there have been so many good and

Fig 164 Inner portal, east face: Purbeck marble capital on the south respond, carved with three lions. *Photograph*: © Richard Foster

saintly kings as in the isle of the English.'[96] Which of these kings might be portrayed in the ten figures of the chapter-house jamb? There is, perhaps, a clue in an anecdote recorded by Matthew Paris for the year 1257, when Henry III paid a week-long visit to St Albans Abbey. Matthew was 'his constant companion in the palace, at the table, and in his chamber, he dictated to him with care and affability … He also named all the holy kings of England who had been canonised. And in order that such a great personage may not have taken the trouble to dictate these matters in vain, we have noted down the saints in this book.'[97]

The eleven saintly kings Henry III recited by heart were: Ethelbert, Edward the King and Martyr, Kenelm, Oswald, Oswin, Neithan, Wistan, Fremund, Eardwulf, Edmund and Edward the Confessor. There being only ten places available in the door jamb, Neithan may be excluded since he was the king of the Picts whose claim to sanctity lay in conforming the Pictish church to the Roman dating of Easter and the manner of monastic tonsures in the early eighth century. Of the remaining candidates, seven also appear among the nine sculptures of martyr-kings identified by Lethaby on the west front of Wells Cathedral.[98] These include Edward, King and Martyr, who must surely find a place among the door-jamb figures since relics of his body had been given to the abbey by Ethelred, Edgar and Canute. Among the saintly kings recited by Henry, three were martyred as boys or youths: Kenelm, Wistan and Edward the Martyr. They appear beardless at Wells, and we may, perhaps, equate them with the bottom two and the fourth figures on the Westminster jamb, also beardless and seeming to have a youthful demeanour. The lack of attributes and missing heads of the remaining figures makes further speculation impossible. However, it can be seen that while the outer figured jamb was intended to represent the contemplative authority of the Church, the inner stood for the authority of the crown under God, the two jambs reflecting the twin functions of the chapter house as envisaged by King Henry.

The voussoirs of the arch springing from the capitals above the door jambs form a foliate trail inhabited by twenty-six seated figures. Much restoration from the nineteenth century is apparent. They would seem to be prophets and sibyls, perhaps formerly identified by lettering painted on their scrolls and books. On either side of the arch stand the chief glories of the chapter house interior: the two commanding figures of the Annunciation (fig 142). The Virgin Mary stands in a trefoiled niche to the north, her right hand raised and her left holding a book (fig 166). Archangel Gabriel is similarly placed to the south, leaning slightly backward and outward to stretch his arms out towards the Virgin (fig 165). The spandrels between them and the arch carry large trefoils with reliefs of censing angels, one taller and one smaller in each. Their presence in a scene of the Annunciation is highly irregular: Gabriel usually flies a solo mission.

The figures of Mary and Gabriel are two of the finest pieces of English sculpture surviving from the thirteenth century; though for many centuries they were not treated with the respect they deserved (see further, p 152). When the chapter house was taken over for the storage of public records, its thirteenth-century sculpture was an inconvenience. The statue of the Virgin Mary was shut up behind the wooden presses that held the many documents – out of sight and out of mind. She was eventually rediscovered by Scott when he came to the office of surveyor of the fabric: 'I was one day on the top of one of these presses, and on venturing to pull away an arris fillet which closed the crevice between it and the wall, I perceived the top of an arched recess in the wall behind the press, and on looking down into it I saw some round object

of stone in the recess below. My curiosity being excited, I let down into it by a string a small bull's-eye lantern, when, to my extreme delight, I saw that the mysterious object was the head of a beautiful full-sized statue in a niche. Permission was speedily obtained for the removal of the press. The statue proved to be a very fine one of the Virgin, and in the spaces adjoining it were angels censing.'[99] To uncover the rest of the doorway Scott noted he had to steal through a mass of parchments and dust ten feet deep. Gabriel's statue had not been boarded up: it leaned out too far. Instead, it was shorn of its wings and taken out of its niche. In 1807, Gabriel stood by the staircase inserted in the vestibule to reach a mezzanine floor at the level of the arch (fig 123).[100] Perhaps it had been set in place recently. If it had been there long, it is surprising that we have no record of such an important sculpture from the usually vigilant antiquary, John Carter. When he took note of the arch's missing tracery in 1799, he would have had to pass the Archangel on the stairs and would surely have

Fig 165 Inner portal, east face: the Archangel Gabriel. *Photograph*: © Richard Foster

Fig 166 Inner portal, east face: the Virgin Annunciate. *Photograph*: © Richard Foster

recognized it as a masterpiece.

The commanding figures of the Annunciation were probably considered slightly larger than life size in the thirteenth century. Gabriel stands at 1.82 m; Mary at 1.89 m, her further height accounted for by an additional stone for the top of her head. Of the four censing angels that hurry between them in the spandrel trefoils, each of the taller pair is 1.07 m. The smaller half-length angels behind the striding pair are just emerging from clouds. Both these secondary angels and the figure of the Virgin are carved of the same poor Reigate stone. The dazzling sculpture of the Archangel owes its still wonderful condition to having been carved in the more robust Caen stone.[101] Despite being made from very different materials, both figures have long been linked to an entry in the building accounts of Henry III for the period between 2 February and 19 April 1253, which records the payment of 53 shillings and 4 pence to William of Ixworth for two statues.[102] Similar finishing on the back of the two figures confirms the view that they must always have been a pair, and were correctly reunited by Scott in 1872. The disparity

in quality may be accounted for by the inferior performance of Reigate stone. When the figures were first carved the arrises of the drapery were probably equally sharp. Cleaning has helped a great deal, showing that the sophisticated fall of the draperies of both figures is closer than used to be apparent to the standard of the angel spandrels below the rose windows just within the abbey's south transept. It is also true that the Virgin here is more sophisticated than her sisters of a decade or two earlier at Wells. Another characteristic shared by the Virgin and Archangel is a boneless curvature of the wrists, very different from the firm angles of the transept angels.

In the same accounting period as William of Ixworth's payment, a later entry records 11 shillings paid to Warin the painter for painting two statues with colour.[103] Given that Peter of Hispania, the king's painter, was on the regular payroll, these statues must have been something exceptional, most likely those provided by William of Ixworth. None other is mentioned in that quarter of 1253. A surprising amount of original painting can still be seen on the Virgin's face (fig 167). Her more visible eye has a

Fig 167 Inner portal: the face of the Virgin.
Photograph: © Richard Foster

yellow-ochre iris and a black pupil; there is ochre again between her eye and black eyebrow, and on strands of her hair; her left cheek has an extensive layer of even pink paint, not one of those unfortunate Gothic blobs; and there is a darker pink on her lips. Using sixty-times magnification, further traces were revealed in a recent examination.[104] There are small traces of pink on the palm of her right hand, the back of her left and on the edge of her undershirt; black in the nostrils; and traces of blue and, perhaps, the remains of gilding on the book she holds in her left hand. Gabriel must have been scrubbed at some point, for now there is only black in his nostrils.

As Paul Williamson has observed, the additional piece of stone for the top of Mary's head recalls the method whereby precious crowns were secured to the heads of ivory Virgins during this period. The Virgin Annunciate does not usually wear a crown. However, there is provision for a diadem just above her hairline, and what may be the indication of a fixing either side where it goes beneath the veil. It is also likely that she had a halo of gilt metal or wood held in place by the joining of the two stones. The two fittings for Gabriel's wings are very apparent, though

not visible from the ground. In his right shoulder is a deep vertical slot, which supported a wing at least a metre long and probably made of gilt wood (fig 168). The other fitting is a wide area cut away from the back of the figure to form a ledge between the left shoulder and the wall behind (fig 169). Into this, the second wing was lodged, splaying across the niche, but not extending more than half the length of the other. Wings of asymmetrical length are not unknown in representations of thirteenth-century standing angels. Dictated perforce by practical considerations, as here by the constriction of the niche, they suggest that the visitant has just landed and not yet furled its wings, the smaller wing being understood as in perspective.

Like the angels on the cloister tympanum, described above, Gabriel's shoulders lean out of the plane of the portal sculpture in order to establish eye contact across the arch with the Virgin (fig 170). This innovation of eye contact is normally associated with the art of Giovanni Pisano and Giotto, working a generation and more later. The Italians must have derived the emotional charge of eye contact, of which they made so much, from northern European sculpture, as they did the sway of Madonna

Fig 168 Inner portal: Gabriel during conservation, showing the slot for the lost right wing. *Photograph*: © Pamela Tudor-Craig

Fig 169 Inner portal: Gabriel, showing the ledge for the lost left wing. *Photograph*: © Richard Foster

Fig 170 Inner portal: Gabriel leaning out of his niche.
Photograph: © Richard Foster

groups, largely through the medium of the highly popular French ivories. Gabriel has another feature not visible from the ground: his mouth is open in speech (fig 171). This is the earliest example we know of Gabriel visibly uttering the words of salutation, written variously on scrolls (as here, and now lost) or lettered across the distance between them. This Annunciation is held in a moment out of time, between the angelic message and the human *fiat*, an interval made fragrant by angels censing the gulf between heaven and earth: the space for the entrance of the Holy Spirit. That overarching gulf was suggested here by the empty quatrefoil over the doorway, so unfortunately filled at the behest of Scott by a seated Christ in Glory, an insertion that makes nonsense of the iconography by forcing the censing angels to turn their backs on Christ.

There is nothing static in this doorway. On the contrary, it conveys the rushing wind of the Holy Spirit described in *Ezekiel*: 'Then the spirit took me up, and I heard behind me a voice of a great rushing saying Blessed is the glory of the Lord.'[105] The dynamism of mid-fourteenth-century portrayals of the Annunciation owes much to Franciscan preaching, as exemplified in the *Meditationes Vitae Christi*,

Fig 171 Inner portal: Gabriel's head, showing open mouth. *Photograph*: © Richard Foster

then attributed to St Bonaventura but written, in fact, in a Franciscan house in Tuscany in the mid-fourteenth century. Its vivid account of the urgency of Gabriel's mission derives from a much earlier work by St Bernard: his *Commentary on the Song of Songs*, begun in 1135 and unfinished at his death in 1153. The commentary was completed by two English Cistercians – John, abbot of Ford, followed by Gilbert of Hoyland[106] – so the work continued to be studied in this country. The fifty-fourth sermon gives Bernard's commentary on chapter 2, verse 8 of the *Song of Songs*: 'See how he comes leaping upon the mountains, bounding over the hills':

> He whose custom was to delegate to others, himself descended to the earth … he uniquely rejoiced like a giant to run his course [*Psalms* 18:6]. For he bounded over Gabriel and preceded him to the Virgin, as the archangel himself witnessed when he says [*sic*] 'Hail Mary, full of grace, the Lord is with thee' [*Luke* 1:8]. What is this? He whom you just left in heaven, do you now find in the womb. He flew, even flew ahead, on the wings of the wind [*Psalms* 17:11]. You are beaten, O Archangel, overleapt by him who sent you ahead.[107]

Here is an explanation for the Westminster Gabriel's unfurled wings, still open in haste; and for the unusual presence of two pairs of censing angels, rushing across their trefoils. 'He bounded over Gabriel and preceded him to the Virgin.' They must cense the Virgin, for the Holy Spirit is with her, attendant upon her assent; they must cense the Archangel, for Christ himself has just overleapt him. In his second sermon on the *Song of Songs,* Bernard wrote, paraphrasing Christ's word to his disciples in *Luke* 10:24: 'O root of Jesse that stands as a signal to the peoples, how many prophets and Kings wanted to see what you see, and never saw it.'[108] Passing through the two doorways into his chapter house, Henry III may have felt thankful. He had seen it.

The beautiful figures of the Annunciation stamp the chapter house itself, as well as its outer entrance, as being under the special care of the Virgin. Richard Crokesley, abbot of Westminster at the time of the building of the chapter house, is recorded as having a particular devotion to the Virgin. In the first year of his abbacy (1246 or 1247) he assembled the whole convent to announce that the feast of the Annunciation was to be celebrated in perpetuity with a solemnity equal to that of the Nativity, *in quinque capis*.[109] Every centrally planned chapter house in England, of which the intent can still be made out,[110] was under the protection of the Virgin as the seat of wisdom,[111] usually as here, by enrichment around the doors, following the declaration of *Proverbs*: 'Does not wisdom cry? … she crieth at the gates, at the entry of the city, at the coming in at the doors.'[112]

The appeal to wisdom to preside over the deliberations guiding religious communities and nations alike is the subject of the illuminated page at the opening of an early fifteenth-century *Bible Historiale* in the British Library (fig 172).[113] The illumination is probably by the Bedford master. God the Father and the Son look down from the empyrean. The third person of the Trinity is not with them: instead, the Holy Spirit is represented by Wisdom, personified as a crowned and winged woman, preaching in an approximation to an octagonal chapter house with aisles. She addresses a gathering of senior clergy and a king with his councillors from a tall pulpit, inscribed with phrases from *Proverbs* Chapter 8: 'counsel is mine, and sound judgement.' In the aisle to the left, Moses expounds the Old Law under a doorway marked *Spes*; to the right, St Paul introduces the New Law under the doorway of *Fides*. The central doorway is inscribed *Caritas*. The Annunciation and the Assumption in the left margin are matched by the descent of the Holy Spirit and the Ascension opposite.

If the iconography of the chapter house's portal sculpture – its Virgin and Child, its Tree of Jesse, its friends of God, its lineage of saintly kings and its Annunciation – has any unifying theme, then it is surely the hope that wisdom should light upon those who sat beneath its lofty octagonal vault. The distinction between 'the Word' as constantly repeated in the choir and sanctuary, and the Word in the chapter house, is that while in the choir the *Opus Dei* was set in stone, in the chapter house everything, from sermons to discipline and debate, was dependant upon fallible human decision, just as the Incarnation depended upon the assent of the Virgin. The invocation of Wisdom, the understanding of Isaiah's words in terms of its transmission from heaven to earth, is nowhere more eloquently expressed than in the Great 'O' Antiphons, dating back to at least the eighth century:[114]

> O Wisdom, coming forth from the mouth of the
> Most High,
> Reaching from one end to the other mightily,
> And sweetly ordering all things:
> Come and teach us the way of prudence…
>
> O root of Jesse, standing as a sign among the peoples;
> Before you kings will shut their mouths,
> To you the nations will make their prayer:
> Come and deliver us, and delay no longer.

There could hardly have been a litany more apt to the lips of a king.

Fig 172 Early fifteenth-century *Bible Historiale*, showing Wisdom preaching. *Photograph*: © The British Library Board; BL MS Add 18856, fol 1r

Appendix A: the provenance and dating of the door-jamb plaster casts in the Victoria and Albert Museum

In 1936 it was still possible to buy casts of the three lowest figures of the outer chapter-house door jamb from the Victoria and Albert Museum at a cost of 7s 6d each.[115] The museum's plaster casts of both jambs were acquired from the disbanded Royal Architectural Museum in 1916, together with other casts of architectural details from the abbey. The RAM's collection held at least thirty-nine casts from the chapter house, including the figures of the Virgin (item no. 24) and the Angel of the Annunciation (item no. 23), which stood on the first floor over the entrance to the museum in Tufton Street.[116] On the ground floor, item no. 320 was described in the museum's catalogue as a 'shaft and enriched jamb' from the vestibule of the chapter house.[117] No reference is made to any figure sculpture. Fortunately, however, item no. 320 was among those photographed around 1877 by the museum's official photographer, Bedford Lemere and Co., whose photograph shows Job, Moses and the figure above them.[118]

The Royal Architectural Museum had opened in 1852. Among its prime movers was George Gilbert Scott, who made substantial donations of plaster casts to the fledgling collection.[119] 'I lent nearly the whole of my large collection, and employed agents and workmen all over the country to get new casts,' he later recalled.[120] Scott's personal collection is likely to have included the Westminster casts, since he had succeeded Edward Blore as surveyor of the fabric at the abbey three years earlier. The plaster casts of the statue of the Virgin and the internal orders of the arch must date from that time or later, since they were hidden behind the wooden presses of the Public Record Office until Scott uncovered them. They were probably the work of the Royal Architectural Museum's usual cast-maker, Domenico Brucciani. The door jambs and outer orders, however, remained accessible while the record office was in occupation, so the casts of these features could have been taken earlier.

A select committee report of 1841, ordered by the House of Commons 'to inquire into the present state of the National Monuments and Works of Art in Westminster Abbey, in St Paul's Cathedral, and in other Public Edifices'[121] gives a valuable insight into the running of the abbey during the years before Scott's appointment. The purpose of the report was to determine whether opening the abbey for free access by all classes of society, 'as a means of moral and intellectual Improvement for the People', would endanger the fabric of the building and its monuments. Four years earlier, Queen Victoria had expressed to the Dean and Chapter, through Prime Minister Lord John Russell, her 'desire that the Abbey Church of Westminster should be open to the public at certain appointed times, without the payment of any fee or gratuity.'[122] The abbey had resisted this royal request, ostensibly on the grounds of organizational difficulties and the possibility of vandalism. The select committee was clearly convened to bring new pressure upon the Dean and Chapter. Part of its enquiry centred upon the practice of taking casts in the abbey and whether this had been a cause of damage.

The dean, John Ireland, was too ill to attend and sent the abbey's treasurer, Henry Hart Milman, in his stead. Milman's answers reveal that the dean, acting alone rather than in chapter, had sanctioned an Italian craftsman called 'Cossomini' to take casts at the abbey about ten years previously, around 1831. This craftsman may be identified as Raphael Cosomini, a 'modeller and moulder', who had established himself in England by the early 1820s and shared premises with a coal merchant at No. 279 High Holborn.[123] However, Milman told the committee there had been no taking of casts during the previous two years since 'it was found rather to damage the statues, and therefore it was discontinued.'[124] Charles Harriot Smith, a sculptor of architectural ornament, informed the committee that when he had need of a cast he 'applied to an Italian of the name of Cosomini, who seems to have the privilege of taking casts from ornaments.'[125] In the sculptor's opinion, the chief cause of damage to the fabric of the abbey had been 'the Westminster scholars, who, from long usage, amuse themselves round the cloisters with playing at football, racket and other violent bodily games.'[126] The committee also interviewed the sacrist, William Hollocombe, who had worked at the abbey for forty years. He confirmed the moratorium on cast-taking since 1839 and added the further information that Cosomini had been employed to make the casts for more than ten years by the architect, Lewis Nockalls Cottingham, a pioneer of the Gothic revival.[127]

Cottingham was well acquainted with the abbey, publishing two volumes of detailed drawings of the recently restored Henry VII's chapel, a work he intended for the use and improvement of 'the Young Architects of Great Britain'.[128] As part of his research for his restoration of the Temple church, he arranged to have the boarded floor of the record office partly lifted to examine the hidden tiled pavement of the contemporary chapter house.[129] John Flaxman, John Carter and Thomas Gayfere, who had worked as Wyatt's mason in the restoration of Henry VII's chapel, were counted among his friends.[130] Cottingham advertised himself as giving 'lessons on civil architecture for which purpose he has made an extensive collection of models and casts from the best remains of Grecian and Gothic buildings.'[131] In 1828, Cottingham moved this collection to No. 43 Waterloo Bridge Road, where he established a museum of medieval art. The first museum to reconstruct period room settings, it rivalled the contemporary museum of Sir John Soane in Lincoln's Inn Fields. The casts taken at Westminster Abbey by Cosomini were, no doubt, destined for his patron's museum. The first gallery reproduced 'the rich subdued tone of an apartment of the Middle Ages, and may be considered the beau ideal of an Architect's Studio,' enthused a contemporary description, 'The Walls are covered with a fine series of Saints, Bishops, etc, with other models and casts of Gothic examples.'[132] Among these casts were some 300 taken from the abbey. Any from the chapter house could only have been made of those architectural details accessible during its occupation by the Public Record Office: that is, the door jambs and outer orders of the arch. Cottingham died in 1847. Four years later, after an unsuccessful campaign to have the collection saved for the nation, the contents of his museum were sold at auction and dispersed among collectors. On the fourth and fifth days of the sale in November 1851, four of the lots included casts of foliage and figure sculpture 'taken from the doorway adjoining the chapter house at Westminster'.[133] The timing was perfect for their acquisition by the new Royal Architectural Museum, either directly or among the casts given on permanent loan by Scott.

So it is possible that the door-jamb casts now in the Victoria and Albert Museum were not made by Brucciani expressly for the Royal Architectural Museum, but came instead from the dissolution of Cottingham's collection at his Museum of Medieval Art. Given the moratorium on cast-taking at the abbey between 1839 and 1841, the casts are likely to be the earlier work of Raphael Cosomini and reproduce the chapter-house door jambs as they appeared at some time between 1831 and 1839.

Appendix B: a note on the conservation history of the portals

During the 1840s, conservation at Westminster Abbey was limited to washing down the monuments once a year and dusting them twice yearly.[134] A generation earlier, the Dean and Chapter had already been berated publicly by John Carter for their neglect of the outer doorway of the chapter house: 'This magnificent portion of the cloister is used as a common tennis wall for the exercise of the college youth, a circumstance which reflects much on the want of

due care in the Reverend Guardians of the sacred pile.'[135]

Things changed when Scott became surveyor. He experimented with a wide range of stone preservation treatments. A snap-shot of the variety of techniques in use at that time, and the competition between the commercial interests and their sometimes secret processes, is given by a debate held at the Royal Institute of British Architects in February 1861 to consider the scandalous problem of the already decaying stonework of the new Houses of Parliament.[136] During the debate, Scott read out a statement detailing the procedures he had employed at Westminster Abbey since 1857, and giving his assessment of their effectiveness. They included water glass (1857–58, 'decay arrested but not perfectly'), Mr Paul's system (using aluminate of potash), Frederick Ransome's technique (using silicate of lime), the secret, silicate-based process of Nicholas Charles Szerelmey (1859, 'much hardened'), Sylvester's treatment (using soap and alum; 'effects appear to have ceased'), shellac in spirits of wine ('admirable indoors, no good in the rain'), white wax dissolved in turpentine (1857, 'failed') and Mr Daines's procedure (using boiling oil and sulphur; 1859, 'almost perfect').[137] Scott considered shellac in spirits of wine – an insect-produced resin dissolved in ethanol – to be the most effective treatment for internal stonework, having used it inside the abbey to his satisfaction for three or four years.

Thanks to the twin depredations of weather and Westminster schoolboys, the outer doorway of the chapter house had been a priority for Scott's treatment. As early as 1854 he had noted flakes of decayed stone, 'which through the winter have been visible on every part of the Cloister pavement.'[138] Four years later, Scott used his shellac treatment in the cloister on what was, in effect, external stonework. The surface of the doorway was so friable that it could not be touched. A pair of bellows with a long flexible tube was used first to blow away the dust. Then the hardening solution of shellac was sprayed over the stonework using a syringe with a perforated nozzle. 'I have, as I trust,' he wrote, 'arrested the progress of disintegration, by a process which I am largely making use of throughout the interior of the church … Its effect is to harden and set the crumbling surface, so as to stereotype the work in the state in which it now is.'[139] Despite Scott's confidence at the time, in later life he was not so certain: 'As to its success in this case, under conditions intermediate between those of external and internal architecture, I am myself very doubtful.'[140] In 1878, *The Builder* complained that the shellac 'has darkened and entirely changed the ancient colour of the building.'[141]

Scott may have started using the same technique inside the chapter house. Examination of the inner folds of the undercut drapery of the reliefs of censing angels reveals dark splashes and dribbles of shellac creeping round the edges against the wall. The fact that the parts of the angels beyond the reach of the shellac spray are now better preserved than the treated parts is testimony to the detrimental long-term effect of Scott's technique, even on internal stonework.[142] By 1906 Lethaby would report that until 'about 1870 the carvings of the entrance to the Chapter House, preserved by their coat of paint, were comparatively perfect, but in a generation they have mouldered out of all form.'[143]

In May 1901 the distinguished chemist, Professor A H Church, was called upon to report on the condition and treatment of the chapter house's stonework to the First Commission of His Majesty's Works. He painted a sorry picture: 'the decay is not confined to the surface, but has in many places penetrated to the depth of two or more inches … the sulphuric acid of the Westminster atmosphere has been the main cause.' Sulphuric acid had gradually converted the calcium carbonate of the limestone into calcium sulphate, which crystallizes as gypsum and forms an impermeable skin, causing the surface to blister and flake off. Another destructive agent was identified as the product of local industry: 'namely, hydrochloric acid, in part derived from the operation of glazing stoneware with salt in the Lambeth potteries.'[144] Church made trials *in situ* and in his laboratory. His recommendation was to treat the stonework with baryta-water, an aqueous solution of barium hydrate.

It appears that Church had already experimented with barium hydrate at the chapter house more than thirty years earlier, under the surveyorship of Scott. At a meeting of the British Association in November 1870, he read a paper giving 'a brief account of a process for preserving stone in which a solution of monocalcic phosphate, barium hydrate, and dialysed silica are successively employed. Very numerous and extensive experiments have been made with this process upon public and private buildings. The new Midland Terminus, St Pancras, has been treated with these solutions, and so have the Chapter House, Westminster, and portions of Canterbury Cathedral and the Houses of Parliament.'[145]

The principle behind Church's treatment with barium hydrate was outlined in the *Journal of the Science of Chemical Industry*: 'The chemistry of the process consists in the conversion of the gypsum in the decayed stone into barium sulphate, with the simultaneous production of calcium hydroxide, which, gradually absorbing carbon dioxide, reconstitutes calcium carbonate.'[146] After cleaning the surface with a blower, the stonework was sprayed with a pneumatic diffuser. The outer doorway was treated four times in the summer of 1901 and again five times in July and August of 1903, using a total of 220 gallons of barium hydrate solution containing around 3 per cent of barium oxide. The hardening proceeded from within outwards and, it was claimed, 'the stone became, not only reconstructed, but even harder than when in its original condition.'

During the 1950s a heavy limewash and gesso mix was applied to the surface of the inner doorway, with the exception of the figures of the Virgin and the Archangel Gabriel. This layer was subsequently removed by air abrasion in the most recent conservation, carried out by Ian Clayton Ltd in 1983. The exposed surfaces were then consolidated with acrylic silane, and major fissures filled with a paste of acrylic silane and Portland stone dust, pigmented to match the original stonework.[147] The same conservation programme found a thick layer of beeswax coating the two full-size figures of the Annunciation. The date of its application is uncertain. It may have been intended to conserve the stonework or to act as a releasing agent when plaster casts were made of the sculptures in the second half of the nineteenth century. The surface of the wax was cleaned and removed in selected areas only, revealing the remains of gesso and pigment layers. Five years later, the figures were removed from the doorway for individual conservation under the supervision of John Larson of the Victoria and Albert Museum. A variety of solvents, appropriate to the differing conditions of the stone and pigment surfaces, was used to remove the thick layer of wax. Friable areas were then stabilized with acrylic silane.

Wall paintings in the chapter house

11

Paul Binski and Helen Howard

The walls of the chapter house, below window-sill level, contain thirty-seven bays of arcading (see Plan 2 for the numbering sequence); painted decoration and sculpture survive in many of these. The wall paintings comprise:

· a Judgement scene (*Judicium*) on the east wall, with a central Majesty flanked by seraphim and probably the Virgin Mary and St John the Baptist (bays 17–21)
· Old Testament figures, forming part of the overall Judgement composition, on the south-east wall (bays 22–24)
· a great Apocalypse cycle (probably originally comprising ninety-six scenes) surviving on the north-west, south-east, south and south-west walls (but now lost from the north and north-east walls: the full scheme originally occupied bays 2–13 and 25–36)
· half-length angel musicians in the top lobes of the wall-arcading, above the Apocalypse and Old Testament figures
· a decorative design of roses at dado-level on the north-west wall and also to the west wall, north of the entrance; superimposed on the roses, immediately above the wall-bench, is a later scheme of confronted beasts.

Additionally, polychromy and gilding survive on the architectural frame of the wall-arcading, especially on the east side, and the figures of the Annunciation over the west portal also retain colour (for which, see pp 176–7).

The imagery of the wall paintings

The monastic chapter was a place of practical discipline. We might conclude from this that English secular or monastic chapter houses generally would have been decorated with art whose purpose was disciplinary. In fact, it was varied in subject-matter and was not governed by one overriding set of topics. The Virgin played an important role: Worcester's round chapter house had a programme of twelfth-century typological paintings stressing Mary's role in the Incarnation; Canterbury's was headed by the coronation of the Virgin within the prior's throne; York and Salisbury – secular chapters – were partly Marian in their imagery, as was the thirteenth-century scheme at Westminster. Common Marian similes at Westminster, such as the rose (*Ut rosa flos florum sic est domus ista domorum*, as the tile pavement says: fig 226 and p 231) or Marian imagery around its portals, make this apparent.[1] These influenced the decoration of the chapter house's interior: the thirteenth-century arcading in the eastern bays is topped by diaper-work, including a rose trellis which retains gilding, either of thirteenth-century origin or derivation. This probably reflected the preferences of Henry III. Here, however, our concerns are with the later medieval murals in its wall arcading, produced under monastic patronage mostly towards and around 1400, and first commented on extensively by Waller in 1873.[2]

The Judgement

Westminster's chapter house paintings are, in fact, at least in part disciplinary in character, and they are unusual. They consist principally of two distinct groups: the Judgement, dominating the five bays (17–21) of the east wall (fig 173) and three bays each of the north-east and south-east walls (bays 14–16 and 22–24; figs 174 and 175);

Fig 173 East wall: painting (bays 17 to 21). Christ in Judgement, with flanking seraphs. *Drawing:* in watercolour by John Carter, before doorways were cut through the first and last bays in 1801; *photograph:* © English Heritage Photo Library

Fig 174 South-east wall: paintings (bays 23 to 25). Three bays of the Judgement scene and two of the Apocalypse. *Photograph*: © English Heritage Photo Library

Fig 175 South-east wall: Judgement. Detail of the group of figures in bay 24. *Photograph*: © Dean and Chapter of Westminster

and the Apocalypse, occupying twenty-four arcades on the north-west, north, parts of the north-east and south-east, as well as the south and south-west walls, beginning in the north-west corner, and running clockwise (fig 180). Finally, confronted images of beasts were added on the lower parts of each wall arcade; these were an afterthought, and we will return to them later.

The first two topics are eschatological, dealing with the Last Things. Their general intent is disciplinary and pedagogic. The Judgement is an artistic reflection of the same gradual process whereby the chapter was hived off from the liturgy to form a separate meeting in a separate building. It relates especially to the *capitulum culparum*, or chapter of faults, which was distinguished from the general *Confiteor* and private confession of sin. The *capitulum culparum* was a means of communal regulation of monastic conduct. A fault may involve a sin (*peccamen*) but was, first, an offence against the rule or customs of the monastic community, declared or otherwise identified in the chapter assembly. A *culpa* could be serious: the tapestries of the Life of Christ donated to the abbey choir

by Abbot Berking in 1246 included the episode of Judas hanging himself; these had the caption *sese suspendit quem culpa gravis reprehendit*; the expression *culpa gravis* is echoed in the prayer offered up by the monk kneeling to St Faith in the picture of that saint in her chapel at Westminster: *Me quem culpa gravis premit erige virgo suavis*.[3] Private auricular confession would be expected of monks too; and it is likely that the Judgement scenes are, at least in part, an unfolding of this process.

The explanation is of a particular kind. At the centre of the east wall (bay 19), Christ is shown as the semi-naked Son of Man (fig 176), cloaked, but revealing his wounds by raising his hands, seated over a rainbow and with his feet placed on a large globe; over him, in turn, are seen the instruments of the Passion raised up as standards by angels to either side. This is not a full Last Judgement because there are no scenes of the last trump, the general Resurrection, the parting of the saved and the damned, the entry to Heaven and Hell, and so on. Rather, Christ is shown as the eternal merciful Judge, as found in contemporary *Horae* at the Seven Requests and penitential psalms.[4] The equipoise of

Fig 176 East wall: Judgement. Christ displaying his wounds, with attendant angels, in bay 19. *Photograph*: © English Heritage Photo Library

his gesture indicates justice. In each adjoining bay is a seraph (or cherub: the terms are not used consistently in medieval terminology) in traditionally feathery raiment, raising its arms as if to echo Christ's gesture; that to Christ's left (bay 20) holds up two crowns, and, like Christ, is surrounded by smaller fiery red seraphs. This gesture recalls that of a thirteenth-century sculpted angel holding up a crown in each hand in the arcade of St Edmund's chapel, and occurs in the thirteenth-century painted seraph on the ceiling of the Painted Chamber in Westminster Palace (now in the British Museum) – images hidden from view by wooden bosses at the time of the execution of the chapter house. The explanation of their presence in the chapter lies in *Isaiah* 6, where the Lord is seated on a high throne between the seraphim with six wings, by which sin shall be cleansed: *et peccatum tuum mundabitur*. This is the *propitiatorium*, or

mercy seat, with the seraphim mentioned in *Exodus* 25:17. The form of the angels with wings and wheel is owed to *Ezekiel* 1. In *Psalm* 79 (*Qui regis*) and *Psalm* 98 (*Dominus regnavit*) the shepherd of Israel is seated upon the seraphim before Ephraim, Benjamin and Manasses, with Moses and Aaron among his priests; God is great in Sion. The venerable figures in the bays (south-east, 22–24) to Christ's left hand represent Sion: one is King David, since he has a harp-morse (fig 175).[5] The witnesses of Sion should be led by the last representative of the Old Law, John the Baptist. His image may have appeared in the blank outer bay (21) of the east wall, on Christ's left. Since the image of the seraph is based upon an Old Testament vision, this ordering is understandable.

The winged seraph on this side (bay 20, fig 177) has, or had, such inscriptions as *dilectio dei*, *dilectio proximi*,

Fig 177 East wall: Judgement. The seraph on Christ's left (bay 20), showing lettering on the margins of the wings. *Drawing*: in watercolour by J G Waller, 1874; *photograph*: © Dean and Chapter of Westminster

puritas mentis, puritas carnis, confessio, satisfactio, simplicitas, humilitas, etc, following a well-known commentary on *Isaiah* 6 in the twelfth-century treatise on penance *De sex alis cherubim*, 'On the Six Wings of the Cherub', attributed to Alan of Lille or Clement of Llanthony.[6] Normally, as in the Lambeth Apocalypse (Lambeth Palace Library MS 209), the De Lisle Psalter (BL Arundel MS 83 (II) and a manual for London priests of *c* 1320 (Cambridge University Library MS Gg.4.32) this quite common image appears as a didactic picture, a chart or epitome of the confessional, which could be used in public or private instruction.[7] At Westminster, it is reinserted into a definite context, being, in effect, superimposed on the *propitiatorium*. So here is a demonstration of God's mercy in the sacrament of penance. The seraph on Christ's right (bay 18), assisted by angels who support a cloth of honour behind it, holds up a crown and rosary, from which we may deduce the presence of the Virgin as intercessor, opposite John the Baptist: the picture would therefore have been a deësis, with the Old Testament to Christ's left, the New, including the church and its saints, to his right. St Jerome had already suggested that a pair of cherubs or seraphs could represent the Old and New Testaments; *De sex alis* makes the connection explicit.[8] It is probably worth recalling that these tremendous angelic presences faced the thirteenth-century sculpted Annunciation to either side of the west door. One of the most beautiful thirteenth-century drawings of the Annunciation, in Cambridge University Library MS Kk.4.25, executed *c* 1230, (illustrating one of the key works of medieval angelology, a homily by Gregory the Great) followed on from the treatise *De sex alis*.[9] In that book the intention was encyclopaedic, to explore the nature of angels. At Westminster, however, the angels accompany a specifically monastic disciplinary regime.

I know at present of no other picture in which the biblical *propitiatorium* includes the lettered seraph. Indeed the only other English chapter house scheme to address the theology of sin and its remedy directly, though by different means, is the Marian portal at Salisbury of around 1260.[10] In Western medieval illustration the general grouping of Christ and seraphim is owed to *Psalm* 98, as in the ninth-century Utrecht Psalter (fol 57, also the *Te Deum* fol 88); another factor, also with reference to *Psalm* 98, may be large rood-loft or high altar compositions showing the Crucifixion between seraphim, as over Westminster's high altar as shown in the Islip Roll.[11] It is legitimate at least to mention Byzantine or Romanesque Last Judgement iconography in which Christ has seraphim to either side, or Mary and John the Baptist, as at twelfth-century

Torcello or Reichenau, or in Greek Gospel books.[12] A seraph accompanies an apocalyptic Christ in the early twelfth-century murals of St Gabriel's chapel at Canterbury.[13] English Romanesque art anticipated the general structure of this deësis, but its details will have been inconceivable before the emergence of the treatise *De sex alis cherubim*, the illustration in Corpus Christi College Cambridge MS 66 of *c* 1190 (of Durham-Sawley origin) being the earliest extant.[14]

A question arises as to the more general importance of *De sex alis* for the Westminster scheme. The text appears early in England in Augustinian circles, most notably in manuscripts attributed to Clement of Llanthony, but had circulated to the Benedictines by 1200. Westminster Abbey did not, as far as we know, possess a copy, but its spread by 1400, as part of such compilations as the *Turris sapientie*, was wide.[15] Its first part is derived from Hugh of St Victor's commentary on *Isaiah* 6 and the *Majestas Domini* in his *De arca Noe morali*. It opens with a commentary upon the text 'I saw the Lord sitting upon a throne high and elevated' (*Isaiah* 6:1), the high throne with the seraphim symbolizing the angels, the elevated throne the souls of the saints enjoying heavenly peace. It continues with *Isaiah* 66:1 in which Heaven is Christ's throne, the earth his footstool; Christ sits in his temple on the throne of eternity: 'by virtue of godliness He surpasses every creature by his timelessness'. All within the temple is subject to him, by which Isaiah means 'the cycle of time and the turning of the ages: for when time returns unto itself in its course, it circumscribes the temple by creating its very circumference'.[16] It is attractive to imagine that this circular image, derived from Hugh's commentary on Noah's Ark, was thought to answer in turn to the shape of the chapter house, or that the Apocalypse and (later) beast images were considered demonstrations of the unfolding of time from beginning to end. However, there is no evidence that the image of the seraph always accompanied the text *De sex alis*; by the fourteenth century its independence is marked.

A modern feature by fourteenth-century standards is the complement of figures ranged to either side of the deësis. These were standing or kneeling saints and angels as witnesses, a general arrangement owed almost entirely to the fourteenth-century Italian All Saints *Maestà* altarpiece or mural, such as those from the circles of Giotto, Duccio and Simone Martini. The Westminster paintings are manifestly trying to look Italian. The remainder of the works – namely the sequence of half-length musical angels under the trilobes of each wall arcade, the Sion figures, and the Apocalypse itself – are in related, but slightly different, styles (figs 178 and 179). Musical angels had become a

Fig 178 South-west wall, bay 33: angel with duct flute. *Photograph:* © Dean and Chapter of Westminster

Fig 179 North-west wall: angel with hurdy-gurdy. *Photograph:* © Dean and Chapter of Westminster

commonplace in English sculpture by *c* 1240 and – in this position, bust-length and at the head of a composition beneath an arch and behind a cloth of honour – were a *cliché* by the fifteenth century. The source is probably *Psalm 97*, *Cantate Domino*, and *Psalm 99*, *Iubilate Domino*: the Gallicanum of *Psalm 99* gives us *introite portas eius in confessione atria eius in hymnis confitemini illi laudate nomen eius* ('enter his gates in praise, his courts with hymns, O give thanks to him and praise his name'). We are reminded of the text recorded above one of the seraphs – *latreia in aula formosa* – an unusual expression, which designates the chapter as itself a heavenly palace.[17]

The Apocalypse and beasts

Pictures from the Revelation of St John, the second group of subjects, were chosen at least in part because of the name of their patron, John of Northampton, to whom we will return.[18] The Apocalypse is unusual in English chapter houses (though it occurs in conventual buildings, such as the Apocalypse bosses in the cloister at Norwich Cathedral): hence at Westminster we may suspect the special inclination of the patron. Noppen and Hansen in particular discussed the pictorial evidence.[19] The pictures on the north-west wall (bays 2–5; fig 180) are the best preserved and tightest stylistically; those on the south have lost most of the inscriptions written on glued vellum, have texts written in a different, squarer hand, show small stylistic differences, and witness St John's beard turning from brown to white: a feature also of Jean Bondol's Angers Apocalypse tapestries (Musée des Tapisseries, Angers) and John Thornton's Apocalypse in the east window at York Minster.[20] These might indicate that the

southern pictures were done in a second campaign, or were compromised by lack of resources or changed personnel reflected in their different state of preservation.

The pictures start (north-west wall) with four scenes from the life of St John, and then four Apocalypse scenes in each trilobed bay, leaping across the Judgement and creating scope for up to 96 pictures in all, paced at about five chapters for each side of the octagon. This substantial total exceeds that of one of the types of model probably known to the painters, the late fourteenth-century Apocalypse, with prefatory and suffixed scenes of the lives of John and St Edward, in Trinity College Cambridge MS B.10.2, closely related in style to the abbey's Litlyngton missal of 1383–84, with 92 images, including St John's life (many scenes are missing after *Revelation* 16).[21] This book is based on thirteenth-century Anglo-Norman prose Apocalypses. In the fourteenth century the Anglo-Norman French metrical version became more influential, as in the case of the cloister bosses at Norwich.[22] Westminster however retained the more old-fashioned prose form. The strong, and often-acknowledged, interest in Europe in Revelation as a theme for monumental decoration in the second half of the fourteenth century, which in England produced *inter alia* the great east window of York Minster *c* 1405, needs little comment. The Westminster murals' style, however, is not that of the English recension, being closer to German (Hamburg or Cologne) or Flemish work towards and around 1400. At least one Cologne painter was a citizen of London in these years, and worked for St Paul's Cathedral.[23]

The same pattern of exchange, from illuminations to murals, may also help in part to account for the fauna that were added late in the fifteenth century, or later, to the bays

Fig 180 North-west wall: Apocalypse of St John and beasts; general view of the surviving scenes in bays 2 to 5. *Photograph:* © English Heritage Photo Library

in the spaces below the Apocalypse panels, in the dossal position. The use of creatures or grotesques in this position on a wall was common in European wall painting.[24] Each bay had two confronted birds or beasts with a bird-filled tree between them, their total number being about forty-eight (twenty-four on each side under the Apocalypse). The animals are identified by skinny *textualis* labels in black or red. The riser of the first step in the north-west bay seems to have depicted sea creatures.[25] Where the Apocalypse marks the end of time, Adam's work in naming the animals was amongst the first of all actions. The birds and beasts were:

North side west wall:
Bay 1, by portal   *[?-lyd-?]* (left)
                Ostrych (right) captions only
                (Beneath the left-hand caption are
                about 15 rows of hitherto unrecorded
                textualis script painted in white on
                black)[26]

North side north-west wall:
Bay 2   *Reynder*
               Ro [*ie* roe-deer]
               (images remain, the intervening tree
               having a nesting bird (woodcock?)
               with four large chicks: fig 181)
Bay 3   *Wylde asse*
Bay 4   *Tame asse*
               (images remain, the intervening tree
               containing a bird: fig 183)
Bay 5   *Dromedary*
               Kameyl
               (images remain, the intervening tree
               having a red crowing cock)

South side south-east wall:
Bay 25   *Lyon* (caption only)

South side south wall:
Bay 29   *Cokedryll*

South side south-west wall:
Bay 33   *Greyho[und]*
               (rear part of the dog remains)

The present writer suggests that the pictures, though fragmentary, are in the tradition of a hybrid version of the bestiary which M R James identified as the 'fourth recension', now represented by only one rather rough surviving book, the *Liber de bestiis* of *c* 1425 (Cambridge University Library MS Gg.6.5) which is more indebted to the *De proprietatibus rerum* of Bartholomeus Anglicus than are other Bestiaries.[27] Though its illustrations do not confront pairs of animals, the couchant position of the *Reynder* with two huge antlers (fig 181) is very close to the stag (*cervus*) on fol 14 (fig 182); the wild ass (*onager*) on fol 32 has the same formidably exposed teeth as the Westminster one and the tame ass (*asinus*), fol 31, has the same neatly combed fringe (figs 183 to 185). Folio 2v of MS Gg.6.5 shows Adam naming the animals with birds sitting in a tree. It also has a dromedary and camel (fol 30, 28v) and, as in the Bestiaries, the camel has two humps and the dromedary scarcely one; however at Westminster the camel has one hump and the dromedary two, a peculiarity shared by the Helmingham Herbal and Bestiary (fols 17v, 19) of *c* 1500.[28]

The abbey's Cosmati sanctuary pavement inscriptions had already connected the ages of certain fauna, including dogs, stags and sea creatures, to the calculation of the date of the end of the world.[29] Again, then, 'the cycle of time and the turning of the ages' might be a theme. The pairings might also suggest a moralization to the effect that monastic life requires a taming of natural appetites. Alternatively, they might just be 'courtly' or palatial in character. Their date is unknown but late. The beasts were painted over a pink ground probably coeval with the Apocalypse, to which had been added some red and white roses visible next to, but earlier than, the *Reynder* and *Ro*.[30] A date of *c* 1500 or later is possible.

Patronage and date

Folio 92v of the *Liber Niger Quarternus* in the abbey muniments records a memorandum, headed *de renovatoribus et benefactoribus capellarum in circuitu infra ecclesiam monasterii* – a composite, since it mentions other works outside the church itself.[31] It includes notice of the *pictura de judicio in fronte domus capitularis*, which John of Northampton, the monk, had had made (*fieri fecit*) by contributing 11 marks, or £7 6s 8d. John professed in 1372, was ordained in 1375, sickened in 1403 and died in 1404. The same memorandum records that he had made the Apocalypse in the Chapter for £4 10s: *Item fieri fecit picturam Apocalipsis … in capitulo nondum completo*; he added a calendar to the cloister for 30s and other paintings at the door (*ad hostium*) of the church for £7; it also notes that he joined John of London in providing a retable for St John the Baptist's chapel – *fieri fecerunt picturam superioris tabule altaris Sancti Johannis Bapitiste pro* – at some point after 1378–79. The subject of this retable will almost certainly have been the altar's dedicatee, St John the Baptist

Fig 181 North-west wall: beasts below the Apocalypse scenes in bay 2; figures of reindeer and roe deer. *Photograph*: © Dean and Chapter of Westminster

Fig 182 Stag (*cervus*). *Photograph*: © the Syndics of Cambridge University Library; Cambridge MS Gg.6.5

himself. This allows us to restate the hypothesis that John the Baptist was shown in the Judgement mentioned earlier. It was not uncommon for patrons called John to commission artworks celebrating both the Baptist and the Evangelist.[32] The memo that John of Northampton also had the Apocalypse painted is unsurprising: the Apocalypse was included in part because of personal devotion to St John the Evangelist, whose life opens the pictures.

A few points are raised by the *Liber Niger*. The Judgment was *in fronte domus capitularis* while the Apocalypse was simply *in capitulo*. *Frons* can mean a facade, but, in this case, it certainly designates a main

interior wall.[33] We find other uses of the term *fronte*, *frons* or *frontispicio* to refer to interior furnishings in the fifteenth century; for instance the Jesse Tree reredos at St Cuthbert's, Wells, designated in its contract as a *fronte*.[34] In the *Liber Niger*, *frons* designates the east face, where the arcading and decoration are altogether richer, marking the abbot's and seniors' seats. *In capitulo* designates the remaining space. The expression *in capitulo nondum completo* may be a slip for *completam*: the Apocalypse, not the chapter house itself, was perhaps unfinished at the time the draft for the entry in the *Liber Niger* was compiled, and that in turn might suggest that, though begun by John, it was still underway in 1403–4 or later: a

Fig 183 North-west wall: wild ass and tame ass among the beasts below the Apocalypse scenes in bays 3 and 4. *Photograph*: © Dean and Chapter of Westminster

Fig 184 Wild ass (*onager*). *Photograph*: Cambridge © the Syndics of Cambridge University Library; Cambridge MS Gg.6.5

Fig 185 Tame ass (*asinus*). *Photograph*: Cambridge © the Syndics of Cambridge University Library; Cambridge MS Gg.6.5

point reinforced by the small stylistic and technical features of the south wall noted earlier.

It is generally assumed that these works were accomplished in 1372–1404. A date after 1377–78, when the chapter house received new buttresses, also seems likely.[35] The *Liber Niger* entry relating to John of Northampton's collaboration in providing a retable with brother John of London *postea reclusus* might be taken to mean that the latter worked with the former before becoming a monk before 1378–79. The term *fieri fecit* could only be used before Northampton's death in 1404. But, as Barbara Harvey has shown in her study of the *peculium*, monks at this time were able to make and save money.[36] Westminster was a wealthy monastery and its monks were paid 'unusually large' wages, as well as surplus issues of the major royal foundations; this implies the existence of an internal market in which monks could accumulate and then plough back capital by patronage. Hence it is important to bear in mind the possibility that John may have to have earned and built up his capital before he could shed it; and that in turn might point to his patronage dating towards the end of his life as a cloister monk, not the beginning. John's benefaction might also have been a partial contribution to the completion of work already in hand, or, given the term *fieri fecit*, to the beginning of a scheme to which others had contributed: £7 seems a modest sum for a fully gilded *Maestà*. It is possible that John himself would have been shown to Christ's left as a kneeling patron-figure, sponsored by John the Baptist, in the now-missing parts of the Judgement. The pictures reveal the significant and growing role of patronage within the monastery and, so to speak, within its internal market, in completing the project begun by the Plantagenets.

Since the *comparanda* are rare and the documents inconclusive, open-mindedness about the stylistic dating of these images is proper. Nothing in the style of these pictures militates against a date towards *c* 1400 or in the first decade of the fifteenth century. The style of the Sion figures looks in keeping with early fifteenth-century painting, and Brian Turner was right to place the Apocalypse pictures in the decade 1400–10.[37] The stylistic gap between the Sion group and the Apocalypse itself is not great; both are freer in handling than the more subtle Judgement. Since there is greater continuity technically and stylistically between the Apocalypse, musical angels and 'Sion' figures than with the central Judgement, and since the 'Sion' figures are also part of the Judgement theme, the gap in execution between all the phases cannot have been great. The probable sequence of execution was: (1) the Judgement (before *c* 1400); (2) the musical angels and Sion images; (3) the Apocalypse, in hand in the 1400s

after the Judgement and possibly finished after 1404.

Analogies of any kind for the Judgement's pseudo-Italianate mode of painting are almost non-existent. The two most important are the mostly lost but certainly very prestigious murals of St Stephen's chapel, Westminster (probably complete by 1363) and the tester of the tomb of the Black Prince at Canterbury, *c* 1380.[38] The radiating form of the gilt haloes of the angels with the seraphim in the chapter house is anticipated in a small halo in one of the Job stories from St Stephen's, and there is a generic relationship with the haloes on the Canterbury tester, though these are closest to the Westminster Litlyngton missal of 1383–84.[39] At Westminster the cusps on the inner circle of the larger haloes are sub-cusped and extended to form rays like the spokes of a rose window, perhaps inspired by the rose window design in the chapter house pavement nearby. This halo is not at all like the haloes of angels in the lost murals of angels holding cloths of honour in St Stephen's chapel: there, the forms were more Italianate. But the general composition of the figures in each bay is nevertheless highly likely to have been informed by the St Stephen's angels which, though more finely garbed, also stood within the lateral wall arcading of the royal chapel. There, as in the chapter house, the same fiction of wall paintings providing a dossal for the actual seated members of the community was apparent. But there is no reason to suppose that the same hands were at work on the two schemes.

Westminster was certainly not alone in cultivating this style. Abbot Thomas de la Mare at St Albans (1349–96) is recorded in the *Gesta abbatum* as commissioning a Majesty (*majestas*) on the main wall (*frons*) of the chapter house; this will have faced the place the *Gesta abbatum* called the *judicium* at the centre of the chapter house.[40] A Majesty is, strictly speaking, more likely to have been apocalyptic in character, so we cannot be sure that this picture was the model for the Westminster *judicium*. But it may have had metropolitan connections. In London, Abbot Thomas also acquired for the high altar of St Albans an Italian altarpiece *in lumbardia pictoratam*, costing over £45.[41] No connection has been made between it and the six-piece polyptych of Lombard manufacture worth £20 which Hugh of St Albans, painter to Edward III, bequeathed in his will of 1361 (proved in 1368) for the support of his widow Agnes.[42] Hugh was presumably a St Albans man, but he had worked on the St Stephen's chapel scheme and indeed supplied its *ordinatio*, or master drawings, in 1350.[43] Since his London business closed after his death, Agnes might have sold this altarpiece, suitably assembled, framed, gilt and polished, to Abbot Thomas at a substantial mark-up around 1370, the two works being one and the same. Presumably there were several vehicles for Italian ideas in the London region, via St Stephen's Chapel, via St Albans, and via circulation of Italian altarpieces, not to mention actual study in Italy.[44] No Italian polyptych would have such imagery as Westminster's paintings, however.

A date around, or after, 1400 would have a further consequence, since the addition of the Apocalypse was particularly responsible for creating the impression that the chapter house is painted all around. We find in *Pierce the Ploughman's Crede* a satirical description of a mendicant chapter house probably in London, with its interior 'As a Parlement-hous y-peinted aboute'.[45] Lethaby posited some connection between this passage and the occasional use before about 1395 of the Westminster chapter house by Parliament.[46] But *Pierce* appears to have been composed between 1393 and 1401, quite possibly after parliamentary use had ceased but before these pictures were begun, completed and inserted into the non-specialist literary imagination. The present writer doubts that there was any connection between these pictures and the history of Parliament. If an allusion to a secular, not monastic, parliament house is intended it might more probably be to the Painted Chamber in the palace, which appears to have doubled as a meeting place for parliament together with the abbey refectory.[47]

Conclusion

In sum, the Westminster scheme is a *unicum*, with no analogy to other medieval European chapter-house paintings.[48] It witnesses the transfer to monumental art of images found in well-developed English traditions of illustration: *De sex alis* and related penitential writing, the Apocalypse and encyclopaedic writing such as *De proprietatibus rerum*. In short, it is 'bookish'. The chapter pictures, though coherent, are a composite. They show no particular system. The only substantial monumental links are to some Last Judgement and *Maestà* compositions which reflect knowledge of Italian antecedents; and the Judgement is certainly quasi-Italian in stylistic stimulus, if not in technique and outcome. [PB]

Wall painting techniques

The examination of these important paintings in 1998–99 was complicated by the damage – both deliberate and accidental – to which they had been subjected, as well as by often harmful conservation treatments undertaken in the past. The analysis of the paintings has previously been published in *Conserving the Painted Past: developing approaches to wall painting conservation*.[49] The present account provides an updated context for these analytical results.

Used as a record office from the 1540s to 1863, the walls were lined with presses and a gallery,[50] and the two principal areas of painting were only rediscovered in 1801 and 1841, respectively.[51] Most of the lower areas of the paintings have been lost, while there is evidence of deliberate scraping in the Apocalypse cycle on the north side. Varnish was applied to the paintings during Scott's restoration of the chapter house in 1866–72,[52] while at the beginning of the twentieth century the paintings on the north-west wall were treated with oil of spike-lavender with a little spirit fresco medium; at the same time the other paintings, as well as the stonework, were treated with barium hydroxide.[53] In the 1920s the paintings were waxed, the surface then being heated with a blow-lamp before cleaning was undertaken (fig 186). At the time it was asserted that there 'is nothing in the wax or in the solvents which can possibly injure the pigments or the media in the paintings'.[54] The results are, however, all too evident, despite some cleaning undertaken in 1985–86, particularly of the best-preserved paintings on the north-west wall.

The Judgement

It has long been noticed that there are substantial differences in style between the Apocalypse and other paintings on the one hand (fig 187), and the Judgement on the other (fig 188).[55] The latter is strikingly Italianate, while the former are much closer to north German paintings of the period around 1400. Scientific examination revealed that the Judgement on the east wall is also technically distinct from the other paintings in the chapter house, a distinction corresponding to the stylistic differences between the two schemes.

Whereas the other paintings in the chapter house are executed on a chalk ground, the Judgement has an overall ground of lead white, a highly reflective surface providing depth and translucency to the paint layers above. This ground was applied directly to the irregularly tooled surface of the masonry (of Reigate stone), though particularly uneven areas and joints between the blocks were first filled with lime plaster roughly tapered to the level of the stone. In the lower zone, beneath the Majesty and elsewhere, preliminary drawing in red earth is clearly visible on the stone surface, and would therefore have been covered by the lead ground before painting commenced.

The palette of the Judgement painting could scarcely be richer, with gold leaf, azurite, indigo, malachite,

Fig 186 South-east wall, bay 24: use of a blow-lamp to aid the penetration of wax into the surface of the wall paintings (*cf* fig 175). *Photograph:* © English Heritage. NMR *c* 1931

verdigris, red lake, vermilion, red lead, red earth, yellow earth, charcoal black, bone white, calcium carbonate white and lead white all being identified. In addition, the presence of lead-tin yellow was suggested by a particle rich in tin and lead within a green paint layer.

Samples taken from the architectural polychromy immediately above the Judgement confirmed the presence of gold leaf, vermilion, a red lake pigment, red earth, carbon black and lead white (fig 34). The gold and red counter-change pattern was achieved by applying

vermilion combined with a red lake pigment for zones of red, and gold leaf on a preparation of vermilion combined with red earth, carbon black and lead white over a lead white ground. The similarity of the palette and application methodology suggest that the architectural polychromy may be coeval with the Judgement.

The already sumptuous palette was further extended by mixing and layering the pigments. For example, the pale flesh tone of the angel in the centre of bay 17 was built up in three layers: first, a grey-green underpaint (of charcoal black and yellow earth in a white matrix), followed by two layers of lead white combined with a little vermilion (the quantity of vermilion varying in each layer). By contrast, the deep red flesh of the angel at extreme right of the next bay (18) was achieved by applying a thin layer of vermilion over red earth on the lead white ground.

In many areas the complexity of the painting is now barely evident. The cloth of honour behind Christ merely appears as an area of dark paint, but examination in infrared light reveals its delicate design of stencilled motifs (figs 189 and 190). These were executed in indigo, on a green background of verdigris combined with lead white. Likewise, the subtle modelling of Christ's red robe is now scarcely apparent, though it was achieved by at least three layers of vermilion combined with varying amounts of lead white. The colour was further enriched by a final red glaze, over which fine linear details were then added in gold (figs 191 and 192).

Fig 187 North-west wall, bay 2: detail of the Apocalypse cycle. *Photograph*: H Howard 1998 © Conservation of Wall Painting Dept, Courtauld Institute of Art, London

Fig 188 East wall, bay 18: detail of Judgement. *Photograph*: H Howard 1998 © Conservation of Wall Painting Dept, Courtauld Institute of Art, London

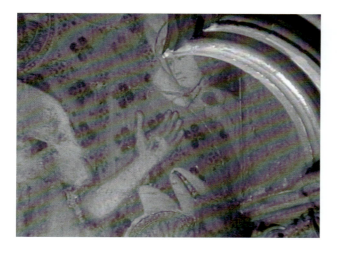

Fig 189 East wall, bay 19: detail of the cloth of honour held by angels behind Christ in the Judgement scene. Examination in near infra-red light revealed the cloth's delicate design of stencilled motifs. *Multispectral imaging*: Foundation for Research and Technology, Hellas © Conservation of Wall Painting Dept, Courtauld Institute of Art, London

Fig 190 East wall: the stencilled motifs were executed in indigo on a green background of verdigris combined with lead white as shown in this paint sample taken from the blue lining of the cloth of honour. The lead white ground is clearly visible at the base of the sample. *Photomicrograph*: H Howard 1998 © Conservation of Wall Painting Dept, Courtauld Institute of Art, London

Fig 191 East wall, bay 19: Christ's red robe embellished with linear detailing in gold and an applied clasp. *Macrophotograph*: H Howard 1998 © Conservation of Wall Painting Dept, Courtauld Institute of Art, London

Fig 192 East wall: cross-section of a sample taken from Christ's red robe. A waxy coating is visible at the top of the sample, and below this a layer of gold leaf on a white oil-based mordant. Multiple layers of red, which were employed to model the cloak, are visible in the lower portion of the sample. The uppermost of these consists of a semi-translucent vermilion layer, applied over three layers of vermilion combined with varying amounts of lead white and some carbon black. A trace of the lead white ground is visible at the base of the sample. *Photomicrograph*: H Howard 1998 © Conservation of Wall Painting Dept, Courtauld Institute of Art, London

The extent and delicacy of the gilding is indeed one of the most striking features of the painting. Whereas the fine lines on Christ's robe were achieved with mordant gilding, perhaps to create a slight relief effect, in other areas water gilding was employed. In the haloes, the gold leaf was applied over a red 'bole' containing red earth and calcium carbonate. Into this bole, concentric circles were incised, which would have remained visible once the gold leaf was applied, and which were used in setting out the intricate black patterns painted on the surface (figs 193 and 194). Luminous effects were achieved by applying translucent glazes over the gold leaf; for example, examination of one of the eyes scattered over the wings of the seraph in the fourth bay (20) revealed the presence of no fewer than three green layers over the gold leaf: a copper green glaze applied over two further layers of verdigris combined with varying quantities of lead white.

One further technical device enhanced the precious effect of the paintings: the use of bold relief for elements such as the crowns held by the seraphim (fig 195), and the

Fig 193 East wall, bay 18: while mordant gilding was employed for linear details such as on Christ's robe (fig 191), the haloes were water gilded on a red bole. Into this bole, concentric circles were incised which would have remained visible once the metal leaf was applied and were used in setting out the intricate black patterns on the surface. *Macrophotograph*: H Howard 1998 © Conservation of Wall Painting Dept, Courtauld Institute of Art, London

Fig 194 Detail of figure 193 showing the incised lines employed to set out the haloes and fine linear details painted in black on the surface of the gold leaf. *Videomicroscopy*: Heritage and Howard 1998 © Conservation of Wall Painting Dept, Courtauld Institute of Art, London

Fig 195 East wall, bay 18: crown held by cherub. *Macrophotograph*: H Howard 1998 © Conservation of Wall Painting Dept, Courtauld Institute of Art, London

brooch clasping Christ's cloak (fig 191). Tool marks in the surface of the best-preserved crown may suggest that these motifs were modelled *in situ*, though it is more likely that they were prefabricated in a tin-lined mould and only finished once they were attached to the wall. The composition of the crown is a mixture of silica and bone white in a lead white matrix, while tiny traces of vermilion, red lead and lead white survive on the surface (fig 196). In Christ's brooch, no doubt the circular central depression was once occupied by a real or imitation jewel.

The Old Testament figures, Apocalypse cycle and angel musicians

By contrast with the Judgement, a chalk ground was employed for all these other paintings. In several samples a single inclusion of azurite is visible, suggesting that a minute quantity of this pigment may have been incorporated to provide a slightly cool appearance to the layer. In the Apocalypse cycle an organic layer approximately 10 μm thick, and incorporating a few particles of red lead, is visible over the ground in some samples, and may represent the remains of a sealant layer to prevent absorption of the binding media from the paint layers above.

Some initial setting out may have been undertaken on the stonework beneath the chalk ground, since, in one sample, red particles are visible at the base of the ground. Elsewhere, traces of summary drawing, in both black and dark red, are visible on the surface of the ground. For example, the tiny angels above the Old Testament figures on the south-east wall appear to have been set out in black, and then, perhaps, refined in red before the final painting, though these areas are so loosely rendered that the painting sequence remains uncertain. There is also some evidence of incised setting out in the chalk ground, in preparation for the application of metal leaf, as for the outline of a sword and shield in *The War of the Beast upon the Saints*. In the final painting, stencils were employed for the motifs on the border of the Apocalypse scenes:

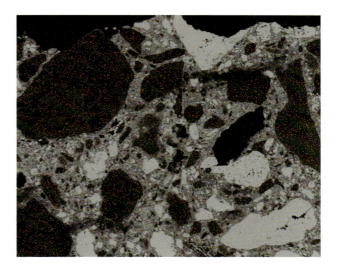

Fig 196 East wall: the body of the relief crown is made from a mixture of lead white, bone white and silica. This SEM micrograph with an X-ray dot map for phosphorus marks the concentrations of phosphorus from the bone white. *SEM micrograph*: H Howard 1998 © Conservation of Wall Painting Dept, Courtauld Institute of Art, London

including little white dogs on the north-west side (fig 197), and rosettes and stars on the south side.

The palette of the paintings is as varied as that of the Judgement, comprising gold leaf, tin leaf, kermes lake (extracted from the insect *Kermes vermilio* Planchon), vermilion, red lead, red earth, azurite, indigo, green earth, verdigris, orpiment, yellow earth, bone white, lead white, chalk and carbon black. Identification of the binding media proved problematic, but GC-MS analysis of a sample of red lead from one of the tiny angels above the Old Testament figures confirmed the presence of linseed oil, and possibly a trace of pine resin. In addition, Fourier transform infra-red (FTIR) analysis of a white alteration product within the red lead layer confirmed the presence of lead carboxylate, indicating soap formation due to a reaction between an original oil medium and the lead pigment (fig 198).[56]

In the Apocalypse, the blue of St John's draperies was

Fig 197 North-west wall, bay 3: Apocalypse. Stencilled border of small white dogs. *Photograph*: © Dean and Chapter of Westminster

Fig 198 Lead soaps have been identified in the chapter house wall paintings. These form due to a reaction between the oil binder and red lead pigment. The increase in volume associated with this alteration and consequent disruption of the surface is clearly visible, particularly at the top right of the cross-section where a large white lead carboxylate 'soap' is present. *Photomicrograph*: H Howard 1998 © Conservation of Wall Painting Dept, Courtauld Institute of Art, London

Fig 199 South-east wall, bay 23. The angel's trumpet appears dark, owing to the partial oxidation of the tin leaf. *Macrophotograph*: H Howard 1998 © Conservation of Wall Painting Dept, Courtauld Institute of Art, London

Fig 200 Cross-section of a paint sample taken from the angel's trumpet shown in figure 199. Tin leaf was applied over an oil-based mordant with tiny red and yellow inclusions. Below the mordant a layer of orpiment is visible on the chalk ground which has a single azurite inclusion. *Photomicrograph*: H Howard 1998 © Conservation of Wall Painting Dept, Courtauld Institute of Art, London

achieved variously with azurite and indigo; for example, with azurite over a grey ground in *The Sixth Vial*, and with indigo both combined with, and applied over, lead white in *The Lamb on Mount Sion*. Similarly versatility is evident in the use of the very expensive kermes lake:[57] combined with lead white for the delicate pink drapery of *The Mighty Angel*, and employed as a glaze over gold leaf for the luminous red of the brooch of one of the Old Testament figures. Gold leaf was used as extensively as in the Judgement, principally for haloes in the Apocalypse scenes, but also for details such as the sword in *The Vision of Christ amid the Candlesticks*. Throughout the cycle it appears to have been applied over an oil-based mordant.

But it is the extensive use of tin leaf in the Apocalypse cycle and musical angels which is particularly striking, and distinct from the Judgement. Now partially oxidized to a dark brown or black, it is difficult to appreciate its original visual impact. Among many examples are the tracery of the church windows in *The Seventh Vial*, made from tin leaf applied over an oil mordant and subsequently glazed; the halo and instrument of the musical angel in the westernmost bay of the north-west wall, now oxidized to black (figs 199 and 200); and the border of the mandorla in the *Majesty and the Twenty-four Elders*, on which linear details were painted in verdigris combined with lead white.

While these paintings show no counterpart to the bold relief elements of the Judgement, they do feature one type of attachment very prominently: the broad strips of parchment employed for the lengthy inscriptions below the Apocalypse scenes (fig 201). Fine ruled lines for setting out the text on the parchment are clearly visible at high

Fig 201 North-west wall, bay 3: scene from the Apocalypse of St John the Divine. The left-hand panel shows Christ in Majesty holding seven stars in his hand, with a sword emerging from his mouth, and flanked by seven candlesticks. The right-hand panel shows Christ in Majesty, surrounded by twenty-four elders playing musical instruments. Below each scene is a text written on a strip of parchment, glued to the wall.
Photograph: © English Heritage Photo Library 1987

Fig 202 North-west wall, bay 3: detail showing the fine ruled lines for setting out the text on the parchment. The surface texture of the material is also clearly visible. *Videomicroscopy*: Heritage and Howard 1998 © Conservation of Wall Painting Dept, Courtauld Institute of Art, London

magnification (fig 202). On some areas of the ashlar support, evidence survives for the painters having wiped red paint from their brushes, in the knowledge that these areas would later be covered by the parchment.

Discussion

Scientific examination has shown that technical differences correlate exactly with the stylistic differences between the two major schemes, with the Judgement executed on an overall lead white ground, and the Apocalypse and associated paintings executed on a chalk ground. Whereas tin leaf is used extensively in the Apocalypse and musical angels, it is absent from the Judgement. Bold raised motifs, such as the crowns, occur only in the Judgement, whereas parchment attachments are employed only in the Apocalypse.

While the Judgement shows Italian influences in its style and iconography, it is entirely northern in its technique. Executed on a lead white ground applied directly to the stone, it is fundamentally unlike Italian wall paintings of the period, which are executed basically in the fresco technique on plaster, however much final detail is added *a secco*. The Judgement painting is medium-rich, multi-layered and translucent on its reflective ground, and thus has a jewel-like quality quite dissimilar to the more opaque Italian paintings.

These characteristics are, however, entirely typical of the finest Gothic wall paintings in England and elsewhere in northern Europe. For example, the surviving fragments of the scheme from St Stephen's chapel in the Palace of

Westminster (1350–63) likewise display red lead grounds bound in oil and oil glazes,[58] while in the late fourteenth-century decoration of the chapel of Our Lady Undercroft in Canterbury Cathedral a reflective layer of red lead was employed beneath vermilion on the vault, and the whole chapel studded with relief elements, including mirrors and glass beads imitating jewels.[59] Similarly, in the paintings of *c* 1395 in the Byward Tower of the Tower of London, an overall lead white ground was employed to provide translucency to the green background of verdigris and lead white in an oil medium. Linseed oil has also been identified in the crimson, red and purple glaze of St Michael's robe.[60] At Westminster Abbey itself, recent analysis of the earlier wall paintings of *c* 1300 in the south transept and St Faith's chapel has confirmed the use of an oil medium.[61] The stylistically similar thirteenth-century paintings in Angers Cathedral have also been shown to employ lead grounds, subtle mixtures of pigments such as lead white, copper blues and red lake, and oil and other binding media.[62] But perhaps the most splendid of all wall paintings displaying such techniques are those on the inner faces of the choir screen of Cologne Cathedral (*c* 1332–49), using mixed media, multiple translucent glazes and vast quantities of gold and other metal foil.[63]

There is no need to look abroad for the authorship of the chapter house Judgement, however, since every aspect of its technique is closely paralleled in other late fourteenth-century painting in England.[64] For example, azurite combined with lead white and red lake was used in the Byward Tower paintings, while the Wilton diptych palette incorporates both azurite and indigo and pigment mixtures including azurite combined with lead white.[65] Isotope ratio studies indicate that the lead used for the production of the lead white in the chapter house painting came from Derbyshire, as has also recently been established for the lead pigments employed in the earlier fourteenth-century Thornham Parva retable.[66] The Judgement displays much less raised ornament than the St Stephen's chapel and Our Lady Undercroft paintings, but the relief crowns are closely paralleled on the painted tester over the tomb of Richard II and Anne of Bohemia in Westminster Abbey, dating from 1395 to 1396.[67] Whereas the motif of the cloth of honour held by angels behind Christ in the Judgement derives from Italian *Maestà* compositions, its alternating stencilled designs revealed by infra-red examination (fig 189) are of a typically English type; the rosettes are similar to those that would have been produced by the unique surviving example of a medieval lead stencil, excavated at Meaux abbey in East Yorkshire.[68] The manner in which this stencilled decoration was applied across the whole expanse of cloth, only for some

Fig 203 Byward Tower, Tower of London: general view of the south wall, to the west of the inserted chimney. *Photograph*: H Howard 2000 © Historic Royal Palaces

then to be concealed when the Instruments of the Passion were added on either side of Christ, is comparable to the painting sequence in the Byward Tower; there, a rich diaper of gilded popinjays, fleurs-de-lis and lions was first applied over the green background, and then partly hidden when the Crucifixion group was painted. Similar heraldic decoration covers a beam extending the length of the room. Recent examination of the Byward Tower paintings has, for the first time, confirmed that the heraldic decoration and figurative elements are coeval. Detailed examination of the final red linear detail around the fleur-de-lis indicates that it is coincident and continuous with the final red linear detail around the halo of St John (figs 203 and 204). In addition the mordant for the gold leaf employed for heraldic decoration on the walls and beam contains characteristic inclusions that are identical to those identified in the mordant employed in the figurative elements of the wall painting.

Also entirely typical of late fourteenth-century painting in England are the complex halo designs in the Judgement, with their radiating tracery surrounded by elaborate borders of quatrefoils and roundels (fig 205). It

Fig 204 Byward Tower, Tower of London: recent scientific examination has, for the first time, confirmed that the heraldic decoration and figurative elements are coeval. This detail shows that the final red linear detail around the fleur-de-lis is coincident and continuous with the final red linear detail around the halo of St John. *Macrophotograph*: H Howard 2000 © Historic Royal Palaces

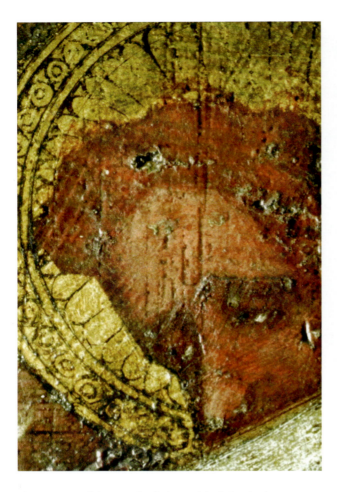

Fig 205 East wall, bay 18: detail of one of the haloes in the Judgement. *Macrophotograph*: H Howard 1998 © Conservation of Wall Painting Dept, Courtauld Institute of Art, London

Fig 206 Canterbury Cathedral: finely wrought black linear details are apparent on the haloes on the painted tester over the tomb of the Black Prince (d 1376). *Photograph*: Marie Louise Sauerberg © Hamilton Kerr Institute, by courtesy of the Dean and Chapter of Canterbury

has been observed that similar borders occurred in some of the haloes of the St Stephen's chapel paintings (1350–63), and that ultimately they derive from those employed by Simone Martini and other Sienese painters from *c* 1320.[69] However, whereas the Italian haloes are in moulded relief, the chapter house haloes are entirely flat, and the designs merely painted. In this, as well as in their combination of Italianate borders with Gothic 'rose window' patterns, they are closely paralleled by the haloes on the painted tester over the tomb of the Black Prince (d 1376) at Canterbury Cathedral, among many factors illustrating the closeness of wall painting and panel painting at this period (fig 206).[70] However, they are even more closely comparable with the almost identical haloes on surviving wall painting fragments from St Stephen's chapel. The way in which the radial spokes, of these and the chapter house haloes, converge to a number of points, clearly off-set from the centre is striking (fig 207).

If the Judgement shows Italian stylistic and iconographical influences modified by northern

Fig 207 Palace of Westminster, St Stephen's Chapel: detail showing one of the haloes in a fragment of wall painting now in the British Museum. The way in which the radial spokes converge to a number of points, clearly off-set from the centre, is strikingly close to those in the Judgement. *Photograph*: © British Museum

intermediaries, the Apocalypse cycle and related paintings are so close in style to north German painting of the late fourteenth century – especially to panel paintings by the workshop of Master Bertram in Hamburg – that the possibility arises that they might even be the work of German painters.[71] The style of the Apocalypse paintings, in particular, is almost identical in the top-heavy proportions of the figures, the facial types, the soft modelling of the draperies, and the predominantly red and blue/green colouring. Evidence for artistic links between England and Germany is abundant at this period,[72] and includes at least two documentary references to German painters actually working in England, one of whom – Herebright of Cologne

– was commissioned in 1398 to paint an image of St Paul and its tabernacle in St Paul's Cathedral.[73]

On the other hand, it has long been recognized that the iconographical model of the Apocalypse cycle is English – most likely a surviving late fourteenth-century manuscript now in Cambridge.[74] In this respect, it is particularly interesting to compare the scene of *Christ and the Twenty-four Elders*, where the wall painter has first followed the horizontal arrangement of the lamps on either side of Christ's head, but at a late stage realized that he need to change this arrangement to make all seven fit (figs 208 and 209). Of course, the use of such a model does not preclude a foreign artist, and it is unfortunate that little analysis

Fig 208 North-west wall, bay 3: changes were made in the design at quite an advanced stage of the painting process. Imaging of the scene of Christ and the twenty-four Elders in near-infrared shows that the painter originally represented only six lamps in the same arrangement as that depicted in a late fourteenth-century manuscript now in Cambridge (Cambridge MS B 10.2 fol 4v). *Multispectral imaging*: Foundation for Research and Technology, Hellas © Conservation of Wall Painting Dept, Courtauld Institute of Art, London

Fig 209 The same detail as in figure 208, but here, in visible light, the painter's correction (*pentimento*) can be seen. All but one of the gilded lamps has been painted over, and a more successful arrangement created, with the lamps suspended around the mandorla. *Multispectral imaging*: Foundation for Research and Technology, Hellas © Conservation of Wall Painting Dept, Courtauld Institute of Art, London

seems to have been undertaken of paintings by the Master Bertram workshop. Nevertheless, evidence from Cologne and elsewhere in Germany shows that there is nothing about their technique that would render impossible their attribution to a German workshop.

Nor, however, is there any aspect of their technique which is unlikely in an English context, underlining the international nature of painting at this period. For example, England was the main producer of tin in the Middle Ages,[75] and there are many examples of its use in polychromy, usually for relief ornament – as in the St Stephen's chapel paintings and for the background of the portrait of Richard II[76] – but also as glazed foil on the Coronation chair at Westminster Abbey.[77] All the pigments employed are paralleled in other English wall paintings of the fourteenth and fifteenth centuries, though it is notable that kermes lake has been identified in both the Apocalypse and Old Testament figures. This was the first time that the use of this particular lake had been identified in English medieval wall painting and, in addition, it is one of the very earliest occurrences of its use, as it has not been identified in any painted work before the end of the fourteenth century.[78] Kermes lake has now also been identified in the portrait of Richard II (Westminster Abbey), dated to the last decade of the fourteenth century, where it was used as a glaze over vermilion for the King's robe,[79] and, most recently, in a sample taken from the frame of the Black Prince's Tester (d 1376).[80] In the latter, both kermes and lac have been identified in the same paint sample, along with a tiny trace of madder.[81]

Although applied inscriptions on parchment occur in, for example, Simone Martini's *Maestà* of *c* 1315–16,[82] an especially close parallel of about the same date as the chapter house Apocalypse is found in London: on Rahere's tomb (*c* 1405) in St Bartholomew's, Smithfield, where texts from *Isaiah* are applied to the open books of the two bedesmen kneeling beside the effigy.[83] Though none survives, there is physical evidence that a material such as

parchment may also have been applied to the tombs of Edmund Crouchback (*c* 1300) and his wife Aveline de Forz at Westminster.[84] Although calcium carbonate, in the form of lime, is commonplace in English wall painting, a chalk ground has only been identified in one other instance; for one of the two early fourteenth-century figures in the feretory of St Albans Cathedral. There, a chalk ground was used for one of the figures, and a lead white ground for the other, indicating – since they are stylistically almost identical – the activity of two different artists within the same workshop.[85]

The technical and other evidence for the chapter house paintings suggests something slightly different: the employment of two distinct workshops, the first executing the Judgement painting, and the second undertaking the Apocalypse cycle and other paintings fairly soon afterwards. The technical differences between the two schemes cannot elucidate their precise dating, though the technical and stylistic break occurring *within* the Judgement, to which iconographically the Old Testament figures belong suggests that little time intervened.[86] But the technical evidence shows that, whatever break did occur in the painting operation, it must have been brief, since the Apocalypse, musical angels, rose dado and Old Testament figures are all essentially one scheme. Although a few of the musical angels are slightly overlapped by the Apocalypse,[87] this merely shows that the painters worked from top to bottom of the wall, as is the usual practice. Such a large operation must have involved a number of different painters, which would account for the relatively minor stylistic differences that are apparent: there is no reason why the angels and Apocalypse scenes, for example, could not have been the responsibility of different hands within a single workshop.

Given the vigorous physical history of these complex paintings, their survival is remarkable, albeit in a compromised condition. We are fortunate indeed that the ongoing deterioration is now being addressed.[88] (HH)

The chapter house decorated tile pavement

12

Laurence Keen

The chapter house, referred to by Matthew Paris as 'incomparable', was nearing completion in 1253, for in that year work was being carried out on the entrance and canvas was purchased for covering the empty windows. At the same time John of St Omer was finishing the wooden lectern which had been commissioned in 1249.[1] Stuart Eborall Rigold, without doubt correctly, observed that the laying of the floor tiles was the final task to be carried out before all of the works on the building were completed, and that this was done before 1259.[2] This *terminus ante quem* is provided by an entry in the Close Roll, dated 20 April, which records that the king gave to Brother Robert, for paving the chapel of St Dunstan, 'all the tiles which remain of the pavement of the chapter [house] of Westminster, and which are now in the belfry of the same place.'[3] So, may one suggest that the pavement was laid in about 1255? Remarkably, for medieval decorated tile floors, these dates are crucial and rare for extant pavements anywhere, and thus give the chapter house pavement an added significance. It is, without doubt, the most important surviving inlaid tiled-floor in Europe. It has never been examined in detail: this is the first attempt. Confronted by designs of the very highest quality, previous writers have assumed that the pavement was a special commission by Henry III in the 1250s. Elizabeth Eames thought that the pictorial tiles were left over from other pavements in the Palace of Westminster.[4] It is proposed here, further, that the pavement, although a special royal commission, is laid entirely with tiles left over from other royal works in the Palace of Westminster. This does not detract from the fact that the pavement consists of tile designs of superlative

quality, ranking with some of the greatest artistic output of medieval ceramic art.

Antiquarian interest in the pavement

After the dissolution of the abbey in 1540 it is well known that the chapter house became a repository for the royal records and it remained so until 1864, when the keys were handed over to HM Office of Works (p 136). It would appear that, from early in its function as an archive repository, the chapter house's thirteenth-century pavement was covered with a wooden floor, which perhaps dated from Wren's work on the building, shortly after 1700.

Whether or not it was known to eighteenth-century antiquaries that the wooden boarding covered a surviving medieval pavement is uncertain. But the first recorded illustrations of some of the tiles were published in 1835: these, at a scale of one third, were engraved by Henry Shaw from drawings by the architect William Caveler.[5] The earliest detailed account appeared in 1841. Lewis Cottingham, in a letter to Sir Henry Ellis, dated 14 January, wrote that, in the context of the restoration of the Temple Church, he examined the chapter house floor 'for specimens of painted tiles'. Having established 'that the patterns of the ancient pavement were laid in strips about three feet six inches wide, from east to west' he and 'my friend Mr. [James] Savage … Directed a portion of the boarded floor to be removed, across the room from north to south, when to our great delight, we found the original pavement in a very perfect state, with scarcely a tile broken, and the colours, in many parts, as brilliant as when first laid'. Cottingham's letter was accompanied by, apparently, nine drawings 'correctly traced and copied from the originals' (the drawings are numbered but are not illustrated). He concluded his letter with the comment that: 'The other designs show great delicacy in the patterns and execution, and the whole floor, when open to view, must have presented a gorgeous display of the exquisite taste of the gothic Architects of the middle ages'.[6]

John Gough Nichols used Cottingham's original drawings, or copies of them, as the basis for twenty-one woodcuts in his *Examples of Decorative Tiles*, published in 1842.[7] Remarkably, the chapter house drawings have recently come to light in the Spruance Library of the Bucks County Historical Society, Doylestown, Pennsylvania, in a volume assembled by Nichols.[8] Cottingham's drawings appear to have been used by Henry Shaw to produce three colour plates in his seminal publication of 1858. There is a double plate showing the eastern half of the whole pavement, and two other plates (without scales) showing some of the designs (figs 210 and 211).[9] The plan is remarkable in that it would appear that not all of the wooden boarding had been removed to record the pavement and so a number of omissions and inaccuracies can be accounted for and allowed. The record presses and cupboards were dismantled in June 1866

Fig 210 Chapter house pavement: the south-east quadrant. *Drawing*: 1850s; after Shaw 1858, plate 4

210

FROM THE CHAPTER HOUSE, WESTMINSTER.

Fig 211 Chapter house pavement: examples of four-tile designs and border tiles; *above*: designs 4 and 21; *below*: designs 6 and 20. *Drawing*: 1850s; after Shaw 1858, plate 6

(p 143), but it is likely that the wooden boarding was left *in situ* to protect the tiles while restoration was in progress. Scott includes a print of the chapter house 'in its present state' by Orlando Jewitt in his *Gleanings*, first published in 1860 (fig 212).[10] This shows the wooden boarding with sections removed to reveal a line of heraldic tiles, their points to the right, suggesting a view to the

south. However, the axis of the tiles has been erroneously turned through ninety degrees, since the view is unambiguously toward the west side of the chapter house. Scott writes that the floor 'is probably the most perfect, and one of the finest encaustic [*sic*] tile pavements now remaining. It is happily, in a nearly perfect state, having been protected by a wood floor'. He notes that: 'Many of

Fig 212 Chapter house interior, view west. This purports to show the lines of heraldic tiles beneath the timber floor, but they are incorrectly orientated. *Drawing*: Orlando Jewitt, 1859; after Scott 1860, page 40

the patterns are most noble in their design, and some of extraordinary delicacy and refinement'. He refers to a number of pictorial tiles and says that: 'Many of the patterns have been pretty correctly copied by Mr. Minton in the pavement of the Temple Church', and that many had been reproduced in Henry Shaw's recent work.[11]

On 12 May 1866, *The Illustrated London News* published a full-page illustration of the chapter house with the wooden boarding and furnishings still intact. The boarding radiates from the central column, with various parts of it removed, and is being inspected by two figures: one, perhaps the dean, the other, no doubt, Gilbert Scott. Another version of the same drawing shows Scott alone inspecting the floor (fig 133). Restoration of the chapter house did not start until early in 1867 (p 143).

The extent of Scott's work on the floor is unclear, but Eames is wrong in stating that Scott 'relaid' the pavement.[12] It would appear that the best preserved of the tiles were retained *in situ*. Where examples were in a sorry state, Scott evidently replaced these with new tiles by Herbert Minton and Sons, as made for the Temple church in the first instance: repointing was carried out in the joints using red cement. The several hundred replica tiles occur randomly all over the pavement. The greatest extent of their use is where the most extreme wear would have occurred, that is at the entrance. Steven Brindle's study of Scott's work has established that he included a provisional sum of £400 for repairing the floor.[13]

Further discussion and a description of the pavement was published by Lethaby in 1906. He opined that 'The tile floor … must be the finest pavement of the kind now existing' and provided illustrations of the 'salmon' [*sic*], one of the border tiles and of seven of the pictorial tiles,[14] which he found 'quite as fine as the otherwise unequalled

Chertsey series, with which they have much in common', and asserted that 'It is clear from the subjects that the tiles were specially designed for Westminster'. Lethaby's drawings of the pictorial tiles are important as they are at a larger scale than those published before, but, as we shall see, they are not entirely accurate. However, he provides an interesting comment on the conservation of the pavement by observing that: 'I fear that the endeavour to protect the tiles by linoleum is not entirely successful. Their surface is turning to dust, and it was only by comparing duplicate tiles that I could make out the subjects'.[15]

The first serious study of the chapter house pavement, and indeed of the abbey tiles generally, was that by Clayton, published in 1912. He provides the earliest published plan of the whole floor, drawn by J O Cheadle, albeit diagrammatically, showing the location of the four sets of pictorial tiles and the six inscriptions in the southern part of the pavement (fig 213). One set of pictorial tiles is planned incorrectly in band 13: it should be in band 14. Recorded is the triangle of 'mixed tiles' in the south-west corner. Clayton observed that the laying of the tiles began on the north side, because a row of fish, present on the north side is missing alongside the royal arms on the south,

and notes the use of specially made triangular tiles with stars against the obtuse angles (fig 214). Only in the triangular area in the south-west are patterned tiles broken to fill the angles. He discusses the use of this triangle and notes that of the nine patterns in this area three do not occur elsewhere in the chapter house.[16]

Clayton published drawings of six decorated designs, one border tile (fish) and three of the pictorial tiles, noting that 'It is high time that special attention were paid to the two sets of figured tiles that lie due south of the central pillar; for they stand in need of special study and preservation'.[17]

In 1924 the Royal Commission on Historical Monuments devoted only a few lines to the pavement, but provided a plate showing all of the eight pictorial tiles, a border tile (one of the pike),[18] six of the patterns, the four tiles showing the arms of England, and ten of the letter tiles.[19] The plate is important in that the drawings of the pictorial tiles are accurate and several show much greater detail than now survives.

A description of the pavement

A fuller appreciation of the chapter house pavement than has been possible hitherto can now be attempted, thanks to a photogrammetric survey carried out by English Heritage in 1998–9 (fig 215),[20] and a complete tile-by-tile drawing of the floor made in 2009 (Plan 2). In 2008 the writer prepared a new set of drawings of the thirty-six tile designs (figs 216 to 222 and Appendix) and the six inscriptions (figs 226 to 228). Here, a brief account of the basic layout of the pavement is given, and some preliminary conclusions will be offered.

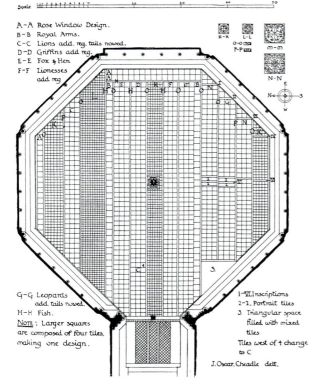

Fig 213 Schematic plan of the pavements in the chapter house and inner vestibule. *Drawing*: after Clayton 1912, fig 1

Fig 214 Tile pavement, band 8: detail of the tiling around the central pillar. Two of the special triangular tiles (design 27) abut the south-west face, and the narrow gaps on the west and south are filled with medieval roof tiles placed on edge. *Photograph*: Warwick Rodwell © Dean and Chapter of Westminster

Fig 215A Photomosaic of the tile pavement in the chapter house, divided into six sections: north east (east is at the top). *Photograph*: © English Heritage Photo Library 1998

Fig 215B Photomosaic of the tile pavement in the chapter house, divided into six sections: east central (east is at the top). *Photograph*: © English Heritage Photo Library 1998

Fig 215C Photomosaic of the tile pavement in the chapter house, divided into six sections: south east (east is at the top). *Photograph*: © English Heritage Photo Library 1998

Fig 215D Photomosaic of the tile pavement in the chapter house, divided into six sections: south west (east is at the top). *Photograph*: © English Heritage Photo Library 1998

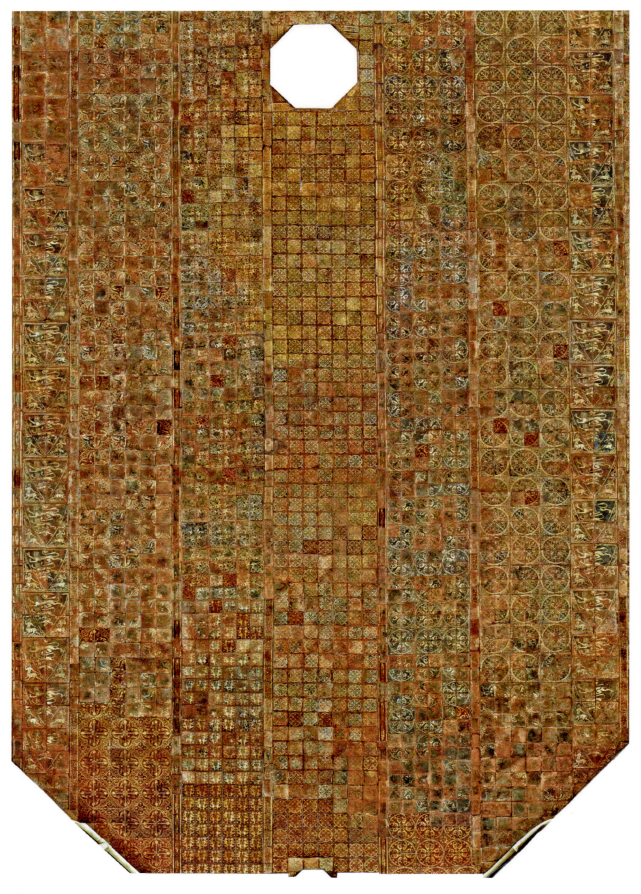

Fig 215E Photomosaic of the tile pavement in the chapter house, divided into six sections: west central (east is at the top). *Photograph*: © English Heritage Photo Library 1998

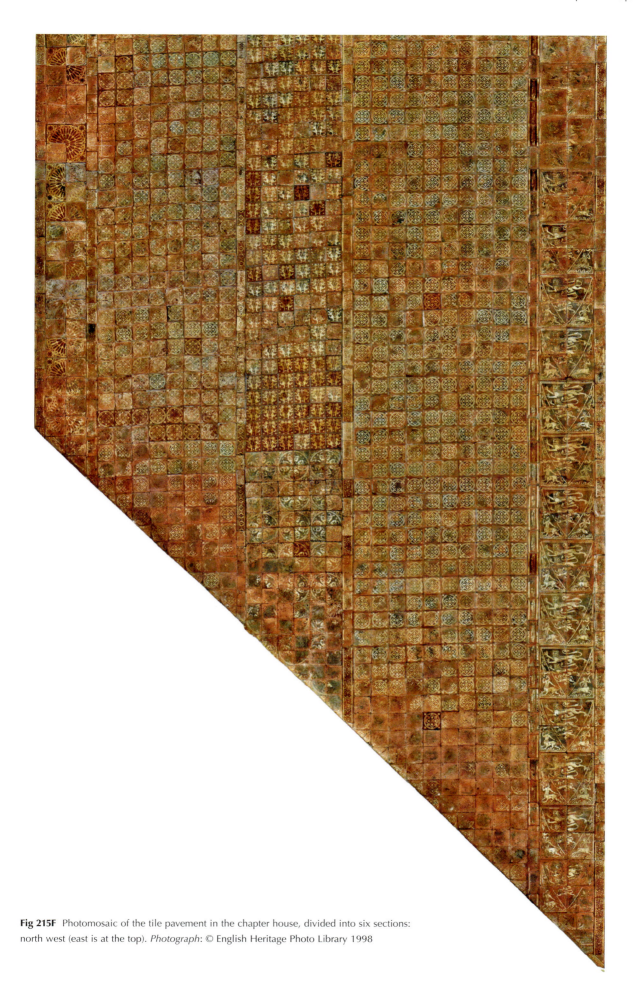

Fig 215F Photomosaic of the tile pavement in the chapter house, divided into six sections: north west (east is at the top). *Photograph*: © English Heritage Photo Library 1998

Fig 216 Four-tile designs 1 to 6. *Drawing*: © Laurence Keen; scale 1:3

7 8 9

Fig 217 Four-tile designs 7 to 9. *Drawing*: © Laurence Keen; scale 1:3

Fig 218 Four-tile designs 10 to 13 (clockwise from top left). *Drawing*: © Laurence Keen; scale 1:3

10–13

Fig 219 Single-tile designs 14 to 19. *Drawing*: © Laurence Keen; scale 1:3

Fig 220 Border tiles, designs 20 to 28. *Drawing*: © Laurence Keen; scale 1:3

29

30

31

Fig 221 Pictorial tiles showing hunting scenes, designs 29 to 31. *Drawing*: left column after Lethaby 1906, figs 19–21; right column © Laurence Keen; scale 1:3

Fig 222 Pictorial tiles, designs 32 to 36. *Drawing*: © Laurence Keen; scale 1:3

The pavement is laid out in fifteen rectangular panels, or bands, on an east–west axis, with all except one separated from the adjacent band by a line of decorated border tiles. Beneath the stone benches along the eastern wall is the only north–south panel. Finally, against the south-west side of the chapter house, the banding is broken by a triangular area of tiling of a wholly different nature from the rest, and the orientation of its components is also north–south. There is no uniformity in the width of each band, the composition of which is as follows.

· *Band 1* contains the four-tile rose window (design 3), with a border (design 20) to north and south; the band is laid in one row alongside the north wall.
· *Band 2* is eight tiles wide, using largely a single-tile design (16); however, the final eleven rows at its western end comprise tiles of design 15. The border on the south is design 23.
· *Band 3* is six tiles wide, mainly consisting of single-tile design 14; the final seventeen rows at the west end comprise sets of a four-tile design (8). The border on the south is design 20.
· *Band 4* is ten tiles wide, made up of design 15.
· *Band 5* uses the four-tile design of the arms of England (designs 10–13) thirty-one times, with borders to north (designs 24 and 25) and south (design 20) (figs 41 and 215). There is a small triangular area of miscellaneous infilling at the western end.
· *Band 6* is made up of a four-tile design, with three sets across the width of the band (design 6; fig 211). The border on the south comprises designs 24 and 25.
· *Band 7* principally comprises three sets of a four-tile design (7) across the width of the band (fig 146). At the western end, however, are twenty-one rows of single tiles of design 14. The border on the south is design 20.
· *Band 8* is the central band and is almost entirely of a single-tile design (16), seven tiles wide. This band is off-centre to the column, which stands adjacent to the north border, with an extra row of tiles along the southern edge (fig 215). On the eastern side of the column is a transverse row of six tiles of design 9. There are special cut tiles of designs 27 and 28 abutting the angles of the column; also some fragments of unglazed medieval roof tile have been used, on edge, to fill narrow gaps (fig 214). There is no archaeological evidence to suggest that Scott disturbed the base of the column: indeed, the tiles indicate that he did not. The border on the south comprises designs 24 and 25.
· *Band 9* contains four-tile designs, arranged three sets wide (design 8). The border on the south is design 20.
· *Band 10* principally contains four-tile designs, arranged

three sets wide (design 5); however, the final twelve rows at the west end are of design 6.
· *Band 11* contains the arms of England, as in band 5, but does not have a row of border tiles to the north (fig 215). However, it is approximately the same distance from the central column as the similar band of arms to the north. The border on the south is design 20.
· *Band 12* consists of four-tile designs (4), three sets wide (fig 211). There is an inscription (I) at the eastern end (fig 40) and a panel of eleven pictorial tiles, arranged in two rows, at the middle (designs 32–36; fig 223). The border on the south is design 22.
· *Band 13* is similarly composed of four-tile designs, but using design 1, laid three sets wide. It has an inscription (II) at the eastern end (fig 42). The border on the south is design 23. Bands 12 and 13 are both truncated on the west by triangular area 17, with a border of design 20 separating them.
· *Band 14* is also largely of a four-tile design (2), three sets wide, with an inscription (III) at the east and another panel of pictorial tiles at the middle. There are twelve pictorial tiles, arranged in two rows, with an inscription (V) between them. The eastern row contains designs 33–36, and the western row comprises two sets of the three-tile hunting scene (designs 29, 30 and 31). The western end of the band comprises five rows of tiles of design 6. The border on the south is design 23.
· *Band 15* is entirely of a single-tile design (15), five tiles wide, with two further inscriptions (IV and VI), one at the east end and the other midway. The border on the south is design 26.

Apart from a few mistakes, the bands are generally consistent in the use of a particular design, although in bands 2, 3, 7, 10 and 14 a second design is used in the western part.

· *North–south band 16* consists of twenty-and-a-half sets of the four-tile rose window design (3), laid in two rows, separated from the rest of the floor by a border of pike (designs 24 and 25) arranged head-to-head and tail-to-tail (fig 215). There is no border against the eastern edge.
· *Triangular area 17* is a triangle of tiling at the end of bands 12 and 13, along the south-western side of the chapter house, arranged in four small bands separated by border tiles, laid north–south. Listing from east to west, the borders are of designs 20, 23, 20 and 23, respectively. The area includes four-tile sets of design 9, part-sets of designs 7 and 8, multiple tiles of designs 14 and 16, and a single example of design 15. It also contains three designs not found elsewhere in the

pavement (designs 17, 18 and 19). The latter are so worn that they can be illustrated only in outline; one has been published previously.[21] The tiling in this triangle appears to be original but the arrangement is strange and the reason behind it is not clear. It has variously been claimed as the site of a tomb, and as the location of the medieval lectern: the former is untenable but the latter is just possible (p 36).[22]

As far as the overall layout is concerned, it is interesting to note how the ends of the bands were treated where they abut the angles of the stone benches and the central column. In the untidy arrangement around the column, a rare design is employed, with apparently specially made tiles with a border design (26) used either singly or twice, with the addition of stamped stars (designs 27 and 28; fig 214). Two different rosette stamps were used and there is evidence that some tiles were scored in half before the stamped decoration was applied. These last are also found along the south-east and north-east sides of the chapter house, and in the very north-west corner. Along the south-east side they occur together with plain diagonally-halved tiles. At the other ends, along the north-east and north-west sides, decorated tiles have been broken or cut to fill the triangular gaps. Some decorated tiles have a diagonally-scored line for producing quarter tiles (mostly design 15). These details suggest not only, as Clayton proposed, that the pavement was laid from the north, but that the tilers also started work from the eastern edge. The lack of a row of border tiles on the northern edge of the southern band (11) of the tiles with the arms of England certainly reinforces

this view. Three other factors need to be taken into account. The first is that, unlike several other thirteenth-century pavements, no use is made of plain tiles in the overall design. Secondly, the decorated designs appear on tiles with a wide range of sizes. Thirdly, the use of seven designs (designs 20–26) for the border tiles is exceptional.

Thirty-six separate designs can be identified, including seven different border tiles. The first border has the most delicate design (20), which must be considered as of exceptional artistic quality. The two images of what is clearly a pike are of superb draughtsmanship (designs 24 and 25). The five-pointed and eight-pointed stars on the facing lions (design 14) are seen also on two of the special triangular-infill tiles (designs 27 and 28), and the small stamp comprising a chequer of five squares occurs on four designs (6, 9, 15 and 16). Of the four-tile designs the most exceptional are those which make up the arms of England (designs 10–13). Remarkably the arms never appear anywhere else with these strange centaurs and dragons. One can observe also the treatment of an internal vein on most of the foliage.

The two panels of pictorial tiles, in bands 12 and 14, which are both meant to be viewed from the west, are of exceptional quality but are no longer in a pristine state, or, indeed, in the condition that they appeared to be in when recorded previously. In band 12 there are two rows of six tiles arranged one above the other, with a border of design 22 between, and borders of design 21 to west and east (fig 223). From north to south, the eastern row comprises: the musicians (design 32); King Edward and the pilgrim (design 33); a bishop or mitred abbot (design 36); the

Fig 223 Pictorial tile group in band 12. *Photograph*: © Dean and Chapter of Westminster 2008

queen with a bird of prey (design 35); a non-pictorial (replacement?) tile of design 4; and another King Edward and the pilgrim (33). The western row has exactly the same sequence for the first four tiles; then there is a tile of a king with a dog (design 34) opposite the non-pictorial tile, and finally another example of the musicians (design 32). The musicians' design is of special interest. The figure on the left holds a three-stringed fiddle; that to the right holds a harp. Neither is depicted in a playing position, so it must be concluded that the design shows two musicians tuning up.[23] None of these designs is now well preserved and to produce drawings is difficult. Shaw's plan shows only ten of these tiles (fig 210), the northernmost two being omitted, presumably because at the time they were still covered by the timber floor. In the place where the non-pictorial tile occurs in the eastern row, Shaw depicts one with the musicians (design 32), which invites the suggestion that the tile was replaced during Scott's restoration. Archaeological evidence, however, suggests otherwise: almost certainly Shaw was mistaken, and there never was a pictorial tile in this position.[24]

Band 14 has two rows of pictorial tiles with inscription V between (fig 224). In the eastern row are six tiles, showing in sequence from north to south: the king and pilgrim (33), the bishop (or abbot, 36), the queen (35), the bishop (or abbot, 36), the king (34), and then another bishop (or abbot, 36). Remarkably, this is not the same sequence as appears in a photograph, possibly of the 1920s, that shows, from north to south, the pilgrim, the

musicians, the queen, the bishop, the king, and then the musicians again (fig 225). *Prima facie*, we appear to have lost two examples of design 32, and gained two of design 36. Losing tiles is one thing, but gaining extra examples of designs as rare as these defies convincing explanation.[25] To the west of this group is the row of six tiles duplicating the three-tile hunting scenes (designs 29, 30 and 31). The outside border tiles are of design 21: those along each side of the inscription are of design 26.

In almost all medieval pavements the tiles are usually of the same size. Here, there is a wide variety of sizes: we note that the single-tile designs are of 135, 140, 145 and 155 mm square. The four-tile designs range from 140, 145, to 160 and then to 180 mm square, with the arms of England being 250 mm square. The pictorial tiles are 180 mm square for the bishop (or abbot), king, queen, the musicians and the pilgrim, whereas the hunting scene tiles are all 190 mm square. Where the two sets occur together in band 14 the difference in sizes requires the untidy insertion of a border tile of design 25.

All previous writers agree on the excellent quality of production and draughtsmanship, which compares favourably with tiles from Chertsey abbey, especially in the case of the pictorial tiles. Three designs perhaps deserve special comment. The rose window (design 3) has often been compared with the rose window in the north transept, considered to be obviously Parisian French, an up-to-date design for 1245, and the tile design is very similar.[26] While tile designs sometimes contain

Fig 224 Pictorial tile group and inscription V in band 14. *Photograph*: © Dean and Chapter of Westminster 2008

Fig 225 Inscription V, flanked by pictorial tiles and hunting scenes. The picture tiles appear to have been enhanced by an unknown hand, and two different designs have been substituted in the upper row. *Photograph*: English Heritage. NMR; probably taken in the 1920s

architectural detail, window tracery is more unusual. Morris has drawn special attention to tiles of *c* 1340 at Neath abbey, with designs spanning a period from the 1270s to the 1330s. He proposes that the tilers had access to an architectural pattern book, which at one stage had been at Exeter.[27] One may wonder whether the tilers producing the Westminster tiles had the same access.

The pike designs (24 and 25) have often invoked comment. Indeed Clayton went to pains to link them with the families of Luca or Lucies, as pike (or luce) is *luceus* or *licius* in medieval Latin.[28] This is wholly unconvincing, however, and Harvey has shown that pike, an expensive freshwater fish, 'was a festal dish … As much part of a major feast day at the Abbey as the ringing of bells and the wearing of copes at the High Mass'.[29] It may come as no surprise, therefore, that the pike should appear represented in a major abbey pavement. Its depiction elsewhere on tiles is unknown, but it does appear in eyelet fillings in a window of *c* 1330–50 at Stanford, Northamptonshire.[30]

The harpist tuning up (design 32) is similar in some respects to the harpists in roundels from Chertsey abbey.[31] But a fiddler and a harpist together is without parallel on tiles. However, one may cite a three-stringed fiddle and harp being played by angels in glass from Gercy, now Varennes-Jarcy (Essone), dated 1220–30.[32]

The inscriptions

Clayton discussed the inscriptions in 1912, noting that 'after a great deal of washing and tracing and magnifying, only one is even conjecturally solved. And this is the more tantalising in that there are quite a number of letters obtainable with study'. He observes that the six inscriptions are in Latin hexameters, that the two halves of each line end with an assonance and that conventional contractions are used. 'Notwithstanding all these data the inscriptions remain unread'. 'Any further attempt will have to proceed on the principle of measuring the breadth of the letter block: an I for instance is on a narrower block than an S'. He then proceeded to attempt readings for the letters that he could decipher.[33]

The inscriptions were revisited by Lethaby in 1925, after the floor had recently been well cleaned, providing drawings of those parts of the inscriptions which were legible. Significantly, some of the letters appeared to be in much better condition than they now are. Lethaby then observed that the tiles appear to be by the same craftsmen responsible for the tiles at Chertsey abbey, where they were probably made, and where kilns (*sic*) had recently been discovered, and also that the figurative tiles in both places are so alike that he thought the same artist was responsible for designing both sets.[34] This is rehearsed in his conclusions of 1913, when he wrote that the Chertsey and Westminster tiles 'stand apart from others in their great and equal excellence … The style of drawing and the rendering of drapery are alike in both sets. The throned kings are almost identical in both, and the two huntsmen at Westminster are closely like the figures of Tristram [at Chertsey]. The harps and hands of the harpers are similar in both'. Lethaby appears ambivalent about where the Westminster tiles were made, as, in 1917, he corrected himself and no longer thought that the tiles were brought by water from Windsor.[35] Importantly, however, Lethaby notes that there is one loose tile at Westminster exactly like one of the large ornamental squares at Chertsey, giving a direct link between the royal works and the Chertsey tiles.[36]

Two scholars have thus examined the inscriptions in detail, without totally satisfactory results. It is agreed that the inscriptions are cast in Leonine hexameters. That means that the final word rhymes with that preceding the midway caesural pause. If the word immediately before the pause can be identified, that gives a clue to the last word. Clayton realized the importance of identifying the width of the letter tiles to determine what the letters might be, but did not appreciate fully that blank letter tiles of a certain width might aid an interpretation. The inscription tiles are all 44–46 mm in height, and range between 14 mm and 30 mm in width. The letter-forms at Chertsey and Westminster are identical, and it seems that the same stamps were used for inscription tiles at the two places.[37]

For the first time, drawings of all of the inscriptions are published here to aid further analysis (figs 226 to 228). There are six inscriptions, but the length of the last two suggests that these comprised two lines in each. The first is

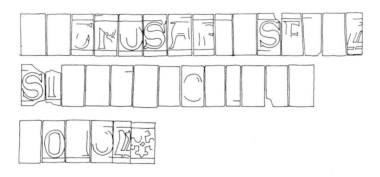

Inscription I

**[.] [U] T R O S A F [L] [O] S F [L] [O] Rum S I [C]
[E] [S] [T] [D] O [M] [I] [S] [T] [A] [D] O [M] O Rum**

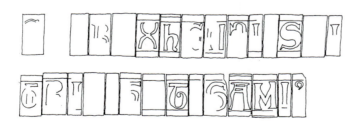

Inscription II

**[.] [ ] [.] R [E] X H E N R I [Cu] S [Sanct] I
T R I [N] [I] T [A] T [I] S A M I Cus**

Fig 226 Tile inscriptions I and II. *Drawing*: © Laurence Keen; scale 1:4

clearly to be read as *UT ROSA FLOS FLORUM SIC EST DOMUS ISTA DOMORUM* (fig 40). The parallel with York Minster, where there is the same inscription to the north of the entrance to the chapter house, is well known; indeed Sarah Brown writes that: 'The emulation of Westminster in the use of an inscription that appears on the tiled pavement was undoubtedly deliberate'.[38]

The second inscription, after a blank start, reads *REX HENRICUS SANCTI TRINITATIS AMICUS* (fig 42). I cannot read the initial *QUAM* provided by Colvin; nor do I read *SANCTE* given by Colvin and Norton,[39] as the tile is not wide enough for an *E*.

The third inscription is more problematic. It starts, after one tile with *CHRISTO*, followed by three blank tiles and the beginning of a verb ending … *BAVIT*. Colvin has *DEDICAVIT*, which seems impossible because of the letter widths. Norton reads only … *AVIT*.[40] Allowing for potential contractions, *LABORAVIT* would be a possibility and produce a rhyme. There is not entire agreement about the readings of the middle of the inscription, but we all agree that the line ends with *AMAVIT*.

The fourth and sixth inscriptions are too worn for any sense to made, but there is a general consensus about those letters which can be suggested. The fifth inscription must clearly refer to the hunting scene (fig 224). It seems to start off with *HI RESONANT CANTUS ISTI CERVIS. CANTUS* would fit with the plural verb *RESONANT*. There are two lines but the second defies interpretation: there appears to be a reference to water.

It should be noted that, although many sites have produced single letter tiles, no other thirteenth-century inscriptions survive *in situ*. The only parallels are two later inscriptions surviving *in situ* in Titchfield abbey, Hampshire. Here, at the entrance to the refectory, the inscription may be translated as 'Before you sit down to meat at your table first remember the poor'. There is a second inscription at the south-east of the cloister, of twelve letters but very incomplete.[41]

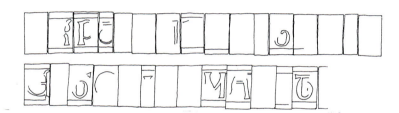

Inscription III

[.] **X P o** [.] [.] [.] [B] [A] [V] [I] [T] [Q] [V] [I] [.]
E [.] [T] [.] **I** [.] [A] **M A** [V] [I] **T**

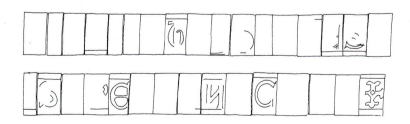

Inscription IV

[.] [.] [.] [.] [.] [I] [S] **T** [.] [.] [.] [.] [.] [.] [E] **S** [S] [I] **S**
[.] [P] **E** [.] [.] [.] **N** [.] **C** [.] [.] [.] **+**

Fig 227 Tile inscriptions III and IV. *Drawing*: © Laurence Keen; scale 1:4

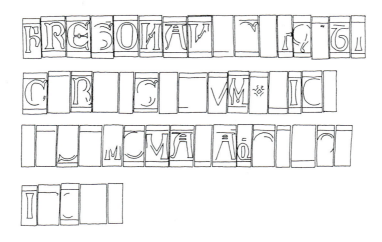

Inscription V

Hi R E S O N A N [T] [C] [An] T Vs [Is] T I
C [E] R [V] [I] S [.] [.] V M + [.] I [.] [I] [I] [.] [S]
[.] M O M A [.] A q [.] [I] [.] Us [.] I [.] [.] [M] [+]

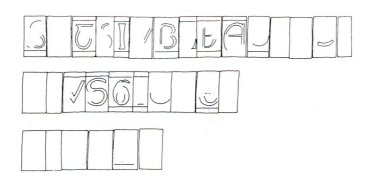

Inscription VI

S [.] T [.] I V B [L] [.] E [.] [.] [.] [.] [.] [.] [.] V S
[.] [.] [.] [.] [E] [.] [.] [.] [.] [.] [.] [.] [.]

Fig 228 Tile inscriptions V and VI. *Drawing*: © Laurence Keen; scale 1:4

Discussion

We need now to try to place the chapter house tiles in context. There can be no doubt that they are of superb quality, including the earliest heraldic tiles in the country. They have frequently been compared with the famous tiles from Chertsey, and Norton has described them as 'some of the earliest two-colour tiles … [and] incomparably the finest, both technically and artistically … [with] no known parallel on the Continent'. It is generally agreed that the Chertsey-type tiles were originally commissioned for some of Henry III's royal works in the 1250s, potentially at Westminster palace, for, as early as 1237 the king ordered that the little chapel in the palace should be paved with *tegula picta*.[42] The Chertsey connexion is perhaps evident in the 1290s when, as Norton suggests, it is possible that the large figure panels were actually designed and first made for the tomb of Queen Eleanor.[43]

The chapter house tiles are beautifully produced, with crisp detail and exquisitely delicate draughtsmanship.

They all have very good inlay (the depth seems to be about 2 mm) and are well fired. The few loose examples in the British Museum and Westminster Abbey Museum show thicknesses of between 36 mm and 47 mm.[44] In her discussion of the Chertsey tiles, Eames observed that, in broken examples, 'whereas the bold lines were made with deep, flat-bottomed and straight-sided projections on the dies, the projections which impressed the finer details were thinner and shorter and were tapered so that they should have the necessary strength'.[45] It is interesting to observe that this seems to have been the case also for some of the Westminster tiles. On the arms of England, where some of the tiles are heavily worn, the lines of inlay are noticeably less wide, suggesting that part of the stamp was tapered. The same technical process is evident on some of the other designs. Like Chertsey, it is clear that the tiles were produced by a specialist workshop, making them to order: we are not dealing here with a tilery with a mass-produced output. It seems possible that some of the designs – those with the chequer of five small squares, for instance – even contain the artist's 'signature'.

It has been noted that there is a wide variety of sizes among the tiles, and that, except along some of the edges, there are no plain tiles.[46] These circumstances are most unusual for medieval pavements generally. It has also been noted that the two panels of pictorial tiles in band 14 are of different sizes and that this caused an untidy and unsatisfactory appearance. For the pictorial tiles and the inscriptions Eames opined that there was no obvious reason for their position in the pavement, and she did not believe that they were originally designed for it. She went on to suggest that it is probable that the pictorial tiles were left over from a pavement laid somewhere in the Palace of Westminster. 'The choice of subjects ceases to be remarkable if one assumes that the tiles were originally designed to pave a royal palace and it is tempting to believe that they were designed for one of Henry III's private chambers in the Palace of Westminster'.[47] I entirely agree with Eames's conclusion, but would go further to suggest that the whole chapter house pavement is not a special commission, but uses stocks of decorated tiles left over from some other operation(s) in the Palace of Westminster, or in the abbey itself.

Norton, in his discussion of the chapter house pavement at Salisbury Cathedral, datable to the later half of the thirteenth century, has noted that the layout there is a considerable improvement on that in the Westminster chapter house. The layout at Salisbury is adapted to the shape of the room with panels radiating from the central column, fanning out to the eight sides of the building (fig 101).[48] One might conclude that, because they were using quantities of left-over tiles, the paviours for the chapter house at Westminster were faced with an unusual and exacting flooring exercise. Confirmation that different batches of the same design were arriving in the abbey is provided by examination of the loose tiles preserved in museum collections. Thus, the same design appears on tiles of markedly different size, as well as thickness; some with and others without keying-scoops.[49] The pavement layout is not at all satisfactory, but might be explained if it is accepted that the tilers were using old stock and that they were more accustomed to paving rectangular rooms and spaces in Westminster palace. Be that as it may, the chapter house pavement, even in its more worn condition than when uncovered in the nineteenth century, is still a remarkable monument and is unique for its survival and the quality of its wide variety of designs. The pavement is, without any doubt, the most important surviving example in Europe: that it is to be seen with the Cosmati pavement in the sanctuary gives it added significance, and places Westminster Abbey as pre-eminent for surviving pavements. Tile studies at the abbey are continuing, and this contribution provides a platform on which those studies might be based.[50]

Appendix: catalogue of tile designs

(by Warwick Rodwell)

The following is a summary of the designs and dimensions (where known) of the tiles used in the chapter house pavement. Where sizes vary by more than ± 1.5 mm, the range is quoted in parentheses. Notes are also included on the small number of other known occurrences of the same designs. Unfortunately, there is no record as to the fate of the many damaged tiles that Scott removed from the pavement in order to insert Victorian facsimiles. Nor is it known what happened to the 'fragments of encaustic tiles of beautiful patterns, similar to some of those in the chapter house … [with] the glaze so fresh as to lead one to think they had never been trodden upon' that Scott found in the vestibule office.[51] Only a very small number of specimens are held by the British Museum and Westminster Abbey Museum.

Design 1   Four-tile design. Facing leopards within an encircled quatrefoil.
Pavement: 180 × 180 × – mm. Used only in band 13 (complete).

Design 2   Four-tile design. Foliage spray.
Pavement: 180 × 180 × – mm. Used only in band 14 (almost complete).

Design 3 Four-tile design. Rose window with octofoils and trefoils in the spandrels.
Pavement: 180 × 180 × – mm (range: 177–184 mm). Used in band 1 (18¼ sets) and band 16 (29 sets).

Design 4 Four-tile design. Foliage spray within two concentric circles separated by a running scroll (fig 211).
Pavement: 180 × 180 × – mm. Used in band 12 (complete).

Design 5 Four-tile design. Stiff-leaf foliage spray within a double-bordered circle.
Pavement: 160 × 160 × – mm. Used in band 10 (largely complete).
Unprovenanced: 160 × 160 × 35 mm; diagonally cut half-tile, probably unused; flaked glaze; inlay 1 mm depth; 4/5 keying scoops; steeply bevelled edges. WA Mus Coll.
A closely similar, derivative design on a smaller tile is found in the 'Westminster' series.[52]

Design 6 Four-tile design. Cock and fox within a double-bordered quatrefoil; also small chequered squares of two sizes used in the field (fig 211).
Pavement: 160 × 160 × – mm. Used in band 6 (complete), band 10 (west end only) and band 14 (west end only).
Chapter house(?): 161 × 161 × 45 mm; no keying scoops. BM: Eames 1980, design 1896.
Chapter house vestibule office: 160 × 160 × – mm; fragment reset in the floor just inside the door.
No. 20 Dean's Yard, Westminster: small fragment found in excavations, 1975–77 (Black 1977, fig 7.13). Mus of London.
Unprovenanced: 160 × 160 × 30 mm; rather soft, oxidized fabric; no keying scoops; very worn on the underside, having been inverted and used as paving or a step. Another similar, very worn on both faces. WA Mus Coll.
Unprovenanced: 164 × 164 × 38 mm; hard, well-fired fabric; flaked orange-brown glaze; unused condition; steeply bevelled edges; no keying scoops. WA Mus Coll.
Unprovenanced: 170 × 170 × 37 mm; fragment in very hard, well-fired fabric; unused condition; 3/5 keying scoops. WA Mus Coll.

Design 7 Four-tile design. Addorsed griffins within a scroll-bordered quatrefoil (fig 146).
Pavement: 145 × 145 × – mm. Used in band 7 (substantially) and in area 17 (7+ examples).
Chapter house(?): 145 × 145 × 39 mm; no keying scoops. BM: Eames 1980, design 1882.

Design 8 Four-tile design. Addorsed regardant lions within a double-bordered circle.
Pavement: 145 × 145 × – mm. Used in band 9 (complete) and in area 17 (few).
Chapter house(?): 143 × 143 × 42 mm; fragment; no keying scoops. BM: Eames 1980, design 1817.

Design 9 Four-tile design. Six-petalled rosettes and small chequered squares within a double-bordered quatrefoil, surrounded by scrollwork.
Pavement: 141 × 141 × – mm. Used only in band 8, alongside the central pillar (six examples) and in area 17 (fifteen examples).[53]

Designs 10–13 Four-tile set, making up the arms of England, with flanking centaurs and dragonesque birds (fig 41).
Pavement: 249 × 249 × – mm. These are very well made tiles, uniform in size, and having 2 mm deep inlay. Used in bands 5 and 11, each containing 31 complete sets: for the potential significance of this number, see p 37, n. 71.

Design 14 Single-tile design. Pair of addorsed regardant lions surrounded by five stars. The stars were not individually stamped on the tiles, but appear to have been incorporated in the die. Notwithstanding, there are two types: the majority of the stars are eight-pointed (design 14A), but there are also many that are five-pointed (design 14B), confirming that there must have been two dies in simultaneous use. The two types of star are never present together on a single tile.
Pavement: 144 × 144 × – mm (range 140–145 mm). Used in band 3 (substantially), and band 7 (west end only).
Pavement: 136 × 136 × – mm. A single example of design 14B in area 17. Also several further examples of both 14A and 14B, all less than 140 × 140 mm, occur in area 17.
Chapter house(?): – × – 42 mm; fragment of design 14B. BM: Eames 1980, design 1813.

Unprovenanced: 154 × 154 × 26 mm. Two fragments, in poor condition, of tiles of a related design, but larger in scale and cruder in execution; there do not appear to be stars in the field. WA Mus Coll.

Design 15 Single-tile design. Geometrical composition of squares within a double-bordered circle, and fleurs-de-lis; also small chequered squares at the corners.

Pavement: 154 × 154 × – mm. Used in band 2 (west end only), band 4 (complete) and band 15 (complete). Some tiles were scored diagonally for breaking into quarters. This seems to have been the only design so treated, and hence examples of half-tiles and quarter-tiles were used to fill small triangular gaps around the margins of the pavement.

Pavement: 136 × 136 × – mm. A single example in area 17. The stamp was made for the larger tile size, and parts of the design were lost around the edges when used on the smaller tiles. Also, the workmanship is markedly inferior in the latter (*cf* design 16). Consequently, this design has been included in the 'Westminster' tile series by Betts.[54]

Chapter house(?): 157 × 157 × 36 mm; part tile with 2/5 keying scoops. BM: Eames 1980, design 2504.

No. 20 Dean's Yard, Westminster: 135 × 135 × – mm. One example found during excavations in 1975 (Black 1977, fig 7.8). Mus of London.

Unprovenanced: 135 × 135 × 27 mm; no keying scoops. One complete and one near-complete example. WA Mus Coll.

Design 16 Single-tile design. Geometrical composition of four small circles within a double-bordered circle, and small leaves; also small chequered squares at the corners.

Pavement: 153 × 153 × – mm. Used in band 2 (substantially) and band 8 (complete).

Pavement: 136 × 136 × – mm. These smaller tiles occur only in the triangular area 17 (five examples). The stamp was made for the larger tile and parts of the design were lost around the edges when used on the smaller tiles. Also, the workmanship is markedly inferior in the latter. Consequently, this design has been included in the 'Westminster' tile series by Betts.[55]

Chapter house(?): 155 × 155 × 41 mm;

fragment with two keying scoops. Another with 2/5 keying scoops. BM: Eames 1980, design 2505.

Unprovenanced: 155 × 155 × 35–39 mm; 3/5 keying scoops. Two fragments. WA Mus Coll.

Design 17 Single-tile design. Foliate composition. Incomplete record of pattern.

Pavement: 135 × 135 × – mm. Only four examples known, all in band 17, and heavily worn.

This design has been included in the 'Westminster' tile series by Betts.[56]

Design 18 Single-tile design. Foliate composition. Incomplete record of pattern.

Pavement: 135 × 135 × – mm. Only three examples known, all in band 17, and heavily worn.

Design 19 Single-tile design. Lion-like creature within a quatrefoil. Incomplete record of pattern.

Pavement: 150 × 150 × – mm. Only eight examples known, all in band 17, and heavily worn.

Design 20 Border tile. Intricate running scroll between parallel lines (fig 211).

Pavement: 175 × 100 × – mm. Used in the northernmost border, and between bands 1 and 2, 3 and 4, 5 and 6, 7 and 8, 9 and 10 and 11 and 12.

Dorter undercroft: 174 × 100 × 30 mm; three keying scoops; steeply bevelled edges (10 degrees). One incomplete and worn example found during excavations in 1986.[57] Mus of London.

Chapter house(?): 175 × 94 × 47 mm; no keying scoops. BM: Eames 1980, design 1264.

Unprovenanced: – × 98 × 30 mm; worn fragment with two out of an original 3/4 keying scoops; steeply bevelled edges. WA Mus Coll.

Design 21 Border tile. Florid cross and circle design; no parallel lines defining the long edges (fig 211).

Pavement: 174 × 82 × – mm (width range 82–85 mm). Used only for the east and west borders of the panels of pictorial tiles in bands 12 and 14 (24¹/₂ tiles in total).

Design 22 Border tile. Running scroll of stiff-leaf foliage between parallel lines.

Pavement: 177 × 80 × – mm (range 175–180 mm). Used between bands 12 and 13; between the pictorial tiles in band 12; and flanking one side of inscription I in band 12.

Design 23 Border tile. Acanthus leaf between parallel lines.
Pavement: 140 × 73 × – mm. Used between bands 2 and 3, 13 and 14 and 14 and 15; as two borders within area 17; also flanking inscriptions IV and VI (on both sides) and inscriptions I and II (on one side only).

Design 24 Border tile. Pike facing right, between parallel lines.
Pavement: 210 × 100 × – mm (length range 210–215 mm). Paired with design 25, and laid head-to-head and tail-to-tail. Used between bands 4 and 5, 6 and 7, 8 and 9 and on the west flank of band 16.
Chapter house: – × 85 × 27 mm; no keying scoops. Incomplete tile, worn and bearing Victorian label 'from chapter house floor'. WA Mus Coll.
South transept: – × 102 × 33 mm. Incomplete tile, very worn, labelled 'found 1969 in E aisle of south transept'. WA Mus Coll.

Design 25 Border tile. Pike facing left, between parallel lines.
Pavement: 210 × 100 × – mm (length range 210–215 mm). Paired with design 24 (see above).

Design 26 Border tile. Upright leaves and dots, between parallel lines.
Pavement: 154 × 66 × – mm. Used on the south flank of band 15 (that is, against the south wall); also flanking inscriptions II, III and V (on both sides).

Design 27 Triangular infill tile. Stamped once with design 26 and individual stars (fig 214).
Pavement: *c* 180 × 180 × – mm, cut and broken diagonally. Ten examples in total: three abutting the central column; three against the north-west wall-bench; three against the north-east; one against the south-east. The eight-pointed stars were stamped individually on each tile (unlike design 14A).

Design 28 Mitred rectangular infill tile. Stamped twice with design 26 and individual stars.
Pavement: 260 × 150 × – mm, cut and broken at 45° at one end. The cut-line contains white clay, indicating that the tile was scored but not broken before being inlaid. Five examples recorded: two abutting central column; two against the north-east wall-bench; one against the north-west wall-bench. The eight-pointed stars were stamped individually on each tile (as with design 27).

Design 29 Pictorial tile. Huntsman on horseback, blowing a horn, facing right; a hunting dog below.
Pavement: 194 × 194 × – mm. Two examples only, both in band 14.

Design 30 Pictorial tile. Archer facing right, with a tree behind.
Pavement: 194 × 194 × – mm. Two examples only, both in band 14.

Design 31 Pictorial tile. Stag with an arrow through its neck, facing right; a hunting dog below.
Pavement: 194 × 194 × – mm. Two examples only, both in band 14.

Design 32 Pictorial tile. Two musicians facing one another; the harpist seated on a stool.
Pavement: 180 × 180 × – mm. Three examples only, all in band 12. Shaw's plan is almost certainly incorrect in showing another occurrence in the eastern row in band 12 (fig 210). An early photograph appears to record two more examples in band 14, where other designs are now present (fig 225); the veracity of the record is dubious (p 228, n 25).

Design 33 Pictorial tile. King Edward giving a ring to a pilgrim (St John the Evangelist in disguise); a tree in the background.
Pavement: 180 × 180 × – mm. Four examples only: three in band 12 and one in band 14.

Design 34 Pictorial tile. Seated king holding a sceptre in his left hand, and a dog jumping into the air.
Pavement: 180 × 180 × – mm. Two examples only: one each in bands 12 and 14.

Design 35 Pictorial tile. Seated queen with a falcon on her left hand; her right hand gesturing.
Pavement: 180 × 180 × – mm. Three examples only: two in band 12, and one in band 14.

Design 36 Pictorial tile. Seated bishop, or mitred abbot, with a crozier in his left hand and his right hand raised in blessing.
Pavement: 180 × 180 × – mm. Five examples: two in band 12 and three in band 14 (but see fig 225 and p 228).

The chapter house glazing

13

Warwick Rodwell

The glazing history of the chapter house has never been studied in detail, and this short contribution is offered as an introduction to the subject. Essentially, there have been three periods of activity. First, the primary glazing of the mid-1250s; second, the Victorian scheme of the 1880s and early 1890s; and, finally, the present scheme, which was completed in 1951.

The medieval glass, which was installed soon after 1253 (p 23), has long been lost, and the occasional subsequent reference to chapter house glazing sheds little light on the subject: windows are mentioned, for example, in the sacrist's roll for 1379/80,[1] and in 1543 a payment was recorded for mending windows in the church and chapter house.[2] The only antiquarian mention of the glass appears to have been by Henry Keepe in his unpublished notes of the 1680s.[3] The sole pictorial representation of the medieval glazing comes from an early seventeenth-century drawing, showing shields in the main lights, bearing the arms of Edward the Confessor, Henry III and the count of Provence (fig 30).[4] The shields are likely to have been incorporated into a field of grisaille glazing, similar to that which remained in part in Salisbury Cathedral chapter house until 1821 (fig 102; p 94). At Westminster, the medieval glass apparently did not survive beyond the mid-eighteenth century when four of the window openings were substantially blocked with brickwork, drastically reducing their size, with a pair of round-headed lights being formed in each. This occurred in *c* 1751, when clear glass in rectangular panes was installed (fig 133; p 128); the remaining two windows had already been lost at an earlier date.

Victorian windows

When the fenestration was restored to its Gothic form by Scott in the later 1860s, he too fitted clear glass, initially, in small rectangular quarries (fig 140). Although the refurbishment of the chapter house was undertaken by HM Office of Works, and not by the Dean and Chapter, Dean Stanley nevertheless urged that the windows be filled with stained glass in 1873. He proposed a scheme of historical scenes relating to the abbey and the history of England, starting with the north window and progressing in a clockwise direction around the chapter house. Scott represented this in his restoration proposal (fig 132), but the funds for commissioning the glass were not forthcoming from the Treasury. The matter was not allowed to rest there, and a scheme to install stained glass was jointly initiated by the Dean and Chapter and Scott. In 1873, the firm of Clayton and Bell supplied an estimate of £6,125 for making and installing a full set of stained glass windows. They went on to prepare a series of cartoons, which were approved by the abbey on 22 May 1876.[5] However, the Treasury insisted that it had not commissioned the work and declined to pay for the new glazing: instead, it offered an *ex gratia* payment of £500 to Clayton and Bell for their designs. The offer was declined.[6] When Dean Stanley died in 1881 there had still been no progress, but his estate defrayed the cost of the first window (the north-east) in the following year.[7] Queen Victoria then paid for another (the east) in his memory. A group of American friends raised the money for a third window (the south-east), and another three were provided out of the abbey's memorial fund (the south, south-west and west). By 1891, only the north window had not been filled, and that was sequentially the first in the iconographic scheme, representing the early legends of the abbey and the life and death of Edward the Confessor. Dean Bradley spearheaded a campaign to complete the glazing as a memorial to Stanley,[8] but only one light out of four had been glazed by 1893.[9] Another panel was added in

that same year,[10] and photographic evidence shows that two further panels were added, but the scheme seems never to have been brought to completion.[11]

The glazing scheme comprised portraits of prominent historical figures in the tracery sexfoils, coats of arms in the quatrefoils, and a series of figures and scenes of important events in the main lights (fig 229). Except on the west, each

Fig 229 Chapter house interior, looking south east, showing the Clayton and Bell glazing in the 1920s. *Photograph*: English Heritage. NMR

light was subdivided into three registers. The uppermost register (a) depicted English monarchs, the middle (b) portrayed scenes from the history of the abbey, and the lowest register (c) carried figures of abbots. Surviving descriptions of the windows, together with the original scheme drawn up by Clayton and Bell, allow the following reconstruction.[12]

An asterisk(*) indicates that the panel is still extant. Square brackets [] indicate the subject-matter of panels that were apparently never installed.

North window

Sexfoil	Venerable Bede*
Quatrefoils	Arms (no record)

1 (a) [King Lucius]; (b) [Thorney Island]; (c) High priest of Apollo*
2 (a) [King Sebert]; (b) [St Peter with fish]; (c) Abbot Orthobright*
3 (a) King Edgar*; (b) Edward the Confessor and the treasury; (c) Abbot Wulsin*
4 (a) [St Edward the Confessor]; (b) [funeral of the Confessor]; (c) Abbot Edwin*

North-east window

Sexfoil	St Anselm
Quatrefoils	Arms (no record)

1 (a) William I*; (b) coronation of William the Conqueror; (c) Abbot Geoffrey*
2 (a) William II*; (b) the miracle of St Wulfstan*; (c) Abbot Vitalis
3 (a) Henry II*; (b) the conflict between the archbishops of Canterbury and York; (c) Abbot Gilbert
4 (a) Richard I; (b) Richard I with a gathering of crusaders; (c) Abbot Laurence*

East window

Sexfoil	Roger Bacon
Quatrefoils	Arms (no record)

1 (a) King John; (b) John signing the *Magna Carta*; (c) Abbot Papillon*
2 (a) Henry III; (b) Henry III examining plans of the new abbey; (c) Abbot Berking
3 (a) Edward I; (b) Alfonso, Prince of Wales; (c) Abbot Wenlok
4 (a) Edward II; (b) Stone of Destiny in the Coronation chair; (c) Abbot Kirtlington

South-east window

Sexfoil	Geoffrey Chaucer
Quatrefoils	Arms: one was of Richard II

1 (a) Edward III*; (b) monks in the chapter house; (c) Abbot Henley*
2 (a) Philippa of Hainault; (b) the Commons meeting in the chapter house; (c) Abbot Bircheston*
3 (a) Black Prince*; (b) the Black Prince in Parliament; (c) Cardinal Langham*
4 (a) Richard III; (b) Richard II and the hermit of Westminster; (c) Abbot Litlyngton

South window

Sexfoil	William Caxton
Quatrefoils	Arms (no record)

1 (a) Henry IV*; (b) death of Henry IV in Jerusalem chamber*; (c) Abbot Colchester
2 (a) Henry V; (b) Henry V's council*; (c) Abbot Kyrton*
3 (a) Henry VI; (b) Henry VI choosing his grave site in the abbey*; (c) Abbot Milling*
4 (a) Edward IV*; (b) Elizabeth Woodville taking sanctuary; (c) Abbot Esteney*

South-west window

Sexfoil	William Shakespeare
Quatrefoils	Arms (no record)

1 (a) Henry VII*; (b) marriage of Henry VII; (c) Abbot Islip*
2 (a) Henry VIII; (b) Wolsey's convocation in the chapter house; (c) Abbot Benson*
3 (a) Edward VI*; (b) Dissolution of the monasteries*; (c) Bishop Thirlby of Westminster
4 (a) Mary I*; (b) funeral of Edward VI*; (c) Abbot Feckenham

West window (fig 230)

Sexfoil	Queen Victoria*
Quatrefoils	Royal arms*; Dean Stanley's arms*

1 Elizabeth I*
2 James I*
3 Charles I*
4 William III*

The two windows on the south side of the inner vestibule were also destined to be filled with stained glass as part of Dean Stanley's scheme: the triple light was to contain depictions of early royalty: Sebert, Edwin, Sulcard,

Fig 230 Chapter house, west window: surviving glazing by Clayton and Bell *c* 1882–3. *Photograph*: © English Heritage Photo Library

Hugolin and Ethelgota. Four noted English scholars were to be represented in the single lancet: Arthur Agarde, Sir Robert Cotton, Thomas Rymer and Francis Palgrave. As far as can be ascertained, the vestibule windows were never made or installed. Instead, an entirely separate scheme was conceived and executed in 1893. The present glazing, together with a tablet on the wall below, constitute a memorial to the American poet James Russell Lowell (1819–91), erected by his English friends. Lowell

was United States Minister at the Court of St James, 1880–85.[13] The single lancet contains a series of four coats of arms, representing institutions with which Lowell was associated (fig 231).[14] The designs in the three-light window incorporate appropriate scenes, such as St Botolph of Boston and the Puritans landing in New England (fig 65).

The Victorian windows were largely unappreciated in the twentieth century, as this comment reveals: 'the present

Fig 231 Chapter house: inner vestibule, south wall. Memorial window to J R Lowell by Clayton and Bell 1893. *Photograph*: © Dean and Chapter of Westminster

Fig 232 Chapter house: the south-east window in 1943, showing bomb damage. *Photograph*: English Heritage. NMR

glass admits but little light and nothing can be said in its favour'.[15] During a German air raid in 1940, a bomb fell in Old Palace Yard, and the blast caused damage to the glazing and tracery of the chapter house windows; only the lights on the west, above the entrance, survived virtually unscathed (figs 232 and 233).

Fig 233 Chapter house: the south and south-west windows in 1943, showing bomb damage. *Photograph*: English Heritage. NMR

Reglazing in the mid-twentieth-century

After the Second World War, the Ministry of Works decided to undertake a comprehensive reglazing of the chapter house, although it is clear that the Clayton and Bell windows had not been destroyed and would have been capable of repair. However, Victorian glass was still deeply unfashionable and there was a desire to increase the volume of natural light entering the chamber by restricting the area of coloured glass. In 1946 Joan Howson was commissioned to prepare cartoons.[16] Howson (1885–1964)[17] was a well-known stained glass artist, operating from a studio at 81 Deodar Road, Putney, Greater London, who received numerous prestigious commissions after the Second World War to reinstate removed and damaged church windows, as well as for designing new glazing (fig 234). Howson was in partnership with Caroline Charlotte

Townshend (1878–1944), until the latter's death, after which her principal assistant was Mary Eily de Putron (fig 235). Although Townshend had no involvement with the chapter house glazing, Howson nevertheless included her in the signed quarries: 'C.C.T. J.H. 1951'.[18] Painted in the small spandrel below the central roundel of the south-west window is a roll-call of Howson's modest workforce, and other persons closely involved in the restoration of the chapter house windows[19] (fig 236).

In 1949 Howson began to execute the chapter house commission – a huge undertaking – which she completed in 1951 (frontispiece and figs 237 and 238).[20] The new glazing was a major attraction at the formal reopening on 17 May. Fortunately, Howson decided to retain the Victorian west window in its entirety (fig 230), while salvaging the least damaged panels of glass from the other windows and incorporating them in a new scheme which

Fig 234 Joan Howson in her Putney studio, firing new panels of glass for the chapter house. *Photograph*: English Heritage. NMR 1949

Fig 235 Mary de Putron drawing one of the shields (arms of Cornwall) for the new glazing in the north-east window. *Photograph*: English Heritage. NMR 1949

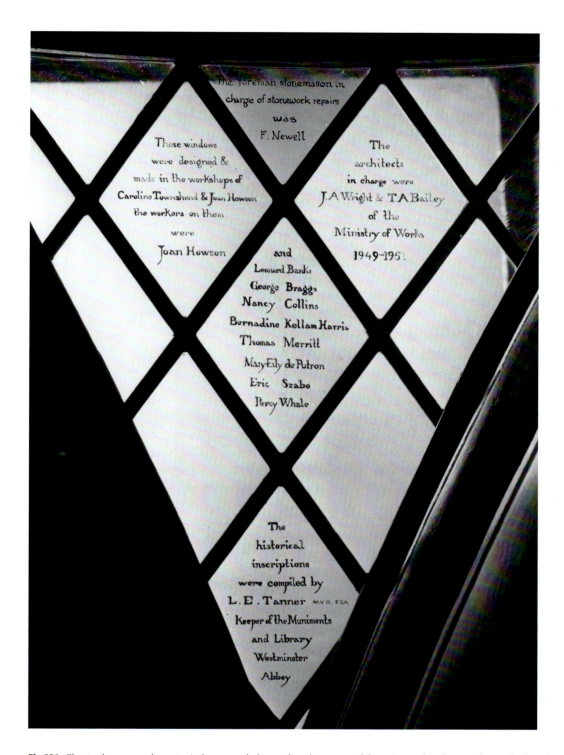

The foreman stonemason in charge of stonework repairs was F. Newell

These windows were designed & made in the workshops of Caroline Townshend & Joan Howson the workers on them were Joan Howson

and Leonard Banks George Braggs Nancy Collins Bernadine Kellam Harris Thomas Merritt Mary Eily de Putron Eric Szabo Percy Whale

The architects in charge were J. A Wright & T. A Bailey of the Ministry of Works 1949-1951

The historical inscriptions were compiled by L. E. Tanner M.V.O. F.S.A. Keeper of the Muniments and Library Westminster Abbey

Fig 236 Chapter house, south-west window: spandrel recording the names of the artists and craftsmen who worked on the new windows. *Photograph*: English Heritage. NMR 1950

embodied large areas of clear glazing. Those panels are now in the windows facing the cardinal directions. The north-east, south-east and south-west windows contain entirely new panels, which include coats of arms of royalty, benefactors, ecclesiastics, architects and First Commissioners of Works, all being connected with the history of the abbey since the thirteenth century. Amongst

the architects represented are Wren and Scott (fig 239).

Howson's reglazing resulted in the interior of the chapter house being much lighter than hitherto. She also abandoned the established convention of including borders around each light. The clear quarries, which are of hand-made glass (some tinted), surrounding the new armorial panels and in the traceries are enlivened by the

Fig 237 Chapter house, north window: Howson's reglazing of 1951, using salvaged panels by Clayton and Bell, derived from several windows.
Photograph: © Dean and Chapter of Westminster 2008

Fig 238 Chapter house, south-west window: Howson's new glazing of 1951. *Photograph*: © Dean and Chapter of Westminster 2008

Fig 239 Chapter house, south-west window: the arms of Sir George Gilbert Scott installed in 1951. The small quarries depict scenes from the Second World War, including a fire in the crossing at Westminster Abbey (bottom left) and the Deanery ablaze (bottom right). *Photograph*: English Heritage. NMR

sporadic inclusion of small painted motifs appropriate to the main subjects in each light. Running across the base of every window is an inscription panel, recording aspects of the history and restoration of the chapter house.[21]

Apart from retaining the west window unaltered, and the roundel of the Venerable Bede in the sexfoil on the north, no other elements of the Clayton and Bell scheme remain *in situ*. The sexfoil of the east window has been made from the former panel depicting Edward the Black Prince (in the third main light), and the south sexfoil is now filled with glass derived from the panel depicting Henry V's council (from the second main light). The remaining three sexfoils, together with the quatrefoils in all the windows, contain modern shields. The main lights are still divided into three registers, the uppermost (a) containing monarchs on the cardinal faces. Only six of the original scenes from the middle register (b) remain, and they have been placed in the two central lights of the north, east and south windows, and are flanked in the outer lights by religious figures imported from the lowest register.[22] Twelve abbots and clerics still remain in the first register (c) – although not in their original locations – bringing the total for their survival to eighteen. Various modern roundels, squares and lozenges are also used as space-fillers between the three registers in each light (figs 47 and 56).

The motifs in the individual quarries mostly follow conventional stereotypes, and include medieval foliate designs, human and animal figures, initials, etc. In the south-east window are copies of designs occurring on the floor tiles of the chapter house. However, the south-west window is different, and its quarries tell a story all of their own. Howson was an ardent socialist and pacifist, and was determined to depict the effect of the recent war on London. Hence, the quarries contain numerous tiny scenes relating to the aerial bombardment and defence of the city during the Second World War. These vignettes were described in the press at the time as depicting 'incidents associated with the Blitz on London, with special reference to the Abbey'.[23]

The south-west window

Although Howson devoted much time and effort to researching the subject matter for all her windows, she unfortunately left hardly any records.[24] Consequently, the sources for and meaning of some of the wartime scenes now elude us, and the south-west window (fig 238) has been dubbed the 'enigma window'.[25] It deserves full study but, briefly, the identifiable scenes may be summarized as follows.[26]

Sexfoil   The central roundel displays the arms of Westminster Abbey, and the surrounding foils contain eighteen scenes of aerial encounter, the details of which are carefully drawn. All the English aeroplanes are identifiable by RAF rings on their wings, and the German by swastikas. One scene shows barrage balloons and another seems to depict a logistical plan.

Quatrefoils   The two roundels contain badges representing medieval architects Henry of Reyns and Henry Yevele, respectively.

Spandrel   In the central spandrel is painted a list of names of the persons involved in the reglazing of the chapter house (fig 236).

Light no. 1   (a) Arms of Sir John Denham (Cavalier, Surveyor to the King).
Quarries: aerial combat scenes, barrage balloons and falling bombs; initials 'JD'; seventeenth-century details, including writing materials.
(b) Royal Arms, Queen Mary (wife of King George V).
Quarries: the initial 'M', twice; firemen tackling a burning building (perhaps the Houses of Parliament).
(c) Arms of Eversley (Baron, First Commissioner of Works).
Quarries: a female volunteer working at a field kitchen, with the caption 'WVS' (Women's Voluntary Service) below;[27] a uniformed man holding a gun stands in front of four anti-tank obelisks, with the caption 'Home Guard' below.

Light no. 2   (a) Arms of William of Wykeham (Bishop of Winchester, Lord Chancellor of England, Surveyor to the King).
Quarries: scenes of aerial conflict; initials 'WW'; medieval details including several tile designs from the chapter house pavement.
(b) Arms of King George VI.
Quarries: Initials 'GVI', twice; king and queen inspecting troops.
(c) Arms of Llanover (peer, First Commissioner of Works).
Quarries: initial 'L', twice (with 'Big Ben' alongside);[28] clusters of falling bombs; two ARP (Air Raid Precautions) wardens, one

carrying a small child; two pilots, one about to climb into his aeroplane; a burning medieval building.

Light no. 3   (a) Arms of Sir John Vanbrugh (Surveyor to the King).

Quarries: scenes of aerial conflict, including enemy planes caught in searchlights; initials 'JV'; hunting scenes.

(b) Arms of Queen Elizabeth (wife of King George VI).

Quarries: initial 'E', twice; scenes of airmen on the ground.

(c) Arms of Sir Gilbert Scott (Surveyor of the Fabric of Westminster Abbey) (fig 239).

Quarries: initials 'GS', twice; clusters of falling bombs; a female ambulance driver getting into her vehicle with the caption 'Ambulance' below; an air raid warden rescuing a child from a building; at the bottom, burning debris inside the crossing of Westminster Abbey (view east), following an incendiary attack, May 1941; part of the west cloister of Westminster Abbey, with the Deanery above on fire (viewed from the east); a female holding a child amongst vegetation, with the caption 'Why?' beneath.[29]

Light no. 4   (a) Arms of Sir Christopher Wren (Surveyor to the King, Surveyor of the Fabric of Westminster Abbey).

Quarries: depictions of aeroplanes, singly, escorting and in formation; initials 'CW'; dome of St Paul's Cathedral on the skyline; rebus comprising a mason's square, dividers and a wren.

(b) Arms of Princess Elizabeth (now Queen Elizabeth II).

Quarries: initial 'E', twice, once against the background of Windsor Castle and once against Edinburgh Castle (below the latter, the initial 'P' for Philip, Duke of Edinburgh; firemen tackling a blaze in a warehouse; dousing incendiary bombs.

(c) Arms of Mount Temple (baron, First Commissioner of Works).

Quarries: at the bottom, a scene in an operating theatre (fig 240), and another inside a telephone exchange; signed and dated half-quarry at the bottom (fig 241).[30]

Fig 240 Chapter house, south-west window: a small quarry depicting a surgeon and two nurses at the operating table. Below is the embellished initial letter of one of the inscriptions explaining the new windows. *Photograph*: © Dean and Chapter of Westminster 2008

Fig 241 Chapter house, south-west window: a small quarry depicting a telephone exchange. Metal helmets and bags containing the gas-masks of the operators hang on the backs of their swivel-chairs. The adjacent half-quarry contains a signature panel. *Photograph*: © Dean and Chapter of Westminster 2008

The chapter house doors and their dating

14

Daniel Miles and Martin Bridge

Most great churches in England retain at least some of their complement of historic timber doors, and Westminster Abbey is no exception. Associated with the abbey church and its former monastic buildings are a number of early medieval doors that have attracted scholarly interest in the past, but hitherto there has been no reliable dating evidence for any of them. Victorian antiquaries principally directed their attentions to the door in the south wall of the outer vestibule of the chapter house, on account of the fact that it displayed remnants of a former covering of skin (door 1; figs 242 and 243; Plan 1).[1] This, it was assumed, must be human, and a mythology grew up linking the skin with the supposed flaying of the robbers who broke into the royal treasury in the abbey in 1303 (chapter 7).[2]

The construction of the door was studied by Cecil Hewett in the mid-1970s, and he was perhaps the first person to appreciate its true significance, observing that its construction was unparalleled in the repertoire of English Romanesque doors. Hewett argued intuitively that the door must be of Anglo-Saxon date.[3] Dr Jane Geddes subsequently included it in her study of early medieval doors, cautiously assigning it to *c* 1100.[4] The need to establish the actual date of this important artefact was self-evident, and a dendrochronology research project to investigate this and several other doors was conceived in 2000. For various reasons, it was not possible to proceed immediately, but in 2005, when Westminster Abbey celebrated the millennium of the birth of Edward the Confessor, attention was once again focused on the vestibule door as a possible survivor from the pre-Norman abbey.[5]

This time the dendrochronology project went ahead, and six doors were sampled, though this chapter is only concerned with the study and analysis of the three surviving medieval doors that are associated with the chapter house complex, attempting also to phase and provenance the timber used in their construction, and to consider their relationship to the perceived sequence of building at the abbey.[6] In common with most other chapter houses, the major portals at Westminster were never designed to receive doors, and hence it was only the subsidiary openings that were fitted with them. In addition to this vestibule door, two further doors (controlling access to the undercroft) are reported upon and discussed here: one hangs in the south-east corner of the south transept (door 3: figs 14 and 250), at the point of entry to the passage, and the other is located at the first of the right-angled turns within it (door 2: figs 14 and 246).

All three doors hang in relatively minor openings: two have been cut down and reused and are not in their original positions. A fourth medieval door once hung in the opening between the outer vestibule and St Faith's chapel (sacristy), but that was probably lost in the sixteenth century, when the doorway was blocked (p 4). The present door there dates only from *c* 1860. Another skin-covered door that formerly hung in the entrance to the same sacristy from the south transept was described in 1723.[7] [WR]

Methodology

Standard dendrochronological techniques were employed to date the samples. In order for tree-ring dating to be used, either physical samples of wood must be obtained, or direct measurements taken from a cleaned section of end-grain. However, conventional sampling was not possible with the Westminster doors, owing to the thin nature of the boards, and the surfaces of the planks being too abraded or damaged to allow the rings to be accurately measured. Since cleaning the surface would have caused unacceptable visual damage to the timberwork, a micro-borer was employed to extract the samples.[8] This was accomplished by using an 8 mm outside diameter hollow drill bit, which extracts a 5 mm diameter core. The drill bit was cooled and cleared of dust with the aid of compressed air, which is channelled through the inside of the cutting tube and clears the waste from around the outside of the bit. The drill bit was accurately aligned by a series of guides fitted to a jig which was clamped to the face of the door. In this manner, the drill can be used to bore through a number of boards as thin as 15 mm thick and as wide as one metre, or more. Hence, in one door, four of the original boards could be drilled in succession with the need to make only a single hole, which was afterwards plugged with an oak pellet, and stained. The cores thus extracted were glued onto grooved timber mounts and prepared, to allow the ring boundaries to be clearly distinguished. The rings were then measured under a ×10/×45 variable-focus microscope, using a travelling-stage, electronically displaying displacement to a precision of 0.001 mm, rounded to the nearest 0.01 mm.

Once a tree-ring sequence has been firmly dated in time, a felling date, or date-range, is ascribed where possible. As none of the boards in the doors retained bark, only an estimate of felling could be given. The number of sapwood rings can be estimated using an empirically derived sapwood estimate, with a stated confidence limit. If no sapwood or heartwood/sapwood boundary survives, then the minimum number of sapwood rings, calculated from the appropriate sapwood estimate, is added to the last measured ring to give a *terminus post quem* or 'felled after' date. A review of the geographical distribution of dated sapwood data from historic building timbers has shown that a 95 per cent confidence range of 9–41 rings is appropriate for the southern part of England; and for Baltic timbers, a similar estimate of 8–24 sapwood rings has been used.[9]

Of all the doors assessed for dendrochronological potential, that in the chapter house vestibule (door 1) had the least promising chances of success.[10] Although the rings were reasonably numerous, there was a band of very narrow rings which it was felt might cause problems in dating. Also, as the planks were tangentially cut, the number of rings in each would not be as great as if they had been radially cut. However, a major redeeming feature

of this door was the presence of sapwood rings on at least two of the boards which, if dated, would produce a felling date-range, which is obviously vital for a door of such importance. The door planks were of sufficient thickness to permit the use of micro-boring. Although the top and bottom edges were too damaged to allow clear *in situ* measurements, or for impressions to be taken, Dr John Fletcher of the Archaeology Research Laboratory at Oxford had managed to take measurements from two of the boards in the late 1970s.

The outer passage door in the south transept (door 3) is constructed from a series of boards that are all slow-grown and are very suitable for dendrochronology; at least one had a clear heartwood/sapwood boundary, which would enable a felling date-range to be produced. This door could be sampled using the long micro-borer through the edge of the vertical boards forming the front. The final door to be assessed (door 2) lay at the landing between the first and second flights of steps in the passage leading to the chapter house undercroft. Both the V-edged planks as well as the framing members were very slow-grown, and two of these timbers retained clear heartwood/sapwood transitions. The thickness of the members made this door ideal for coring using the micro-borer.

Apart from the door in the chapter house vestibule, all the boards used in the various doors were slow-grown, suggesting that many of them might have been imported from the Baltic region, or from other non-local sources.

Chapter house vestibule office door (door 1)

This door (figs 242 and 243) opens from the south side of the outer vestibule into the understair office-store. It probably once led into the Pyx chamber, although there has been no access by this route since the early fourteenth century (p 4) and it is thus unfortunate that the term 'Pyx door' has entered the literature in modern times.[11] It should not be confused with the two large doors opening directly from the east cloister into the Pyx chamber or treasury, and it will, therefore, be referred to here as the chapter house vestibule office door (Plan 1). At present, the door is just over 4 ft (1.27 m) in width and 6½ ft (1.98 m) in height (fig 244). It is constructed from five boards about 1½ in (40 mm) thick and ranging in width from 9 in (225 mm) to 15½ in (390 mm). The boards are rebated, without stops, for half their thickness by 1⅜ in (35 mm). Although Hewett stated that the planks were riven, closer inspection found that they were all converted tangentially by sawing through-and-through.[12] Nevertheless, the boards were fully seasoned before

Fig 242 Chapter house vestibule: the setting of the reused eleventh-century door 1 in the south wall. The original rear face of the door is presented in this view. *Photograph*: Warwick Rodwell © Dean and Chapter of Westminster

Fig 243 Chapter house vestibule, door 1: the original outer face (now reversed). *Photograph*: © English Heritage Photo Library 2002

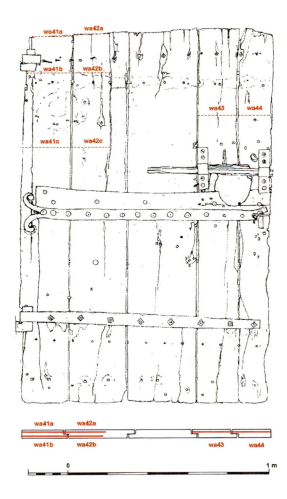

Fig 244 Chapter house vestibule, door 1: measured drawing of the original outer face and section showing the sampling locations. *Drawing*: Angela Thomas (with additions)

jointing, as the deformation typically found with through-and-through conversion was not evident here.[13]

The boards are connected by three flush inset ledges in the shape of two opposed dovetails, the edges cut slightly concave and secured by pegs. There are also about three edge-dowels 1/2 in in diameter per joint, which pass through the centre-line of the rebate. Two ledges were placed at the top and bottom on the back of the door, and one in the middle on the front. There still remains a central iron strap with a split curl on the original front (figs 243 and 244).[14] There are also impressions of two Romanesque C-and-strap hinges with split-curl terminals at the top and bottom of the door, respectively.[15] The front of the door was originally covered with animal skin, of which some fragments still survive beneath the central iron strap. Although this skin has repeatedly been claimed by antiquaries as human, modern re-examination has shown that it is vegetable-tanned cow hide.[16]

The door has been reduced by about 4 in (100 mm) in width, and by an unknown amount in height: Hewett was probably correct in suggesting that it would originally have been round headed (fig 245). There is no reason to doubt

that the door was cut down and hung in its present position in the 1250s, when the chapter house and its vestibules were constructed. The plain upper strap-hinge is thirteenth century, and the lower one is a nineteenth-century replacement. It is not known where in the abbey the door would originally have been located, although the entrance to the Confessor's chapter house is an attractive possibility.[17]

The primary objective of the research project was to ascertain whether this door is eleventh century, and if so, whether it dates from the period of Edward the Confessor, or later. In the 1970s, Fletcher was commissioned to date the door,[18] and he made two visits to measure the tops of the boards *in situ*.[19] At the time, the two measured boards were found to cross-match together, but failed to provide a date reliable enough for publication. As part of the current analysis, the 1970s data was found in punch-card form in the Fletcher archives, and was manually keyed in.[20] Now,

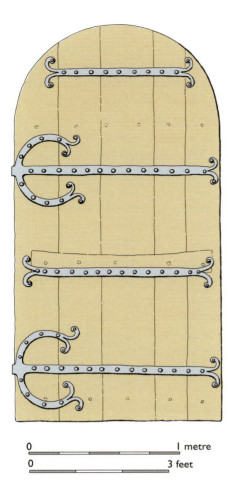

chronologies and was found to be datable, spanning the years AD 924 to 1030. The number of chronologies matched was limited, which is unusual considering the wealth of Norman chronologies for the London area. However, the site master matched exceptionally well with the chronology from Greensted church, Essex, and with another from a series of boards from the Tower of London. Whilst dendro-provenancing is not realistic based on so few chronologies, it does illustrate that the timber used in this door originated from a source near to London, and which was subject to unusual climatic or management trends.

Remarkably, this door retained some sapwood on the two planks that were dated. One had a clear heartwood/sapwood boundary at 1026, and another sample had ten rings of sapwood with a heartwood/sapwood boundary datable to 1020. By taking the average heartwood/sapwood boundary date of 1023, a felling date-range of 1032–64 has been produced. This makes the vestibule door the oldest securely dated door in Britain, and the earliest example of post-Roman sawn timber boards. As such, it is of Anglo-Saxon origin, and must have been part of the abbey complex built by Edward the Confessor between c 1050 and 1065. Dendrochronology has shown that the timber was of English origin. The date-range produced by this door has pushed back the earliest known examples of square-rebated boards by about half a century.[21]

Door in the chapter house undercroft passage (door 2)

By the reign of Edward I, the undercroft to the chapter house was being used as a royal treasury and, although the documented burglary of 1303 has generally been thought to relate to the Pyx chamber, recent research suggests that it took place in the undercroft, through a window (chapter 7). It has been established that originally there was no door in the present position in the undercroft passage, and the outline on the walls of a former flight of steps discounts a previous theory of a 'pit-fall' and drawbridge beyond (fig 17; p 113).

The next oldest door studied is that situated at the first right-angled turn in the passage leading to the undercroft from the south transept. It is a large door that has been cut down and reused from elsewhere. It measures 4 ft (1.21 m) wide by 6 ft 4 in (1.93 m) high, and is square topped. The outer face consists of four old planks abutting a replaced hanging-stile (fig 246). It is uncertain whether the door was re-formed and placed in its present position by Sir Gilbert Scott, c 1865, when he was restoring the north

Fig 245 Chapter house vestibule, door 1: suggested reconstruction of the original external face, based on the evidence of surviving ironwork and hinge-scars on the boards. *Drawing*: Warwick Rodwell © Dean and Chapter of Westminster

nearly thirty years on, encouraging matches have been found with the reference chronologies, but clearly more material was needed to bolster the t-value matches to acceptable limits.

Therefore, during the 2005 analysis, four out of five boards making up this door were sampled using the micro-borer. The board not sampled was the middle plank, with only thirty rings, which derived from one of the outer slabs of the tree when it was converted. Radial splits in the first two boards required additional core samples to be taken, to ensure that the breaks were covered. The three unbroken sequences from the first two boards were found to match each other, as well as with the direct graticule measurements taken by Fletcher. Since matches between the samples suggested that they had originated from the same parent tree, the individual sequences were combined to form the 107-ring site master. This was compared with over 1,300 British reference

Fig 246 Undercroft passage, door 2: outer face, showing also the sampling location. *Photograph*: Warwick Rodwell © Dean and Chapter of Westminster

transept, from whence it originated. Alternatively, the door may have been installed when the undercroft was restored by W R Lethaby in 1909 (p 31). The planks are about 1½ in (30 mm) in thickness, tapering to ¾ in (20 mm), and have 2 in (50 mm) deep V-edged joints. The inside face of the door consists of a 5 in (130 mm) by 1¾ in (45 mm) thick locking-stile, a bottom rail slightly thinner and wider, and braces averaging 1½ in (38 mm) and 1¾ in (45 mm) in thickness. The boards are fixed to the framing by large 1 in (25 mm) diameter flat-headed clout nails, which form a lozenge pattern on the front of the door. The bottom rail is dovetail-lap jointed into the stile. A significant feature of this door is the use of diagonal braces/ledges, which are set at different angles (figs 247 and 248).

Seven timbers were sampled from this door: two planks and five of the framing members. Once all the individual same-timber and same-tree means had been

produced, they were combined to form a 183-year site master. This was compared with the reference chronologies and was found to span the years 1000–1182, and matched best with English chronologies. Five of the timbers from this door were thus dated. The timbers with the latest heartwood-ring dates are the external boards, two of which were found to originate from the same tree and produced a 'felled-after date', or *terminus post quem*, of 1224, taking into account the last unmeasured rings in the V-groove joints. Inspection of the tip of the feather-edged V-groove on the inside of one board, lower down from the point of sampling, showed clear evidence for a heartwood/sapwood boundary. Although this could not be directly related to the sequence of rings sampled, it confirms that the *terminus post quem* of 1224 is probably within ten years of the actual felling date-range. The bottom rail and locking-stile produced *termini post quos* of after 1190 and after 1207, respectively. These four last heartwood-ring dates are consistent with each other, and suggest felling in the period around 1250.

However, one of the braces yielded a clear heartwood/sapwood boundary date of 1111. This would give a felling date-range of 1120–52, which is a full century earlier than the other dated elements of the door. Closer inspection of this brace showed that there is a peg-hole in it, filled with a plug, suggesting that the timber was reused (fig 249). Further peg-holes in this and some other braces that have not been dated may also signify secondhand timber. Dendrochronology shows that the timber is local in origin.

The dating of this reused door to *c* 1250 suggests that it was originally from one of the main doors in the central part of the abbey, rebuilt during the reign of Henry III. A drawing of the door was prepared, and the lines of the cross-braces projected beyond the later hanging-stile and the truncated top; this produced a reconstruction of the door as originally built (fig 248). It would have measured approximately 4 ft (1.22 m) wide, and just over 8 ft (2.40 m) high. All of the existing door openings in the abbey were then measured, and only one seemed potentially to be the original location of the door. That is the door to the western aisle of the north transept. The opening there housed two leaves 4 ft (1.22 m) wide and 12 ft (3.65 m) high, with a square top. The abbey possesses a painting, dating to *c* 1740, which shows the western leaf of this door extending to two-thirds of the height of the opening, which is virtually identical in size to the drawn reconstruction of the door.[22] Determining whether the painting depicts the original thirteenth-century door leaves is not straightforward. A dark, internal view of the same doorway in 1812 shows that the inner faces of the doors had been panelled.[23]

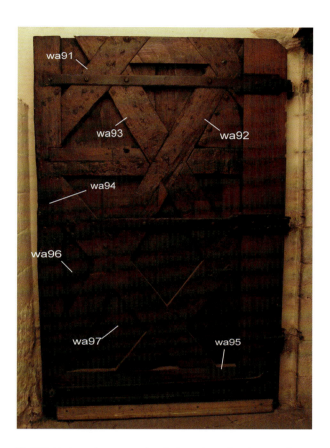

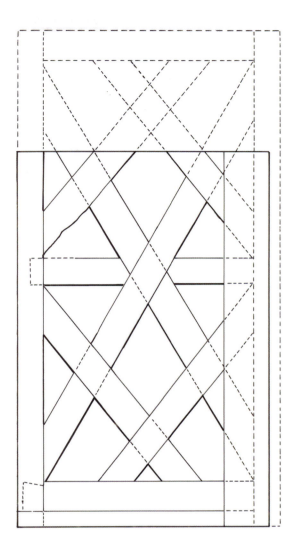

Fig 247 Undercroft passage, door 2: inner face, showing sampling locations. *Photograph*: Warwick Rodwell © Dean and Chapter of Westminster

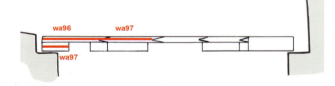

Fig 248 Undercroft passage, door 2: measured drawing of the inside (south) face of the door, reconstructing its original form; and a detailed section showing the line of sampling. *Drawing*: © Daniel Miles

However, all is made clear by Lethaby, who wrote 'when the repairs of Wren's time were done, older wooden doors were new cased'. In the accounts of Wren's works at the church is an item, under 1700, for 'mending Solomon's Porch doors'. These were broken up and thrown aside in the more thorough restoration of later days. A considerable fragment of one of those that remained has recently been adapted as a door to the stair of the chapter house undercroft. It has diagonal framing covered with plain boarding, and such doors are shown at the North Transept in one of the seventeenth-century views of the interior.[24]

Fig 249 Undercroft passage, door 2: detail of a peg inserted into a brace (wa91) reused in the construction of the door. *Photograph*: © Daniel Miles 2007

Fig 250 South transept, outer passage door 3: outer face, showing the sampling location. *Photograph*: Warwick Rodwell © Dean and Chapter of Westminster

Fig 251 South transept, outer passage door 3: inner face. *Photograph*: Warwick Rodwell © Dean and Chapter of Westminster

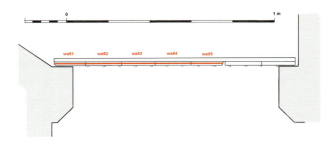

Fig 252 South transept, outer passage door 3: section drawing of the door and jambs, showing the line of sampling. *Drawing*: © Daniel Miles

Outer passage door, Poets' Corner, south transept (door 3)

Here, the research aim was to try and determine the date of the door leading from the transept to the south-east stair vice and the undercroft, and also to compare its dating to the similar door to the sub-crypt in the White Tower, Tower of London, which is of mid-fourteenth century date.

This door, as seen from the transept, has a series of seven vertical square-edged boards, clench-nailed in a square pattern to twelve horizontal boards on the back, of which one is a replacement (figs 250 and 251). The door is slightly wider than its counterpart in the north transept, being 3³/₄ ft (1.15 m) wide, and 7 ft (2.13 m) high, again with a two-centred head. The boards measure between 6 in (150 mm) and 7 in (175 mm) in width and are ³/₄ in thick (fig 252). The two layers of boards are fixed together by clenched nails, arranged in a 3 in (75 mm) grid, some of which accidentally align with the joints in the boards in order to maintain symmetry.

Five boards from this door were sampled. The last sample fractured during coring, which is particularly regrettable as it retained a heartwood/sapwood boundary. Combining three of the samples, a 169-year site master was constructed and compared with reference chronologies: it was found to be datable, and spanned the years 1162–1330. This matched best with Baltic chronologies, showing that the timber was imported. One additional sample failed to match the others of the site master, but did date individually. This also matched with Baltic chronologies, spanning the years 1168–1328. It is likely that this timber came from a slightly different region of the Baltic.

The four dated boards yielded last measured-ring dates ranging from 1314 to 1330. None of the dated boards retained evidence for sapwood, and therefore only a *terminus post quem* of 1338 can be given for the door. This is almost identical in date to the sub-crypt door in the White Tower, which produced similar last heartwood-ring dates. Unfortunately the fifth board with some sapwood failed to date. The analysis suggests an eastern Baltic origin for the timber.[25]

A summary of the data collected is given in figure 253, and the results are interpreted graphically in figure 254.

Fig 253 Westminster Abbey doors: summary of tree-ring data

WESTMINSTER ABBEY DOORS

Sample number & type		Timber & position	Dates AD spanning	H/S bdry	Sapwood complement	No of rings	Mean width mm	Std devn mm	Mean sens mm	Felling seasons & dates/date ranges (AD)
Chapter House: Outer Vestibule										
*wa41a	g	Board 1 from fore edge (JMF)	924–1024			101	1.49	0.64	0.306	
*wa41b	mc	ditto	951–1026	1026	H/S	76	1.59	0.64	0.263	
*wa41c	mc	ditto	925–996			72	1.72	0.77	0.325	
wa41		Mean of **wa41a+wa41b+wa41c**	924–1026	1026	H/S	103	1.54	0.66	0.290	
*wa42a	g	Board 2 from fore edge (JMF)	938–1030	1020	10	93	1.57	0.65	0.234	
wa42b1	mc	ditto	949–966			18	1.40	0.83	0.346	
wa42b2	mc	ditto	980–1009			30	1.67	0.35	0.150	
wa42b3	mc	ditto	1013–1029	1020	9	17	1.13	0.25	0.189	
*wa42c	mc	ditto	940–999			60	1.73	0.80	0.247	
wa42		Mean of **wa42a+wa42c**	938–1030	1020	10	93	1.57	0.65	0.234	
wa43a1	mc	Board 4 from fore edge	–			19	1.09	0.33	0.266	
wa43a2	mc	ditto	–			5	1.93	0.42	0.214	
wa43a3	mc	ditto	–			6	1.39	0.24	0.187	
wa43a4	mc	ditto	–		8	38	1.63	0.61	0.201	
wa44a1	mc	Board 5 from fore edge	–			5	2.24	0.45	0.311	
wa44a2	mc	ditto	–			28	2.45	0.56	0.201	
* = WMNSTR1 Site Master (English)			**924–1030**	**1023 Avg. H/S bdy**		**107**	**1.57**	**0.61**	**0.246**	**1032–64**
Chapter House Undercroft: Inner Passage Door										
wa91a1	mc	Top left brace	–			17	1.31	0.12	0.126	
wa91a2	mc		1000–1109			110	1.10	0.22	0.125	
wa91b	mc		1054–1111	1111	H/S	58	1.08	0.18	0.154	
*wa91		Mean of **wa91a2+wa91b**	1000–1111	1111	H/S	112	1.09	0.20	0.130	1120–52
wa92a	mc	Middle left brace	–			72	1.55	0.39	0.168	
wa92b	mc		–		H/S	42	1.83	0.44	0.230	
wa92	mc	Mean of **wa92a+wa92b**	–		H/S	78	1.60	0.42	0.174	
wa93a1	mc	Middle right brace	–			52	1.04	0.17	0.119	
wa93a2	mc		–			10	0.71	0.14	0.141	
wa93a3	mc		–			13	0.54	0.08	0.146	
wa93a4	mc		–			91	0.72	0.18	0.142	
wa94	mc	Locking stile	1083–1198			116	1.09	0.44	0.185	After 1207
wa95	mc	Bottom rail	1097–1181			85	1.59	0.59	0.184	After 1190
wa96a1	mc	Board from fore edge	–			21	2.11	0.37	0.211	
wa96a2	mc		1056–1165		110+22 NM		1.76	0.38	0.189	(After 1224)
wa97	mc	Board 2 from fore edge	1042–1182		141+33 NM		1.79	0.39	0.182	After 1224
wa967		Same tree mean of **wa96a2+wa97**	1042–1182			141	1.82	0.37	0.176	
* = WMNSTR6 Site Master (English)			**1000–1182**		**183+33 NM**		**1.49**	**0.35**	**0.148**	**After 1224**
South Transept: Outer Door to Passage										
*wa81	mc	Board 1 from fore edge	1162–1314			153	0.99	0.35	0.269	
*wa82	mc	Board 2 from fore edge	1184–1330			147	1.14	0.30	0.162	
wa83	mc	Board 3 from fore edge	1168–1328			161	0.99	0.28	0.157	
*wa84	mc	Board 4 from fore edge	1172–1322			151	1.15	0.26	0.158	
wa85a1	mc	Board 5 from fore edge	–			48	1.98	0.40	0.185	
wa85a2	mc		–		H/S	27	1.74	0.32	0.168	
* = WMNSTR5 Site Master (Baltic)			**1162–1330**			**169**	**1.07**	**0.25**	**0.135**	**After 1338**

Key: * = sample included in site-masters; g = graticule reading; JMF = John Fletcher Measurements from punch card

H/S bdry = heartwood/sapwood boundary – last heartwood ring date; std devn = standard deviation; mean sens = mean sensitivity.

Sapwood estimate (95% confidence) of 9–41 used for English timbers (Miles 1997a); 8–24 for Baltic oak boards (Tyers 1998).

Given the lack of any heartwood/sapwood boundaries, a *terminus post quem* date has been given for each board by adding the minimum number of sapwood rings to the last measured ring date, as adjusted by adding any unmeasured core segments beyond (+NM).

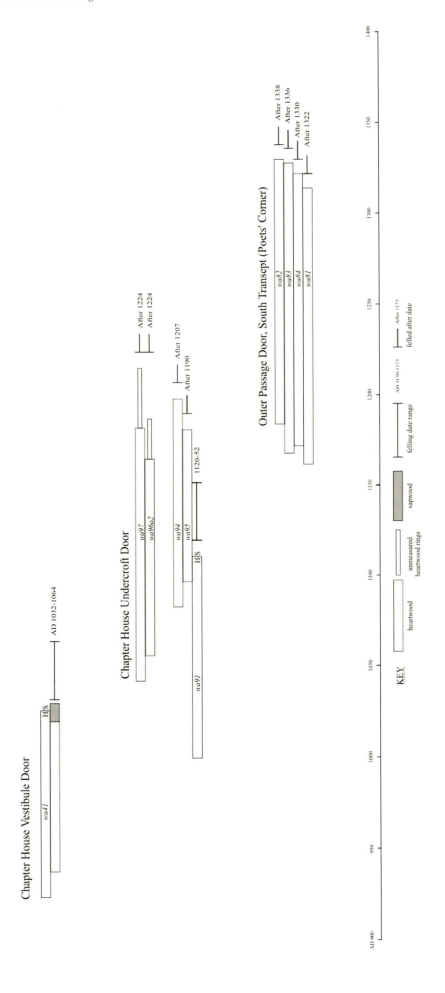

Fig 254 Bar-chart showing dated timber samples from the doors in chronological order. *Drawing:* Michael Worthington

Notes to chapters

CHAPTER 1 (pp 1–31)

1   Scott 1860; 1861, 31–7; 1863, 39–46; 1867; 1879, 284–6.

2   For example, Stanley 1864–7; Lethaby 1906, 37–54 and *passim*; Bond 1909, 284–9; Lethaby 1925, 98–132.

3   RCHME 1924, 79–81, pls 155–9.

4   Noppen 1935 (reprinted in 1936), followed by Noppen and Rigold 1949 (with further editions in 1952, 1953 and 1961), then by Rigold 1976 (with a new English Heritage edition in 1985, reprinted in 1987, 1988 and 1990), by Anon 1987 and by Rodwell 2002.

5   Brayley 1823, II, 286; Noppen 1935, 14. Polychromy on the central image bracket was still legible in the early 20th century when it was recorded by Lethaby (fig 148): WAM, Lethaby MSS.

6   Pennant 1790–[1820?], II, 53.

7   Ackermann 1812, II, 261–2.

8   For a plan, elevation of bays 2 and 3 of the south wall, and profiles of the columns, drawn in 1804, see Carter 1795–1814, I, 50, pl 70.

9   The condition of the medieval bosses is now much worse than it was in the 19th century. For rudimentary sketches, see Carter 1795–1814, I, 50, pl 70, items S, R and Q respectively. The latter two bosses were carefully drawn by Caveler (1839, pl 23, nos 7 and 6, respectively).

10   This arrangement was possibly adopted because the floor of the sacristy is higher than that of the vestibule; there is a flight of three modern steps immediately north of the doorway. Alternatively, the door may have been hung like this as a security feature; the same applies to the doorway in the north wall of the sacristy, which opens into the transept. Outward-opening doors with deep reveals are more difficult to force; on the other hand, a door opening into the sacristy from the vestibule could easily have been made impregnable by fitting internal draw-bars, so no fully satisfactory explanation for this odd arrangement (as seen from the vestibule) can be offered.

11   The jambs of the rear-arch have shallow pockets cut into them; these received the ends of the timber studs carrying the lath-and-plaster blocking.

12   Brayley 1823, II, 298. By 'old' the writer meant 11th century. On their plan of 1820, this space is labelled 'An old staircase to the private apartments of the abbots'.

13   Several views exist of the east cloister in the early 19th century, and they all show the blocked doorway to the former day-stair: eg Ackermann 1812, II, pl T.

14   Scott (1863, 49–52) describes the chamber as he found it in 1849, and again in 1859, just before he restored the day-stair.

15   The step, which appears in Carter's drawing of 1782 (fig 149), and many subsequent views, was eliminated by ramping the cloister floor in 2004. Previously, the threshold formed an upstand, *over* which one stepped to enter the vestibule, its floor being at the same level as the cloister paving. The whole of the vestibule floor has been raised: the wall-benches are now uncomfortably low and their tops are not parallel to the paving.

16   NMR F870008/5.

17   Feasey 1899, pl 13. The kerb was 19th century, and was introduced when the split level was created in the vestibule. By raising the floor in the southern bays, the up-over-and-down step at the outer entrance was eliminated. In 1981, when the first English Heritage shop was constructed in the south-east bay of the vestibule, the floor in the northern half was raised by inserting a timber deck. That was removed when the shop was rebuilt in 1987. The various floor arrangements appear in several photographs held by the NMR.

18   Plate-glass doors were installed in front of the gates in 1988, and removed in 2003: they are seen in Rodwell 2002, 6.

19   In the early 20th century, glazed panels were fitted to the fronts of the gates, but were subsequently removed (RCHME 1924, pl 156).

20   Various architectural students have made measured drawings of this vestibule and the innermost portal: for example, M Allen, 1880 (Royal Academy Prize Medal); E C Shearman, 1880 (*The Builder*, 14 March 1885); E G Hardy, nd. Copies in WAM.

21   T Tatton-Brown, 'Westminster Abbey: Chapter House inner vestibule and St Faith's Chapel roof'. MS report, March 1995: copy in WAM.

22   A very slight step at the entrance to the vestibule possibly marks the site of an eleventh full step which was expunged by raising the floor in the outer vestibule (see note 17 above).

23   The authenticity of its design was questioned by Lethaby (1925, 124).

24   At some time, a hole was broken through the back of the locker, to the outside, and subsequently refilled with brickwork. The two compartments now have separate oak doors, which are modern.

25   Summerly 1842, 40.

26   Betts (2002, 64) noted five designs amongst the reset medieval tiles. It is doubtful whether 'Westminster' tiles could be as early as the 1250s, and hence they mark a replacement or enhancement of the vestibule floor within half a century of its completion.

27   The wall core was reported to consist of chalk and flint rubble (Brayley 1823, II, 299). Until the 1980s, a vertical band of original Reigate ashlar remained on the north side, adjacent to the Poets' Corner entrance, where it formed part of the newel stair at the interface between the chapter house and transept; but that has since been refaced with Portland stone. In 2009 just one original Reigate ashlar survived on the south face, at undercroft level.

28   The capitals, bases, responds and king-mullions are mainly carved in Devonshire marble, some of which is markedly

striped in colour. Most of the smaller mullions and the three freestanding shafts that flank each respond are of grey carboniferous limestone, probably from Kilkenny (Ireland). There are, however, some striking inconsistencies: for example, a few mullions contain mixed stone types and some bases are not of Devonshire marble (fig 12). Several other stone types are present in very small quantities (eg Northamptonshire ironstone).

29 Scott followed the same course of action at Salisbury Cathedral: 'The decayed shafts, capitals and bases of the numerous windows … were originally of Purbeck marble, a material peculiarly liable to decay. It was therefore resolved … to employ … Devonshire marble, as being more durable and less costly than Purbeck. The juxtaposition of these two kinds of marble, differing as they do in external appearance, offended the eye. In order to soften the contrast, a process of rubbing and oiling the surfaces of both is now being employed … with a view to assimilating, as nearly as possible, the colour of the new to that of the old material' (*The Builder*, 15 May 1869, 384).

30 The evidence is recorded in photographs, eg the ashlar face of the stair-turret in Poets' Corner was intact in 1969: NMR G13.743/5. Similarly, there were still parts of the plinth of the chapter house and medieval mouldings on the inner face of the north-east flying buttress in 1959: NMR G22799/26 and G7565/9.

31 The east and north windows carry florets (fig 11), and the north east has stiff leaves. The three southern windows have no decoration on their hood-mouldings.

32 Rackham 1909–10, 39 n. 1.

33 Tatton-Brown (note 21 above) wondered whether the change was associated with repairs following the fire of 1298 which destroyed the roof of the dorter. It is not known whether the roof of the inner vestibule was also consumed, but if it was the adjacent window tracery is likely to have been damaged too.

34 Colvin *et al* 1976, 415.

35 Brayley 1823, II, pl 60.

36 The figure of Christ is possibly a replacement for a previous sculpture, but since the bracket in the base of the quatrefoil upon which it sits is also Victorian, it is feasible that originally there was only painted decoration here (Brown 1999, fig 20, pl 4). It is not known what the bracket on the west side held, but the width suggests a figural composition, perhaps an Annunciation (ibid, fig 146).

37 Jordan 1980, 68.

38 Photographs of the outer portal in 1907 reveal the surface of the tympanum as heavily blackened and spalling: NMR BB74/3532. It has subsequently been cleaned.

39 Jordan 1980, 72: *contra* Noppen (1935, 7, 16), who asserted that Scott 'took down the pillar and substituted a copy; but his reason for so doing has never been discovered'. The originality, or otherwise, of the column has caused much anxious comment: eg Clayton 1912, 52 n. 1; Lethaby 1925, 104.

40 The radiating bars were certainly not introduced in the 18th century, as suggested by Wander (1977, 80).

41 Close access to these features has not been possible. It is apparent (from fig 143) that most of the hooks on the pillar have a rounded basal angle, but one or two are more sharply right-angled and are possibly replacements. The differences may, however, be inconsequential.

42 Summerly 1842, front cover (copy in Westminster Abbey Library). His illustration is taken from bay 20. Comparison may be made with the polychromy and gilding on the mouldings of the pulpitum screen at Salisbury Cathedral (Brown 1999, pl 1).

43 The full scheme is set out in Noppen 1935. For the musical instruments depicted in this and the next scene, see Montagu 1988.

44 Loftie 1891, 206.

45 I owe this date to Dr Steven Brindle FSA; see also Noppen 1936, 29.

46 Photographs of visitors donning the overshoes in 1951 are held by the NMR PK175A.

47 Noppen 1936, 30–1. Photographs held by WAM, and those in innumerable publications, show various display and visitor-management arrangements in the chapter house: see, for example, RCHME 1924, pls 157–8.

48 Colvin *et al* 1976, 414 n. 2. This must have been the west or south-west window; probably the latter. Illustrations show that both were infilled with brick, and plastered.

49 Colvin *et al* 1976, 414. Two bakehouses are marked on a plan of 1818; one of these probably started life as a brewhouse (Sir John Soane's Museum: 37 (1) 19).

50 The Gothic windows were still present when William Morgan drew his map of Westminster, published in 1682 (fig 31).

51 Colvin *et al* 1976, 415.

52 The upper part of the chapter house shows well in a drawing of Westminster Abbey from the south by William Capon, 1819: British Library, Prints and Drawings, *Crace Views of London*, portfolio XIV, no. 86. This is reproduced in Wander 1977, fig 7. For a photograph of the chapter house from the south west in 1860, see Lethaby 1925, fig 24.

53 Scott 1867, 155.

54 Ibid 152, quoting from the text of an unpublished lecture on chapter houses delivered by Clutton, who was the architect responsible for beginning the restoration of Salisbury Cathedral chapter house in 1855 (Brown 1999, 47). No authority for his statement regarding the alleged removal of Westminster's chapter house roof in 1714 has been traced.

55 For an annotated photographic record of repairs carried out between 1948 and 1951, see NMR AL1091 (Westminster Abbey, Blue Album).

56 For a photographic record of work carried out in the 1970s, see NMR file PK175C.

57 Harrod 1873, 373.

58 RCHME 1924, 81.

59 The paving of the first passage is Yorkstone and the steps are Reigate stone; the latter are medieval, although repaired. The landing is paved with small rectangular slabs, potentially medieval, but reused.

60 Some of the lintels were given extra support by flat iron bars which are longitudinally channelled into their undersides.

61 The medieval steps in passage A are reused, as are the three

remaining stone steps in passage B: they are all in secondary medieval positions. Only the steps in passage C are primary and unaltered.

62 At two other points, headroom was less than 1.6 m. Similarly, headroom of only *c* 1.5 m occurs in the intramural stair-passages at triforium level in the south transept. The steps there are also steep, having a rise of 250 mm and tread of 290 mm.

63 Jewitt's plan of 1859 shows the closely spaced steps of the timber stair in the middle of the passage (fig 29), confirming that it was Scott who reopened the passage.

64 Some commentators have speculated that the timber steps might conceal a pit which formed part of the medieval security arrangements, but that is not so.

65 This drum is in two halves, and has an internal piecing-in. It may have started as a single drum which fractured during the hollowing process. The compartment is 670 mm in diameter by 310 mm high.

66 RCHME 1924, pl 159.

67 The compartment is 610 mm in diameter by 47 mm high.

68 Scott 1863, 46. The hollowness of the column had been remarked upon by earlier writers, eg Brayley 1823, II, 299.

69 Foundation deposits, generally in the form of collections of bones, are sometimes encountered during archaeological excavations, although usually in buildings of earlier date.

70 The full profile is preserved on the north and there was no neck-ring.

71 The condition of these does not allow the number of blocks of which they are made to be ascertained. The base appears to comprise two blocks, there being a visible joint on the west.

72 Jewitt (1863, 196) claimed that the capitals once had neck-rings and that these had disappeared through decay. Although the lower parts of the capitals are eroded, and the sprue resulting from running the lead into the joint is exposed in most instances, there is no compelling evidence to support the assertion that there were neck-rings (unlike the capitals in the outer vestibule, with which Jewitt drew comparison).

73 The Purbeck marble base in the angle between the east and south-east sides has a crisp profile but has been renewed; the others are all heavily eroded.

74 The north-east and south-east sills were neatly paved with stone in the early 20th century.

75 They are associated with refitting the undercroft as a sacristy, replacing earlier casements which possibly dated from 1909 (glimpsed in RCHME 1924, pl 159).

76 The existing ferramenta are seemingly all Victorian or later replacements. On the south-west, the grille is certainly 20th century; moreover, there was still an entrance to the crypt via the south-east window opening until 1909, confirming that the grille there cannot be earlier.

77 Where the jambs have not been renewed, plugged holes for the ends of the horizontal bars are still preserved. There were two or three bars per window, and there would also have been at least two stanchions. The evidence is not completely preserved anywhere, but most can be gleaned from the south-west window. Similar ferramenta also occur in the Pyx chamber, and were formerly present on the treasury windows at Salisbury Cathedral (p 85, fig 96).

78 In plan, the recess measures 2.65 m wide by 1.3 m deep; it has a segmental head.

79 For views of the interior of the crypt in 1932, before and after the fixtures were installed, see *Westminster Abbey Kalendar 1934*, 71 and 72: WAM VI.21(6ᵃ).

80 The aumbry is glimpsed in an early photograph (fig 21).

81 Noted in RCHME 1924, 81. Both aumbry and piscina are shown on plans by Carter and Jewitt.

82 Clayton 1912, 44 n. 2. He did not see the screed, but based his interpretation on information supplied by the Clerk of the Works.

83 Harrod 1873, 375; Clayton 1912, 44, citing Pipe Roll for 32 Ed I. See also p 116 below.

84 Medieval tiles in usable condition were frequently reclaimed, as seen in the Pyx chamber: there, a floor laid *c* 1300 was patched at a much later date using tiles that were probably made in the 11th century. Vestigial traces of the mortar bedding remaining after tiles have been reclaimed are often encountered in archaeological excavations, but the evidence is fragile and easily destroyed.

85 Jewitt 1863, 196.

86 Scott 1863, 46n; 1867, 145–6. Bond (1909, 72) argued that the dimension of the chapter house had been increased during construction, by thickening the outer walls. He supposed this marked 'the intention to use the crypt as the royal treasury', failing to observe that the 'strong doors' which supposedly made it a secure chamber were later introductions.

87 In fact, the octagonal Purbeck marble base probably continues all the way down to the capital of the column below. Certainly, the chapter house column could not have been erected on rubble-and-mortar infilling in the conoid of the undercroft vault. The load imposed by the chapter house vault, through this single column, demanded support on a solid uncrushable stone core.

88 TNA: E 101/466/30.

89 *Civitas Londinium*, the map of London and Westminster commonly attributed to Ralph Agas, was drawn *c* 1562, but survives only in copies made in 1633 (Guildhall Lib).

90 Carter 1795–1814, I, 50, pl 70; Brayley 1823, II, pl 60.

91 Carter 1786, pl 29; Brayley 1823, II, pl 46.

92 Pencil drawings by Carter, *c* 1780, show the figures and foliage scrolls on the wall-arch above the portal (WAM VI.15(19)). Watercolours of the entrance by W Capon, 1779, and J C Buckler, *c* 1830, are in the Guildhall Library (Wakefield Coll, p5428530 and p5431294, respectively). The library of the Society of Antiquaries has a crude and unfinished watercolour of the early 19th century (Red Portfolio, Westminster Abbey, fol 12a), and a pen-and-wash reconstruction drawing of the portal sculpture, attributed to Flaxman (ibid, fol 27; here fig 152).

93 A small amount of material is also held by Sir John Soane's Museum.

94 Hardy 1869–85. *Foedera* was published in parts between 1704 and 1713.

95 Ibid, I, xxx. I am indebted to Dr Barney Sloane FSA for

[96] *Gent's Mag*, 1799, **69**(2), 578. Called 'The pursuits of architectural innovation no. XII', this is one in a series of articles by 'An Architect' (J Carter) on Westminster Abbey.

[97] Carter 1786, 7–8, pl 29.

[98] Carter 1795–1814, I, 50, pl 70.

[99] Brayley 1823, II, 299.

[100] Caveler 1839, 60, pl 24. Herbert Minton's first pattern-book of encaustic tiles (1835) also included examples from the chapter house (MS in Stoke-on-Trent City Archives).

[101] Summerly 1842, 42.

[102] Summerly (ibid, 37) confirms that access to the chapter house by antiquaries was possible: 'permission to examine minutely its many great curiosities, both architectural, decorative and historical, can only be obtained from the authorities of the Public Record Office, at the Rolls House, in Chancery Lane'. See also Nichols 1842 and Minton 1842.

[103] Shaw 1858.

[104] Scott 1863, pl 9. See also Pearson 2000, app 3.

[105] One view looks west and shows a hexagonal table fitted around the central column; it also indicates a row of tiles with the arms of Henry III, but this is incorrectly orientated: the rows run east–west, not north–south, as implied by the drawing. Jewitt's second view is towards the north east and clearly shows the radial-segmental construction of the timber floor. Two versions of this exist: one shows Scott alone, with a measuring tape in his right hand; and the other shows two men conversing, one of whom is a cleric (perhaps the Dean).

[106] Smith 1807, 226n; Eastlake 1847, I, 123. Had the existence of the paintings been known in 1799, Carter (see above, note 96) would certainly have mentioned them.

[107] Although the painting is unsigned, pencil marginalia are unequivocally in Carter's hand; neither is it dated, but it cannot be after 1801, when parts of two panels were destroyed by the new doorways. The watercolour, measuring 628 mm by 265 mm, is owned by English Heritage (Accn 88291754). From at least the early 1920s, until 1998, it was displayed in a frame which was clipped to a heating pipe on the east side of the chapter house. It appears in RCHME 1924, pl 157; also noted in Lethaby 1925, 101. I am indebted to Robert Gowing for assistance with the study of this watercolour.

[108] Brayley 1823, II, 298–9. See also Waller 1873.

[109] Eastlake 1847, I, 123, 180–1.

[110] Summerly 1842, front cover.

[111] Pennant 1790–[1820?], I, 79; II, 54. Now No. 2 Little Cloister.

[112] Brayley 1823, II, 299. Their description copied in part that of Ackermann (1812, II, 274).

[113] WAM. The illustrations are not signed or dated, but the handwriting on them is distinctively Carter's.

[114] The draughtsman failed to synchronize the relationship between the exterior and the interior, and thus he has the entrance passage opening into the north-west bay instead of the west.

[115] WAM. Only the southern half of the chapter house is shown on this plan: the remainder appears on an additional sheet prepared by Hawksmoor in 1731, although that records less detail and omits minor structures.

[116] Three mortices for the framing of the cupboard-front are preserved in the soffit of the wall-arch above the recess. Jewitt mistook these for evidence of a screen 'placed before the altar', as did Scott (Jewitt 1863, 195; Scott 1867, 156). There are also five smaller pockets in the soffit of the north-east bay, indicating that this too had had a timber cupboard-front erected.

[117] Lethaby 1925, 127.

[118] Published in Scott 1863, 195–7, pl 29.

[119] At an unknown date, *c* 0.9 m of soil had been dumped in the undercroft; the consequent erosion line in the Purbeck marble of the central column is readily apparent.

[120] This chapter draws heavily on the collective knowledge of all who have studied the building, and I am greatly indebted to my fellow contributors for exchanging ideas and discussing aspects of the chapter house with me, in some cases over the course of many years. Jim Vincent, Clerk of the Works at Westminster Abbey, kindly arranged for the new survey drawings of the chapter house, vestibules, undercroft and tile pavement to be made by The Downland Partnership. Through the good offices of Jeremy Ashbee FSA, Anna Keay and Robert Gowing, English Heritage commissioned the cleaning of the tile pavement in 2008, thus enabling it to be studied more precisely. Angus Lawrence of Nimbus Conservation Ltd, who carried out the external conservation and repairs in 2009–10, kindly arranged access for me to study the chapter house from the scaffolding, and I am grateful to Tim Tatton-Brown for his observations on the geology of the masonry.

CHAPTER 2 (pp 32–39)

[1] Luard 1872–84, V, 195; Vaughan 1958, 65.

[2] Madden 1866–9, III, 94 (where, however, Paris adds a passage about the gifts Henry had conferred on the abbey); Vaughan 1958, 61.

[3] Madden 1866–9, III, 318; Vaughan 1958, 113–14. See also chapter 3, n. 1.

[4] I have here come independently and more emphatically to the same view as Christopher Wilson: 'it seems possible that Henry III always intended the chapter-house to be available for use by gatherings summoned on his orders to discuss public business', gatherings before which he himself might appear: Wilson 2008, 65. I hope this chapter may be seen as a small companion piece both to Wilson's article, which explores how Henry influenced the design of the abbey, and also to Binski 1986 (ch 2), which shows how the paintings in Henry's great chamber at Westminster reflected and proclaimed his ideas. See also Binski 2004, 15–26, 28–9, 32 and 185–92, for the decoration of the chapter house, including the 14th-century paintings.

[5] For a general survey of Henry's reign, see Carpenter 2004, chapters 10 to 12 (with chapters 1, 2, 13 and 14 dealing, over the period between 1066 and 1300, with national identity, the economy, religion and society) and Prestwich 2005, chapter 4 with Part III on society and people. Mortimer 1994 covers politics, government, society and culture in the

period 1154–1258. Binski 2004 explores art and imagination in England between 1170 and 1300. For a discussion of ritual, which relates to some of the points made in this chapter, see Weiler 2003.

6   Barron 2004, 238, and the works cited there. For Westminster itself, see Rosser 1989.

7   The transformation of the economy is discussed in the essays in Britnell and Campbell 1993. For markets and fairs see Letters 2003, I, 26–36.

8   Echoing Powicke 1947, II, 588.

9   Carpenter 1996, ch 14; Maddicott 1994, 230–2.

10 CPR *1247–58*, 506; Stacey 1988; Huscroft 2006, 101–2.

11 Thus one might seek to qualify Powicke's poetic final verdict: 'The old man left his kingdom greater than it was when, a fair-faced child, he rode from Devizes to be crowned at Gloucester. England was more united, more prosperous, more richly endowed, more beautiful in 1272 than it was in 1216': Powicke 1947, II, 588.

12 The definitive work on Magna Carta is Holt 1992.

13 Richardson and Sayles 1967.

14 Treharne and Sanders 1973, 111. For an introduction to the development of Parliament in this period, see Carpenter 1996, ch 19, where much other relevant work is cited. Understanding will be transformed with the publication of John Maddicott FSA's Ford lectures (see note 37 below).

15 Work on Henry's personal rule includes Stacey 1987; Maddicott 1994; Carpenter 1996; and Howell 1998.

16 For Eleanor, see Howell 1998.

17 Wilson 2008, 64–9.

18 Recent work on the abbey includes Wilson *et al* 1986; Binski 1995; Carpenter 2001 (for the period between 1258 and 1269) and Wilson 2008. H M Colvin in Brown *et al* 1963, I, 93–109 (on Henry and his works), 130–56 (on the abbey) and 141–3 (on the chapter house) is indispensable.

19 Luard 1864–9, IV, 77.

20 For Henry and Louis, see Carpenter 2005.

21 For the legislative reforms, see Brand 2003.

22 For de Montfort, see Maddicott 1994.

23 For recent work relating to Henry's piety, see Dixon-Smith 1999; Vincent 2001 and 2004; and Carpenter 2005.

24 Luard 1872–84, III, 290; IV, 231–2.

25 Carpenter 2007a, 39–40. See Dixon-Smith 1999.

26 Carpenter 2007b.

27 Ibid.

28 Colvin 1971, II, 226, 236. The original steps in the inner vestibule do not survive, and there are now seven in the main flight and another two just inside the inner portal.

29 Luard 1872–84, IV, 362. For a further use of the refectory in 1252 see Bémont 1884, 342 (a reference I owe to John Maddicott FSA).

30 Luard 1872–84, IV, 365. Meetings in both St Catherine's and the refectory are noticed in Westlake 1923, II, 329–31, 389.

31 Luard 1872–84, V, 360–1 (this refers to 1237, not 1253 as is sometimes thought).

32 Luard 1861, 230–1.

33 Duffus Hardy 1833–4, I, 502–2b. For this episode, see Carpenter 2008, 45.

34 Stubbs 1879–80, I, 324. St Catherine's was the scene of the farcical episode in 1176 when, in a dispute over seating between the archbishops of Canterbury and York, the latter was knocked to the ground: Stubbs 1867, I, 112–13.

35 I have calculated this (excluding the four years in which Henry was all or some of his time on the continent) from the tables compiled by Steven Brindle and included in his introduction to Craib 1923 (14–22); see also Brindle's own page 3 figures. One should add that the minority government between 1218 and 1227 spent a considerably higher proportion of time at Westminster and clearly based itself there, a point I wish I had appreciated when writing Carpenter 1990. Indeed Brindle (Craib 1923, 3) calculates that between 1220 and 1229 Henry spent nearly 50 per cent of his time at Westminster, although down to the end of 1223 this is really the time of Henry's ministers rather than of Henry himself, of whose whereabouts one cannot be sure. Henry travelled more once he began to emerge from the minority, but on nowhere near the scale of his predecessors.

36 I owe these figures (which are for the time John was in England, and exclude 1215 and 1216) to Julie Kanter, who is working on a thesis on the itineraries of the 13th-century English kings. For Henry's neglect of the Tower, see Carpenter 1996, ch 10.

37 I owe these figures to John Maddicott FSA who has kindly sent me his detailed list of parliamentary assemblies between 1235 and 1257, which will be printed as an appendix to his Ford lectures in Maddicott forthcoming. This list supersedes that in Fryde *et al* 1986, 536–40. I have assumed that the meetings said to be in London were, in fact, at Westminster. See also Maddicott 1999a, 25–6 and n. 46.

38 Close Rolls *1253–4*, 114–15; see Maddicott 1999b.

39 For the composition of these assemblies, and for the suggestion that the summoning of lesser tenants in chief could bring to Parliament those of knightly status, see Maddicott 1999a.

40 For the Commons using the chapter house in the 14th century see Barbara Harvey, below, pp 110–11.

41 Luard 1864–9, I, 386 (where the editorial date of 1256 is wrong).

42 Stapleton 1846, 71; Maddicott 1994, 318.

43 Clanchy 1968, 215–16; Carpenter 1996, ch 7.

44 Luard 1872–84, IV, 362, 365. The newsletter has been discovered by Nicholas Vincent and will appear in a forthcoming publication. I am most grateful to Nicholas Vincent for allowing me to see a copy of his transcription.

45 Luard 1872–84, V, 20. That Paris has the gist of Henry's words correctly is suggested by the Song of Lewes: Kingsford 1890, lines 485–526.

46 Luard 1872–84, IV, 362, 365. Paris speaks of the meeting being in 'the infirmary, namely in the chapel of St John the Evangelist' but this is almost certainly a mistake as the infirmary chapel was St Catherine's. It did, however, contain an image of St John the Evangelist: Thompson 1902–4, II, 246. The newsletter simply mentions the meeting as taking place 'in the chapel which you [the addressee] know'.

47 Luard 1872–84, V, 180 and 57 for a speech Henry made in

the great hall at Winchester. For Henry III recalling how 'in his own person' he had entered the chapter house of Holy Trinity Canterbury and prohibited the prior and monks 'in full convent' from pursuing a plea in the courts Christian, see Hector 1979, no. 136D.

48 Close Rolls *1247–51*, 203, 245 (Colvin 1971, 190–1).

49 Colvin 1971, 236–7, 266–7.

50 Close Rolls *1254–6*, 416. This would fit with Paris having written his comment after 1255.

51 Clayton noticed that the tiles west of the central column retain an unusual amount of glaze and wondered whether this was because they had been protected by the lectern. However, he also observed that 'the convenience of the position is open to question' (Clayton 1912, 52); if the lectern was there it would have meant the central column was between it and the president. If, on the other hand, the lectern was placed east of the central column, then the reader might have had his back to some of the audience so this position too has its problems. See below, pp 104 and 227.

52 Galbraith 1927, 80–1. The translation is that found in Myers 1969, 118. For the readings at the lectern see Thompson 1902–4, II, 182.

53 Luard 1872–84, V, 180.

54 Close Rolls *1256–9*, 366. John was also to convey the *patibulum* in the infirmary chapel to the house where Master William worked. Perhaps this was a frame used in the manufacture of the lectern. Brown *et al* 1963, II, 142 n. 5, mentions the second lectern but without comment.

55 Geddes 1987, 174–5 and nos 364–6, and, of course, more generally Geddes 1999.

56 In January 1259, the king told the Exchequer to give 50 marks to the keepers of his Wardrobe for work on an altar frontal, a lectern, the tomb of his daughter Catherine, and various pictures: CLR *1251–60*, 448. The exchequer *liberate* roll and receipt roll show that the order was obeyed: TNA: PRO E 403, 1217, m.2 and E 403/ 17B, m.2 (references I owe to Richard Cassidy who is editing the Pipe Roll of 1258–9, and allied material, for the Pipe Roll Society). The wardrobe accounts reveal that between July 1258 and July 1261 the keepers passed £333 6s 8d to the king's goldsmith, William of Gloucester, for the lectern and these other works: TNA: PRO E 361/1, m.1. The accounts of William of Gloucester himself do not mention work on the lectern but they were rendered by his executors after his death and were far from complete: TNA: PRO E 372/ 116, m.32d, partly printed in Scott 1863, 113–14. In 1258 Henry possessed another lectern, made of silver. This was in the custody of the keepers of the Wardrobe and it remained there until the king's death in 1272: TNA: PRO E 361/ 1, m.1d E 372/ 116, m.1d. This lectern weighed under ten pounds, which, given its lightness, suggests it was not of full length. See also CLR *1251–60*, 262. The Wardrobe accounts of the reign of Henry III have been edited by Dr Ben Wild and will be published by the Pipe Roll Society.

57 Close Rolls *1259–61*, 112.

58 See note 43 above.

59 *Ad honestam frontem*, Close Rolls *1242–7*, 273; Brown *et al* 1963, I, 503–4.

60 As Barbara Harvey suggests in Chapter 6, the *gradus* before which monks prostrated themselves was probably the lowest step in front of the president's seat. It was not, therefore, a structure which would have interfered with the positioning of Henry's lectern. The monks might sit to receive discipline, rather than lying prostrate (Thompson 1902–4, II, 191), but the bench on which they sat was probably movable. I am assuming that Henry's lectern was likewise movable and was not intended to be a permanent feature of the chapter house.

61 Carpenter 2007a, 43. The £229 was the cost of food, drink, stables and almsgiving on both the vigil and the day of the feast, but Henry fasted on the vigil (Luard 1872–84, V, 48) so the costs on that day would have been small.

62 Maddicott 1994, 200–1, and see Ridgeway 1988, 230, 241.

63 For Henry's contribution to the church as a whole, see Wilson 2008.

64 Lethaby 1925, 125. Lethaby suggests the glass was grisaille with 'a bright shield of arms set in each light' (see fig 30).

65 Wilson 2008, 79–80.

66 For the way the windows go beyond their French models in letting in light, see Wilson *et al* 1986, 86–7.

67 Lethaby 1925, 107–9, 120; Binski 1995, 190 and pl 248.

68 See note 89 below.

69 See chapter 12. For a different interpretation of the floor from that offered here, see Binski 1995, 187.

70 Clayton 1912, 51.

71 The plan of the floor in Clayton 1912, 49 (by J O Cheadle), is not exact. Warwick Rodwell suggests to me that there were thirty-one royal shields in each band as an allusion to the commencement of the chapter house in Henry's thirty-first regnal year (October 1246 to October 1247).

72 For example CLR *1226–40*, 268; *1240–5*, 205, 227; *1245–51*, 151; *1251–60*, 113; and see Binski 1995, 77.

73 For recent debate about the nave shields, see Wilson 2008, 92 n. 72.

74 If there were baronial shields in the windows of the chapter house, then that would have given visual testimony to the place of the community there. However the only recorded shield is that of Provence, and is in effect, therefore, the shield of the queen: Lethaby 1925, 125.

75 On the inscription see here chapter 12, pp 230–1 (inscription II).

76 A king and queen, presumably Henry and Eleanor, are also depicted in the two short bands of small portrait tiles in the floor: Clayton 1912, 49, 66–7.

77 Luard 1872–84, VI, 388. This was in line with the long cross coinage introduced in 1247 where the 'Henricus' which had appeared on coins since the reign of Henry II (including those of Richard and John) was now qualified by 'tercius' or 'III'.

78 Binski has argued that the date on this inscription is 1279 and I have accepted this, but I now suspect it is intended to stand for 1269 and is thus Henry's work: Binski 1990, 14–15, 22, 15 nn. 41 and 42; Carpenter 1996, 418–19.

79 The Confessor appears on one of the tiles giving his ring to the pilgrim: Clayton 1912, 49, 70. See tile design 33 on page 225.

80 Wickham Legg 1891–7, I, 388–9.

81 See, for example, the Parliament of 1244: Luard 1872–84, IV, 362–6; Carpenter 2004, 357.

82 Wilson 2008, 65.

83 Eg Luard 1872–84, IV, 182, 366; V, 330.

84 For the entrance from the east cloister turret, see Wilson 2008, 65; for its location, see Plan 1. I am grateful to Richard Mortimer FSA for accompanying me on an inspection.

85 If Henry used the 'pew', I would see it as having this kind of function as much as being a place where he attended or viewed services.

86 Stapleton 1846, 42. It was in the great hall in 1253 that sentence of excommunication against violators of Magna Carta was pronounced: Luard 1872–84, V, 375. For the capacity of the great hall, see Dixon-Smith 1999, 87.

87 Westlake 1923, II, 387.

88 Tout 1920–33, III, 291 and n. 1. See Loach 1991, 44 (a reference I owe to Barbara Harvey), which suggests that the Commons normally stood when meeting in the Westminster refectory.

89 Including the upper tier from which the wall arcading springs, there are three tiers in six of the bays, and four in the eastern presidential bay as a result of the upper tier under the arcading being set higher than in the other bays. However, in the six bays, only the top two tiers are really usable as benches for sitting, the bottom tier being so low as only to permit squatting. The calculation of sixty-three assumes that five people sat on the upper tier, each under a separate arch of the wall arcade (of which there are five per bay), and four on the bench below, the smaller number being because of the dangling feet of those above. In the presidential bay it may be that no one sat on the tier immediately below the top seat, thus creating a fitting distance between the *seniores* there and those below. It would be good to make practical experiments today as to the capacity of the chapter house, not least to see the effects on the acoustics.

90 Luard 1872–84, V, 48.

91 Ibid, 6–7.

92 Maddicott 1994, 200–1.

93 I am most grateful to Barbara Harvey FSA and John Maddicott FSA for commenting on a draft of this chapter.

CHAPTER 3 (pp 40–65)

1 Madden 1866–9, III, 318. Because the reference occurs under the year 1250, it has sometimes been claimed that Paris wrote it then. However, the chronicle in question, the *Abbreviatio Chronicorum*, was probably compiled between 1255 and 1259 (Vaughan 1958, 114) and if the entry for 1250 was written in the late 1250s, as is very likely, Paris might by then have seen the eastern parts of the abbey church built to full height and been able to appreciate that they had a different character from the chapter house. Be that as it may, it is important to note that his writings contain not a single evaluative comment on the architecture of the rebuilt church. We can only speculate as to what exactly Paris intended by placing his notice that the king built an incomparable chapter house at Westminster under 1250. Perhaps he believed 1250 to be the year when the building reached structural completion. Such a dating would be compatible with the frequently cited reference to the temporary filling of the windows with canvas in 1253, and with the evidence that the adjacent and structurally integral south wall of the south transept was the part of the church which progressed most rapidly from 1246. The only other works of art to which Paris applied the epithet 'incomparable' were the early 13th-century shrine of St Thomas at Canterbury Cathedral and an early 12th-century two-volume missal at St Albans, both destroyed; Lehmann-Brockhaus 1955–60, I, no. 864, II, no. 3840. It can be assumed that Paris regarded these objects as being of quite outstanding quality and ambition.

2 Between 1216 and 1245 Henry III had visited Worcester at least twenty-five times.

3 The literature on the Lincoln chapter house, as on the cathedral generally, is sparse. For the most recent account see Draper 2006, 141.

4 These visits took place on 6 January 1230 and 2 October 1236.

5 On the Abbey Dore chapter house see Harrison 1997 and Hillaby 1997. On the Beverley chapter house see Bilson 1895. Henry III is not known to have visited either Abbey Dore or Beverley and he certainly saw neither the dodecagonal-plan chapter house at Cistercian Margam Abbey in Glamorgan (which is a slightly later and more elaborate version of that at Abbey Dore) nor the octagonal example at Augustinian Holyrood Abbey, Edinburgh. The small and relatively undistinguished chapter house built on an elongated octagonal plan at Lichfield Cathedral around 1240 will doubtless have been known to the king, who had visited Lichfield several times before 1245.

6 Buttresses of this kind occur at Amiens and Salisbury cathedrals, both of which Master Henry had studied carefully, as his work at Westminster clearly reveals.

7 The fundamental problem in the planning of the Westminster chapter house was the fact that the 13th-century church at Westminster had transepts much longer than those of its 11th-century predecessor, a change which made the destruction of the north end of the 11th-century east claustral range unavoidable. Presumably it was not so much reluctance to demolish part of the fabric of the Romanesque east range as the desire that the chapter house entrance be close to the traditional position approximately at the centre of the east cloister walk which ruled out the possibility of setting the whole chapter house one bay further south, an option which would have avoided blinding the north-west window of the main room.

8 The vault responds and central pier rise to one-and-a-half times the height of their Lincoln counterparts. The utility of the Lincoln-Westminster comparison was demonstrated by Peter Kidson in Kidson, Murray and Thompson 1965, 99, 101.

9 Examples of single shafts carrying multiple ribs include the nave of the Temple church in London (late 1150s), the

Trinity chapel of Salisbury Cathedral (after 1220) and the west porch of Ely Cathedral (before 1215?). In the Westminster chapter house the gauge of the peripheral shafts is considerably greater than that of the shafts on the central pier.

10 Other recent buildings which are possible sources for the extreme slenderness of the central pier are the eastern (Trinity) chapel at Salisbury Cathedral and the refectory of Saint-Martin-des-Champs, Paris.

11 Wilson 2008, 75–7.

12 The accuracy of George Gilbert Scott's reconstruction of the vault from 1866 can be relied on, in part because the original springers and wall ribs survived the demolition of most of the vault in the mid-18th century, but also because a very large number of rib voussoirs were found to have been used to stop up the windows of the chapter house. Many of these voussoirs were incorporated into the reconstructed vault, a method of validation used by Scott in other of his restorations. The only detail of Scott's reconstructed vault whose accuracy must be doubted is the French-style concavity of the webs, which has no counterpart elsewhere in the abbey. On the relation of the vault to the windows see Kidson, Murray and Thompson 1965, 99; Wilson, Tudor-Craig, Physick and Gem 1986, 86–7; Wilson 1992, 182. Only at Chichester Cathedral, Beverley Minster and Fountains Abbey are there high vaults over central vessels that pre-date Westminster and that lack stilted wall ribs and obscured clearstorey windows; Wilson 1991, 189, pls 17, 23, 28.

13 For the easternmost chapels on the north side of the nave of Notre-Dame see Kimpel 1971, 37–41, 85–6; Kimpel and Suckale 1985, 344, and Bouttier 1987, 366, 374.

14 The other example of concentricity with some claim to have pioneered the concept is the blind tracery on the east walls of the outer aisles of the choir of Beauvais Cathedral. This belongs to the second campaign of work on the Beauvais choir and dates from the early 1240s; Murray 1989, 59, 71–4, 83, figs 98, 112. For the eastern nave bays of Châlons-en-Champagne see Ravaux 1976, 206–17. Only a few years later than Châlons are the concentric window heads and vaulting in the choir aisles of the parish and pilgrimage church of Saint-Sulpice-de-Favières near Etampes; Kimpel and Suckale 1985, ill. 440. For the relationship between the clearstorey and high vault at Saint-Urbain in Troyes, see Wilson 2007, 109, figs 2, 3.

15 Bony 1979, 4. These words were also intended to apply to the eclecticism of the abbey church at Westminster. Bony attempted to account for the formal differences between the church and the chapter house by attributing the latter to Master Aubrey; Bony 1979, 3–4. Lethaby's more plausible explanation for the highly unusual situation of two men styled Master being simultaneously present is that Henry was the architect responsible for the whole project whereas Aubrey was the contractor for the chapter house; Lethaby 1925, 130. The fact that Aubrey appears at Westminster only in Henry's final years as master mason (which are likely also to have been the final years of his life) raises the possibility that Aubrey was drafted in to share the burden of directing

the works. For evidence of the common authorship of the design of the chapter house and the abbey church see note 22 below.

16 Kunst 1968, 122, 139; Wilson, Tudor-Craig, Physick and Gem 1986, 25–6; Wilson 2008, 77–81.

17 At Beverley most of the chapter house has been destroyed, but the remaining and recorded elements confirm that it was of a piece stylistically with the contemporary eastern parts of the church.

18 Luard 1872–84, v, 475; Wright 1839, 67; Binski 1995, 45–6.

19 For Binham see Wilson, Tudor-Craig, Physick and Gem 1986, 27–8; Thurlby 1991; Wilson 1987, 76–7. I hope in the future to present a detailed case for attributing Binham to Master Henry. For the French-derived components of St Edward's chapel, Windsor, see most recently Wilson 2008, 81.

20 For example, the piers of the main arcade, the moulding profiles of which include numerous beaked rolls, and the curious way in which the wall ribs of the high vault emerge from the vault cells instead of springing at the same level as the other ribs.

21 It is extraordinary that there should be no discussion of tracery orders or even of mouldings in the only monograph ever devoted to the beginnings of Rayonnant architecture, namely Branner 1965. For hierarchized multi-order tracery see Bouttier 1987, passim, and Wilson 1992, 122. The lateral windows of the Sainte-Chapelle appear to have been pioneering in their use of tracery orders, for the concept is used in a much less systematic fashion in other approximately contemporary Parisian buildings, such as the west window of the refectory of Saint-Germain-des-Prés, the lateral nave chapels of Notre-Dame in Paris and the four-light blind traceries on the interior of the north transept terminal wall of the same church. The most recent discussion of the Sainte-Chapelle, which concurs with the general consensus that the architect was not inventive either formally or technically, includes no comment on tracery orders; Gasser 2007, 170.

22 However, the very fine-gauge mouldings included in the outer parts of the smaller order at the chapter house were undoubtedly modelled on those in the Sainte-Chapelle's apse windows (figs 50, 55, 56). The mouldings at the inside edge of each of the large sexfoiled circles do not conform to the profile given to the larger tracery order as a whole, a variation only made possible because this part of the tracery is not connected to any other. The profile used here is almost exactly the same as that used for the heads of the clearstorey tracery in the abbey church. Henry's profiles differ from the general run of early 13th-century English mouldings on account of their unusually great reliance on regular circular sections and their relatively restrained use of roll mouldings of complex profile. The latter achieve prominence at Westminster only on the archivolts of the central door of the north transept, where they are small in scale. For the motif of mouldings dying into cylindrical springer blocks, see Jansen 1982. The mouldings of the chapter house windows were drawn in 1859 by R J Johnson; WAM CN.3.I.23.

23 Branner 1964, 13, 15.

24 The only reference in print to this feature is in Lethaby 1925, 106.

25 Arcading with pointed trefoiled heads had steadily gained ground in England during the early 13th century. Major examples of the half-quatrefoil type from that period are to be seen in the extension to the east arm of Winchester Cathedral and in the west porch of Ely Cathedral.

26 For a discussion of possible English influences on Amiens Cathedral see Sandron 2004, 84. The half-quatrefoil arches of the wall arcade in the nave at Amiens might have had an English source, but they are more likely to have been influenced by the choir triforium at Noyon Cathedral. For the influence on Master Henry of French sources that approximate to forms favoured in England see Wilson, Tudor-Craig, Physick and Gem 1986, 53; Wilson 1987, 78; Wilson 1992, 181; Wilson 2008, 76–7.

27 Lethaby 1925, 109, 124.

28 Bony 1983, 384.

29 The loss of much of the portal's original tracery left the way open to including speculative embellishments rather than confining the new work to the reinstatement of the missing elements of the design. As was pointed out by Lethaby, the reliefs inserted into the portal tracery greatly darken the inner vestibule and St Faith's chapel, and are nonsensical in relation to the iconography of the original 13th-century imagery round the portal; Lethaby 1925, 115–16, 119.

30 For a recent exposition of this generally accepted connection see Nussbaum and Lepsky 1999, 204. Westminster's only concession to the idea that its vault is the aggregate of eight triangular compartments is the placing of the sides of the octagonal capital and base of the central pier parallel to the walls. This means that the notionally compartment-bounding ribs are enabled to project from the clustered rib springings somewhat more than the ribs within the compartments (fig 47).

31 Scott 1861, 40.

32 Lethaby 1925, 105. I am most grateful to Tim Tatton-Brown for clarifying the nature of the evidence for Salisbury's iron ties, first mentioned in 1668. The problem of how many of the iron ties in the abbey church are 13th century requires further investigation, but see Wilson, Tudor-Craig, Physick and Gem 1986, 63. The incidence of wooden and iron ties is usefully plotted in Binski 1995, 22, fig 19.

33 For iron and wooden ties in French Gothic churches and medieval churches generally see Viollet-le-Duc 1858–68, II, 402–3; Fitchen 1961, 275–9; Müller 1990, 303–4; Nussbaum and Lepsky 1999, 58–9, 329 n. 172. Lethaby's treatment of the problem was almost certainly influenced by aesthetic preferences based on progressive notions of structural honesty.

34 Viollet-le-Duc 1858–68, V, 387–8; Scott 1879, 285. In December 1725 the Office of Works ordered that the chapter house 'be secured by a cirb or iron chain'; Wander 1977, 80. Pace Wander, it is clear from several entries in OED that 'cirb' signifies not a 'crib' but a 'curb', a ring of iron or timber placed around a circular structure to strengthen it and hold it together. Whether or not the 1725

order was executed, the record is of interest for its implication that no major structural ironwork encircled the chapter house at an earlier date. Nevertheless, I hesitate to follow Wander's suggestion that the order's existence calls into question the 13th-century dating of the hooks above the capital of the central pier.

35 As can still be seen in numerous English medieval vaults, high vaults especially.

36 Lethaby 1906, 44.

37 For a reference to the finding of a fragment of what was supposed to be an octagonal pinnacle from the chapter house, see Scott 1879, 477.

38 Comparanda for these lozenges are at Lincoln Cathedral (the door on west side of south-west transept), St Radegund's priory, Cambridge (the chapter house facade), the Dominican friary, Gloucester (the south range) and the parish churches of Wyck Rissington (Glos) and Langford (Oxon).

39 Jean Bony compared this design to the revised triforium design introduced into the transepts of Amiens Cathedral in the late 1240s; Bony 1983, 72 n. 8. Bony's comparison with the windows of the lateral choir chapels of the parish church at Vailly-sur-Aisne does not carry conviction, not least because his dating of c 1230 is much too early; compare Sandron 2001, 423. Nikolaus Pevsner thought that the window belonged to the repairs executed after the fire of 1298; Pevsner 1957, 407. Presumably he was thinking of designs such as the west windows of the nave aisles at Tintern Abbey.

40 Branner 1964, 11–12.

41 An example of what is being avoided here can be seen in the chapel undercroft of Lambeth Palace, which probably dates from around 1220.

42 Brieger 1957, 187.

43 Unless one includes the high east choir wall of Romsey Abbey, to all appearances the first phase of an abortive remodelling of the upper levels of the choir; Wilson 2007, 120 n. 31.

44 To the best of my knowledge there is no substantial discussion in print of the design of this remarkable building.

45 Brown 2003, 47–85.

46 Lethaby 1925, 110–11. Although the York chapter house is covered by a wooden vault without any central support, it is clear both from the inclusion of stone springers and from the steep curvature of their constituent ribs that a stone vault borne on a central pier was the original intention.

47 As measured between the floor and the intradoses of the vault ribs. Although the first stone of York Minster's nave was laid in April 1291, demolition work needed to clear the site was under way by 1289; Brown 2003, 88. Evidence for regarding at least the intention to rebuild as approximately contemporary with the start of work on the chapter house is the fact that the replacement of the aisleless (and hence exceptionally inadequate) late 11th-century nave will have seemed a far more obvious priority than building a new chapter house.

48 Harvey 1984, 274. Simon is documented as the architect of

the York nave, and since the nave and chapter house share many stylistic traits and are more strongly influenced by French Rayonnant than are any other English buildings of their time, there is no reason why the chapter house should not be attributed to him. No doubt the York chapter will have felt the need to compete not only with Westminster Abbey but also with St Mary's Abbey in York, whose church was completely rebuilt in a very grand, though not particularly up-to-date, fashion between 1270 and 1294.

49 In a so-far unpublished paper on the choir of St Augustine's, Bristol, delivered to the conference 'An enigma explored: medieval art and architecture at Bristol Cathedral', University of Bristol, 19–21 September 2008. See also Wilson 2007, 118. In Wilson 1992, 196–204, the account of the York chapter house fails to acknowledge its role as the forerunner of St Stephen's chapel, Westminster Palace, the building from which the concept of an architecture of multiple modes was diffused through southern England.

50 The early or mid-13th century chapter house vestibule of St Werburgh's Abbey, Chester (now Chester Cathedral) has a vestibule which arguably equals the Westminster vestibules in the degree to which its treatment contrasts with that of the main room.

51 Wander 1978, 43; Wilson 2007, 114–15.

52 The only example of great church architecture conforming to the traditional basilican format which can be placed amongst the first rank of Decorated buildings artistically is the main vessel of the choir of Wells Cathedral, probably begun c 1330.

53 In one sense the Sainte-Chapelle foreshadows the Westminster chapter house's hierarchy-transgressing role, for enormously tall windows imitating those of its upper chapel were soon to be incorporated into the clearstoreys of great churches such as Beauvais and Cologne; Wilson 1992, 125–6. Nevertheless, the posterities of the two buildings could not have been more different, as the Sainte-Chapelle did not herald the rise of an experimental and exploratory architecture; indeed northern French Rayonnant of the late 13th and early 14th centuries is notable for its fidelity to ideas that had been more or less fully worked out by the middle years of the 13th century; Branner 1965, 137.

54 Prague, Archiv Pražského Hradu, Knihovna metropolitní kapituly, H.15, fol. 92v); reproduced in Suchý 2009, 11E.

CHAPTER 4 (pp 66–90)

1 Bilson 1895.

2 Harvey 1974, 75, 212–13, 251. See also Stratford 1978, 51–3.

3 Both the interior and the exterior were originally circular, but the latter was re-formed into a buttressed decagon in the late 14th century: it measures 21.3 m (70 ft) across the sides.

4 The early 13th-century chapter house is circular internally, but a buttressed dodecagon externally; Robinson 2006, figs 138, 139, 173.

5 Robinson 2006, fig 169.

6 Worcester and Lincoln each measured 20.75 m (68 ft) across the external faces, and were the two largest chapter houses

until they were eventually outstripped by York (21.3 m; 70 ft).

7 Stratford 1978.

8 Bilson 1895, 429.

9 Rickman 1848, opp 130.

10 Bilson 1895, 426.

11 Bilson (1895, 429) opted for c 1230.

12 Bilson 1895, 426.

13 Summers 1988, pl 24.

14 Roper 1886; VCH 1914, 105–6.

15 Similarly, on the north-west face at Westminster.

16 Britton 1836a, pls 12–15.

17 Rodwell 1989, 291–3.

18 VCH 1990, 47–51. Antiquarian suggestions that the vestibule was conceived as a rectangular chapter house have not found general favour.

19 Rodwell 1993, 31–3.

20 Rodwell 1989, 285–8.

21 There was a brick building adjoining the north side of the nave which served as a library until it was demolished in 1763; but it was a 15th-century addition and therefore has no bearing on the present discussion: VCH 1990, 56, fig 9.

22 VCH 1970, 151.

23 Even though access to the crypt has been improved, it still 'leaves much to be desired on the practical side. The space is uncomfortably cramped, and the inconvenience of the position and the difficult approach can well be imagined in relation to the handling of such things as long frontals' (Russell 1946, 23–4).

24 Howe 2006a.

25 Another, substantial sacristy was constructed outside the north aisle of the nave, probably in the 1260s: see RCHME 1924, folding plan.

26 Biddle and Kjølbye-Biddle 1980.

27 Two stone coffins with removable lids were incorporated in the design and fabric of the Cosmatesque pavement in the sanctuary: one was used for the burial of Richard de Ware (abbot 1258–83) and the other for Walter de Wenlok (abbot 1283–1307). See generally Grant and Mortimer 2002, *passim*.

28 Rodwell 2001, 144–5, fig 279.

29 Colchester and Harvey 1974; Rodwell 2001, 127–45.

30 *Vernacular Architect*, 2003, **34**, 117.

31 Geddes 1999, 179–80, fig 5.62.

32 A tree-ring date for the door indicates that it was added after 1456: *Vernacular Architect*, 2003, **34**, 117.

33 The door was originally the entrance to a small sacristy (one of a pair with the south transept), which must have been demolished to make way for the chapter house (Rodwell 2001, 138, fig 115B). Almost certainly, there was an unfulfilled intention to replace this modest door with a pair of openings occupying the full width of the stairs.

34 Colchester and Harvey 1974, 205. A single tree-ring date with a bracket of 1294–1324 was obtained by Michael Worthington in 2001 from a roof timber (pers comm Michael Haycraft).

35 Colchester and Harvey 1974, 205.

36 Investigations by the writer in 1988, when the chapter house was undergoing restoration.

37 Hewett 1985, 110, fig 106.

38 'Glasgow Cathedral', *The Builder*, 1 July 1893, 11–13.

39 Fawcett in Williamson *et al* 1990, 109.

40 C E M, 'Llandaff Cathedral', *The Builder*, 7 May 1892, 358–60.

41 In the early 14th century the east side was breached and a quire aisle formed.

42 It has further been suggested that the vestibule was originally intended as the basement storey for a lateral tower (Newman 1995, 244, 254). See also Thurlby 2006.

43 Cragoe in Keene *et al* 2004, 139. Although there was a chapter house at St Paul's in the 13th century, nothing is known about its structure.

44 Roberts 2002, 83–5; Cragoe in Keene *et al* 2004, 139.

45 Keene *et al* 2004, 183 with refs. The foundations of the chapter house have been partially preserved beneath the churchyard, and have recently been laid out to public view in a new garden.

46 Dugdale 1658, pls 127 and 161; reproduced in Roberts 2002, 84, 88.

47 Martin Stancliffe FSA kindly provided a plan of the foundations.

48 Hollar's plan shows four square plinths, which presumably carried moulded columns.

49 For the mouldings, see Harvey 1978, 15, fig 1.

50 Dr John Schofield FSA very kindly shared information with me on St Paul's in advance of his own publication, *Archaeology of St Paul's Cathedral: Excavation and Survey up to 2006* (in prep).

51 RCHME 1925, 120 (plan), 123–4, pls 179, 184–8; Brown *et al* 1963, 526–7; Thomas *et al* 2006, 105–6, 113, 160.

52 I am greatly indebted to Tim Tatton-Brown for the benefit of extended discussions about Salisbury Cathedral, and for arranging access to roofs and other closed spaces.

53 Cocke and Kidson 1993, 7, pls 14–16.

54 This is a curious omission, but could be explained if there was initially an intention to incorporate a sacristy in the main south transept, or to attach one to it, as had been designed at Wells (Rodwell 2001, 139–40, fig 279).

55 There was a small, L-shaped projection of uncertain date on the east side: it was demolished in the late 18th century (Brown 1999, figs 14, 15).

56 Three of the four original doors survive: the outer one to the treasury is missing.

57 Brown 1999, fig 46. In order to enter the muniment room from the transept, no less than five secure doors had to be negotiated.

58 Norton 1996. The support structure was completely renewed in the 1930s, without dismantling the tile pavement (Brown 1999, 168). The roof was renewed at the same time, following the original design.

59 Luard 1858, 90; Brown *et al* 1963, 16.

60 Biddle and Kjølbye-Biddle 1980, fig 7.

61 Anderson 1989. For a plan showing these in 1723, then probably still in their medieval positions, see Dart 1723, I, 70. The monuments have since been repositioned.

62 That is, the room that later became known as 'the Pyx chamber'. It contains a 13th-century stone altar, perhaps indicating that it was a chapel closely associated with the chapter house (Rodwell 2002, 16). Since the sacristy to the north contained the altar of St Faith, it possibly demonstrates an intention to flank the vestibule with two chapels. However, by the early 14th century, at the latest, the Pyx chamber was separately walled-off from the space under the day-stair: that became a small store, which it remains to this day.

63 Wilson 2008; see also p 33.

64 Seven of the faces are pierced by ten openings, each comprising a square aperture that passes through the thickness of the wall and is fitted with a moulded quatrefoil externally.

65 Brown 2003, 294–8.

66 Ibid, 58. The full inscription reads: *Ut rosa flos florum sic est domus ista domorum* ('As the rose is the flower of flowers, so is this the house of houses').

67 As Consultant Archaeologist to Westminster Abbey, Wells Cathedral and until recently Lichfield Cathedral, I owe a huge debt of gratitude to their respective Deans and Chapters for allowing me unrestricted access to study their two-storeyed chapter houses over the course of many years. I am also grateful to the numerous colleagues with whom I have discussed chapter houses – and learned much from them – over more than three decades. I have particularly benefited from collaboration with the Revd Canon Tony Barnard, Philip Dixon FSA, Diane Gibbs-Rodwell, Michael Haycraft, the Very Revd Patrick Mitchell KCVO FSA, Frances Neale FSA, Alan Rome FSA, John Schofield FSA, Martin Stancliffe FSA, Tim Tatton-Brown and Pamela Tudor-Craig FSA.

CHAPTER 5 (pp 91–101)

1 Chilmark stone was not used in London until brought there by the railway after *c* 1860 (Tatton-Brown 1998, 39–46).

2 Brown 1999, 28–31.

3 Scott 1861, 31.

4 Ibid, 32–3.

5 Brown *et al* 1963, 137.

6 This two-storeyed building, with its outer lobby, had probably been added to Salisbury Cathedral by 1245, when services in the new eastern end were commenced.

7 Burges 1859, 109; this evidence was used most recently in Blum 1991, 22.

8 For a partial discussion of the dating, see Kemp and Tatton-Brown 2008, 94–103; see also Brown 2001.

9 On 16 Nov 1270, the men of Wiltshire swore an oath of fealty to the Lord Edward and his infant son, John of Windsor, *in capitulo Sarum*. See Howlett 1885–90, II, 557–8. I am grateful to Dr John Maddicott FSA, for this reference.

10 The external buttresses on the north, east and south were enlarged only in the 1855–6 rebuilding.

11 Some of the fifty-one prebends were, by the mid-13th century, attached to the principal persons, so the fifty-two seats were more than enough. In 1255, for example, the prebend of Potterne was attached to the bishopric.

12 See discussion in Brown 2003, 58. In March 1297 Parliament probably met in the chapter house at Salisbury.

13 For Salisbury, see Brown 2001.

14 For this technique, see Alexander 2005.

15 Cocke and Kidson 1993, pl 47. Sargent's watercolour of 1852 (fig 101) and Britton's drawing of 1820 (fig 102) both show the centrally crossed bars that are present today; hence, these were presumably added sometime between 1810 and 1820, perhaps when new clear glazing was put in. This followed the progressive removal of the medieval glass, the last of which disappeared in 1821 (Brown 1999, 88–90). Marked differences in the arrangement of the ferramenta in some of the main lights of the south-west, west and north-west windows are evident by comparing Buckler's and Sargent's views.

16 Wren's survey is dated 31 Aug 1668; it is published in Bolton and Hendry 1934, 26.

17 Francis Price, in his fine book about the cathedral (Price 1753), does not discuss any repairs to the chapter house, but when the neighbouring library building was partially demolished and reconstructed, soon after 1758, repairs may have been carried out also on the chapter house.

18 All the iron ties used by Price in roof carpentry, etc, seem to have been secured with forelock bolts.

19 Quoted by Lethaby (1925, 104). Carter's first recorded visit to Salisbury was in 1784 (Rodwell and Leighton 2006, 4). The iron bars are not shown in J M W Turner's watercolour of the interior of the chapter house of 1799 (Cocke and Kidson 1993, frontispiece), in Buckler's view of 1810 (Cocke and Kidson 1993, pl 47), nor in Britton 1835, pl 49.

20 Each angle-pier at Westminster has thirteen shafts attached to it, seven internally (including the central main shaft), and two triplets externally. At Salisbury, there are also thirteen shafts, nine of which are internal and have en délit Purbeck marble shafts. Externally, only the capitals, shaft-rings and bases are of Purbeck marble; the shafts are of engaged, coursed masonry.

21 Also at Westminster, similar continuous bars run through the triforium openings at abacus level.

22 For the architectural differences, see pp 51–62.

23 See also Lethaby 1906, 139–40, fig 58; 1925, 103–5.

24 Lethaby 1906, 44.

25 For a fine drawing of this roof, see Hewett 1985, fig 105.

26 Lethaby 1906, 44.

27 Hewett 1985, 107.

28 Small scale dendrochronology by the University of Nottingham on the Salisbury chapter house roof, commissioned by Dr Pamela Blum, yielded no precise felling dates, but a date in the early 1260s was considered to be the most likely: *Vernacular Architect*, 1996, **27**, 79 and 81.

29 View by R Thacker, c 1671, reproduced in Cocke and Kidson 1993, pl 34.

30 As shown by Hearne's pre-1798 view, reproduced in Cocke and Kidson 1993, pl 36.

31 See also Brown 1999, figs 20, 22.

32 Lethaby 1925, 104–5.

33 I am very grateful to my sister, Fanny Middleton, for word-processing my text, and to Warwick Rodwell FSA for his helpful comments on the manuscript and for filling out the final paragraphs.

CHAPTER 6 (pp 102–111)

1 Dobson 1973, 108; and for the priory's net income at this time of c £2,000 per annum, see ibid 250.

2 See chapter 2.

3 Below, pp 110–11.

4 In other words, still under instruction. For the custom at Canterbury and its acceptance as the norm, see Knowles and Brooke 2002, 158–9, 214–15, and Pantin 1931–7, II, 69–70. *Cf* Thompson 1902–4, II, 190. The fourth and only surviving part of the customary of Westminster Abbey cited here (and subsequently) was written by William Haseley, sub-prior and master of the novices, under the direction of Abbot Richard Ware (1258–83) and probably finished in 1266 (Thompson 1902–4, II, vi–vii).

5 Tolhurst 1942, 50–4.

6 McCann 1952, chs 24–5.

7 As demonstrated in Gransden 1973, 82–6. Logan 1996, 147–55 is indispensable.

8 Gransden 1963, 87; Thompson 1902–4, I, 243–4; II, 204–6. See also McCann 1952, ch 23; Knowles and Brooke 2002, 152–3.

9 Butler 1949, 119; cf Dunbabin 2002, 145–6.

10 Knowles 1963, 411–17. For a rare example of the exact ordering of a chapter's business, see Tolhurst and McLachlan 1936, 74–85.

11 Butler 1949, 30.

12 McCann 1952, chs 3, 66.

13 Morgand 1963, 235–8.

14 Symons 1953, 17–18, where a separate room is envisaged; Knowles and Brooke 2002, 164–6; Rollason 2000, 238–9.

15 For Wulfsige, reputedly the first abbot of this foundation, see Knowles, Brooke and London 2001, I, 76.

16 Or, in the case of cathedral priories such as Norwich, between the bishop and the chapter. For the claims made by such chapters, see Crosby 1994, 371–92.

17 Thompson 1902–4, II, 185, 196–7; cf Knowles and Brooke 2002, 148–9, 168–9.

18 Thompson 1902–4, II, 181.

19 Ibid, 127 (where 'ad insulam' is La Neyte), and 183.

20 Ibid, 187.

21 Harvey 1965, 38–9.

22 WAM Muniment Book 11, fol 28; and for Belsize, Harvey 2002, 16.

23 Thompson 1902–4, II, 181; Knowles and Brooke 2002, 166–7. Here and elsewhere, secular business might be discussed when 'talking' took place in the cloister, in sessions now sometimes described as 'parliaments'. As in chapter, French was the language of discourse. Thompson 1902–4, II, 161, 164, 197–8; Pantin 1931–7, I, 73; Tolhurst and McLachlan 1936, 74. For later use of the outer vestibule of the chapter as a parlour (that is, for informal conversation), see below, p 110.

24 For a vivid example of the impossibility of deciding an election controversy in chapter, see Thomson 1974, 14–23.

25 For glimpses of the two sides, see Thompson 1902–4, II, 174, 185, 195; and for the same system in operation at Thorney Abbey at the Lenten distribution of books in the early 14th

century, Sharpe 2005, 243–63.

26 For the lien on seats of absentees hinted at in arrangements at Thorney Abbey, see ibid, 253–63.

27 Thompson 1902–4, II, 49–50. In the later Middle Ages, erratic expenditure on mats for the chapter house is recorded from year to year in the sacrist's accounts, and it is possible that, in several years in the 15th century, none were bought; see, for example, WAM 19702–5, WAM 19714–19715*. In two years the length of matting purchased is recorded: 40 yards (*virgate*) at 2d per yard in 1514–15 and 30 yards at the same price in 1518–19 (WAM 19773, 19777). I am indebted to Warwick Rodwell for the information that 40 yards would be needed to provide individual mats for each bay in the step from which the wall arcading springs and 53 yards to cover the middle step continuously.

28 Thompson 1902–4, II, 148–9, 176–7.

29 Ibid, 50. These mats, referred to as *mattule*, were evidently small. For the long, wide mat (*matta longa et larga*) provided in a parlour for monks recovering from a blood-letting, see ibid, 176.

30 See note 89.

31 Galbraith 1927, 81; *cf* Gransden 1973, 86.

32 Thompson 1902–4, II, 182.

33 BL Add MS 8167, fol 2; Pantin 1931–7, I, 46. For the decrees of the papal visitors, see Graham 1912, 737–9, and for the relevant statutes of the General Chapter, Pantin 1931–7, I, 15–21 and 34–45.

34 Thompson 1902–4, II, 184.

35 Ibid, II, 189.

36 That is, he prostrated '*ad gradum*' but not on it (ibid; *cf* Knowles and Brooke 2002, 126–7).

37 BL Add MS 8167, fol 2; Pantin 1931–7, I, 46.

38 Harvey 1965, 22.

39 WAM 19339.

40 Bliss and Twemlow 1902, IV, 523; Pearce 1916, 119.

41 Dobson 1973, 70.

42 Cheney 1931, 450–1.

43 For Laurence's grant of Sawbridgeworth church (Herts), confirmed by Alexander III in 1161, see Mason 1988, nos 170, 283; for Walter of Winchester's grant of Benfleet church and manor, with Fanton and Paglesham (Essex), between 1175 and 1190, ibid, no. 299; and for William Postard's grant of 21 marks (£14) per annum from the churches of Oakham and Hambleton (Rutl) to the infirmary, between 1191 and 1200, ibid, no. 321. In 1161, the abbey possessed less than the actual rectory of Sawbridgeworth, and the same may be true of its interest in Benfleet church at the time of Walter of Winchester's grant.

44 Harvey 1965, 217–22.

45 The first of these two agreements is undated but can be assigned to the period 11 Nov 1225 to 3 Feb 1226 (ibid, 222–5). For the second agreement, see Kemp 2000, no. 396, and for the full text, Harvey 1965, 225–7.

46 Harvey 1965, 218–19.

47 Ibid, 227–8. The arbiters were William of Bitton I, bishop of Bath and Wells (1248–64) and John Mansell, a royal servant and councillor described here as provost of Beverley.

48 Ibid, 230, 236. The common seal was applied to the

ordinance of 1283 on 31 December 1283, but additions were enacted on 2 January 1284. Walter de Wenlok, Ware's successor, was elected on the former date.

49 McCann 1952, ch 33; Robinson 1909, 118; Harvey 2002, 139.

50 For the testimony of some senior monks in 1307 that before his death Ware had sealed a document committing himself and his successors to observance of the compositions, see WAM 9497. Such an undertaking implies previous controversy.

51 Harvey 1965, 17–24.

52 Ibid, 22–3.

53 WAM 19996, 19998–9. In each case the chapter consented to the deposit of £3 6s 8d, the sum received annually from St Stephen's chapel in the palace of Westminster, in part settlement of an earlier dispute between the chapel and the abbey. For earlier references to common chests, see Knowles 1955, II, 328.

54 For two such grants in 1319, see WAM 5912 and 5914 (Harvey 1993, 244, nos 29–30); see also Harvey 1965, 236.

55 WAM 5456; Widmore 1751, 193; and for Norwych see Harvey 2004–9a.

56 I am indebted to Dr Paul Brand for advice about grants of corrodies. For explicit reference to the chapter in the normal formula of consent to leases by the abbot and convent of Westminster at the end of the 15th century, see, for example, WAM Reg. Bk I, fols 2v–3, 20, 73.

57 Harvey 1993, 117, 136; and for irregularities in diet, which were free of serious restraint here from the mid-14th century, and the decline of commensality, see ibid, 41–2. For a wider view of changes in Benedictine life in this period, see Clark 2002, 10–12.

58 Pantin 1931–7, II, 39–40. Such a statute is more likely to have followed than preceded local moves to secure privacy.

59 WAM 19716, 19729*, 19731. The sacrist's apparently erratic purchase of mats for the chapter house in this period is also relevant in this context; see note 27.

60 Wilkins 1737, II, 594.

61 For the sacrist's purchase in 1473–4 of green pigment '*pro tabulis in claustro*' and other purposes, see WAM 19720; and for his obligation, Thompson 1902–4, II, 49.

62 TNA: PRO E33/1, fol 83. For definitive comment on the four indentures bipartite to which Abbot Islip took an oath on behalf of the abbey on 4 November 1504, and of which the indenture of abstract is the third, see Condon 2003, 66–78; and for comment in the present essay on the layout and furnishing of the chapter house, see above, p 104.

63 Robinson 1909, 83; see below, pp 108–9. *Cf* Rodwell 2009, 155. For the date of Edwin's death, see Knowles, Brooke and London 2001, I, 76.

64 Robinson 1909, 84, and Knowles, Brooke and London 2001, I, 76.

65 Robinson 1909, 85, 87, 88, 91, 94, 96, 98 and 102; for essential discussion of Flete's references, see Anderson 1989, 4–11; and for the explicit suggestion that the three grave slabs now in the south cloister were formerly in the old chapter house, Badham 2007, 199.

66 Robinson 1909, 100.

67 Luard 1890, II, 146–7, the source of the account in Robinson 1909, 100. For the new work in the Lady Chapel, see Harvey 2003, 14.

68 Below, p 109. For the chronology of the new work, see Lethaby 1925, 98, and Brown *et al* 1963, I, 141.

69 Robinson 1909, 106.

70 For the obligations and privileges of confraternity, as set out in the admission ceremony, see Thompson 1902–4, II, 232–4; for a late 12th-century reference to burial in the abbey as though it were a privilege distinct from confraternity, Mason 1988, no. 388.

71 For the suggestion that construction of the monastic buildings of the Confessor's church probably began *c* 1065 and continued for twenty or thirty years, see Gem 2003, II, 439. Sulcard does not refer explicitly to the date of construction of these buildings.

72 Chibnall 1969–80, III, 134, 166; IV, 336–8.

73 Mason 1988, no. 436; for comment, see Mason 1996, 221–2; and for the date of Alice de Mandeville's death, Bates 1998, no. 399.

74 '*ad introitum domus praedictae ex parte australi*' (Robinson 1909, 83). The phrase refers the reader to the earlier part of the sentence, where the chapter house ('*domus capitularis*') is mentioned. On this phrase, see below, p 110.

75 Robinson 1909, 40–3; Scholz 1964, 82–6; and for Sulcard's work see below, p 109.

76 '*in tabula plumbea infra tombam marmoream*' (Robinson 1909, 83). *Cf* the lead nameplates made for the tombs of the Anglo-Saxon bishops of Wells, formerly inlaid but now separated from the tombs (Rodwell 1979, 407). I am indebted to Professor Michael Lapidge FSA for help in translating this epitaph.

77 Barlow 1997, 166.

78 Robinson 1909, 45; and for Osbert of Clare's influential identification of Saebert as the founder of the first church at Westminster, see Bloch 1923, 83. Writing many years after the event, Thomas Walsingham gives 1307 as the date of Sebert's translation to Henry III's church (Riley 1863–4, I, 114).

79 Barlow 1997, 166. For Hugh, see also Harmer 1952, 564.

80 Scholz 1964, 90–1. Sulcard's own name for his work was '*codex memorialis*' (ibid, 61). For his debt in the final passage to the *Anonymous Life of King Edward*, see Barlow 1992, 110–11.

81 Carpenter 2007b, passim.

82 Above, pp 13–22. In the following discussion of the site of the marble tomb, I am greatly indebted to Warwick Rodwell FSA.

83 *Cf* Clayton 1912, 53 where it is suggested that the area accommodated a tomb.

84 Camden 1600, fol 38v.

85 Robinson 1909, 129.

86 Given-Wilson 2005, V, 297, 399.

87 Edwards 1979, 5–7. For further important comment, see Hawkyard 2002, 65–6.

88 For the use of the chapter house by Simon de Montfort's Great Parliament of 1265, see above, pp 35 and 39.

89 For the certain occasions, the Parliaments of Jan 1352, Apr 1376, Jan 1377 and Nov 1384, see Given-Wilson 2005, V, 41, 297, 399; VI, 386. For other possible occasions, in Nov 1381, Oct 1382, and Jan 1395, for which, again, the evidence is provided by the official record, see VI, 215, 283, and VII, 286. We should note also that, in Oct 1377, the Commons were evidently sent to the chapter house before they had assembled before the king, to hear an address by Richard Scrope, steward of the king's household (VI, 10). The sacrist's references to damage inflicted by the Commons on the mats in the chapter house occur in his accounts for, respectively, 28 Sept 1377 – 29 Sept 1378 and 28 Sept 1379 – 29 Sept 1380 (WAM 19637, 19639). We do not know at which point in the year he normally replaced damaged mats with new ones: damage in one year of account and replacement in another is a possibility. On the damage, see also above, p 104.

90 Carpenter 2003, 357.

91 Galbraith 1927, 80–91; and for the significance of this Parliament, see Harriss 2005, 441–4.

92 Robinson 1909, 128.

93 WAM 23454–9; Robinson 1911, 9–12, 16–20; and for Litlyngton see Harvey 2004–9b.

94 Robinson 1911, 11.

95 Harvey 1993, 89.

96 I am greatly indebted to the Dean and Chapter of Westminster for permission to cite their muniments in this paper.

CHAPTER 7 (pp 112–123)

1 Some of the material for this chapter is derived from the writer's doctoral thesis: Ashbee, J A 2006. 'The Tower of London as a royal residence, 1066–1400'. Unpubl, University of London, esp 275–87.

2 Tout 1920–33, esp II, 52–8.

3 To avoid confusion between the two undercrofts under discussion, the lower chamber of the chapter house will be referred to as the 'basement'.

4 Published as 'A medieval burglary' in Tout 1934, III, 93–115.

5 Tout 1920–33, II, 58.

6 For treatments of the physical space of the chapter house basement, see, for example, Scott 1861, esp App, 39–43, 'On some discoveries in connection with the ancient treasury at Westminster', by Joseph Burtt, and ibid, 1–10; Harrod 1873, 373–82; Tout 1934, 93–115; Lethaby 1925, 127–30.

7 Scott 1863, 46.

8 It should be noted that this would be unlikely to deceive a careful searcher. The lower compartment is restricted to the height of a single course; the upper compartment, opening eastward, is tall enough to involve a break in two masonry courses of the drum. Such a break could, of course, be concealed with render, but no sign of this can now be seen on the column.

9 Rodwell 2009, 155–9.

10 The documentary evidence for the wardrobe stores in the reign of Henry III is provided by Ben Wild, to whom I am grateful for his generosity in sharing this material and for discussing its interpretation.

11 Close Rolls 1902–38, VIII, 62.

12 Sandys 1925, 147–62.

13 Ibid. I am very grateful to Ben Wild for discussing the significance of the New Temple material in the wider context of safe storage of jewels and other materials.

14 TNA: E101/351/9, m5 onwards.

15 Chancery Rolls 1912, 275; Robinson 2006, 250–3.

16 Harvey 1993, 88 n. 69.

17 Ibid, 3.

18 Tout 1920–33, II, 51.

19 For example: TNA: E101/354/12; E101/354/13; Cole 1844, 277–84, in which chests are labelled as 'de Turri Londoniarum'.

20 'et in domo thesaurarie garderobe regis subtus capitulum Westmonasterii pavando, hostiis et aliis reparandis, anno xix.' See Harrod 1873, 373–82, esp 375; Tout 1920–33, II, 53. Examination of the manuscripts of the Pipe Roll has not identified the entry in question.

21 'omnibus jocalibus eiusdem regis et aliis (inventis) in thesauraria garderobe regis subtus capellam monachorum ibidem'; TNA: E101/357/13.

22 These include Scott 1861, 6; Hall 1898, 29; and Lethaby 1925, 127–30.

23 Lethaby 1925, 127–30.

24 For example, the documentation for the Tower of London uses 'subtus' for a postern across the road from the king's chamber, and at York Castle, for 'the mills under the castle'; TNA: E101/467/9 m2, temp Edward I for Tower of London; E101/501/13, temp Richard II, for York Castle.

25 Lethaby 1925, 129, discussing BL Cotton MS Nero D ii, fol 194r.

26 Tout 1920–33, II, 54.

27 TNA: E101/357/13.

28 TNA: E101/5/18 no. 11 (part 3).

29 TNA: E101/354/12.

30 Taylor 1986, 119.

31 Among the more exotic manuscripts listed are 'a book of (polyphonic) organum chant beginning alleluia' and 'a cloth called Mappa Mundi'.

32 Tout 1920–33, II, 55.

33 CPR 1898, 192; TNA: E101/323/8.

34 CPR 1898, 195.

35 The principal documents from the inquisition into the robbery are collated in TNA: E101/323/8.

36 Ibid, memorandum recording an indenture of 22 June 1303 concerning the investigation of the robbery. A similar description of the keeper's inspection, together with a full list of items left in the treasury, and those subsequently recovered, is given in Cole 1844, 277–84.

37 Tout 1920–33, II, 55.

38 Sandys 1925.

39 'Si commenca viii jours avaunt le Nowel de enter pur debruser la ove les ustiz qil aveit a ceo purveu, cest a saver deux tarrers un greynur et meindre et coteaux et autres menuz engins de fer, e issint fust entour le bruser par heez de nut quant il pureit entendre et vist son penit des viii jours avaunt le Nowel iesqes a la quinzeyne de pasqe suaunt qe a doncs le primes aveit le entre par la nut de un mescredi la veille seint mark et tot le iour seint

mark demora leinz et ordena ceo qil voleit enporter, et quant qil enporta il enporta la nut suaunt hors de leinz, et de ceo partie lessa dehors la brecke iesqes lautre nut suaunt et le remenaunt si porta ove li taunt qe dehors la porte derere la eglise seint margarete'; TNA: E101/323/8, un-numbered fol beginning 'le dit Richard Podelicote'.

40 Ibid. 'E mesme le jour qe le Rei seu parti de la ou il geust vers bernes le nut guamt le dit Richard solom ceo qil aveit espie trova un eschele estaunt a une meson qe fust en coveraunt prede la porti du Paleys vers Labbaye, e mist cel eschele a une fenestre du chapitre qe se overi et clost par une corde e la evera par mesme cele corde en valaunt e de illeks ala al eaux del Refreyter e le trova clos de Lok e de son cotel le overi e entra leinz e trova vi hanaps en un aumori derere le eaux e quilers dargent trente e plus en un autre aumorie e les hanaps de mazere de souz un baunk cheskun pres de autre e touz ces enporta e clot les eaux apres li saunz fermer de la lok…Par ceo qil savoit les estres del Abbeye et ou la tresorie esteit et coment ili poeit avenir.'

41 'Estre ceo il dient qe unt grant suspecion ver les Moynes avantdistz pur ceo qe ja quatre aunz passe si feust meme cele Tresorie comence a bruser dens leur cloistre nomement desouz le eus de mesme la Tresorie enver la cloistre'; TNA: E101/323/8. This reference to a previous robbery is discussed by modern writers, such as Palgrave 1836, I, 288; Harrod 1873, 373–82, esp 379; Hall 1898, 29; Lethaby 1925, 127–30.

42 CPR 1895, 218.

43 BL MS Cotton Nero D ii, fol 194r.

44 Lethaby 1925, 129.

45 For a less pessimistic interpretation of the evidential value of the drawing, see above, p 24.

46 Harrod 1873, 380; this point is made in the context of discussing whether or not the monks were complicit in the robbery.

47 'in certo et securo loco poni faciatis'; TNA: E101/323/8, writ of Edward I, 6 June.

48 Ibid, tripartite indenture.

49 TNA: E101/380/7.

50 Vivian Galbraith had interpreted 'the great chapel' as Saint John the Evangelist in the White Tower, and 'the tower' as the Wardrobe Tower, lying east of its apse: Galbraith 1925, 231–47, esp 238. The 'great chapel' however, makes much more sense as St Peter ad Vincula. For confirmation that 'magna capella' indicates St Peter's, rather than St John's; see, for example, TNA: E101/4/10, in which Ralph of Sandwich accounts for rebuilding the chapel, and E101/470/1 m6, with a repair to a window on its north side, irreconcilable with St John's.

51 'de quel toriel les ditz tresorier et les chamberleyns ount devers eux les cliefs des huys foreins et le dit gardein des almaries ou les ioelx sount enclos les queux ioelx vessel draps et autres choses furent del auncien estor de la garderobe et liverez as ditz tresorier et chaumberleins'; TNA: E101/380/7.

52 For a recent summary, see Ashbee 2008, 141–59, esp 150–3.

53 The status of the cross-wall is complicated by the apparent existence of some kind of partition from the 12th century, similar to those indicated elsewhere in the dormitory undercroft by the patterns of moulded decoration in the

column capitals.

54 For the doors, see Miles and Bridge 2005. An archaeological study of the chamber and pavement is in preparation by Warwick Rodwell.

55 '*la tresorie de Westmoustre desouth le dortoir*'; TNA: E101/333/3.

56 TNA: E101/332/26.

57 '*in una cista in thesauraria regis infra claustrum Westmonasterium iuxta capitulum*'; Palgrave 1836, I, 156.

58 Ibid, 179. The locations of the Exchequer of Receipt and Accountant's chamber are given on pages 171 and 189.

59 TNA: E101/333/28.

60 Ibid, II, 316, 332.

61 Carpenter 1996, 427–61, esp 429.

62 Ibid, 448–56 and particularly n. 138 and n. 162.

63 Of the many people who have assisted in the production of this paper, I must make special acknowledgement of Ben Wild, who with great generosity shared his unpublished researches into Henry III's wardrobe. I am also indebted to Warwick Rodwell FSA for arranging access into the chapter house basement and for discussing the interpretation of its features: sections of the text describing the physical fabric of the building are based exclusively on his work.

CHAPTER 8 (pp 124–138)

1 Scott 1863, 39.

2 TNA: PRO MPB 2/1.

3 John Carter, writing in the *Gent's Mag*, 1799, quoted in Lethaby 1925, 100. Others were more nuanced in their views. In 1866 an anonymous commentator (probably William Burges), writing in *The Ecclesiologist*, described it as 'excellent, though alas, sadly dilapidated', and added that 'we dread any attempt at restoration lest damage should be done to its precious fragments'. Ibid, 102.

4 See Hallam 1986.

5 Roper and Hallam 1978, esp 73–4.

6 Hallam 1979, 3–10.

7 TNA: PRO 4/7, fols 104–13.

8 Hallam 1990, esp 27. See also above, p 115.

9 See above, pp 115–18.

10 See above, pp 103–5.

11 I am grateful to Dr Charles Knighton FSA for his advice on this matter.

12 See Wren 1750, 158.

13 Hawkyard 2002, esp 77, n. 121; Knighton 1997–9, I, xxiii, n. 41 quoting WAM 37046, fol 6v where a payment in 1543 is mentioned for mending the windows in the church and chapter house.

14 Hawkyard 2002, 77, nn. 122–3; TNA: E407/68/2–3. See also Green 1974–7, 26.

15 Hawkyard 2002, 76–7.

16 CSPD 1871, 312, 556. In 1574, a William Davidson was granted the office of keeper of the records in the Treasury House, Westminster.

17 Stow 1754–5, II, 631–2 (the chapter house is said to have needed 'reparations both in glass and lead'); Wernham 1956, esp 19.

18 Bodleian Library, MS Rawlinson C. 704, fol ii.

19 Sainty 1983, 164, 176.

20 Macray 1878, 358; McKisack 1971, 85–94.

21 Hallam 1987, 141, n. 2; Hallam 1997.

22 Sainty 1983, 164, 176.

23 Agarde's 'Compendium of the Four Treasuries' is printed in Powell 1631; Palgrave 1836, II, 311–35.

24 Powell 1631, 34–91.

25 Powell 1631, 92–120. From later sources it is likely that the Pyx chamber had just received these records; Parliamentary Archives HL/PO/JO/10/6/67/2029: memo of 1704 by John Lowe stating that the 'leagues and treaties' were moved into the Chapel of the Pyx in 1610. There is a later description of the opening of a box kept in the Pyx chamber in 1734, which contained coinage and measures dating from 1696, TNA: E36/253, 324.

26 Stanley 1869, 428.

27 CSPD 1864, 147.

28 Sainty 1983, 171, 177.

29 The two also disputed about the seating arrangements in the Tally Court and over access to Domesday: Hallam 1986, 127–30; TNA: SP 46/139, fols 16–80.

30 Condon and Hallam 1984, esp 352–8; Williams 1955–9, 125–31. Hunter 1830, I, 296.

31 Hunter 1830, I, 296.

32 John Lawton, formerly a deputy chamberlain, was appointed sole keeper of the records in 1727 at an annual payment of £200 plus a further £220 for three clerks; TNA: E101/337/17.

33 TNA: E36/253, 294.

34 CTB 1952, 196, 599.

35 *Lords Journal 1767–*, XVIII, 135–6; Parliamentary Archives HL/PO/CO/1/7: Minutes of Committees, fol 143v; CSPD 2006, 90, no. 534.

36 It was estimated that £776 was needed to repair it and to make another gallery and presses for records: TNA: WORK 6/16, fols 58, 73v.

37 TNA: E36/253, 328; WORK 6/16, fol 122; at a cost of £151.

38 TNA: E36/253, 332; WORK 6/16, fols 169r–v.

39 TNA: WORK 6/17, fol 74.

40 TNA: E36/253, 332; WORK 6/16, fols 169r–v; see below, see figs 120–3 and pp 130–3.

41 TNA: E36/253, 169.

42 Parliamentary Archives HL/PO/JO/10/6/67/2029, fol 18.

43 TNA: E36/253, 332; WORK 6/16, fols 169r–v.

44 TNA: E36/253, 296; CTB 1936, 336.

45 Musing on the Gothic style and his plans for completing the abbey's central tower and spire, Wren wrote: 'to deviate from the old form would be to run into disagreeable mixture, which no person of good taste would relish' adding that 'I have prepared perfect draughts and models such as I conceive may agree with the original scheme of the old architect, without any modern mixtures to shew my own inventions'; see Wren 1750, 298, 302; see also Tinniswood 2002, 336–7.

46 Rigold 1976, 9.

47 Parliamentary Archives HL/PO/JO/10/6/67/2029.

48 *Lords Journal 1767–*, XXI, 141–2.

49 This was at an estimated cost of £390; TNA: E36/253, 316–18; Parliamentary Archives HL/PO/JO/10/6/296: 15 Jan 1719/20. But it was recommended by Lawton, and repeated to a committee of the House of Commons in 1732, that the records of the Courts of Wards and Requests should be moved there as well as Rymer's papers; see *Lords Jnl*, XXXIII, 281–2; CHCR 1801, I, 1715–35, 508–35.

50 At a cost of £370 6s 9d; TNA: WORK 6/17, fol 142v.

51 Rigold 1976, 9.

52 Colvin *et al* 1976, 414–15.

53 Hallam 1986, 135–6; TNA: IND 1/17175, fol 18.

54 See Condon and Hallam 1984, 373–82.

55 Society of Antiquaries of London, Minute Book, VII, 228–30: meeting of 18 December 1855; 244–9: meeting of 19 February 1756; Commons Journal 1742– , XXXI, 196, 201, 411.

56 Hallam 1986, 134–40; Condon and Hallam 1984, 373–82.

57 Ibid, 382.

58 CPRR, 1800, 1.

59 For a more contemporary but partial view, see Cole 1884, I, 11–12.

60 Cantwell 1991, 1–12; Walne 1960–64, 8–16.

61 CPRR, 1800, 1–14.

62 See Thorne 2004–9.

63 Searches in Domesday Book were charged at 6s 8d each and for 4d a line for copies, the same level as in 1638. Other fees had increased since that time: for example searches in other records had risen from 7s to 8s 4d. The annual income was £25 17s, but 'it has not been the custom to take fees where the object of enquiry has been to illustrate points of history, curiosity or general law; in all such cases, the best assistance has usually been given gratuitously'; CPRR, 1800, 37–52, esp 43.

64 CPRR, 1800, 42.

65 CPRR, 1800, 52; CPRR, 1800–19, 42; TNA: WORK 14/51, letter from T Duffus Hardy to Rivers Wilson dated 27 February 1862; after this lease expired the PRO would pay £10 1s 4d per annum for the two offices.

66 RIBA drawing SC 82/11.

67 CPRR, 1800, 11.

68 TNA: OBS 1/692 with extracted plans in MPB 1/2; a third copy was deposited in the British Museum.

69 See DKR, VII, 1846, 26–7.

70 Fig 126: WAM (P) 377; Soane Museum, Prints and Drawings, Drawer 37, set 1, no. 19 (1794) and 39 (1826).

71 TNA: OBS 1/692, basement storey.

72 TNA: OBS 1/692, Index.

73 BL Add MS 42,780A, fol 35; and the Black Book of the Exchequer, *Liber A* and *Liber B*.

74 The 'closet' was the medieval locker in the south wall of the inner vestibule.

75 TNA: PRO 1/1, 14 June 1835; PRO 36/49, 17–24, at p 22.

76 DKR, VII, 1846, 26–7.

77 As of 1823: Brayley 1823, II, 289–99; see also Scott 1863, 194–7, pl 29 (reproduced here as fig 29).

78 CPRR, 1800–19, 5–9.

79 TNA: WORK 14/4/1, 1816–17.

80 Forde 1986, 28.

81 CPRR, 1837, General Report, 9–67; TNA: PRO 36/7, for

example, 92–4, 113–15, 241, 282–6. For the 'County Bags' see IND 1/17175 (list of searches in the chapter house and Agarde's catalogues at note 23 above. For Caley see Goodwin 2004–9.

82 For Palgrave see Martin 2004–9.

83 Cantwell 1991, 23.

84 DKR, I, 1846, 17–18.

85 TNA: PRO 2/91, 328–9.

86 TNA: PRO 1/1, 14 June 1835; PRO 36/49, 17–24, at p 22.

87 The poor quality of Charles Devon's work may be seen in BL Add MS 24,713: a muddled and unsystematic catalogue of records in the chapter house. This he sold to the British Museum in 1862.

88 TNA: PRO 36/49, 5, 19–24 *et passim*.

89 CPRR, 1837, General Report, x.

90 TNA: WORK 14/1/1, 1832, referring to 1826; WAM (P) 377 (fig 126) illustrates this graphically and gives the names of the owners of the buildings.

91 Thornbury 1878, III, 453–4. Years later, in 1865, Dean Stanley recounted Palgrave's account of that night to a meeting of the Society of Antiquaries. He was standing on the roof of the chapter house with Dean Ireland, 'looking at the flames, when a sudden gust of wind seemed to bring the flames in that direction. Sir Francis implored the Dean to allow him to carry Domesday Book and other valuable records into the Abbey, but the Dean answered that he could not think of doing so without first applying to Lord Melbourne'. Stanley 1869, 428–9.

92 DKR, VII, 1846, 26–7.

93 Cantwell 1991, 13–55.

94 Ibid, 120–38.

95 DKR, VI, 1845, 15–16 and App I. In the 1848 Report, Joseph Burtt's work in cataloguing the miscellanea is singled out as showing his excellent 'archaeological skill', and in 1856 he is again praised for discovering and identifying many strays: DKR, IX, 1848, 2–3; ibid, XVII, 1856, 7.

96 DKR, IV, 1843, App I, 4–5.

97 DKR, XV, 1855, 18–19.

98 For example, a certified copy of a Domesday folio signed by the head of the chapter house branch record office, Frederick Devon, in 1847: LRRO 67/190, no. 49; see Cantwell 1991, pl 4.

99 DKR, I, 1840, 17–18; ibid, X, 1849, App; XX, 1859, App. In 1838 the fees were set as follows: a search in Domesday Book was 6s 8d, but for a search in any other record the greater sum of 8s 4d was charged. Copies of Domesday were 4d a line and those of any other record, 1s per 200 words, with an extra 2s for certification: ibid, I, 1840, 66.

100 Cantwell 1991, 48–9, 57–8; DKR, I, 1840, 17–18; ibid, II, 1841, 4–5; TNA: PRO 4/2, fol 94.

101 Cantwell 1991, 190; the returns by Devon are in TNA: PRO 4/1–PRO 4/6.

102 TNA: PRO 2/91, 194–5, 302–3, 238–9, 351–2, 354–5.

103 Cantwell 1991, 48–9, 57–8; DKR, I, 1840, 17–18; ibid, II, 1841, 4–5; TNA: PRO 4/2, fol 94.

104 TNA: PRO 2/91, 194–5. See also Cole 1884, I, 20–1.

105 Cantwell 1991, 72, 80–1; TNA: PRO 4/4, fol 216; PRO 4/3, fol 198.

106 TNA: PRO 4/1, fols 169–96; PRO 4/3, fol 198; PRO 4/5, fol 172.

107 TNA: PRO 4/5, fol 173.

108 TNA: PRO 4/4, fol 230.

109 TNA: PRO 4/2, fol 152; PRO 4/6, fol 81. In 1841 Henry Cole had proposed to Lord Langdale that Domesday be put on display at the chapter house; Devon was clearly most unsupportive of this idea, which was squashed by Palgrave: PRO 2/89, 244–8, 255.

110 TNA: PRO 4/5, fol 169.

111 TNA: PRO 4/1, fol 178; Scott 1863, 41.

112 TNA: PRO 4/3, 254; Scott 1863, 51.

113 Cantwell 1991, 124–5, 190; TNA: PRO 4/6, fols 79–81.

114 WAM Fabric Vouchers, 1858, bill for £50 from Henry Poole, mason for cleaning and 'indurating' the stonework; WAM RCO4, 18 March 1854, notes of meeting of Scott and Gladstone and letters on the state of the abbey and chapter house. See also below, pp 182–3.

115 DKR, XX, 1859, xvi; ibid, XXI, 1860, xiii–xiv.

116 DKR, XXI, 1860, xiii–xiv.

117 Scott 1863, 9; see also 48–50.

118 See Jenning 1974. The chests are, anti-clockwise from the left, TNA: E 27/CASE3, CASE7, CASE6, CASE5.

119 In 1879 the Pyx chamber was handed over by Standards Dept to the Office of Works. Several oak presses, where the treaties were kept, and several ancient chests still remained there, according to a letter of H W Chisholm, Warden of the Standards. TNA: WORK 14/51, 1879.

120 TNA: PRO 4/7, fols 104–13.

121 TNA: PRO 4/7, fols 54–112.

122 TNA: PRO 8/61, 98; *Illustrated Times*, 25 February 1860.

123 DKR, XXII, 1861, x; ibid, XXIII, 1862, 36.

124 DKR, XXXIII, 1862, 36; Cantwell 1991, 203.

125 TNA: WORK 14/51, letter from T Duffus Hardy to Rivers Wilson, dated 27 February 1862.

126 TNA: WORK 14/51, 14 June 1864.

127 *Gent's Mag*, 1862, **132**(1), 676.

128 Stanley 1869, 429.

129 Society of Antiquaries of London, Minute Book, XLIII, 7 December 1865; TNA: WORK 6/432 contains correspondence with Scott relating to the restoration.

130 See above, notes 7 and 9.

131 Similarly the Jewel Tower nearby, used for the records of the House of Lords from 1621, was from 1864 replaced by the grandiose Victoria Tower in the Palace of Westminster, which still houses the Parliamentary Archives today.

132 The author would like in particular to thank Adrian Ailes FSA, Mark Collins, Dorian Gerhold FSA, Charles Knighton FSA and Caroline Shenton FSA for their helpful comments on earlier drafts of this paper.

CHAPTER 9 (pp 139–157)

1 Scott 1879; Cole 1980.

2 WAM, Surveyor of the Fabric's Reports: the reports from 1827 to 1906, edited by Christine Reynolds, are pending publication in the Westminster Abbey Record Series.

3 Cocke 1995, 65–72.

4 WAM, Fabric vouchers 1858, dated 13 January 1859.

5 Previously published as a series of articles in the *Gent's Mag* (Scott 1860).

6 Cocke 1995, 74.

7 Ibid, 72.

8 His biographer, David Cole, lists 879 known works; at the time of Scott's death in 1878 his office had sixty projects in progress; Cole 1980, 182, 205.

9 WAM, report by Scott to the Dean and Chapter, 18 Feb 1871; Reynolds forthcoming, no. 58.

10 Cocke 1995, 75–7.

11 Scott 1861, 31–7, includes the fruits of his investigations undertaken c 1849–55. These investigations formed the basis of his restoration of the building in 1866–72. The second essay was written as he was finishing the work (Scott 1867); and the third, a much shorter account, is in Scott 1879, 284–6, written long after he had completed the restoration: 'My work here has been very much a matter of investigation, and up to a certain date is fairly chronicled in "The Gleanings". Since that time, however, many other things have come to light'.

12 WAM, Fabric vouchers.

13 WAM, RCO 4, letter from Thynne to Scott.

14 WAM, RCO 4, letters concerning abbey restoration, 1854–8.

15 Scott 1863, pls 13, 14.

16 WAM, RCO 4, memo dated 14 June 1864.

17 Scott 1863, 39.

18 TNA: WORK 14/51, memo from Office of Works to Scott, 29 Jan 1866.

19 Ibid, memo from Scott to the First Commissioner of Works, 3 Feb 1866.

20 Ibid, memo by John Taylor, Office of works, 22 June 1866.

21 Ibid, estimate by John Lee, undated [1866].

22 Ibid, letter from Scott to the First Commissioner, 2 July 1866.

23 Ibid, letter from Henry Poole and Sons to the First Commissioner, 2 July 1866.

24 Ibid, letters from the Office of Works to Scott, 3 July 1866, and Scott's reply, 5 July 1866.

25 Ibid, memo from Hunt to the First Commissioner, 26 Sep 1866; memo from Hunt to Scott, 29 Oct 1866; note from the Office of Works to the Treasury, 3 Nov 1866; memo from the Treasury to the First Commissioner, 7 Nov 1866; letter from the Office of Works to Scott, 12 Nov 1866; memo from the Treasury to the First Commissioner, 8 Dec 1866.

26 Ibid, letter from Office of Works to Scott, 19 Dec 1866.

27 Ibid, letter from Scott to the First Commissioner, 26 Mar 1866. Scott also requested the first £135 of his fee.

28 W S Weatherley, a colleague in Scott's office, said of Kaberry: 'a more careful level-headed Yorkshireman I never met'; quoted in Lethaby 1925, 108. Kaberry is listed by David Cole as one of Scott's clerks of works for the period 1873–8: it would seem that he had actually joined the office, or at any rate was well-known to Scott, before then; Cole 1980, 236.

29 TNA: WORK 14/51, correspondence between Scott and Office of Works, June 1866.

30 Ibid, correspondence between Scott and Office of Works, 5 Nov 1868, 12 Dec 1868, 16 Dec 1868.

31 WAM, Surveyor of the Fabric's Reports; Reynolds forthcoming, no. 49.

32 TNA: WORK 14/51, correspondence between Poole, Scott and Office of Works, June to October 1869.

33 Ibid, Scott to Office of Works, 12 Oct 1869.

34 Ibid, correspondence between Office of Works and Scott.

35 Ibid, correspondence between the Office of Works and Scott; memoranda between the Treasury and the Office of Works.

36 Ibid, correspondence between the Office of Works and Scott. A copy of the contract was sent to Henry Poole and Sons on 16 November.

37 Ibid, correspondence between the Office of Works and Scott.

38 Ibid.

39 Ibid.

40 The following relies substantially on accounts published in Scott 1863 and 1879.

41 Scott 1863, 46.

42 TNA: WORK 14/51, letter from Scott to the Office of Works, 12 Oct 1869.

43 Scott 1879, 285.

44 Lethaby 1925, 104–5.

45 Scott 1879, 285.

46 TNA: WORK 14/51, letter from Scott to the Office of Works, 16 Aug 1870.

47 Skempton *et al* 2002, II, 590–2, article on Ordish by J Clarke and T Swailes: the article misunderstands the nature of Ordish's work at Westminster, interpreting his framing as a repair to carry an old vault, rather than a new one.

48 TNA: WORK 14/51, Scott to Office of Works, 16 Aug 1870.

49 TNA: WORK 14/51.

50 Lethaby 1925, 104.

51 Scott 1863, 40.

52 TNA: WORK 14/51, letter from Scott to the Office of Works, 12 Oct 1869.

53 Scott 1863, 41.

54 Scott 1879, 285–6.

55 Scott 1863, 43–4.

56 Scott 1863, 42.

57 Article in *Gent's Mag*, 1799, quoted in Lethaby 1925, 100.

58 Scott 1863, 40.

59 Lethaby 1925, 104.

60 TNA: WORK 14/51, specification dated July 1866; letter to the Office of Works explaining the costs incurred, 16 Aug 1870.

61 Scott 1863, 42.

62 Lethaby 1925, 108.

63 Scott 1863, 42–3.

64 TNA: WORK 14/51.

65 Scott 1879, 284.

66 WAM, RCO 5; Reynolds forthcoming, no. 66.

67 Pevsner 1957, 409.

CHAPTER 10 (pp 158–183)

1 Thompson 1902–4, II, 183–4. Quoted in Binski 1995, 219 n. 124. The phrase is an insertion into the text and may be of a slightly later date, but its import remains valid.

2 See chapter 2.

3 WAM CN.8.II.A(3): this drawing, now in the Westminster Abbey Muniments, was the basis for a print of 1786; Society of Antiquaries Brown Portfolio, Westminster, fol 83.

4 Keepe 1683, 177–8.

5 Binski 1995, 186.

6 'Pro tasha introitus capituli xxv li'; see Colvin 1971, 227.

7 Malcolm 1802, 199–200.

8 Storer and Greig 1805, II, no pagination. A view of the cloister entrance to the chapter house is included among the plates drawn by John Greig and engraved by James Storer.

9 WAM CN.4.I.iii(19).

10 Dart 1723, 128.

11 Brayley 1823, II, 285.

12 Crook 1995. See also Crook 2004–9.

13 Evans 1956, 182 and n. 8, 207–11.

14 *Gent's Mag*, June 1799, **69**(1), 447.

15 Carter 1786, between 6 and 7.

16 Westminster Abbey Library Langley Collection VI.9(4), see also Carter 1795–1814, II, pl 5.

17 *Architectural Association Sketchbook*, 1873–4, VII, pl 48.

18 The corbel is semicircular in plan and measures only 600 mm by 300 mm. Despite this, Scott thought the Virgin had been seated, see Scott 1863, 43.

19 Compare the action in the mid-13th century Chichester roundel.

20 Compare, for instance, the ivory angels either side of the reliquary of St Romain at Rouen, a composite ensemble including two attendant angels of *c* 1300; see Taralon 1965, catalogue no. 209, 107–8 and pl 140.

21 BL MS Arundel 83, fol 131v; Sandler 1983, pl 16. See also Lethaby 1925, 121 and fig 74.

22 Hubel 1975, 18.

23 Another parallel is with the central medallion of the Agnus Dei on the reverse of the Croix du Paraclet in the treasury of Amiens Cathedral where the whole design was carried out in low relief; see Hubel 1975, catalogue no. 60, 29–30, pls 116–17. The 13th-century reliquary processional cross of Nailly, now in the treasury of Sens Cathedral, is entirely covered in a tight filigree of gold foliage against a black enamelled ground; see Hubel 1975, catalogue no. 820, 45, and pl 118.

24 Hubel 1975, catalogue no. 414, 227 and pl 60. For the full effect of figures in three dimensions against a background of patterns, including trails of foliage in champlevé enamels, a precedent can be seen in the Eltenburg reliquary from Cologne, of *c* 1180, Victoria and Albert Museum no. 7650-1861; see Williamson 1986, 144–5 and front cover.

25 John Flete's second relic list was published by Robinson (1909, 68–73). The 1520 list (WAM 9485) was published by Westlake (1923, 499–551).

26 Carter 1795–1814, II, opp 62.

27 Our thanks go to Tony Platt for sharing this, and other treasures, with us.

28 Rodwell 2001, 143, figs 119, 120.

29 Ibid, 277–9.

30 The drawing was given to Pamela Tudor-Craig FSA by Mrs Croft-Murray and is now on permanent loan to the Society of Antiquaries (Westminster Abbey Red Portfolio, fol 27).

31 The Soane Museum has a Flaxman sketch of architectural features of Henry III's work in the abbey, including geometric tracery and the parapet (drawer 42, set 21).

32 Brayley 1823, pl 46.

33 *The Builder*, 28 April 1855, 199.

34 Victoria and Albert Museum, RIBA Collection, P B 458/14.

35 In her youth, Pamela Tudor-Craig was asked by Stephen Dykes Bower to advise him in such an endeavour. She did not encourage him. He was neither the first surveyor of the fabric, nor probably the last, to ponder such an enterprise.

36 *The Graphic*, 13 August 1881, in Westminster Abbey Library, Langley Collection VI.15(36).

37 Scott 1850, 32. Scott's 'plea for the faithful restoration of our ancient churches' was a paper read before the first meeting of the Buckinghamshire Architectural and Archaeological Society in 1848. He later recalled: 'It was a somewhat impassioned protest against the destructiveness of the prevailing restorations, and was preceded by an address from the Bishop of Oxford in which he took almost the contrary line, inveighing against popish arrangements, etc., etc. I was so irate at his paper that my natural timidity vanished, and I gave double emphasis to all I had written'; Scott 1879, 149.

38 Westminster Abbey Library, Langley Collection VI.B.15(19).

39 Malcolm 1802, 199–200.

40 Sauerländer 1970, 462.

41 Binski 1995, 39–42.

42 *Isaiah* 11:1–5.

43 Evans, E 1956, ch 21, verse 25. See Evans, J 1956, 72–3.

44 *Jerome*, Book IV, ch 13, lines 12–16 in Gryson 1993, 436; 'For we understand the rod of Jesse [to be] Saint Mary the Virgin'.

45 Watson 1934, 1 *et seq*. Watson's list in all media could not hope to be complete. It omitted, for example, the putative Tree of Jesse up the stem of the central column of the Worcester chapter house of the 12th or early 13th century, which would provide another example of a Jesse tree associated with a chapter house; see Stratford 1978, 57–8. Stratford argues that the column was a 13th-century replacement, but this does not affect its importance in Jesse-tree iconography.

46 *Matthew* 1:6–10.

47 *Luke* 3:23–38. See Johnson 1969. Nathan the prophet, third son of David, founded the prophetic genealogy.

48 See Oursel 1926, 44–7, 79.

49 Douai Bibliothèque Municipale, MS 340, fol 11.

50 For a table of the prophets and other figures, such as Virgil and a Sibyl, flanking trees of Jesse, see Watson 1934, 148–9.

51 Watson 1928, 458. For a more recent view, see also the collected papers in Mews 2001.

52 BL MS Arundel 44, fol 114v.

53 *Proverbs* 9:1, 'Wisdom hath built her house, she hath hewn out her seven pillars'.

54 *Proverbs* 8:22.

55 'This double archway has had its dividing column in the centre with nearly all its open tracery … cut away'; John Carter quoted in Lethaby 1925, 99–100.

56 Lethaby 1906, 242.

57 The inner jamb is museum no. A. 1916–277 and the outer, A. 1916–278. The unusual asymmetry of the doorway jambs misled the Victoria and Albert Museum into labelling the casts as left-hand and right-hand doorway jambs.

58 The Christian depiction of Moses with ram's horns on his forehead derives from a medieval mistranslation of *Exodus*, ch 34. In the Latin text of the *Vulgate*, St Jerome took the literal meaning of a Hebrew word with the root meaning of a 'horn', translating it as *cornuta*, rather than using its metaphorical sense, a 'ray of light', intended to describe the face of Moses shining with extreme radiance after his encounter with God.

59 Lethaby 1906, 242. According to *Exodus* 4:22, Tubal Cain, son of Lamech, was the prototypical blacksmith, 'instructor of every artificer in brass and iron'.

60 Lethaby 1925, 118.

61 For an extended discussion of the iconography of Job, see Terrien 1996.

62 For example, 1:15 'I am king of this land'; and 7:24 'Are you, indeed, Job, our fellow-king?' See James 1897.

63 *Job* 29:14; Rivington and Rivington 1844–7, I, 153.

64 Bibliothèque de Bordeaux, Bible de la Sauve Majeure, MS 1 fol 250v.

65 Rivington and Rivington 1844–7, I, 153.

66 A copy from 1200 is preserved in the British Library: Royal MS 7 A.VIII.

67 Hutten 1926, 64.

68 Celano II, 3, para. 95 in Armstrong *et al* 1999–2001, I, 265.

69 Corpus Christi College, Cambridge, MS 16, fol 70v (formerly fol 66v). The feeding of the birds appears in the left-hand margin and the reception of the stigmata in the bottom margin.

70 '*Reliquiarum philacteriae super altare matutinale posita sunt*'; (Thompson 1902–4, II, 62) quoted in Bond 1909, pt 3, 48.

71 Westminster Abbey Library MS 37.

72 Fol 254r. For discussion of this letter, see Tudor-Craig 1998, 102–19.

73 For a full list of the abbey's relics see Robinson 1909, 68–73.

74 Robinson 2004, 44–5 and pl 7.

75 See, for example, St John's College, Cambridge, MS B.18 fol 13r, a 12th-century psalter from Reims, and University College London Library MS Lat 6 fol 19r, a fragment of a 13th-century missal.

76 Manuscripts of the *Speculum Humanae Salvationis*, dating from 1324 onwards, would pair the image of Esther before Ahasuerus with that of Mary before Christ as anti-type and type of intercession.

77 *Job* 19:25–26.

78 *Exodus* 33:11. St Francis was already called 'friend of God' by Thomas of Celano (1230–2) and by Roger of Wendover before 1235; see Armstrong *et al* 1999–2001, I, 235 and 600. The theme was developed, including Old Testament examples, by the Franciscan David of Augsburg (died 1272); see McGinn 2005, 408–9.

79 Giles 1854, III, 383.

80 Scott *c* 1876, 8.

81 Lethaby 1925, 118.

82 Rigold 1976, 21.

83 *Exodus* 28:33.

84 *Song of Songs* 4:3.

85 Dove 1997, 232.

86 Cambridge University MS Ee.3.59, fol 3v.

87 Collard 2007, 23, quoting Close Rolls 1902–38, VII, 283.

88 Chetham's Library, Manchester, MS 6712, cols. 486, 514.

89 Hollaender 1944, 23.

90 King Arthur, col. 185; Edward the Confessor, cols. 433–4; Henry I, col. 486; Richard I, col. 524; King John, col. 549.

91 A photograph of a cast of the lion capital appears in Bedford Lemere and Co's catalogue of the Royal Architectural Museum. It is labelled item 155, and was probably among the casts dating back to the 1830s (Lemere, B and Co *c* 1877, pl 147). W R Lethaby had confirmation of the originality of the capital in a letter from Mr C Burgess, who had worked on the Gilbert Scott restoration: 'The capital with the lions is old; most of the others in the arcade are modern, also the heads'; Lethaby 1906, 119.

92 Rigold 1976, 16.

93 'The statues of our ancient Kings that formerly stood in Niches near the Tops of these Buttresses and attracted Admiration, [are] for the most part removed, and their broken Fragments lodged in the roof of Henry VIIth's chapel, where they are buried from the public Eye forever'; Newberry 1753, 6.

94 Lethaby 1925, 241.

95 Lethaby 1906, 163.

96 Fenster and Wogan-Browne 2008, 27.

97 Giles 1854, III, 220.

98 St Edwin, St Edmund, St Kenelm, St Edward King and Martyr, St Oswin, St Oswald, St Ethelbert, St Ethelred and St Wistan; see Hope and Lethaby 1904, 158.

99 Scott 1863, 41.

100 The figure can be made out in a cross-section of the converted chapter house drawn for the Record Commissioners in 1807; TNA: OBS 1/692 with extracted plans in MPB 1/2; see fig 123.

101 For the information which came to light in 1988 when the pair of the Annunciation were professionally examined after the 'Age of Chivalry' exhibition at the Royal Academy, see Williamson 1988, 123–4, 928. See also Williamson 1995, 204–6, 285–6. We are grateful to Paul Williamson FSA for having drawn our attention to the analysis of the stones by F G Dimes, which has cleared up a long-established error.

102 'Item Willelmo Yxeworth pro ij ymaginibus liij sol iiijd'; Colvin 1971, 227. The entry does not specify the chapter house, though other entries nearby do. Lethaby ascribed the first suggestion that it refers to the Annunciation figures to Edward S Prior and Arthur Gardner; Lethaby 1906, 155.

103 'Warino pictori pro ij ymaginibus pingendis cum colore xj sol'; Colvin 1971, 229.

104 September 2008, by Richard Foster and Signe Hedegaard of the abbey's conservation team, using a DinoLite portable microscope with a digital camera.

105 *Ezekiel* 3:12–13.

106 Walsh and Edmunds 1979, I, xi–xii.

107 Ibid, III, 68–70.

108 Ibid, I, 13.

109 'Iste autem abbas ob reverentiam beatae dei genitricis Mariae, primo anno suae creationis, ex unami voluntate totius conventus in pleno capitulo statuit ut annuntiato beatae Mariae eodem modo et ordine celebretur in perpetuum quo illius celebratur nativitas, videlicet in quinque capis'; Robinson 1909, 109.

110 The Virgin and Child on the *trumeau* of the entrance to the chapter house at York; the coronation of the Virgin on the tympanum of the doorway at Salisbury; the Assumption painted on the inside wall over the entrance to the chapter house at Lichfield; the coronation of the Virgin carved around the abbot's throne at Canterbury; the Jesse tree probably painted up the central column of the chapter house at Worcester.

111 See Tudor-Craig 2002, 110–27.

112 *Proverbs* 8:1–3.

113 BL Add MS 18856. See Tudor-Craig 2002, pl 38.

114 For a bibliography of the 'O' Antiphons, see Cross and Livingstone 1997, 169.

115 Victoria and Albert Museum 1936, 57.

116 For a complete list of the casts, see Anon 1877.

117 Ibid, 22.

118 Lemere, B and Co *c* 1877, pl 45. Casts of the Archangel Gabriel and the Virgin Mary appear on pls 70 and 71, respectively.

119 See various entries for 1854–60 in the minute books of the Royal Architectural Museum held by the Architectural Association, AA B401 1851-1903, described in Bottoms 2007.

120 Scott 1879, 166.

121 HMSO 1841, iii.

122 Ibid, question 778.

123 Post Office 1851, I, Street Directory 304; II, Commercial and Personal Directory 680; III, Court Directory 1586.

124 HMSO 1841, question 1031.

125 Ibid, question 1541.

126 Ibid, question 1544.

127 Ibid, questions 1182–4.

128 Cottingham 1822–9, I, preface.

129 He communicated his findings in a letter of 14 January 1841, published in *Archaeologia*, **25**, 122–6.

130 According to Cottingham's obituary in *The Art-Union*, October 1847, 377–8, quoted in Myles 1996, 169.

131 Cottingham 1822–9, I, preface.

132 Christie and Manson 1850, 2. This memoir was written after Cottingham's death as part of an unsuccessful campaign by his family and friends to persuade the government or the British Museum to acquire the collection for the nation.

133 Shaw 1851, 40–1.

134 According to the evidence of William Hollocombe, the Abbey's Sacrist given to the Select Committee, HMSO 1841, question 1195.

135 Carter 1795–1814, II, 3.

136 The debate was reported in detail in *The Builder*, 16 February 1861, 103–5.

137 For the full list see Jordan 1980, 68.

138 Surveyor's Report, 22 February 1854, WAM RCO.4.

139 Scott 1863, 44.

140 Scott 1879, 153.

141 *The Builder*, 7 September 1878, 931.

142 In the early 1990s, Professor Robert Baker went round the ambulatory of the Abbey with Pamela Tudor-Craig, tapping with his delicate fingers the bases of the tombs that had received Scott's treatment. They all rang hollow: the shellac had penetrated about half an inch, and beneath that was a void.

143 Lethaby 1906, 241.

144 Church 1904, 3–4.

145 Reported in *Nature*, 10 November 1870, 37.

146 Sonstadt 1904, 824.

147 For a complete account of the 1983 conservation programme, see Taylor, Gradwell and McGrath 1998, 219–27.

CHAPTER 11 (pp 184–208)

1 The tag has numerous variants: '*Ut rosa flos florum sic est liber iste librorum*' (Alan of Lille's *Anticlaudianus*, IX) is one; see Bossuat 1955, 198. For the chapter house's fabric see Lethaby 1906, 43–54, 276–8; and Lethaby 1925, 98–132. For chapter house decoration see, *inter alia*, for Westminster, Wilson 1983, 120, n. 51; Binski 1995, 185–93; for Worcester, Heslop 2001.

2 For earlier discussions of the paintings see Waller 1873; Noppen 1932; Hansen 1939; Tristram 1955, 201–6; Turner 1985.

3 'From the burden of my heavy sin, sweet Virgin, deliver me.' Robinson 1909, 26; the tapestries are discussed by Binski 1991; for St Faith, Binski 1995, 167–71.

4 Wieck 1988, 97, 103; figs 64, 73.

5 Waller 1873, 386.

6 Waller 1873, 380–3 for the inscriptions; see Carruthers and Ziolkowski 2002, 83–102.

7 Morgan 1990, 59–61 and 254–5; Evans 1982, 23; Sandler 1983, 80, pl 23 (noted also in Waller 1873, 380). For MS Gg.4.32 see Hanna 2005, 5–6, 10, 13, 14, 27–8, 73, 150, 176.

8 Waller 1873, 385 for the rosary; Carruthers and Ziolkowski 2002, 85, 90.

9 Morgan 1982–8, I, n. 53 with bibliography to 1982.

10 Binski 2004, 188–9, figs 155, 156.

11 De Wald 1932, pls 91, 138; Binski 2004, 236–7.

12 See, for example, Demus 1970, pl 242; Lowden 1997, fig 176.

13 Demus 1970, pl 235; see also figs 197, 202, 208.

14 Binski and Panayotova 2005, no. 145.

15 The only MS recorded at Westminster which might have contained such a diagram on the model of other manuals of penance is the non-extant *Modus confitendi*, Robinson and James 1909, 33 no. 146 (list B, at 47 no. 88; list C, at 55 no. 140).

16 See Carruthers and Ziolkowski 2002, 87–90.

17 Noted in Waller 1873, 383.

18 Noppen 1932; Turner 1985, 94–7.

19 Noppen 1932; Hansen 1939. Recently discovered fragments of Apocalypse pictures formerly in the now-lost chapter house at Coventry indicate that their occurrence may have been more common: see Gill 2007.

20 Some further points are noted in Turner 1985, 94–5.

21 Noppen 1932; for MS B.10.2 and its context Sandler 1986, no. 153; Binski 1991; Binski 1995, 56, 192–3.

22 Rose 1999; N J Morgan has prepared studies of the Norwich and York Apocalypse recensions to which I am indebted.

23 Lethaby 1930, 792.

24 Demus 1970, pls 42, 78, 85, 92, fig 35 (chapter house at San Pedro de Arlanza, for which see also Cahn 1992).

25 Waller 1873, 415–16; Noppen 1932, 159.

26 The script, probably later 14th century in date, is fragmentary and indistinct but appears to be in Latin and may relate to the Annunciation images above; further technical examination is required but I am grateful to Vanessa Simeoni for enabling me to examine it under bright light.

27 Scott 1996, no. 64; Abeele 2000. Noppen 1932, 159 unhelpfully remarks that S C Cockerell advised him about a source in 'a later and rarer book' which he does not specify; Hansen 1939, 79–81 assists by identifying Cockerell/Noppen's source as Bodleian Library MS Ashmole 1504 and the Helmingham Herbal and Bestiary (see now Barker 1988): these sister manuscripts are arranged alphabetically with English captions, but, aside from the point about camels noted below (note 28) are not as close as MS Gg.6.5 in relation to actual representation.

28 Barker 1988.

29 Wander 1978, 141, 146–7.

30 Turner 1985, 97–8.

31 'Renovators and benefactors of the chapels round the inside of the abbey church'. Stanley 1869, 640–1; Turner 1985, 89; Binski 1995, 187–8.

32 Compare the frescoes in the Peruzzi Chapel, Santa Croce, Florence or the patronage of Jean Duc de Berry; see Meiss 1967, I, 91–2 no. 57 and II, fig 494.

33 Lehmann-Brockhaus 1955–60, V, 183 for entries under *frons*. Gervase of Canterbury uses the term in reference to an east end, Stubbs 1879–80, I, 15.

34 Serel 1875, 20–1.

35 Rackham 1909–10, 39 n. 1.

36 I refer to B F Harvey's paper 'The Monks of Westminster and the *Peculium*' to appear in a festschrift for R Pfaff; I am grateful to her for allowing me to see it.

37 Turner 1985, 95, 98.

38 Tristram 1955, 148, 206–19, pls 1–6, 13–14.

39 Wilson 1995, 496–7; for the Missal, for example, fol 157v, Sandler 1986, no. 150, fig 402.

40 Riley 1867–9, I, 245; III, 386.

41 Riley 1867–9, III, 381.

42 Namely '*unam tabulam de vj peciis de lumbardy*': Harvey 1947 at 305 (appendix).

43 Tristram 1955, accounts from 282.

44 Binski and Park 1986, 34–41; Martindale 1994.

45 Barr 1993, 70 at line 202.

46 Lethaby 1925, 125; Tristram 1955, 47.

47 Butt 1989, 266.

48 Gardner 1979; Boskovits 1990.

49 Howard 2003.

50 Scott 1861, 32–3. See also chapters 8 and 9.

51 Eastlake 1847, 123, 180; Lethaby 1925, 100–1.

52 Waller 1873, 379; Church 1904, 8.

53 Church 1904. Scanning electron microscopy with energy dispersive X-ray analysis (SEM/EDX) and proton induced X-ray emission (PIXE) analysis detected barium, originating from the barium hydroxide applied to consolidate the schemes. Elemental mapping indicated that the barium has collected at the interface between paint layers, in the interstices of the paint layers, and at the interface of the painting and ground, which may help to explain the poor condition of the painting.

54 Anon 1929, 380.

55 See art historical contribution by D Park in Howard 2003.

56 This analysis was kindly undertaken by M Spring and C Higgitt of the National Gallery's Scientific Department.

57 Records of the purchase of pigments for St Stephen's Chapel, Westminster Palace in 1351–4 indicate that red lakes were among the most expensive; see Salzman 1952, 168. Imported kermes would have been costly in comparison with madder, which was produced more locally; see White and Kirby 2006.

58 Spring and Higgitt 2006, 223–5; Geersdaele and Goldsworthy 1978.

59 Howard 1993a.

60 White 1993; Babington 1993; J Spooner and H Howard have work in progress on the recent examination of these paintings.

61 Instrumental analyses suggest the use of linseed oil: see Howe 2006b, 97, 103; also Tristram 1950, 121–4.

62 Demailly et al 1998.

63 Professor Adrian Heritage of the Fachhochschule Köln is currently researching the technology of these paintings for his PhD: 'Cologne Cathedral choir screen paintings: materials, techniques and physical history', Courtauld Institute, University of London; see also Maul 1992.

64 The only exception is the bone white identified as a component of one of the relief crowns. Otherwise, bone white has only so far been identified in English medieval wall paintings in one of the Apocalypse scenes in the chapter house, where it was combined with yellow earth and other materials beneath tin leaf.

65 Roy 1997, 80.

66 Bucklow 2003, app 4.

67 Tristram 1955, 199.

68 Park 1986, 194 and pl 82.

69 Martindale 1994, 111 n. 20.

70 Tristram 1955, pls 13–14. I am grateful to Marie Louise Sauerberg of the Hamilton Kerr Institute, who has undertaken the recent conservation of the tester, for discussing this work with me and for providing figure 206.

71 Dorner 1937; Hansen 1939.

72 Rogers 1986, 220–2.

73 Harvey 1961, 11 n. 1.

74 Noppen 1932.

75 Hatcher 1973. A detailed discussion of tin relief decoration, including the methods of manufacture, types of moulds employed and the relationship between makers of relief decoration and metal workers, is given in Nadolny 2001, esp 313–19.

76 Nadolny 2001; and Nadolny and Roy 2006.

77 Rees Jones 1952–54, 103; Sauerberg 2005.

78 I am much indebted to Jo Kirby of the National Gallery for this identification by high performance liquid chromatography (HPLC). In one sample a minute quantity of brazilwood lake was also identified, but this is probably a residue from manufacturing the kermes lake in a dyebath of cloth clippings; see White and Kirby 2006, 218.

79 Ibid, 218.

80 Elsewhere at Westminster lac lake has generally been identified; for example, analysis by J Kirby confirms that lac lake was employed on the Retable of c 1260–70 (Sauerberg et al, 2009), in wall paintings of c 1260–70 in the south transept and of c 1300 in St Faith's chapel (Howe 2006b, 97, 103–4), on the tomb of Aveline de Forz (wife of Edmund Crouchback) dated to c 1295 (J Kirby, pers comm, 2006), on the tomb of Edmund Crouchback (Howard 2009) and on the painted sedilia (Wrapson 2006).

81 Analysis by HPLC, J Kirby, pers comm, 2009.

82 Borsook 1980, 21.

83 Webb 1921, I, 72.

84 Howard 2009.

85 Howard 1993b.

86 Binski 1995, 190–1.

87 Turner 1985, 93.

88 Paul Binski is grateful to Barbara Harvey FSA for reading a draft of this paper, and to Nigel Morgan for advice. Helen Howard's work on the paintings was commissioned by English Heritage, and she is grateful to Robert Gowing and Adrian Heritage for help of various kinds. Helen is especially grateful to David Park FSA for advising on the art-historical context of the paintings, and both he and Sharon Cather FSA for their contribution to all aspects of the study. Particular thanks are due to Jo Kirby of the Scientific Department at the National Gallery for carrying out high performance liquid chromatography of the organic colorants, Dr Sophie Stos-Gale of the Isotrace Laboratory, Oxford, for lead isotope analysis, Geoff Grime, of the Scanning Proton Microprobe Unit, University of Oxford, for proton induced X-ray emission (PIXE) analysis, the Foundation for Research and Technology Hellas and Adrian Heritage for multispectral imaging, Marika Spring and Catherine Higgitt, of the National Gallery Scientific Department, for FTIR and GC-MS analysis of red lead samples, Marie Louise Sauerberg, of the Hamilton Kerr Institute, for her generosity in sharing her findings during the conservation of the Black Prince's tester; and Jane Spooner, of Historic Royal Palaces, for collaboration at the Byward Tower, Tower of London.

CHAPTER 12 (pp 209–236)

1 Brown et al 1963, 141–2; 1971, 236; Rigold 1976, 3.

2 Rigold 1976, 3.

3 Clayton 1912, 36–73 at 43; Close Rolls 1902–38, X, 377: totam tegulam que remansit de pavimento capituli Westmonasterii, et que nunc est in berfrario ejusdem loci. St Dunstan's chapel lay just to the south of the chapter house,

opening off the dorter undercroft.

4   Eames 1980, 163.

5   Caveler 1839, 60, pl 24.

6   Cottingham 1842.

7   Nichols 1842.

8   Reed 1996. There are several mistakes in Minton's copies, notably the omission of the dog to the king's right hand in the pictorial tile; ibid, 8.

9   Shaw 1858, pls IV, V and VI.

10 Scott 1860, 465; republished in Scott 1863, 40.

11 Scott 1863: the plate is on p 40 and the description pp 45–6, with tiles illustrated on pls VIII and IX. Scott's original account appeared in *Gent's Mag* (Scott 1860), where tiles are discussed on p 355, and illustrated between 356 and 357.

12 Eames 1980, 172.

13 Clayton 1912, 56, n. 1 notes that it was unfortunate that Scott did not order the preservation of the broken or defaced tiles, and that Minton's office did not supply any contract with Scott, or their earlier dealings with Cottingham. Some tiles seem to have been salvaged from Scott's work, for eight tiles became part of the Rutland collection now in the British Museum. Eames (1980) lists her design nos 1256 (here design 7), 1257 (design 20), 1258 (design 6), 1259 and 1260 (design 16), 1261 (design 15), 1688 (design 14) and 1721 (design 8). I owe thanks to Dr Brindle for extracts from his unpublished notes.

14 Lethaby 1906, figs 17 (fish), 18 (border), 19 to 25 (pictorial).

15 Lethaby 1906, 47–9 and figs 17 to 25. His fig 17 is design 25 here; fig 18 is design 20; figs 19 to 21 (the hunting scene) are designs 28 to 30. The four pictorial tiles are fig 22 (the king), design 34; fig 23 (the queen), design 35; fig 24 (the musicians), design 32; and fig 25 (the ring giving), design 33.

16 Clayton 1912, 48–73 for the chapter house.

17 Ibid, 64. The patterned tiles are figs 2 to 4, 6 to 8, the fish border tile fig 5 and the pictorial tiles figs 9 to 11.

18 The two border tile designs portraying fish represent pike, not salmon as is sometimes claimed.

19 RCHME 1924, 81 and pl 16.

20 I owe thanks to Dr Steven Brindle FSA for a copy of the survey, and to Dr Jeremy Ashbee FSA for providing a CD of the pavement.

21 Lethaby 1925, fig 69. The design is shown complete, whereas now only part of it is visible on the few examples surviving.

22 Clayton 1912, 53; Hawkyard 2002, 67.

23 This view benefits from discussion with Jerry Bird, who knows more about medieval instruments than I do. For instruments depicted in the wall paintings, see Montagu 1988.

24 A pocket to receive the end of a post, 70 mm square, had been cut into the floor, removing part of this tile and part of the adjacent one to the north. This must have occurred during the record-office era, and the damaged area was subsequently patched with mortar by Scott. Hence, it is likely that there were only ever eleven pictorial tiles in this group.

25 I am grateful to Warwick Rodwell FSA for the following note. Although held by the NMR, the pedigree of the photograph reproduced in figure 225 is unknown. Close inspection reveals that all the pictorial tiles appear to be in much better condition than they are today, whereas the inscription and border tiles show precisely the same degree of wear as at present. To suggest that the pictorial tiles alone were subjected to heavy abrasion during the 20th century, while the adjacent borders were not, carries no conviction. It is further apparent that the joints around the two 'rogue' tiles of design 36 are not commensurate in appearance with those around the other tiles in the photograph. In particular, they each exhibit thin white lines along two edges, and dark shadow-lines along the other two. I therefore contend that this is not a true photograph of the 1920s, but a photo-montage: two retouched pictures of design 36 have been overlaid on those of design 32, and the remaining pictorial tiles have all been substantially enhanced by an artist, while the borders and inscription remain untouched. An unaltered photograph of the same group of tiles (potentially printed from the same negative), taken in the 1920s, shows the ensemble looking very much as it does today (copy in WAM). In the 1950s, the Ministry of Works was still selling heavily retouched postcard photographs of the pictorial tiles (set in WAM).

26 Wilson *et al* 1986, 47; Draper 2006, 243.

27 Morris 2006, 127–8.

28 Clayton 1912, 60.

29 Harvey 1993, 46–7 and 226 n.

30 Marks 1998, 252.

31 Eames 1980, drawings 478 and 495.

32 The window is now in the Musée National du Moyen Age, Paris.

33 Clayton 1912, 70–3.

34 Lethaby 1925, 110–14, figs 62 to 66. He provided drawings of two decorated tiles (figs 67, 69).

35 Lethaby 1917, 133.

36 Lethaby 1913, 69–80, pp 77–9 for Westminster. The confusion about the place of manufacture is discussed by Norton 1981, n. 14. A grisaille window design from Westminster is illustrated by Norton 2002, 20–2 and fig 30. Brown *et al* 1963, 142 discusses the water transport and writes, 'there is nothing to show that the chapter house tiles were not made on the spot at Westminster'.

37 For the Chertsey series, see Eames 1980, designs 1118–1174. Eames's designs 1141, 1147, 1151, 1152, 1155, 1157, 1159 and 1163 are found at Westminster, and possibly also 1164 and 1172.

38 Brown 2003, 50, 58.

39 Brown *et al* 1963, 143; Norton 2002, 22.

40 Ibid.

41 Green and Green 1949. The inscriptions are discussed at pages 9 and 15 and the refectory inscription is illustrated on pl A1.

42 This section owes much to Norton 2002, 20–1. He cites the chapel paving being ordered in 1238. The 1237 date derives from Lethaby 1913, 79.

43 Norton 1981, 109–12. See also Keen 2007, 315–17 and Cherry 1987, 181–2 who writes on the chapter house pavement, referring to one of the most outstanding designs there as the four-tile design of the royal arms with figures of dragons and centaurs in the space left by the curve of the

shield, suggesting that they may have been designed for a floor in the royal palace.

44 Eames 1980, 172.

45 Gardner and Eames 1954, 32.

46 A few plain tiles, diagonally halved and all heavily worn, occur only as infill against the south-east and south-west sides. In the few instances where any glaze or slip remains, it is yellow.

47 Eames 1980, 163.

48 Norton 1996, 95 and fig 4.

49 For example, tiles bearing design 6 vary between 159 mm and 170 mm square, by 30–45 mm thick; design 14, as well as being variously stamped with five- and eight-pointed stars, varies between 144 mm and 154 mm square, by 26–42 mm thick. Dimensional variations in the order of 10 mm would not permit tiles to be laid together in the same panels.

50 Professor Warwick Rodwell FSA and I have shared many discussions about this pavement. I thank him for his invitation to produce this paper and for making arrangements for me to spend many hours on my knees in the chapter house, continuing an examination of the pavement which, from my notes, had started in 1980. At that time, it had been suggested by Dr Arnold Taylor FSA that a paper on the pavement might be published as a supplement to *The History of the King's Works*. Mr J Thorne helped me with access and research, but, alas, neither he nor Dr Taylor has lived to see the result. This piece is an offering to the archaeological and art historical analysis of the abbey as a tribute to the memory of Dr Thomas Cocke FSA, with whom I had the privilege to share so much academic work.

51 Scott 1863, 52.

52 Betts 2002, design W92.

53 For the same design from Chertsey abbey, but larger in scale, see Eames 1980, design 2756. See also Betts 2002, designs W146 and W147.

54 Betts 2002, design W104; 135 mm square. Examples recorded from Bermondsey abbey and the Guildhall chapel.

55 Betts 2002, design W105. A fragment from Bermondsey abbey.

56 Betts 2002, design W100. A fragment from St Mary Spital priory.

57 Mills 1995, 99, fig 14.29.

CHAPTER 13 (pp 237–250)

1 WAM 19639.

2 WAM 37046. Hawkyard 2002, 77, n. 121; Knighton 1997–9, xxiii, n. 41.

3 Unfortunately, Keepe, who was primarily interested in monuments and heraldry, did not include a description of the glass in his *Monumenta Westmonasteriensia* (1683). However, in his manuscript notes and addenda to his printed work, Keepe records the arms of Henry III and Richard of Cornwall 'in the windows of the Chapter House': Cambridge University Library, Dd.8.39, p 115. I am indebted to Dr Richard Mortimer FSA for this reference. For

Keepe, see Doggett 2004–9.

4 Bodleian Library, MS Rawlinson C.704, fol iii. See also Brown *et al* 1963, 142, n. 1. Three heraldic shields dating from the 13th century, and possibly from the chapter house, have survived. Depicting the arms of Henry III, Eleanor of Provence and Richard of Cornwall, they are now in St Edmund's chapel, but were only placed there in 1938. Prior to that, the shields were in the windows of the sanctuary apse, where they had probably been installed by Wren, who may have salvaged them from the chapter house when he carried out improvements there at the beginning of the 18th century; see Reynolds 2002, 16.

5 WAM (P)79.

6 A large volume of correspondence on this subject exists: TNA, WORK 14/51. I owe the references to Dr Steven Brindle FSA.

7 I have been unable to discover why the implementation of the glazing scheme began with the north-east window, rather than the north, which was left until last.

8 The cost of filling that window was estimated at £975. A lengthy article, based on a lecture by Bradley, appeared in *The Times* (5 June 1891). The article was reprinted as Bradley 1891.

9 This was the no. 3 light (Bradley 1895, 365). See also 'Westminster Abbey re-examined. Chapter house: sculpture, glass and painting', *The Builder*, 4 July 1924, 19–22.

10 Murray Smith 1906, 362. This panel told the story of the remission of Danegeld by Edward the Confessor: according to the original scheme, it was in the no. 3 light, so some confusion is apparent here: *cf* n. 9.

11 A photograph of 1914 attached to the RCHME record card for the chapter house shows the tracery lights completely filled, one panel each at the bottom of the first and second lights, the third light complete, and no stained glass in the fourth light. The same arrangement appears in 1932 (NMR AA49/744) and in views down to 1943. However, a panel depicting Abbot Edwin survives, and that should, according to the original scheme, have been at the bottom of the fourth light.

12 Descriptions of the glazing in the upper and middle registers are given by Farrar (1893, 34–8), who observed, 'As the Abbots of Westminster placed in the lowest compartments of the window are comparatively little known, I will not trouble the reader with their names'.

13 For contemporary news cuttings, see WAM VI.15(9). Lowell was the equivalent of the American ambassador to the UK.

14 The glazing of the single lancet is contained in an oak sub-frame which is set into an external rebate in the masonry surround; this probably reflects the original arrangement. The 13th-century practice of mounting glazing in timber sub-frames is found in other small lancets at Westminster Abbey (in the triforium, for example), but is best known at Salisbury Cathedral, where all the major windows were treated in this manner.

15 Noppen 1935, 11.

16 NMR PK175A.

17 For an obituary (by M E de Putron), see *The Times*, 12 June 1964, 15.

18 The dated initials are accompanied by a seagull, which was their trademark. Townshend and Howson were the founders of the Seagull Pottery. Howson, who died twenty years, to the day, after her partner, always included Townshend's initials in her work.

19 Howson's partner was now Mary Eily de Putron. The full team is also recorded in a photographic album compiled by the Ministry of Works, 1948–51: NMR AL1091.

20 It should be remembered that some wartime restrictions were still in force, which slowed down the work: Howson, for example, was only permitted to fire her electric kiln after 6 pm.

21 Two errors in the inscription should be noted: bomb damage occurred in 1940 (not 1941), and Howson's glazing was installed early in 1951 (not 1950).

22 In general, the glass in the middle register seems to have suffered more damage than in the upper and lower registers. Also, very little glass has survived at all from the east window, which was worst affected by the bomb blast.

23 Notes accompanying the Ministry of Works' press release for the reopening in 1951.

24 Confirmed by her niece, Mrs Jane O'Leary, and great-nephew, Mark Westcott, July 2009.

25 Rodwell 2002, 10. It was further suggested to Diane Gibbs-Rodwell by the late Mrs Anne Campbell (née Howson, niece of Joan Howson), in c 2000, that some of the motifs in the lower part of the window were related by encoding to elements of the inscription running across the bottoms of the four lights.

26 Close access has not been possible, and full identification and description of the quarries must await such a future opportunity.

27 Howson is known to have painted some of her scenes from contemporary photographs, and the precise shot used for this scene has been identified. The WVS is now the Women's Royal Voluntary Service (WRVS).

28 St Stephen's tower was erected during Llanover's period in office.

29 Apparently an allusion to the Egyptian pharoah's daughter rescuing Moses from the bullrushes.

30 I am grateful to Anna Eavis and her colleagues at the National Monuments Record for assistance with researching the post-war glazing programme, and to Jane O'Leary and Mark Westcott, who provided much valuable information on Joan Howson and the workings of her studio. I am also indebted to Christine Reynolds for guiding me to relevant sources in the Westminster Abbey Muniments, and to my wife, Diane Gibbs-Rodwell, for her help in studying and interpreting the 'enigma' window.

CHAPTER 14 (pp 251–260)

1 Scott 1863, 50.

2 This is recounted in innumerable guide books and general works on the abbey of the nineteenth and twentieth centuries. See also Swanton 1976, 25; Geddes 1999, 13–14.

3 Hewett 1978, 214, figs 14, 15; 1980, 26, figs 23, 24; 1985,

155, fig 149.

4 Geddes 1999, 22, 344, fig 2.5.

5 Rodwell 2009, 163–6.

6 Full details of the investigation on all six doors will be found in the Centre for Archaeology Report 38/2005 (Miles and Bridge 2005).

7 Dart 1723, I, 64. By the 1850s the door had gone (Scott 1863, 47–8). In this instance, mythology linked the skin with sacrilegious Danes who had been flayed.

8 This system was initially developed for work on the medieval doors at the Tower of London, commissioned by the Historic Royal Palaces Agency.

9 Tyers 2001.

10 An assessment of the dating potential of the doors was carried out by Daniel Miles in 2001.

11 The term first appeared in Hewett 1978, and has subsequently been repeated by others, including Rodwell et al 2006.

12 Hewett 1985, 155–6.

13 Miles 1997.

14 The door was reversed when it was cut down and hung in its present position in the mid-13th century; consequently the original front is now inside the office-store.

15 Geddes 1999, 344; Rodwell 2002, 7.

16 Swanton 1976, 25; Geddes 1999, 14.

17 Rodwell et al 2006, 25. Hewett's suggestion that the door was 'once part of the Pyx Chapel of Edward the Confessor's building' is untenable (Hewett 1978, 214). The Trial of the Pyx was not instituted until the reign of Henry II, and the term 'Pyx Chapel' is a Victorian appellation.

18 By the Historic Buildings and Monuments Commission, the precursor of English Heritage.

19 He was assisted by F S Walker, Margaret Tapper and Dr Jane Geddes.

20 The material in the archive is confusingly labelled 'Chapter House Undercroft'.

21 Geddes 1999, 28–9.

22 Oil on canvas, signed by P(ietro) Fabris.

23 Ackermann 1812, II, pl 57.

24 Lethaby 1925, 78.

25 The authors are grateful to the Dean and Chapter of Westminster and to John Burton, Surveyor of the Fabric, for facilitating the project; and for the assistance of the staff of the Works Department who carefully lifted the vestibule door off and back onto its pintles. Research by Christine Reynolds, Assistant Keeper of the Muniments, was instrumental in confirming the provenance of the door now leading to the chapter house undercroft. Warwick Rodwell FSA liaised between parties and assisted during the sampling. Michael Worthington provided the bar-charts. Acknowledgement is also due to English Heritage and Sheffield Dendrochronology Laboratory for supplying published and unpublished data; Cathy Groves kindly ran the imported material against their European database to bolster the chronology matches. The work was funded by English Heritage and co-ordinated by Alex Bayliss FSA and Derek Hamilton both of whom, with Cathy Groves, provided useful discussion and comments on the report.

Bibliography

Abbreviations

BL	British Library
CUP	Cambridge University Press
HMSO	His/Her Majesty's Stationery Office
NMR	National Monuments Record, English Heritage, Swindon
ODNB	*Oxford Dictionary of National Biography: online edition*
OUP	Oxford University Press
PRO	Public Record Office
RCHME	Royal Commission on the Historical Monuments of England
TNA	The National Archives
WAM	Westminster Abbey Muniments
WA Mus Coll	Westminster Abbey Museum Collection

Abeele, B van den 2000. 'Un bestiaire à la croisée des genres: le manuscrit Cambridge UL Gg.6.5', *Reinardus*, **13**, 215–36

Ackermann, R 1812. *The History of the Abbey Church of St Peter's Westminster, its Antiquities and Monuments*, 2 vols, London

Alexander, J 2005. 'Solid as a rock: poured lead joints in medieval masonry', in R Bork (ed), *De Re Metallica: the Uses of Metal in the Middle Ages*, 255–65, Aldershot: Ashgate

Alexander, J and Binski, P (eds) 1987. *The Age of Chivalry: Art in Plantagenet England 1200–1400*, London: Royal Academy of Arts

Anderson, F 1989. 'Three Westminster abbots: a problem of identity', *Church Monuments*, **4**, 3–15

Anon 1877. *Royal Architectural Museum: Catalogue of Collection*

Anon 1929. 'Method of preserving mural paintings in the chapter house, Westminster Abbey', *Mus J*, **28**, 375–81

Anon [A Harvey and R Mortimer] [1987]. *The Chapter House, Pyx Chamber and Treasury, the Undercroft Museum, Westminster Abbey*, London: Dean and Chapter of Westminster

Armstrong, J, Hellman, J A W and Short, W J 1999–2001. *Francis of Assisi: Early Documents*, 3 vols, London: New City

Ashbee, J 2008. 'The Structure and Function of the White Tower, 1150–1485' in E Impey (ed) *The White Tower*, 140–59, London: Yale

Babington, C 1993. 'Byward Tower, Tower of London: technique of the wall paintings', unpublished report, English Heritage

Badham, S 2007. 'Edward the Confessor's chapel, Westminster Abbey: the origins of the royal mausoleum and its Cosmatesque pavement', *Antiq J*, **87**, 197–219

Barker, N 1988. *Two East Anglian Picture Books: a Facsimile of the Helmingham Herbal and Bestiary and Bodleian MS Ashmole 1504*, London: Roxburghe Club

Barlow, F (ed and trans) 1992. *The Life of King Edward who rests at Westminster*, Oxford: OUP

Barlow, F 1997. *Edward the Confessor, 1042–1066*, London: Yale

Barnwell, P S and Pacey, A 2008. *Who Built Beverley Minster?* Reading: Spire

Barr, H 1993. *The Piers Plowman Tradition*, London: Dent

Barron, C 2004. *London in the Later Middle Ages. Government and People 1200–1500*, Oxford: OUP

Bates, D 1998. *Regesta Regum Anglo-Normannorum. The Acta of William I (1066–87)*, Oxford: OUP

Bémont, C 1884. *Simon de Montfort Comte de Leicester*, Paris

Betts, I M 2002. *Medieval 'Westminster' Floor Tiles*, London: MoLAS Monogr 11

Biddle, M and Kjølbye-Biddle, B 1980. 'England's premier abbey: the medieval chapter house of St Albans Abbey, and its excavation in 1978', *Expedition*, **22**, 17–32

Bilson, J 1895. 'On the discovery of some remains of the chapter-house of Beverley Minster', *Archaeologia*, **54**, 425–32

Binski, P 1986. *The Painted Chamber at Westminster*, London: Society of Antiquaries

Binski, P 1990. 'The Cosmati at Westminster and the English court style', *Art Bull*, **72**, 6–34

Binski, P 1991. 'Abbot Barking's tapestries and Matthew Paris's *Life of St Edward the Confessor*', *Archaeologia*, **109**, 85–100

Binski, P 1995. *Westminster Abbey and the Plantagenets: Kingship and the Representation of Power 1200–1400*, London: Yale

Binski, P 2004. *Becket's Crown: Art and Imagination in Gothic England 1170–1300*, London: Yale

Binski, P and Massing, A (eds) 2009. *The Westminster Retable: History, Context and Conservation*, Cambridge: Hamilton Kerr Institute and London: Harvey Miller

Binski, P and Panayotova, S (eds) 2005. *The Cambridge Illuminations: Ten Centuries of Book Production in the Medieval West*, London: Harvey Miller

Binski, P and Park, D 1986. 'A Ducciesque episode at Ely: the mural decoration of Prior Crauden's Chapel', in W M Ormrod (ed), *England in the Fourteenth Century. Proceedings of the 1985 Harlaxton Symposium*, 28–41, Woodbridge: Shaun Tyas

Black, G 1977. 'The redevelopment of 20 Dean's Yard, Westminster Abbey 1975–7', *Trans London Middlesex Archaeol Soc*, **28**, 190–210

Bliss, W H and Twemlow, J A (eds) 1902. *Entries in the Papal Registers relating to Great Britain and Ireland 1362–1404*, 4 vols, London: HMSO

Bloch, M (ed) 1923. 'La Vie de S. Édouard le Confessor par Osbert de Clare', *Analecta Bollandiana*, **40**, 64–131

Blum, P 1991. 'The sequence of the building campaigns at Salisbury', *Art Bull*, **73**(1), 6–38

Bolton, A T and Hendry H D 1934. *The Wren Society Vol XI*, London

Bond, F 1909. *Westminster Abbey*, Oxford: OUP

Bony, J 1979. *The English Decorated Style: Architecture Transformed 1250–1350*, Oxford: OUP

Bony, J 1983. *French Gothic Architecture of the Twelfth and Thirteenth Centuries*, Berkeley: University of California Press

Borsook, E 1980. *The Mural Painters of Tuscany*, Oxford: OUP

Boskovits, M 1990. 'Insegnare per immagini: dipinti e sculture nelle sale capitolari', *Arte Cristiana*, **78**, 123–42

Bossuat, R 1955. *Alain de Lille, Anticlaudianus*, Paris: Textes Philosophiques du Moyen Age

Bottoms, E 2007. 'The Royal Architectural Museum in the light of new documentary evidence', *J Hist Collections*, **19**, 115–39

Bouttier, M 1987. 'La reconstruction de l'abbatiale de Saint-Denis au XIIIe siècle', *Bull Monumental*, **145**, 357–86

Bradley, E T 1895. *Annals of Westminster Abbey*, London: Cassell

Bradley, G G [1891], *The Westminster Chapter House and the late Dean Stanley*, London

Brand, P 2003. *Kings, Barons and Justices: The Making and Enforcement of Legislation in Thirteenth-Century England*, Cambridge: CUP

Branner, R 1964. 'Westminster Abbey and the French court style', *J Soc Architectural Historians*, **23**, 3–18

Branner, R 1965. *St Louis and the Court Style in Gothic Architecture*, London: Zwemmer

Brayley, E W 1823. *The History and Antiquities of the Abbey Church of St Peter, Westminster*, 2 vols, London: J P Neale

Brieger, P 1957. *English Art 1216–1307*, Oxford: OUP

Britnell, R H and Campbell, B M S 1993. *A Commercialising Economy: England 1086–1300*, Manchester: Manchester University Press

Britton, J 1835. *The Architectural Antiquities of Great Britain*, 2nd edn, 5 vols, London: Nattali

Britton, J 1836a. *The History and Antiquities of the See and Cathedral Church of Lichfield*, 2nd edn, London: Nattali

Britton, J 1836b. *The History and Antiquities of the Cathedral Church of Wells*, 2nd edn, London: Nattali

Brown, R A, Colvin, H M and Taylor, A J 1963. *The History of the King's Works: the Middle Ages*, 2 vols, London: HMSO

Brown, S 1999. *Sumptuous and Richly Adorn'd: the Decoration of Salisbury Cathedral*, London: HMSO

Brown, S 2001. 'The thirteenth-century stained glass of the Salisbury Cathedral chapter house', *Wiltshire Archaeol Natur Hist Mag*, **94**, 118–38

Brown, S 2003. '*Our Magnificent Fabrick*': an Architectural History of York Minster, c 1220–1500, London: English Heritage

Bucklow, S 2003. 'Lead isotope ratios', in A Massing (ed) *Painting and Practice: the Thornham Parva Retable: Technique, Conservation and Context of an English Medieval Painting*, 226, Cambridge: Hamilton Kerr Institute

Burges, W 1859. 'The iconography of the chapter-house, Salisbury', *Ecclesiologist*, **20**, 109

Butler, H E 1949. *Chronicle of Jocelin of Brakelond*, London: Nelson

Butt, R 1989. *A History of Parliament*, London: Constable

Cahn, W 1992. 'The frescoes of San Pedro de Arlanza', in E C Parker (ed) *The Cloisters: Studies in Honor of the Fiftieth Anniversary*, 87–109, New York: Metropolitan Museum of Art

[Camden, W], 1600. *Reges, reginae, nobiles, et alii in ecclesia collegiata B Petri Westmonasterii sepulti*, London: E Bollifantus

Cantwell, J 1991. *The Public Record Office 1838–1958*, London: HMSO

Carpenter, D 1990. *The Minority of Henry III*, London: Methuen

Carpenter, D 1996. *The Reign of Henry III*, London: Hambledon Continuum

Carpenter, D 2001. 'Westminster Abbey in politics 1258–69', in M Prestwich, R Britnell and R Frame (eds), *Thirteenth-Century England VIII: Proceedings of the Durham Conference 1999*, 49–58, Woodbridge: Boydell

Carpenter, D 2003. *The Struggle for Mastery: Britain 1066–1284*, Oxford: OUP

Carpenter, D 2004. *The Struggle for Mastery: Britain 1066–1284*, London: Penguin

Carpenter, D 2005. 'The meetings of Kings Henry III and Louis IX', in M Prestwich, R Britnell and R Frame (eds), *Thirteenth-Century England X: Proceedings of the Durham Conference 2003*, 1–30, Woodbridge: Boydell

Carpenter, D 2007a. 'The household rolls of King Henry III', *Historical Research*, **80**, 22–46

Carpenter, D 2007b. 'King Henry III and Saint Edward the Confessor: the origins of the cult', *Engl Hist Rev*, **122**, 865–91

Carpenter, D 2008. 'The struggle to control the Peak: an unknown letter patent from January 1217', in P Brand and S Cunningham (eds), *Foundations of Medieval Scholarship: Records Edited in Honour of David Crook*, 35–50, Heslington: Borthwick Institute

Carruthers, M and Ziolkowski, J M 2002. *The Medieval Craft of Memory: an Anthology of Texts and Pictures*, Philadelphia: University of Pennsylvania Press

Carter, J 1786. *Specimens of Ancient Sculpture and Painting*, London

Carter, J 1795–1814. *The Ancient Architecture of England*, 2 vols, London

Caveler, W 1839. *Select Specimens of Gothic Architecture, comprising the Ancient and most Approved Examples in England*, 2nd edn, London

Chancery Rolls 1912. *Calendar of Chancery Rolls, Various, 1277–1328*, London

Chaplais, P 1994. *Piers Gaveston: Edward II's Adoptive Brother*, Oxford: OUP

CHCR 1801. *Reports from the Committees of the House of Commons*, 16 vols, London

Cheney, C R 1931. 'The papal legate and English monasteries', *Engl Hist Rev*, **46**, 443–52

Cherry, J 1987. 'Tiles', in Alexander and Binski (eds) 1987, 181–2

Chibnall, M 1969–80. *The Ecclesiastical History of Ordericus Vitalis*, 6 vols, Oxford: OUP

Christie and Manson 1850. *Descriptive Memoir of the Museum of Medieval Architecture and Sculpture*, London

Church, A H 1904. *Copy of Memoranda by Professor Church FRS, Furnished to the First Commission of His Majesty's Works*

Concerning the Treatment of the Decayed Stone-work in the Chapter House, Westminster Abbey, London: HMSO

Clanchy, M T 1968. 'Did Henry III have a policy?', *History*, **53**, 203–16

Clark, J G 2002. 'The religious orders in pre-Reformation England', in J G Clark (ed), *Religious Orders in Pre-Reformation England*, 3–33, Woodbridge: Boydell

Clayton, P B 1912. 'The inlaid tiles of Westminster Abbey', *Archaeol J*, **69**, 36–73

Close Rolls 1902–38. *Close Rolls of the Reign of Henry III 1227–1272*, 14 vols, London

CLR 1916–64. *Calendar of Liberate Rolls, Henry III, 1226–1272*, 6 vols, London

Cocke, T 1995. *900 Years: the Restorations of Westminster Abbey*, London: Harvey Miller

Cocke, T and Kidson, P 1993. *Salisbury Cathedral: Perspectives on the Architectural History*, London: HMSO

Colchester, L S and Harvey, J H 1974. 'Wells Cathedral', *Archaeol J*, **131**, 200–14

Cole, D 1980. *The Work of Sir Gilbert Scott*, London: Architectural Press

Cole, H 1844. *Documents Illustrative of English History in the Thirteenth and Fourteenth Centuries*, London

Cole, H 1884. *Fifty Years of Public Work of Sir Henry Cole, KCB*, London: Bell

Collard, J 2007. '*Effigies ad Regem Angliae* and the representation of kingship in thirteenth-century English royal culture', eBLJ, <http://www.bl.uk/eblj/2007articles/article9.html> (14 November 2009)

Colvin, H 1971. *Building Accounts of Henry III*, Oxford: OUP

Colvin, H, Crook, J M, Downes, K and Newman, J 1976. *The History of the King's Works, Volume V: 1660–1782*, London: HMSO

Commons Journal 1742– . *Journals of the House of Commons 1547–*, London

Condon, M 2003. 'God Save the King! Piety, propaganda and the perpetual memorial', in Tatton-Brown and Mortimer (eds) 2003, 59–97

Condon, M M and Hallam, E M 1984. 'Government printing of the public records in the eighteenth century', *J Soc Archiv*, **7**, 348–84

Cottingham, L N 1822–9. *Plans, Elevations, Sections, Details and Views of the Magnificent Chapel of Henry VII at Westminster Abbey Church, etc*, 2 vols, London: Priestley and Weale

Cottingham, L N 1842. 'Tile pavement of the chapter house at Westminster', *Archaeologia*, **29**, 390–1

CPR 1895. *Calendar of the Patent Rolls, 1292–1301*, London

CPR 1898. *Calendar of the Patent Rolls, 1301–1307*, London

CPR 1906–13. *Calendar of Patent Rolls 1232–1272*, 4 vols, London

CPRR 1800–37. *Reports from Commissioners of the Public Records*, London

Craib, T 1923. 'The itinerary of Henry III 1216–1272', volume in the Map Room at the National Archives, Kew, edited and annotated by S Brindle and S Priestley

Crook, J M 1995. *John Carter and the Mind of the Gothic Revival*, London: Society of Antiquaries

Crook, J M 2004–9. 'Carter, John (1748–1817)', in ODNB (eds H C G Matthew and B Harrison), <http://www.oxforddnb.com/view/article/4791> (21 November 2009)

Crosby, E U 1994. *Bishop and Chapter in Twelfth-Century England: a Study of the Mensa Episcopalis*, Cambridge: CUP

Cross, F A and Livingstone, L A 1997. *The Oxford Dictionary of the Christian Church*, Oxford: OUP

CSPD 1864. *Calendar of State Papers Domestic, Interregnum, 1655–6*, London

CSPD 1871. *Calendar of State Papers Domestic, Elizabeth, VII, Addenda*, London

CSPD 2006. *Calendar of State Papers Domestic, Anne, IV*, Woodbridge and London

CTB 1936. *Calendar of Treasury Books, XVIII, 1703*, London

CTB 1952. *Calendar of Treasury Books, XX, 1705–06*, London

Dart, J 1723. *Westmonasterium, or the History and Antiquities of the Abbey Church of St Peter's Westminster*, London

Demailly, S, Hugon, P, Stefanaggi, M and Nowik, W 1998. 'The technique of the mural paintings in the choir of Angers Cathedral', in A Roy and P Smith (eds) *Painting Techniques: History, Materials and Studio Practice*, 10–15, London: International Institute for Conservation of Historic and Artistic Works

Demus, O 1970. *Romanesque Mural Painting*, London: Thames & Hudson

Dixon-Smith, S 1999. 'The image and reality of almsgiving in the great halls of Henry III', *J Brit Archaeol Ass*, **152**, 79–96

DKR 1846. *Annual reports of the Deputy Keeper of the Public Records*, London

Dobson, R B 1973. *Durham Priory 1400–1450*, Cambridge: CUP

Doggett, N 2004–9. 'Keepe, Henry (1652–1688)', in ODNB (eds H C G Matthew and B Harrison), <http://www.oxforddnb.com/view/article/15250> (21 November 2009)

Dorner, A 1937. 'Ein Schüler des Meisters Bertram in England', *Jahrbuch der Preussischen Kunstsammlungen*, **58**, 40–4

Dove, M 1997. 'In Canto Cantorum': *Glossa Ordinaria*, Turnhout: Corpus Christianorum Continuatio Mediaevalis 22

Draper, P 2006. *The Formation of English Gothic: Architecture and Identity*, London: Yale

Duffus Hardy, T 1833–4. *Rotuli Literarum Clausarum in Turri Londinensi Asservati*, 2 vols, London

Dugdale, W 1658. *The History of St Paul's Cathedral in London*, London

Dunbabin, J 2002. *Captivity and Imprisonment in Medieval Europe c 1000–c 1300*, Basingstoke: Palgrave Macmillan

Durand, G 1901. *Monographie de l'Eglise Notre-Dame Cathédrale d'Amiens*, 2 vols, Paris: Persée

Eames, E S 1980. *Catalogue of Medieval Lead-Glazed Earthenware Tiles in the Department of Medieval and Later Antiquities, British Museum*, London: British Museum

Eastlake, C 1847. *Materials for a History of Oil Painting*, 2 vols, London

Edwards, J G 1979. *The Second Century of the English Parliament*, Oxford: OUP

Evans, E (trans) 1956. *Tertullian's Treatise on the Incarnation*, London: SPCK

Evans, J 1956. *A History of the Society of Antiquaries*, Oxford: OUP

Evans, M 1982. 'An Illustrated Fragment of Peraldus's Summa of Vice: Harleian MS 3244', *Journal of the Warburg and Courtauld Institutes*, **45**, 14–46

Eyre-Todd, G (ed) 1898. *Glasgow Cathedral: a History and Description*, Glasgow: Morison Brothers

Farrar, F W 1893. 'Westminster Abbey', *Our English Minsters*, **1**(1), London: Isbister

Feasey, H J 1899. *Westminster Abbey Historically Described*, London: George Bell

Fenster, T S and Wogan-Browne, J 2008. *Matthew Paris, The History of St Edward the King*, Medieval and Renaissance Texts and Studies 341, Tempe, Arizona

Fitchen, J 1961. *The Construction of Gothic Cathedrals: a Study of Medieval Vault Erection*, Oxford: Oxford University Press

Forde, H 1986. *Domesday Preserved*, London: HMSO

Fryde, E B, Greenway D E, Porter S and Roy I 1986. *Handbook of British Chronology*, Cambridge: CUP

Galbraith, V H 1925. 'The Tower as an Exchequer record office in the reign of Edward II', in A G Little and F M Powicke (eds), *Essays Presented to Thomas Frederick Tout*, 231–47, Manchester

Galbraith, V H (ed) 1927. *The Anonimalle Chronicle 1333–1381*, Manchester: Manchester University Press

Gardner, J 1979. 'Andrea di Bonaiuti and the chapter house frescoes in Santa Maria Novella', *Art History* **2**(2), 107–38

Gardner, J S and Eames, E 1954. 'A tile kiln at Chertsey abbey', *J Brit Archaeol Ass*, **17**, 24–42

Gasser, S 2007. 'L'architecture de la Sainte-Chapelle. Etat de la question concernant la datation, son maître d'œuvre et sa place dans l'histoire de l'architecture', in C Hediger (ed), *La Sainte-Chapelle de Paris: Royaume de France ou Jérusalem Céleste?*, 157–70, Turnhout: Brepols

Geddes, J 1987. 'Decorative wrought iron', in Alexander and Binski (eds) 1987, 174–5

Geddes, J 1999. *Medieval Decorative Ironwork in England*, London: Society of Antiquaries

Geersdaele, P C van and Goldsworthy, L J 1978. 'The restoration of wall painting fragments from St Stephen's Chapel, Westminster', *The Conservator*, **2**, 9–12

Gem, R 2003. *Studies in English Pre-Romanesque and Romanesque Architecture*, 2 vols, London: Pindar

Giles, J S 1854. *Matthew Paris's English History from the Year 1235 to 1273*, London

Gill, M 2007. 'Monastic murals and lectio in the later Middle Ages', in J G Clark (ed), *The Culture of Medieval English Monasticism*, 55–71, Woodbridge: Boydell

Given-Wilson, C (ed) 2005. The *Parliament Rolls of Medieval England 1275–1504*, 16 vols, Woodbridge: Boydell

Goodwin, G (rev B Nurse) 2004–9. 'Caley, John (bap 1760, d 1834)', in ODNB (eds H C G Matthew and B Harrison), <http://www.oxforddnb.com/view/article/4389> (21 November 2009)

Graham, R 1912. 'Visitation of Bury St Edmunds and Westminster in 1234', *Engl Hist Rev*, **27**, 728–39

Gransden, A 1963. 'Customary of the Benedictine Abbey of Eynsham in Oxfordshire', *Corpus Consuetudinum Monasticarum*, **2**, Siegburg: F Schmitt

Gransden, A 1973. *Customary of the Benedictine Abbey of Bury St Edmunds in Suffolk*, London: Henry Bradshaw Society

Grant, L and Mortimer, R (eds) 2002. *Westminster Abbey: the Cosmati Pavements*, Aldershot: Ashgate

Green, E 1974–7. 'The management of Exchequer records in the 1560s', *J Soc Archiv*, **5**, 25–30

Green, P M and Green, A R 1949. 'Medieval tiles at Titchfield Abbey, Hants, afterwards Place or Palace House', *Proc Hampshire Fld Club Archaeol Soc*, **17**, 6–30

Gryson, R (ed) 1993. *Commentaires de Jérôme sur le Prophète Isaï, Livres I–IV*, Freiburg: Herder

Hall, H 1898. *The Antiquities and Curiosities of the Exchequer*, London: E Stock

Hall, P 1834. *Picturesque Memorials of Salisbury*, Salisbury

Hallam, E 1979. 'The Tower of London as a record office', *Archives*, **61**, 3–10

Hallam, E 1986. *Domesday Book Through Nine Centuries*, London: Thames & Hudson

Hallam, E 1987. 'Annotations in Domesday Book since 1100', in A Williams and R Erskine (eds), *Domesday Book Studies*, 136–50, London: Alecto

Hallam, E 1990. 'Nine centuries of keeping the public records', in G H Martin and P Spufford (eds), *The Records of the Nation: the Public Record Office 1838–1988*, 23–42, Woodbridge: Boydell

Hallam, E 1997. 'Arthur Agarde and Domesday Book', in C J Wright (ed), *Sir Robert Cotton as Collector*, 233–61, London: British Library

Hanna, R 2005. *London Literature 1300–1380*, Cambridge: CUP

Hansen, C 1939. *Die Wandmalereien des Kapitelhauses der Westminsterabtei in London*, Würzburg: Triltsch

Hardy, T D 1869–85. *Syllabus of the Documents relating to England and other Kingdoms contained in the Collections known as 'Rymer's Foedera'*, 3 vols, London: PRO

Harmer, F E 1952. *Anglo-Saxon Writs,* Manchester: Manchester University Press

Harrison, S 1997. 'The cloistral range and a fresh look at the chapter house', in Shoesmith and Richardson 1997, 113–24

Harriss, G L 2005. *Shaping the Nation: England 1360–1461*, Oxford: OUP

Harrod, H 1873. 'On the crypt of the chapter house, Westminster Abbey', *Archaeologia*, **44**, 373–82

Harvey, B 1965. *Documents Illustrating the Rule of Walter de Wenlok, Abbot of Westminster 1283–1307*, London: Royal Historical Society

Harvey, B 1993. *Living and Dying in England 1100–1540: the Monastic Experience*, Oxford: OUP

Harvey, B 2002. *The Obedientiaries of Westminster Abbey and their Financial Records c 1275–1540*, Woodbridge: Boydell

Harvey, B 2003. 'The monks of Westminster and the old Lady Chapel', in Tatton-Brown and Mortimer (eds) 2003, 5–31

Harvey, B F 2004–9a. 'Norwych, George (b before 1405, d 1469)', in ODNB (eds H C G Matthew and B Harrison), <http://www.oxforddnb.com/view/article/20366> (21 November 2009)

Harvey, B F 2004–9b. 'Litlyngton, Nicholas (b before 1315, d 1386)', in ODNB (eds H C G Matthew and B Harrison), <http://www.oxforddnb.com/view/article/16775> (21 November 2009)

Harvey, J H 1947. 'Some London painters of the fourteenth and fifteenth centuries', *Burlington Mag*, **89**, 303–5

Harvey, J H 1961. 'The Wilton Diptych – a re-examination', *Archaeologia*, **58**, 1–28

Harvey, J H 1974. *Cathedrals of England and Wales*, London: Batsford

Harvey, J H 1978. *The Perpendicular Style 1330–1485*, London: Batsford

Harvey, J H 1984. *English Medieval Architects: a Biographical Dictionary down to 1550*, Gloucester: Sutton

Hatcher, J 1973. *English Tin Production and Trade before 1550*, Oxford: OUP

Hawkyard, A 2002. 'From Painted Chamber to St Stephen's Chapel: the meeting places of the House of Commons at Westminster until 1603', *Parliamentary History*, **21**, 62–84

Hector, L C 1979. *Curia Regis Rolls of the reign of Henry III*, *xvi*, London: HMSO

Heslop, T A 2001. 'Worcester Cathedral chapter house and the harmony of the Testaments', in P Binski and W Noel (eds), *New Offerings, Ancient Treasures:. Studies in Medieval Art for George Henderson*, 280–311, Stroud: Sutton

Hewett, C A 1978. 'Anglo-Saxon carpentry', *Anglo-Saxon England*, **7**, 205–29

Hewett, C A 1980. *English Historic Carpentry*, Chichester: Phillimore

Hewett, C A 1985. *English Cathedral and Monastic Carpentry*, Chichester: Phillimore

Hillaby, J 1997. 'Superfluity and singularity', in Shoesmith and Richardson 1997, 103–12

Hillam, J, Morgan, R A and Tyers, I 1987. 'Sapwood estimates and the dating of short ring sequences', in R G W Ward (ed), *Applications of Tree-ring Studies: Current Research in Dendrochronology and Related Areas*, 165–85, Oxford: BAR Int Ser 333

HMSO 1841. *Report from the Select Committee on National Monuments and Works of Art in Westminster Abbey, in St Paul's Cathedral and in Other Public Edifices*, London: HMSO

Hollaender, A 1944. 'The pictorial work in the Flores Historiarum of the so-called Matthew of Westminster', *Bull John Rylands Lib*, **28**, 361–81

Hollerich, M J 1999. *Eusebius of Caesarea's Commentary in Isaiah: Christian Exegesis in the Age of Constantine*, Oxford: OUP

Holt, J C 1992. *Magna Carta*, Cambridge: CUP

Hope, W H St-J and Lethaby, W R 1904. 'The imagery and sculptures on the west front of Wells Cathedral church', *Archaeologia*, **59**, 143–206

Howard, H 1993a. 'The chapel of Our Lady Undercroft, Canterbury Cathedral, and the relationship of English and Bohemian painting techniques in the second half of the fourteenth century', *Technologia Artis*, **3**, 31–4

Howard, H 1993b. 'Workshop practices and the identification of hands: Gothic wall paintings at St Albans', *The Conservator*, **17**, 34–45

Howard, H 2003. 'Technology of the painted past: recent scientific examination of the medieval wall paintings of the chapter house of Westminster Abbey', in R Gowing and A Heritage (eds), *Conserving the Painted Past: Developing Approaches to Wall Painting Conservation*, 17–26, London: James & James

Howard, H 2009. 'Edmund Crouchback: technique of the tomb of a crusader', in Binski and Massing 2009, 319–40

Howe, E 2006a. 'Painting and patronage at Westminster: the murals in the south transept and St Faith's Chapel', *Burlington Mag*, **148**, 4–14

Howe, E 2006b. 'Wall painting technology at Westminster Abbey c 1260–1300', in Nadolny 2006, 91–113

Howell, M 1998. *Eleanor of Provence: Queenship in Thirteenth Century England*, Oxford: OUP

Howlett, R (ed) 1885–90. *Chronicles of the Reigns of Stephen, Henry II and Richard I*, London: Longmans

Hubel, A 1975. *Dom Schatzmuseum Regensburg*, Munich: Schnell und Steiner

Hunter, J 1830. *The Diary of Ralph Thoresby*, 2 vols, London: Henry Colburn and Richard Bentley

Huscroft, R 2006. *Expulsion: England's Jewish Solution*, Stroud: Tempus

Hutten, E 1926. *The Franciscans in England 1224–1538*, London: Constable

James, M R 1897. 'The Testament of Job' in *Apocrypha Anecdota II: Texts and Studies: Contributions to Biblical and Patristic Literature*, **5**(1), lxxii–cii and 103–37, Cambridge: CUP

Jansen, V 1982. 'Dying mouldings, unarticulated springer blocks and hollow chamfers in thirteenth-century architecture', *J Brit Archaeol Ass*, **135**, 35–54

Jenning, C 1974. *Early Chests in Wood and Iron*, London: HMSO

Jewitt, O 1863. 'The Crypt', in Scott 1863, 195–7

Johnson, M D 1969. *The Purpose of Biblical Genealogies*, Cambridge: CUP

Jordan, W J 1980. 'Sir George Gilbert Scott, RA, Surveyor to Westminster Abbey, 1849–1878', *Architect Hist*, **23**, 60–87

Keen, L 2007. 'Christ crucified, Christ risen: medieval ceramic tiles', in *Pagans and Christians – from Antiquity to the Middle Ages; Papers in Honour of Martin Henig, presented on the occasion of his 65th birthday*, 313–17, Oxford: BAR Int Ser 1610

Keene, D, Burns, A and Saint, A (eds) 2004. *St Paul's: the Cathedral Church of London 604–2004*, London: Yale

Keepe, H 1683. *Monumenta Westmonasteriensia*, London

Kemp, B R 2000. *English Episcopal Acta, 19: Salisbury 1217–1228*, Oxford: OUP

Kemp, B R and Tatton-Brown, T 2008. 'The date of the cloister at Salisbury Cathedral', *J Brit Archaeol Ass*, **161**, 94–103

Kenyon, J R and Williams, D M (eds) 2006. *Cardiff: Architecture and Archaeology in the Medieval Diocese of Llandaff*, Leeds: Maney

Kidson, P, Murray, P and Thompson, P 1965. *A History of English Architecture*, Harmondsworth: Penguin

Kimpel, D 1971. 'Die Querhausarme von Notre-Dame zu Paris und ihre Skulpturen', unpublished doctoral dissertation, University of Bonn

Kimpel, D and Suckale, R 1985. *Die gotische Architektur in Frankreich 1130–1270*, Munich: Hirmer

Kingsford, C L (ed) 1890. *The Song of Lewes*, Oxford: Clarendon Press

Knighton, C 1997–9. *Acts of the Dean and Chapter of Westminster 1543–1609*, Woodbridge: Boydell

Knowles, D 1955. *The Religious Orders in England*, 3 vols, Cambridge: CUP

Knowles, D 1963. *The Monastic Order in England*, Cambridge: CUP

Knowles, D and Brooke, C N L 2002. *Monastic Constitutions of Lanfranc*, Oxford: OUP

Knowles, D, Brooke, C N L and London, V C M 2001. *Heads of Religious Houses: England and Wales 940–1216*, 2 vols, Cambridge: CUP

Kunst, H-J 1968. 'Der Chor von Westminster Abbey und die Kathedrale von Reims', *Zeitschrift für Kunstgeschichte*, **31**, 122–42

Lehmann-Brockhaus, O 1955–60. *Lateinische Schriftquellen zur Kunst in England, Wales und Schottland vom Jahre 901 bis zum Jahre 1307*, 5 vols, Munich: Prestel

Lemere, B and Co *c* 1877. *Architectural Photographs: Catalogue of Photography Taken from Specimens in the Royal Architectural Museum, Westminster*, London

Lethaby, W R 1906. *Westminster Abbey and the King's Craftsmen: a Study of Medieval Building*, London: Duckworth

Lethaby, W R 1913. 'The Romance tiles of Chertsey abbey', *Walpole Society*, **2**, 69–80

Lethaby, W R 1917. 'English Primitives V', *Burlington Mag*, **30**, 45

Lethaby, W R 1925. *Westminster Abbey Re-examined*, London: Duckworth

Lethaby, W R 1930. 'Old St Paul's? VIII', *The Builder*, **139**, 791–3

Letters, S 2003. *Gazetteer of Markets and Fairs in England and Wales to 1516*, List and Index Society, <http://www.history.ac.uk/cmh/gaz/gazweb2.html> (15 November 2009)

Loach, J 1991. *Parliament under the Tudors*, Oxford: Clarendon

Loftie, W J 1891. *Westminster Abbey*, London: Seeley

Logan, F D 1996. *Runaway Religious in Medieval England c 1240–1540*, Cambridge: CUP

Lords Journal 1767– . *Journals of the House of Lords 1509–* , London

Lowden, J 1997. *Early Christian and Byzantine Art*, London: Phaidon

Luard, H R (ed) 1858. *Lives of Edward the Confessor*, London: Longmans

Luard, H R (ed) 1861. *Roberti Grosseteste Epistolae*, London: Longmans

Luard, H R (ed) 1864–9. *Annales Monastici*, 5 vols, London: Longmans

Luard, H R 1872–84. *Matthaei Parisiensis Chronica Majora*, 7 vols, London: Longmans

Luard H R (ed) 1890. *Flores Historiarum*, 3 vols, London: HMSO

Macray, W 1878. *Catalogi Codicum Manuscriptorum Bibliothecae Bodleianae, Partis Quinti*, Oxford

Madden, F 1866–9. *Matthaei Parisiensis Historia Anglorum*, 3 vols, London: Longmans

Maddicott, J R 1994. *Simon de Montfort*, Cambridge: CUP

Maddicott, J R 1999a. '"An infinite multitude of nobles": quality, quantity and politics in the pre-reform parliaments of Henry III', in M Prestwich, R Britnell and R Frame (eds), *Thirteenth-Century England VII: Proceedings of the Durham Conference 1997*, 17–46, Woodbridge: Boydell

Maddicott, J R 1999b. 'The earliest known knights of the shire: new light on the parliament of April 1254', *Parliamentary History*, **18**, 109–30

Maddicott, J R forthcoming. *The Origins of the English Parliament, 924–1327*, Oxford: OUP

Malcolm, J P 1802. *Londinium Redivivum*, London

Marks, R 1998. *The Medieval Stained Glass of Northamptonshire*, Corpus Vitrearum Medii Aevi Great Britain Summary Catalogue 4, Oxford: OUP

Martin, G H 2004–9. 'Palgrave , Sir Francis (1788–1861)', in ODNB (eds H C G Matthew and B Harrison), <http://www.oxforddnb.com/view/article/21157> (21 November 2009)

Martindale, A 1994. 'St Stephen's Chapel, Westminster, and the Italian experience', in D Buckton and T A Heslop (eds), *Studies in Medieval Art and Architecture presented to Peter Lasko*, 102–12, Stroud: Sutton

Mason, E 1988. *Westminster Abbey Charters 1066–c 1214*, London Record Society, 25, <http://www.british-history.ac.uk/source.aspx?pubid=580> (15 November 2009)

Mason, E 1996. *Westminster Abbey and its People c 1050–c 1216*, Woodbridge: Boydell

Maul, G 1992. 'Geschichte, Konservierung und Technologie der Chorschrankenmalereien', *Kölner Domblatt*, 239–60, Cologne: Central-Dombau-Verein zu Köln von 1842

McCann, J 1952. *The Rule of St Benedict in Latin and English*, London: Burns Oates

McGinn, B 2005. *The Harvest of Mysticism in Medieval Germany 1300–1500*, New York: Crossroad

McKisack, M 1971. *Medieval History in the Tudor Age*, Oxford: Clarendon

Meiss, M 1967. *French Painting in the Time of Jean de Berry: 2 vols*, London: Phaidon

Mews, C J 2001. *Listen, Daughter: the Speculum Virginum and the Formation of Religious Women in the Middle Ages*, London: Palgrave Macmillan

Miles, D H 1997. 'The interpretation, presentation, and use of tree-ring dates', *Vernacular Architect*, **28**, 40–56

Miles, D W H and Bridge, M C 2005. *The Tree-Ring Dating of the Early Medieval Doors at Westminster Abbey, London*. English Heritage Centre for Archaeology Rep 38/2005

Mills, P 1995. 'Excavations at the dorter undercroft, Westminster Abbey', *Trans London Middlesex Archaeol Soc*, **46**, 69–124

[Minton, H] 1842. *Examples of Old English Tiles Manufactured by Minton and Co, Stoke upon Trent*, Minton archives MS 1366, Stoke-on-Trent

Montagu, J 1988. 'The restored chapter house wall paintings in Westminster Abbey', *Early Music*, **16**, 239–50

Morgan, N J 1982–8. *Early Gothic Manuscripts*, 2 vols, London: Harvey Miller

Morgan, N J 1990. *The Lambeth Apocalypse*, London: Harvey Miller

Morgand, D C 1963. 'Memoriale Qualiter I (saec viii fin–ix med)', *Corpus Consuetudinem Monasticarum*, **4**, 177–283, Siegburg: F Schmitt

Morris, R K 2006. 'Later Gothic architecture in South Wales', in Kenyon and Williams (eds) 2006, 102–35

Mortimer, R 1994. *Angevin England 1154–1258*, Oxford: Blackwell

Müller, W 1990. *Grundlagen gotischer Bautechnik: Ars Sine Scientia Nihil*, Munich: Deutscher Kunstverlag

Murray, S 1989. *Beauvais Cathedral: Architecture of Transcendence*, Princeton: Princeton University Press

Murray Smith, A 1906. *Westminster Abbey: its Story and Associations*, London: Cassell

Myers, A R (ed) 1969. *English Historical Documents 1327–1485*, London: Eyre & Spottiswoode

Myles, J 1996. *L N Cottingham 1787–1847: Architect of the Gothic Revival*, London: Lund Humphries

Nadolny, J 2001. 'The techniques and use of gilded relief decoration by northern European painters *c* 1200–1500.' Unpublished PhD thesis, Courtauld Institute of Art, University of London

Nadolny, J (ed) 2006. *Medieval Painting in Northern Europe: Techniques, Analysis, Art History: Studies in Commemoration of the Seventieth Birthday of Unn Plahter*, London: Archetype

Nadolny, J and Roy, A 2006. 'The original technique of the Westminster Abbey portrait of Richard II', in Nadolny 2006, 137–47

Newberry, J 1753. *The Historical Description of Westminster Abbey, its Monuments and Curiosities*, London

Newman, J 1995. *The Buildings of Wales: Glamorgan*, London: Penguin

Nichols, J G 1842. *Examples of Encaustic Tiles*, London:

Noppen, J G 1932. 'The Westminster apocalypse and its source', *Burlington Mag*, **61**, 146–59

Noppen, J G 1935. *Chapter House and Pyx Chamber, Westminster Abbey*, London: HMSO

Noppen, J G and Rigold, S E 1949. *The Chapter House, Westminster Abbey*, London: HMSO

Norton, C 1981. 'The British Museum collection of medieval tiles', *J Brit Archaeol Ass*, **134**, 107–19

Norton, C 1996. 'The decorative pavements of Salisbury Cathedral and Old Sarum', in L Keene and T Cocke (eds), *Medieval Art and Architecture at Salisbury Cathedral*, 90–105, Leeds: Maney

Norton, C 2002. 'The luxury pavement in England before Westminster', in Grant and Mortimer 2002, 7–27

Nussbaum, N and Lepsky, S 1999. *Das gotische Gewölbe:. Eine Geschichte seiner Form und Konstruktion*, Munich: Deutscher Kunstverlag

Oursel, C 1926. *La Miniature du XIIe siècle à l'Abbaye de Citeaux*, Dijon

Palgrave, F 1836. *Ancient Kalendars and Inventories of the Exchequer*, London

Pantin, W A 1931–7. *Documents Illustrating the Activities of the General and Provincial Chapters of the English Black Monks 1215–1540*, 3 vols, London: Royal Historical Society

Park, D 1986. 'Cistercian wall painting and panel painting', in C Norton and D Park (eds), *Cistercian Art and Architecture in the British Isles*, 181–210, Cambridge: CUP

Pearce, E H 1916. *The Monks of Westminster*, Cambridge: CUP

Pearson, L 2000. *Minton Tiles in the Churches of Staffordshire*, a report for the Tiles and Architectural Ceramics Society, <http://www.tilesoc.org.uk/cummingpage.htm> (15 November 2009)

Pennant, T 1790–[1820?]. *Some Account of London, Westminster and Southwark*, 2 vols, London

Pevsner, N 1957. *The Buildings of England London I: The Cities of London and Westminster*, Harmondsworth: Penguin

Post Office 1851. *Post Office London Directory for 1851*, 3 vols, London

Powell, T 1631. *The Repertorie of Records*, London

Powicke, F M 1947. *King Henry III and the Lord Edward: the Community of the Realm in the Thirteenth Century*, 2 vols, Oxford: Clarendon

Prestwich, M 2005. *Plantagenet England 1225–1360*, Oxford: OUP

Price, F 1753. *A Series of … Observations … upon … the Cathedral-church of Salisbury*, London

Rackham, R B 1909–10. 'The nave at Westminster', *Proc Brit Acad*, **4**, 35–93

Ravaux, J-P 1976. 'La cathédrale gothique de Châlons-sur-Marne', *Mémoires de la Société d'agriculture, commerce, sciences et lettres du département de la Marne*, **111**, 171–227

RCHME 1924. *An Inventory of the Historical Monuments in London Vol I: Westminster Abbey*, London: HMSO

RCHME 1925. *An Inventory of the Historical Monuments in London Vol II: West London*, London: HMSO

Reed, C 1996. 'A discovery in Pennsylvania: the "tiles" Guardbook of John Gough Nichols', *J Tiles Architect Ceramics Soc*, **6**, 3–12

Rees Jones, S 1952–54. 'The coronation chair', *Studies in Conservation*, **1**, 103–14

Reinhardt, H 1937. 'Le jubé de la Cathédrale de Strasbourg et ses origines rémoises', *Bulletin de la Société des Amis de la Cathédrale de Strasbourg*, 2nd ser, **6**, 19–28

Reynolds, C 2002. *Stained Glass of Westminster Abbey*, Norwich: Jarrold

Reynolds C (ed), forthcoming. *Reports and Letters of the Surveyors of the Fabric, Westminster Abbey, 1827–1906*, Woodbridge: Boydell

Richardson, H G and Sayles, G O 1967. 'The earliest known official use of the term "parliament"', *Engl Hist Rev*, **82**, 747–50

Rickman, T 1848. *An Attempt to Discriminate the Styles of Architecture in England*, London: John Henry Parker

Ridgeway, H 1988. 'King Henry's grievances against the council in 1261', *Historical Research*, **61**, 227–42

Rigold, S E 1976. *The Chapter House and Pyx Chamber, Westminster Abbey*, London: HMSO

Riley, H T (ed) 1863–4. *Thomas Walsingham's* Historia Anglicana, 2 vols, London: Longmans

Riley, H T (ed) 1867–9. *Gesta Abbatum Monasterii Sancti Albani*, 3 vols, London: Longmans

Rivington, J G F and Rivington, J (trans) 1844–7. *Morals on the Book of Job by St Gregory the Great*, 3 vols, Oxford: John Henry Parker

Roberts, M 2002. *Dugdale and Hollar: History Illustrated*, London: University of Delaware Press

Robinson, D M 2006. *The Cistercians in Wales: Architecture and Archaeology 1130–1540*, London: Society of Antiquaries

Robinson, J 2004. *The Lewis Chessmen*, London: British Museum

Robinson, J A (ed) 1909. *The History of Westminster Abbey by John Flete*, Cambridge: CUP

Robinson, J A 1911. *The Abbot's House at Westminster*, Cambridge: CUP

Robinson, J A and James, M R 1909. *The Manuscripts of Westminster Abbey*, Cambridge: CUP

Rodwell, W 1979. 'Lead plaques from the tombs of the Saxon bishops of Wells,' *Antiquaries Journal*, **59**, 407

Rodwell, W 1989. 'Archaeology and the standing fabric: recent studies at Lichfield Cathedral', *Antiquity*, **63**, 281–94

Rodwell, W 1993. 'The development of the quire of Lichfield Cathedral: Romanesque and Early English', in J Maddison (ed), *Medieval Art and Architecture at Lichfield Cathedral*, 17–35, Leeds: Maney

Rodwell, W 2001. *Wells Cathedral: Excavations and Structural Studies 1978–93*, 2 vols, London: English Heritage

Rodwell, W 2002. *Chapter House and Pyx Chamber, Westminster Abbey*, London: English Heritage

Rodwell, W 2009. 'New Glimpses of Edward the Confessor's abbey', in R Mortimer (ed), *Edward the Confessor: the Man and the Legend*, 151–67, Woodbridge: Boydell

Rodwell, W and Leighton, G 2006. *Architectural Records of Wells by John Carter FSA, 1784–1808*, Taunton: Somerset Record Society

Rodwell, W, Miles, D, Hamilton, D and Bridge, M 2006. 'The dating of the Pyx door', *Engl Heritage Hist Rev*, **1**, 24–7

Rogers, N J 1986. 'The Old Proctor's Book: a Cambridge manuscript of *c* 1390', in W M Ormrod (ed), *England in the Fourteenth Century, Proceedings of the 1985 Harlaxton Symposium*, 213–23, Woodbridge: Boydell

Rollason, D 2000. *Symeon of Durham, Libellus de Exordio atque Procursu istius, hoc est Dunhelmensis Ecclesie*, Oxford: Clarendon Press

Roper, M R and Hallam, E M 1978. 'The capital and the records of the nation', *London J*, **4**, 73–94

Roper, W O 1886. 'Cockersand Abbey', *Trans Lancashire Cheshire Archaeol Soc*, **4**, 26–34

Rose, M 1999. *The Norwich Apocalypse: the Cycle of Vault Carvings in the Cloisters of Norwich Cathedral*, Norwich: University of East Anglia

Rosser, G 1989. *Medieval Westminster 1200–1540*, Oxford: OUP

Roy, A 1997. 'The technique of the Wilton Diptych', in D Gordon, L Monnas and C Elam (eds), *The Regal Image of Richard II and the Wilton Diptych*, 74–81, London: Harvey Miller

Russell, A L N 1946. *Westminster Abbey: A Guide to the Buildings and the Monuments*, London: Chatto and Windus

Sainty, J C 1983. *Officers of the Exchequer*, List and Index Society special ser, **18**, London

Salzman, L F 1952. *Building in England Down to 1540: a Documentary History*, Oxford: OUP Reprints (1992)

Sandler, L F 1983. *The Psalter of Robert de Lisle*, Oxford: OUP

Sandler, L F 1986. *Gothic Manuscripts 1285–1385*, 2 vols, Oxford: OUP

Sandron, D 2001. *Picardie Gothique; Autour de Laon et Soissons: les édifices religieux*, Paris: Picard

Sandron, D 2004. *Amiens: La cathédrale*, Paris: Zodiaque

Sandys, A 1925. 'The financial and administrative importance of the London Temple in the thirteenth century', in A G Little and F M Powicke (eds), *Essays in Medieval History Presented to Thomas Frederick Tout*, 147–62, Manchester

Sauerberg, M L 2005. 'The Coronation Chair – revisited', *Studies in Conservation*, **50**, 230–1

Sauerberg, M L, Roy, A, Spring, M, Bucklow, S and Kempski, M 2009. 'Materials and Techniques' in Binski and Massing 2009, 233–251

Sauerländer, W 1970. *Gothic Sculpture in France 1140–1270*, London: Thames & Hudson

Scholz, B W 1964. 'Sulcard of Westminster: "Prologus de Constructione Westmonasterii"', *Traditio*, **20**, 59–91

Scott, G G 1850. *A Plea for the Faithful Restoration of our Ancient Churches*, London

Scott, G G 1860. 'Gleanings from Westminster Abbey', *Gentleman's Mag*, new ser, **8**, 250–7, 351–61, 462–9, 577–84; new ser, **9**, 33–40

Scott, G G 1861. *Gleanings from Westminster Abbey*, Oxford and London: John Henry and James Parker

Scott, G G 1863. *Gleanings from Westminster Abbey*, 2nd edn, Oxford and London: John Henry and James Parker

Scott, G G 1867. 'The chapter-house of Westminster', *Old London: Papers Read at the London Congress, July 1866*, 141–57, London: Archaeological Institute of Great Britain and Ireland

Scott, G G *c* 1876. *A Guide to the Royal Architectural Museum*, London

Scott, G G 1879. *Personal and Professional Recollections*, London: Sampson Low Marston Searle & Rivington

Scott, K L 1996. *Later Gothic Manuscripts 1390–1490*, London: Harvey Miller

Serel, T 1875. *Historical Notes on the Church of St Cuthbert in Wells*, Wells: J M Atkins

Sharpe, R 2005. 'Monastic reading at Thorney abbey 1323–1347', *Traditio*, **60**, 243–78

Shaw, H 1851. *Catalogue of the Museum of Medieval Art, etc.*, compiled for Messrs Foster and Sons, London

Shaw, H 1858. *Specimens of Tile Pavements*, London: B M Pickering

Shoesmith, R and Richardson, R (eds) 1997. *A Definitive History of Dore Abbey*, Woonton Almeley, Herefordshire: Logaston

Skempton, A W, et al 2002. *Biographical Dictionary of Civil Engineers in Great Britain and Ireland 1500–1830*, London: Thomas Telford

Smith, J T 1807. *Antiquities of Westminster*, London

Sonstadt, E 1904. 'Decayed stone-work in the chapter house, Westminster Abbey: treatment of', *J Soc Chemical Industry*, **23**, 16

Spring, M and Higgitt, C 2006. 'Analyses reconsidered: the importance of the pigment content of paint in the interpretation of the results of examination of binding medium', in Nadolny 2006, 223–9

Stacey, R 1987. *Politics, Policy and Finance under Henry III, 1216–1245*, Oxford: OUP

Stacey, R 1988. '1240–1260: a watershed in Anglo-Jewish relations', *Bull Inst Hist Res*, **61**, 135–50

Stanley, A P 1864–7. ['Proceedings', 2 December 1865] *Proc Soc Antiq London*, ser 2, **3**, 183–94

Stanley, A P 1869. *Historical Memorials of Westminster Abbey*, 3rd edn, London

Stapleton, T 1846. *De Antiquis Legibus Liber: Cronica Maiorum et Vicecomitatum Londoniarum*, London

Storer, J and Greig, J 1805. *Select Views of London and its Environs*, 2 vols, London: Vernor and Hood

Stow, J 1754–5. *A Survey of the Cities of London and Westminster*, 6th edn, J Strype (ed), 2 vols, London

Stratford, N 1978. 'Notes on the Norman chapter house at Worcester', in G Popper (ed), *Medieval Art and Architecture at Worcester Cathedral*, 51–70, London: British Archaeological Association

Stubbs, W (ed) 1867. *Gesta Regis Henrici Secundi Benedicti Abbatis*, 2 vols, London: Longmans

Stubbs, W (ed) 1879–80. *The Historical Works of Gervase of Canterbury*, 2 vols, London: Longmans

Suchý, M 2009. 'England and Bohemia in the time of Anne of Luxembourg: dynastic marriage as a precondition for cultural contact in the late Middle Ages', in Z Opačić (ed), *Prague and Bohemia: Medieval Art, Architecture and Cultural Exchange in Central Europe*, 8–21, London: British Archaeological Association

Summerly, F (the *alias* of H Cole) 1842. *A Hand-Book for the Architecture, Sculpture, Tombs, and Decorations of Westminster Abbey*, London: George Bell

Summers, N 1988. *A Prospect of Southwell*, revised edn, Southwell: Kelham House Publications

Swanton, M J 1976. '"Dane skins": excoriation in early England', *Folklore*, **1**, 21–8

Symonds, T 1953. *Regularis Concordia Angliae Nationis Monachorum Sanctimonialiumque*, London: Thomas Nelson

Taralon, J 1965. *Les Trésors des Eglises de France*, Paris: Hachette

Tatton-Brown, T 1998. 'The building stones for Salisbury Cathedral', *Hatcher Review*, **5**(45), 39–46

Tatton-Brown, T and Mortimer, R (eds) 2003. *Westminster Abbey: the Lady Chapel of Henry VII*, Woodbridge: Boydell

Taylor, A J 1986. *The Welsh Castles of Edward I*, London: Hambledon

Taylor, K, Gradwell, C and McGrath, T 1998. 'The cleaning and consolidation of the stonework to the Annunciation door, chapter house, Westminster Abbey', in J Ashurst and F G Dimes (eds), *Conservation of Building and Decorative Stone*, 2nd edn, 219–27, London: Butterworth

Terrien, S 1996. *The Iconography of Job Through the Centuries*, Pennsylvania: Pennsylvania State University Press

Thomas, C, Cowie, R and Sidell, J 2006. *The Royal Palace, Abbey and Town of Westminster on Thorney Island*, London: Museum of London Archaeology Service

Thompson, E M (ed) 1902–4. *Customary of the Benedictine Monasteries of Saint Augustine, Canterbury, and Saint Peter, Westminster*, 2 vols, London: Henry Bradshaw Society

Thomson, R M 1974. *Chronicle of the Election of Hugh, Abbot of Bury St Edmunds and Later Bishop of Ely*, Oxford: Clarendon Press

Thornbury, W 1878. *Old and New London*, 6 vols, London: Cassell

Thorne, R 2004–9. 'Rose, George (1744–1818)', in ODNB (eds H C G Matthew and B Harrison), <http://www.oxforddnb.com/view/article/24088> (21 November 2009)

Thurlby, M 1991. 'The west front of Binham priory, Norfolk and the beginnings of bar tracery', in W M Ormrod (ed), *Harlaxton Medieval Studies New Ser I: England in the Thirteenth Century*, 155–65, Donington: Shaun Tyas

Thurlby, M 2006. 'The early Gothic fabric of Llandaff Cathedral', in Kenyon and Williams 2006, 60–85

Tinniswood, A 2002. *His Invention so Fertile: a Life of Christopher Wren*, London: Pimlico

Tolhurst, J B L 1942. *Monastic Breviary of Hyde Abbey, Winchester*, London: Henry Bradshaw Society

Tolhurst, J B L and McLachlan, L 1936. *Ordinal of St Mary's Abbey, York*, London: Henry Bradshaw Society

Tout, T F 1920–33. *Chapters in the Administrative History of Medieval England: the Wardrobe, the Chambers and the Small Seals*, 6 vols, Manchester: Manchester University Press

Tout, T F 1934. *The Collected Papers of Thomas Frederick Tout*, Manchester: Manchester University Press

Treharne, R F and Sanders, I J 1973. *Documents of the Baronial Movement of Reform and Rebellion, 1258–67*, Oxford: OUP

Tristram, E W 1950. *English Medieval Wall Painting: the Thirteenth Century*, Oxford: OUP

Tristram, E W 1955. *English Wall Painting of the Fourteenth Century*, London: Routledge & Kegan Paul

Tudor-Craig, P 1998. 'The large letters of the Litlyngton Missal and Westminster Abbey in 1383–4', in M P Brown and S McKendrick (eds), *Illuminating the Book: Makers and Interpreters; Essays in Honour of Janet Backhouse*, 102–19, London: British Library

Tudor-Craig, P 2002. 'The iconography of wisdom and the frontispiece to the Bible Historiale, BL Add 18856', in C Barron and J Stratford (eds), *Harlaxton Medieval Studies New Ser XI: The Church and Learning in Later Medieval Society: Essays in Honour of R B Dobson*, 110–27, Donington: Shaun Tyas

Turner, B 1985. 'The patronage of John of Northampton. Further studies of the wall-paintings in Westminster chapter house', *J Brit Archaeol Ass*, **138**, 89–100

Tyers, I 1998. 'Tree-ring analysis and wood identification on timbers excavated on the Magistrates Court Site, Kingston upon Hull, East Yorkshire', unpublished report no. 410 for ARCUS (the Archaeological Research and Consultancy at the University of Sheffield)

Tyers, I 2001. 'Appendix 2. Tree-ring analysis of the Roman and medieval timbers from medieval London Bridge and its environs', in B Watson, T Brigham and T Dyson (eds), *London Bridge: 2000 Years of a River Crossing*, London: Museum of London Archaeology Service

Vaughan, R 1958. *Matthew Paris*, Cambridge: CUP

VCH 1914. *Victoria County History: Lancashire Vol 8*, London

VCH 1970. *Victoria County History: Stafford Vol 3*, London

VCH 1990. *Victoria County History: Stafford Vol 14*, London

Victoria and Albert Museum 1936. *Catalogue of Plaster Casts*, London

Vincent, N 2001. *The Holy Blood: King Henry III and the Westminster Blood Relic*, Cambridge: CUP

Vincent, N 2004. 'King Henry III and the Blessed Virgin Mary', in R N Swanson (ed), *The Church and Mary*, 126–46, Woodbridge: Boydell

Viollet-le-Duc, E 1858–68. *Dictionnaire raisonné de l'Architecture française du Xe au XVIe siècle*, 10 vols, Paris: Librairie-imprimeries réunies

Wald, E T de 1932. *The Illustrations of the Utrecht Psalter*, Princeton: Dept of Art and Archaeology of the Princeton University

Waller, J G 1873. 'On the paintings in the chapter house, Westminster', *Trans London Middlesex Archaeol Soc*, **4**, 377–416

Walne, P 1960–64. 'The Record Commissions, 1800–37', *J Soc Archiv*, **2**, 8–16

Walsh, K and Edmunds I M (trans) 1979. *Bernard of Clairvaux; Sermons on the Song of Songs*, 4 vols, Kalamazoo: Cistercian Publications

Wander, S H 1977. 'The restorations of the Westminster Abbey Chapter House', *RACAR, Canadian Art Rev*, **4**, 78–90

Wander, S H 1978. 'The Westminster Abbey Sanctuary pavement', *Traditio*, **34**, 137–56

Watson, A 1928. 'The *Speculum Virginum*, with special reference to the Tree of Jesse', *Speculum*, **3**(4), 445–69

Watson, A 1934. *The Early Iconography of the Tree of Jesse*, Oxford: OUP

Webb, E A 1921. *The Records of St Bartholomew's Priory and of the Church and Parish of St Bartholomew the Great, West Smithfield*, 2 vols, Oxford: OUP

Weiler, B 2003. 'Symbolism and politics in the reign of Henry III', in M Prestwich, R Britnell and R Frame (eds), *Thirteenth-Century England X: Proceedings of the Durham Conference 2001*, 14–42, Woodbridge: Boydell

Wernham, R B 1956. 'The public records in the sixteenth and seventeenth centuries', in L Fox (ed), *English Historical Scholarship in the Sixteenth and Seventeenth Centuries*, 11–30, Oxford: OUP

Westlake, H F 1923. *Westminster Abbey: the Church, College, Cathedral and Convent of St Peter, Westminster*, 2 vols, London: P Allen

White, R 1993. Unpublished National Gallery scientific report, 3 November 1993

White, R and Kirby, J 2006. 'Some observations on the binder and dyestuff composition of glaze paints in early European panel paintings', in Nadolny 2006, 215–22

Wickham Legg, J 1891–7. *Missale ad Usum Ecclesie Westmonasteriensis*, 3 vols, London: Henry Bradshaw Society

Widmore, R 1751. *An History of the Church of St Peter, Westminster*, London

Wieck, R S 1988. *Time Sanctified: the Book of Hours in Medieval Art and Life*, Baltimore: Walters Art Gallery

Wilkins, D 1737. *Concilia Magnae Britanniae et Hiberniae, AD 446–1717*, 4 vols, London

Williams, N 1955–9. 'The work of Peter le Neve at Chapter House, Westminster', *J Soc Archiv*, **1**, 125–31

Williamson, E, Riches, A and Higgs, M 1990. *The Buildings of Scotland: Glasgow*, London: Yale University Press

Williamson, P 1986. *The Medieval Treasury*, London: Victoria and Albert Museum

Williamson, P 1988. 'The Westminster Abbey Annunciation group', *Burlington Mag*, **130**, 123–4 and 928

Williamson, P 1995. *Gothic Sculpture 1140–1300*, London: Yale University Press

Wilson, C 1983. 'The original setting of the apostle and prophet figures from St Mary's Abbey, York', in F H Thompson (ed), *Studies in Medieval Sculpture*, 100–21, London: Society of Antiquaries

Wilson, C 1987. 'The English response to French Gothic architecture c 1200–1350', in Alexander and Binski 1987, 74–82

Wilson, C 1991. 'The early thirteenth-century architecture of Beverley Minster: cathedral splendours and Cistercian austerities', in P R Coss and S D Lloyd (eds), *Thirteenth-Century England III: Proceedings of the Newcastle Conference 1989*, 181–95, Woodbridge: Boydell

Wilson, C 1992. *The Gothic Cathedral: the Architecture of the Great Church 1130–1530*, revised edn, London: Thames & Hudson

Wilson, C 1995. 'The medieval monuments', in P Collinson, N Ramsay and M Sparks (eds), *A History of Canterbury Cathedral*, 415–510, Oxford: OUP

Wilson, C 2007. '"Not without honour save in its own country?" Saint-Urbain at Troyes and its contrasting French and English posterities', in A Gajewski and Z Opačić (eds), *The Year 1300 and the Creation of a New European Architecture*, 107–21, Turnhout: Brepols

Wilson, C 2008. 'Calling the tune? The involvement of King Henry III in the design of the abbey church at Westminster', *J Brit Archaeol Ass*, **161**, 59–93

Wilson, C, Tudor-Craig, P, Physick, J and Gem, R 1986. *Westminster Abbey*, London: Bell & Hyman

Wrapson, L 2006. 'The materials and techniques of the c 1307 Westminster Abbey sedilia', in Nadolny 2006, 114–36

Wren, S 1750. *Parentalia, or Memoirs of the Family of the Wrens*, London

Wright, T 1839. *The Political Songs of England*, London: Camden Society

Index

Illustrations are denoted by page numbers in *italics* or by *illus* where figures are scattered throughout the text. Locations are in Westminster Abbey and London unless specified otherwise.

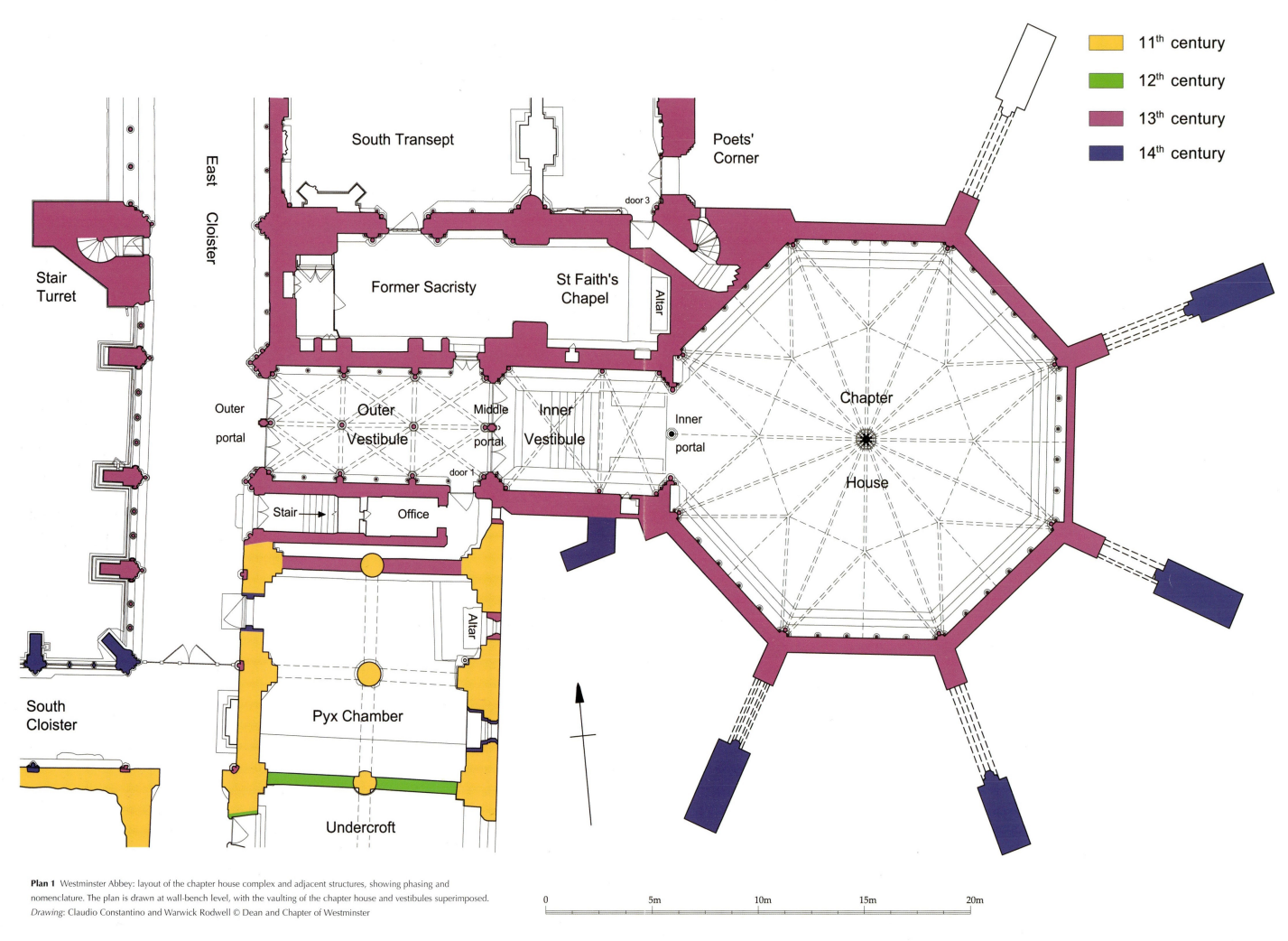

Legend:
- 11th century (yellow)
- 12th century (green)
- 13th century (pink/magenta)
- 14th century (dark blue)

Stair Turret

East Cloister

South Transept

Poets' Corner

Former Sacristy

St Faith's Chapel

Altar

Chapter House

Outer portal

Outer Vestibule

Middle portal

Inner Vestibule

Inner portal

door 3

door 1

Stair

Office

Altar

South Cloister

Pyx Chamber

Undercroft

Plan 1 Westminster Abbey: layout of the chapter house complex and adjacent structures, showing phasing and nomenclature. The plan is drawn at wall-bench level, with the vaulting of the chapter house and vestibules superimposed. *Drawing*: Claudio Constantino and Warwick Rodwell © Dean and Chapter of Westminster

0   5m   10m   15m   20m

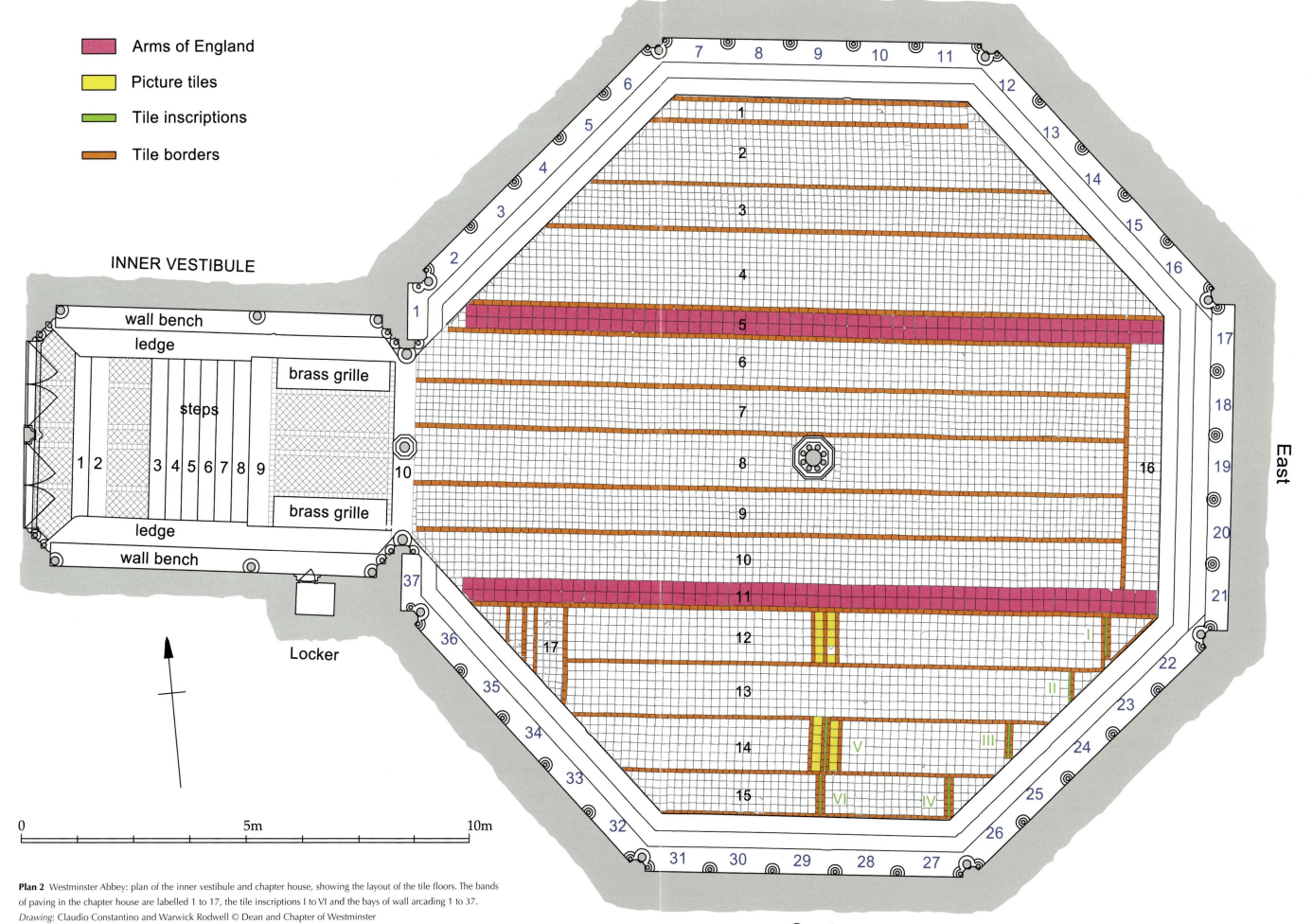

North

- Arms of England
- Picture tiles
- Tile inscriptions
- Tile borders

INNER VESTIBULE

wall bench
ledge
steps
brass grille
1 2 3 4 5 6 7 8 9
10
ledge
brass grille
wall bench

Locker

East

South

0   5m   10m

Plan 2 Westminster Abbey: plan of the inner vestibule and chapter house, showing the layout of the tile floors. The bands of paving in the chapter house are labelled 1 to 17, the tile inscriptions I to VI and the bays of wall arcading 1 to 37.
Drawing: Claudio Constantino and Warwick Rodwell © Dean and Chapter of Westminster